Data Communications and Computer
for Computer Scientists and Engineers

Second Edition

PEARSON
Education

We work with leading authors to develop the
strongest educational materials in engineering,
bringing cutting-edge thinking and best learning
practice to a global market.

Under a range of well-known imprints, including
Prentice Hall, we craft high-quality print and
electronic publications which help readers to
understand and apply their content,
whether studying or at work.

To find out more about the complete range of our
publishing, please visit us on the World Wide Web at:
www.pearsoneduc.com

Data Communications and Computer Networks

for Computer Scientists and Engineers

Second Edition

Michael Duck
and
Richard Read

Harlow, England • London • New York • Boston • San Francisco • Toronto • Sydney • Singapore • Hong Kong
Tokyo • Seoul • Taipei • New Delhi • Cape Town • Madrid • Mexico City • Amsterdam • Munich • Paris • Milan

Pearson Education Limited
Edinburgh Gate
Harlow
Essex CM20 2JE
England

and Associated Companies throughout the world

Visit us on the World Wide Web at:
www.pearsoneduc.com

First published 1996
Second edition 2003

© Pearson Education Limited 1996, 2003

ISBN 0 130 93047 4

British Library Cataloguing-in-Publication Data
A catalogue record for this book is available from the British Library

Library of Congress Cataloging-in-Publication Data
Copy to follow

10 9 8 7 6 5 4 3 2 1
07 06 05 04 03

Typeset in 10/12pt Times by 35
Printed and bound in Great Britain by Henry Ling Ltd, at the Dorset Press, Dorchester, Dorset

To Marlon

Contents

Preface

....

Aims and objectives

Data communications underpins all forms of distributed computer-based systems and computer networks and may be defined as the process of sending data reliably between two or more communicating parties. Data itself may represent a wide range of information such as the contents of a computer file, a digitized signal representing an image in a webcam system or telemetry measurements sent from a remote site to a central base for monitoring and control purposes. Data communications has successfully emerged from the telecommunications industry by tailoring and adapting traditional communication methods and systems to convey a digital signal rather than earlier, and increasingly historical, analogue signals which predominantly carried telephone conversations.

As computing has developed, a need to interconnect distant computer systems has emerged and this has given rise to the computer networks of today. There are now an enormous number of such networks as well as a variety of different types and arrangements, or configurations. In general, computer networks comprise a number of interconnected end-stations, possibly one or more intermediate networks used to interconnect the networks to which communicating stations are connected and the communication links connecting distant points within each network. Data communications is primarily concerned with techniques used to communicate at a distance. As such they are predominantly concerned with signalling and sets of rules, or protocols, to govern communication to ensure that interconnected parties achieve successful communication. Computer networks build upon data communications and are concerned with a higher level view than mere data communications. Such networks encompass the physical layout of a network, or topology, and the various underlying protocols to support networking and enable, as far as possible, seamless interaction between a user's application and the network over which it is to be run. To some extent a distinction between data communications and computer networks is artificial as without the latter, there would not be a network. However, the distinction is useful in explaining different aspects of networking and also to break down the complex tasks of computer networking into more manageable elements.

This book examines a wide range of techniques, technologies and systems used in data communications and computer networks. In particular it addresses a variety of data transmission methods used to convey data between physically distant locations. A number of types of network are considered and which may interconnect a few or many thousands of users on either a permanent or temporary, switched basis. In order to support successful communication, a set of rules and procedures has been developed, many of which are embodied in internationally agreed standards. We shall look at the standard bodies and their standards and recommendations and also how they are used in practice.

The book concentrates upon the techniques used in both data communications and computer networks rather than on specific issues relating to use. Attention is also given to the engineering aspects of these subjects. A key feature of this book, and indeed the industry, is the strong emphasis in breaking down the various functions and tasks of computer communications into a series of manageable subtasks, each of which may be defined as one of a series of layers. With this in mind many of the topics are dealt with in a layered manner, and usually relate closely to prescribed layered models which have been formulated within the discipline.

Intended audience

The book has been written to position itself within the marketplace midway between a number of excellent texts in this subject area which may be regarded as comprehensive, and almost reference works, and a number of other texts which are rather brief and tend to be merely primers. Reference texts can be too detailed and large for a newcomer to the topic and the primer type of text can lack information and be rather bland for many readers. With this in mind the book is written to appeal to two broad ranges of readers:

1. Students on computer science and engineering undergraduate and postgraduate courses who are studying data communications and/or computer networks.
2. Professional engineers, managers and users who work with computer networks in their everyday work. Here the book may be used either as an introductory text for personnel moving into the field or for updating in cases where previous experience has predominantly been in the area of traditional telecommunications.

Changes to the first edition

This new edition contains the original detail on data communications, with some minor updating, but greatly extends the work on computer networks. Recent developments in speech and video encoding have been added.

The techniques used for end-stations and customers to gain access to national and international networks have been extended and now include details of high-speed digital access such as ADSL. Earlier time-division multiplexing has also been extended to include SDH/SONET developments which exploit the high speeds of modern optical transmission systems. Local area network treatment now includes details of higher speed Ethernet operation at 100 and 1000 Mbps and coverage of the IEEE wireless LAN standards. In the area of packet-switched networks, the emphasis has shifted towards the Frame Relay networks that have been so successfully deployed as core wide area networks. A separate chapter on the most recent wide area network technology, asynchronous transfer mode, has been included. The other major area in which the second edition has been substantially extended is in devoting a full two chapters of detail to the operation of the Internet. Generic considerations to be borne in mind when internetworking are presented. Substantial detail then follows on the TCP/IP suite of protocols and how they are deployed, as well as consideration of routing strategies employed for the successful routing of traffic across an internet. In addition a number of related topics such as Voice over IP and how IP may be implemented in conjunction with other networking protocols, currently very topical, are considered. Linked with the treatment of IP is a much strengthened consideration of security in terms of guarding against eavesdropping and unauthorized access and activities as well as security strategies required for e-commerce over the Internet. The final chapter on network management has been updated to include a widely used practical network management system.

Summary of chapters

Chapter 1   Introduction

This chapter commences with a review of the development of data communications which, although of interest in its own right, is used as a vehicle to set the scene, and introduce a number of basic concepts which are developed in later chapters. After outlining how data communications have developed we then turn our attention to the different forms of data and see some examples of where such data originates. The general concept of communications models is introduced as a tool to support design, implementation and understanding of communications networks and systems. The case is then made for the need for standards and the major standards organizations are discussed. The ISO's communications model, the Open Systems Interconnection (OSI) Reference Model, is examined in detail. Another set of standards, developed by the Institute of Electrical and Electronic Engineers, which have influenced the design of a number of different types of computer networks are covered. The chapter concludes with a brief introduction to the ubiquitous TCP/IP suite of protocols which are the linchpin of today's Internet and makes comparisons between each of the communications models, and their associated standards, offered by the various standards organizations.

Chapter 2   Data communications

This chapter looks at the various different ways in which data may be transmitted and how the speed of transmission, or data rate, is measured in bits per second. An example is presented of how data is represented by a unique pattern of bits. This gives rise to the notion of how data is encoded into a binary representation. In practice, the sequence of bits transmitted may suffer corruption in transmission, leading to some, or even all, of the bits arriving at a receiver in error. Errors, and how they may be overcome, are introduced in this chapter and explored in depth later in Chapter 4. In practice, networks typically comprise a number of users and intermediate connection points. The chapter continues by examining how a network physically interconnects points together to form a topology. A brief review follows of the media available for transmission of data, namely metallic conductors, optical fibre or radio transmission. The chapter concludes by discussing how data signals may be directly applied, by means of appropriate coding, to metallic media, a form of transmission known as baseband signalling. The point is made that baseband transmission is not possible over fibre and radio channels but rather modulation must first be employed, as discussed in Chapter 6.

Chapter 3   Information theory

Chapter 2 explores a number of techniques and considerations for the transmission of data. The fundamental purpose of a communications system is not to send data but primarily to convey information between two, or more, parties. This raises the twin questions, both of which are addressed in this chapter, of what is information and how may it be represented in a communications system? The chapter commences with a more theoretical approach to define information and indicate how it is measured. Source coding is then presented as the process of mapping information into suitable data representations. This leads naturally into the topic of data compression which is concerned with ensuring that data contains the minimum number of bits to adequately contain the information it represents. There then follows explanations of two major areas in data communications which employ source coding and compression, namely facsimile and image transmission. The emergent MPEG standards are included here.

Chapter 4   Error control

This chapter discusses the impairments that can lead to errors in a communications link. The principles of error control, which is employed in order to overcome the effects of these impairments, are introduced. The principles of two fundamental methods of error control, namely forward error control and feedback error control, are discussed. The use of codes in forward error control systems is covered in some detail, culminating in the cyclic codes and convolutional codes that are used extensively in data and computer networks. Finally, different feedback error control strategies are discussed.

Chapter 5   Data link control

This chapter starts by looking at the measurement of the flow of data over a link and link throughput and utilization are defined. The concepts of link management and flow control are introduced. Link management involves the setting up and disconnecting of a link. Flow control ensures that data in the form of frames or packets is transmitted in an orderly fashion. The chapter concludes by examining a commonly used data link layer protocol, namely the High-level Data Link Control (HDLC) protocol and a further protocol developed from it known as the Point-to-Point Protocol (PPP) and which is used widely throughout the Internet.

Chapter 6   Modems

Chapter 2 makes mention that not all signals are transmitted in baseband form. Rather, some signals use modulation before they are sent over the transmission medium. The chapter commences by explaining the principal methods of modulation used for transmission of data and continues by an examination of the effect of noise upon such signals. Channel capacity is introduced where the effects of noise and bandwidth place an upper bound upon the maximum data rate possible. Practical modems are then discussed in terms of their principal elements and how they generally conform to internationally agreed standards to ensure that interoperating modems are compatible. Finally, other types of modem for use with radio-based systems and cable TV are also considered.

Chapter 7   Access networks

This chapter is concerned with how customers may gain digital, and ideally high-speed, access to networks. It commences with the examination of a modern all-digital network capable of supporting a range of integrated services and known as an Integrated Services Digital Network (ISDN). Such a network supersedes earlier non-digital telephone networks and, apart from being digital, differs in that ISDN networks are designed to carry any type of communication service rather than simply voice calls. Customer access arrangements are discussed in some detail. Next we consider a development of ISDN, namely Broadband ISDN, for which many standards have been defined by the ITU. Broadband ISDN was conceived to support very high-speed transmission for data and video-based services to customers. Finally a number of high-speed digital services, generically known as xDSL, are described whereby high-speed digital access may be delivered over standard telephone lines to customers' premises. These services are especially attractive for high-speed Internet and video services and form part of the broadband revolution.

Chapter 8   Transport networks

This chapter describes the mechanism of time-division multiplex (TDM) used to aggregate many digital bit streams into a single, higher speed bit stream. This is used to gain efficiency advantages in terms of sharing expensive equipment and line plant as well as to exploit fully the bandwidth of physical media used to transport digital signals within transport networks. A key 'building block' in telephone-based networks which is described is pulse code modulation (PCM) used to digitize analogue telephone signals. Ultimately, when all-digital access networks are developed, PCM systems may eventually disappear, but there is no immediate prospect of this happening. Finally, practical implementations of TDM, namely SDH and SONET, which are used to exploit the high speed of modern optical transmission links, are described.

Chapter 9   Introduction to local area networks

Local area networks (LANs) are computer networks commonly used in networking within a single site. They are confined to a relatively small, or local, physical area of no more than a few kilometres' radius. This chapter introduces the topic of LANs which are further examined in the following two chapters. LANs typically have a single medium which all stations must share. The principal Medium Access Control techniques that enable stations to gain access to the physical medium used are examined. There are two principal techniques known as Carrier Sense Multiple Access with Collision Detection and Token operation. The chapter concludes with performance comparisons of these two techniques.

Chapter 10   LAN standards

This chapter examines the three principal LAN standards which have been, or continue to be, used in practice. Emphasis is placed upon the dominant standard known as IEEE 802.3 and referred to as Ethernet. Treatment of Ethernet in this chapter is restricted to 10 Mbps operation which, although rather dated, serves to illustrate much of the important detail regarding the Medium Access Control protocol used in the higher speed Ethernet LANs which are discussed in the next chapter. Finally the chapter concludes with a description of the IEEE 802.11 Wireless LAN standard and which is proving to be increasingly popular.

Chapter 11   High-speed LANs and metropolitan area networks

This chapter is devoted to higher speed LANs, not covered in Chapter 10, and also related networks known as metropolitan area networks (MANs) which are used to interconnect over much larger physical distances, typically spanning an area up to that of a major city. The chapter commences with an explanation of an optical-fibre-based high-speed LAN in the form of the Fibre Distributed Data Interface standard. High-speed developments of the IEEE 802.3 Ethernet LAN discussed in the previous chapter are then explored. The chapter concludes with the IEEE 802.6 and emerging IEEE 802.17 MAN standards.

Chapter 12   Packet-switched and frame relay networks

This chapter looks at the way in which carriers operate wide area, switched packet data networks. The relative merits of circuit-switched and packet-switched networks are described. The Frame Relay wide area network standard is covered in some detail, as is the original X.25 packet-switched protocol. Two important concepts in the operation of data communications networks, namely traffic management and congestion control, are introduced.

Chapter 13   Asynchronous transfer mode

This chapter introduces the most recent wide area network technology, asynchronous transfer mode. This is the predominant WAN technology used in the cores of the majority of the world's largest data networks and has been an important contributor in the drive towards data and voice convergence. The topics of traffic management and congestion control, introduced in the previous chapter, are expanded upon.

Chapter 14   Internetworking

This chapter explores the generic aspects of techniques used for the interconnection of two or more networks, generally known as internetworking. Firstly the general issues and problems relating to internetworking are set out. Techniques to facilitate internetworking are then discussed, principally the use of repeaters, bridges and routers, and the differences between them. One of the key tasks that a router performs, as its name suggests, is to decide upon the route over which an incoming packet must be forwarded. To this end routing tables are introduced along with how they may be constructed from knowledge of a network's topology. An outline of the Internet, the network of choice for many to achieve internetworking, in terms of its history and organizational structure, is presented. Technical details of the Internet, although introduced here, are described explicitly in the next chapter. Finally, the chapter concludes with consideration of some of the techniques used to improve upon security in an internet.

Chapter 15   Internet protocols

The various internetworking devices, such as routers and bridges, that were discussed in Chapter 14 need to interoperate using a common group of protocols. This chapter examines the Internet Protocol (IP), which is a key protocol used within the Internet for internetworking. The topic of subnetting, which is used to compartmentalize a single IP network to provide efficient and more easily managed subnetworks, is discussed. Routing protocols, which are used to organize efficient routing of data within large internets, are then examined. The chapter continues by examining the transport layer protocols: the Transmission Control Protocol (TCP) which is connection oriented and used to overlay reliable transmission of data upon IP to ensure data is not lost or corrupted, and the UDP which is a lighter weight protocol popular in low-priority applications in which guaranteed delivery of data is not essential. In addition, a number of other associated protocols commonly used in the Internet for a variety of reasons are discussed. Virtual private networks, which are, as the name suggests, private networks and based upon a common IP-enabled core network, are discussed. The chapter continues an examination of real-time operation, including Voice over IP (VoIP) which is proving very popular. The use of Multi Protocol Label Switching to enable IP to operate efficiently over wide area network technologies such as ATM is introduced. In similar vein mention is made of how IP traffic may be carried over SDH/SONET-based networks. The chapter concludes with a further examination of security measures used in IP networks based around approaches collectively known as IPsec.

Chapter 16   Network management

The concepts of data flow measurement and link management introduced in Chapter 5 are extended, culminating in an introduction to network management systems. Network management standards are discussed with an emphasis on ISO and TCP/IP environments. Finally, a practical network management system is presented.

Appendices

Appendix 1 deals with encryption. It commences with an outline of possible security threats and then takes the reader through the processes of symmetrical and asymmetrical encryption techniques. This leads naturally to a discussion of secure distribution of encryption keys. Finally Secure Socket Layers, which are widely used in TCP/IP e-commerce applications, are introduced.

Appendix 2 deals with line coding. The *raison d'être* for line coding has already been outlined in Chapter 2. The purpose of this appendix is to decouple the large degree of detail of line codes from this chapter to ease its flow. In this way it frees the reader from such detail within the chapter and leaves the option of studying the topic within the appendix. The topic itself is vast and restricted here to an indication of the various classes of line codes, an introduction to the subject's nomenclature, an outline of contemporary codes used today and some comparisons between them.

Appendix 3 deals with the topic of queuing theory that is so important in the design of data communications networks.

Supplementary material

A solutions manual containing answers to the end-of-chapter exercises is available for lecturers to download from: www.booksites.net/duck_datacomm

Acknowledgements

··

The authors wish to acknowledge the assistance of the following in the preparation of this book: Mike Oxborrow, consultant, for his assistance in the development of new material on Synchronous Digital Hierarchy; Tony Dunne, Vosper Thorneycroft, for advice given on the X.25 protocol; Peter Doonan, Nortel Networks, for proof-reading material on Frame Relay; Chris Aubrey, consultant, for advice regarding asynchronous transfer mode; Eric Ogsten, Nortel Networks, for his assistance in the development of new material on the TCP/IP suite; Professor Fred Halsall for his continued cooperation in permitting the use of some of his glossary contained in *Data Communications, Computer Networks and Open Systems*, fourth edition.

Finally, the authors particularly wish to extend their appreciation to Peter Bishop who co-authored the first edition of this text. Inevitably, Peter has indirectly assisted in the development of the second edition as much of his original material continues to appear here. Appreciation is also extended for his assisting in the preparation of this edition, in particular proofreading Chapter 3, and numerous useful suggestions, which have enhanced this second edition.

Publisher's acknowledgements

We are grateful to the following for permission to reproduce copyright material:

Figures 2.20, 2.21, 2.22, 2.23, 2.24, 6.1, 6.3, 6.4, 6.5, 6.6, 6.7, 6.8, 6.9, 6.10, 6.13, 8.1 and 8.2 from *Essence Communications* (Read, R. 1998), reprinted by permission of Pearson Education Limited; Figures 9.1 and 9.6 from *Data and Computer Communications*, 3rd edn by Stallings, William, © 1991, pp 350, 416–17 and Figure 13.17 from *Computer Networks*, 3rd edn by Tanenbaum, Andrew, © 1996, p 154. Reprinted by permission of Pearson Education, Inc., Upper Saddle River, NJ; Figures 13.7, 13.8,

13.9, 13.10, 13.11, 13.13, 13.18, 15.7, 15.12, 16.5, 16.6, 16.7, 16.8 and 16.9 reprinted by permission of Nortel Networks Limited.

In some instances we have been unable to trace the owners of copyright material, and we would appreciate any information that would enable us to do so.

Chapter 1

Introduction

This chapter commences with a review of the development of data communications which, although of interest in its own right, is in fact used as a vehicle to set the scene, and introduce a number of basic concepts, for later chapters in the book. Having established how data communications have developed we then turn our attention to the different forms of data and offer some examples of where such data occurs in practice. The general concept of communications models, which are a tool to enable design, implementation and understanding of communications networks and systems, is introduced. The case is then made for standards and the major standards organizations are discussed. A communications model which has greatly influenced current network philosophy is the Open Systems Interconnection (OSI) Reference Model for which standards have already have been produced and many others are under development. After introducing this model, later chapters explore how the model is used in practice, generally through a particular standard. The Institute of Electrical and Electronic Engineers, although not a standards organization in its own right, is discussed, as is its influence on the design of computer networks. A comparison then follows which relates standards of various organizations. The chapter concludes with a brief introduction to the ubiquitous TCP/IP standard which is the linchpin of today's Internet.

1.1 The development of data communications

A brief overview of the development of data communications follows to enable the reader to appreciate the more complex concepts of later chapters. The appearance of digital electronics in the early 1960s led to the widespread use of digital computers. Three main communities which rapidly deployed computers were large financial institutions such as banks and building societies in order to automate and reduce staffing, universities for the solution of complex problems and large commercial organizations to improve management and efficiency. Early computers, despite having relatively limited computing power compared with those of today, were expensive. Their use was therefore shared, often by many users. This raised the issue of how users gain access to computers. The issue of computer access which is both secure and fairly apportioned continues to be a topic of great importance and will be developed further in later chapters.

Another issue which appears in communications is that of a protocol. This is nothing more than a set of rules to govern an activity. Consider two people holding a conversation. A simple protocol, often observed by some cultures, is that only one person speaks at a time. A person wishing to speak waits for a pause in the conversation before commencing. Some computer networks also use this protocol, in which case it is called stop-and-wait. In the case of a floppy disk, there clearly needs to be an agreed system for formatting and reading disks in order that they can be interpreted and processed by a computer. In other words, there needs to be a communication protocol.

One of the key features of a communications system is that of transmission speed. The principal measure of the speed of transmission of data is bit per second (bps). It is found by dividing the total number of bits transmitted by the time taken to complete such a transfer. Transmission speeds in some networks, which we shall explore in Chapter 11, may be as high as one thousand million bits per second (Gbps), or more.

The emergence of modems in the early 1960s changed data communications dramatically. A modem is a device that converts digital data into analogue signals and therefore allows digital signals of computers to be converted into analogue-type signals suitable for transmission over the then almost universal analogue circuits of the telephone network or Public Switched Telephone Network (PSTN). This opened up the possibility of remote terminals being electrically connected to a distant or **host** computer, either permanently or temporarily, by means of a PSTN. This is an early example of on-line operation, which paved the way for interactive operation in which the stations at either end of a link can interact with each other. It would be an understatement to say this greatly speeded up data transmission and hence processing! On-line operation also opened up new opportunities and applications, for example remote access of databases or resource sharing.

With the introduction of on-line operation, new protocols became necessary to format and control the flow of data. The possibility then existed of interconnecting a number of different computers, each of which may operate a different protocol. Networking, which is the technique of connecting two or more user systems together, was in its infancy and the emergence of the need for standards soon became evident.

Computer terminal equipment is generally called data terminal equipment (DTE). Modems, as has been suggested above, may be used to interconnect a DTE to a telephone line. A modem is an example of equipment that terminates the end of a communication network. Such equipment is referred to as data circuit terminating equipment (DCE). The connection between a DCE and a DTE is an example of an interface. Standard interfaces have been defined which govern the physical and procedural arrangements for connection. We shall consider the details of some standard interfaces in later chapters.

By the mid-1960s networks had advanced to the point that, instead of one DTE connecting with a single host computer, DTEs, or users, began communicating with each other. This enabled resource sharing and intercommunication to occur. To support such activity, users are assigned an address in the same way as a telephone line or house has a unique identity. Such addresses enable a network to successfully route messages from a send station to a receive station across a network. In order that communication networks are able to route connections they must contain either **switches** or **routers** to select the paths, or routes, a connection must follow. Hence many networks are called switched networks.

Simple DTE to host computer communication commonly uses a continuous connection for the duration of the message transfer. This is known as **circuit switching**, where a physical, or fixed path, is dedicated to a pair of devices for the duration of the communication. A dial-up modem arrangement to connect a DTE to a host computer is a good example of a circuit-switched connection.

New data networks began to be experimented with towards the end of the 1960s and operated on a packet basis whereby data messages, unless very short, are subdivided into a number of separate blocks of data, known as packets, each containing hundreds of bytes. Each packet may flow through the network independently of other packets. This now meant that each packet must contain some addressing information. Connections may be **connection oriented** where a route through the network, known as a logical connection, is established (not necessarily a fixed end-to-end physical connection) for the duration of the message exchange and over which all subsequent packets flow. Connection-oriented operation is similar to circuit-switched operation. Once a logical connection is established, data is then transferred, using as many packets as is necessary, until the data transfer is complete. The connection may then be terminated.

Connection-oriented operation is used extensively in data communications. An alternative method of operation is that of connectionless operation, which has become extremely popular in recent years. Here each packet is considered by the network as a unique entity and separate from any other packets, even though it may form part of the same message transfer. This means that each packet must contain full address information so that it can be routed through a network independently. This contrasts with connection-oriented operation where, once a route is set up, subsequent packets follow the same route and do not have to be independently addressed. Packet switching will be explored in detail in Chapter 12. Public telephone and packet networks are generally operated on a national basis and cover a very large geographical area. It is for this reason that they are called **wide area networks** (WANs).

In contrast to the 1960s, the 1970s saw computers become both available and affordable to society as a whole and appear in everyday industrial and commercial environments. Local intercommunication between computers may, as has already been discussed, be provided by a WAN, be it a telephone or packet network. However, local interconnection using a WAN is unwieldy and expensive. **Local area networks** (LANs) appeared in the mid-1970s. These networks today often comprise a number of personal computers (PCs) confined to a relatively small, or local, physical area and are suitable for a single site or complex. The appearance of LANs offered the facility of economically connecting machines together in, say, an office using a dedicated communication network. Where a connection is required between more distant users, for example users on separate LANs, connection may be made using an intermediate WAN.

The 1980s saw the development of **metropolitan area networks** (MANs) that connect a number of sites and typically span an area the size of a metropolitan region, or city. Optical fibre, rather than a metallic conducting medium, is generally used to support the relatively high data rate found in MANs over distances of the order of tens of kilometres. A MAN is often used as a backbone network to interconnect a number of physically disparate LANs. Both LANs and MANs are dealt with in later chapters.

The 1990s witnessed a rapid increase in popularity in internetworking. Just as packet switching grew out of a need to bring together a number of disparate systems into a network, a need has been perceived to bring together different networks. Although a user may not be aware of the existence of more than one network, the different networks that are interconnected in this way retain their own individuality and characteristics. Such a grouping of networks is often referred to as an **internet**.

1.2 Types and sources of data

The previous section has already alluded in part to the nature of data and where it originates. In general, there are three main types of signal required to be transmitted: speech, video and data. Although speech and video signals are analogue in nature, the technology now exists to digitize virtually any signal at source. Once this process has occurred, any signal, irrespective of the type of information it represents, may, from then on, be regarded merely as data. Video signals are in the main found in videophones, video conferencing, multimedia applications, broadcast TV, cable TV, satellite and surveillance systems. Analogue operation continues today in some instances, even though the technology may be obsolescent, because it continues to provide adequate quality and the technology used continues to perform satisfactorily.

Although many different networks have evolved, there is increasing pressure for data transmission, through the introduction of standards, to operate at preferred speeds or rates. Speeds which are commonly used are 1200, 2400, 4800, 9600 bps, or multiples, and submultiples, of 64 kbps. A higher range of speeds of 1.5/2, 8, 34, 52, 155, 622 or 2488 Mbps are widely available in the long-haul communication links of WANs offered by Post, Telephone and Telecommunications operators (PTTs).

Figure 1.1 illustrates the major types of services currently found and their accompanying data rates. Additionally the services are also categorized into audio, visual and data. Services operating at under 2 Mbps are termed **narrowband** whereas higher rates are categorized as **broadband**. These themes will be developed further in Chapters 7 and 8.

Some of the services are self-explanatory. Video telephony is commercially available in the form of a 'videophone' where an image of the telephony user appears at

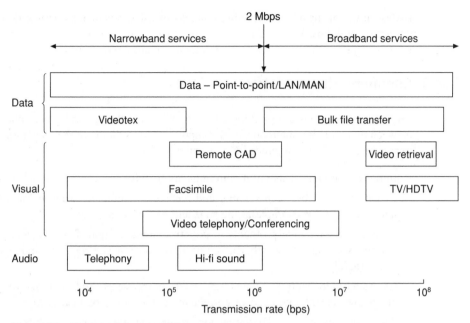

Figure 1.1   Types and sources of data.

the distant videophone. Video conferencing is a method of conferencing using TV cameras and monitors between two or more sites. It attempts to provide a conferencing facility and atmosphere without the need for participants to travel to the same venue for a traditional conference or meeting. Speech and images are relayed and close-ups may be included to view documents, photographs and drawings.

High-definition television (HDTV) is an extension of existing traditional TV services, the higher definition leading to greater picture detail and sharpness. To facilitate improved information content a higher bit rate is necessary. Videotext is a service which transmits alphanumeric and fairly simple graphics information. It is commonly found as an additional service offered within TV broadcast services or for remote booking services used, for instance, by travel agents for flight and holiday bookings. As indicated in Figure 1.1, Videotex has a relatively low data rate of up to 100 kbps or so.

Remote computer-aided design (CAD) simply occurs when CAD information is required to be transmitted. Such information occurs in a variety of CAD applications often associated with engineering design and may be design drawings, instructions for programs, etc. Bulk file transfer transmission occurs at a fairly high data rate and is used to pass very large files of information between sites. An example is where large amounts of stored computer information are passed to a second computer for back-up purposes in the event of the first computer failing. These back-ups are, of necessity, performed quite frequently to maintain integrity and because of the large volume of data involved they must be performed at high speed.

Data has already been discussed in terms of the need to transmit at a distance, or more locally as in a LAN. Dependent upon the application, data may be transmitted at very slow speeds of, say, the order of tens of bps typical of some telemetry applications.

LANs, however, have relatively high speeds of the order of tens, hundreds or even thousands of Mbps.

1.3 Communications models

Data communications are predominantly associated with supporting communications between two, or more, interconnected computer systems. Some of the main tasks necessary for successful communication are listed below:

- Initialization and release of a communications link.
- Synchronization between sending and receiving stations in order to interpret signals correctly, for example at the start and end of a packet.
- Information exchange protocols to govern communication. For instance, a protocol needs to indicate whether a station may transmit and receive simultaneously, or alternately.
- Error control to determine if received signals, or messages, are free from error. Where errors are evident some sort of corrective action should be instigated.
- Addressing and routing. These functions ensure that appropriate routing occurs within a network so as to connect a sending station successfully to a receiving station with the correct address.
- Message formatting. This is concerned with the formatting or coding used to represent the information.

Although the above list is not exhaustive it does illustrate something of the range of complexity involved in a data transfer between communicating parties. In order to build a system, the communication task must be broken down into a number of manageable subtasks and their interrelationships clearly defined. A common approach to such analysis is to represent the tasks and their interrelationships in the form of a conceptual communications model. If the model is sufficiently well defined then the system may be developed successfully.

Although a given communications system may be modelled in a number of ways, computer communications models lean heavily towards layered models. Each layer of the model represents a related series of tasks which is a subset of the total number of tasks involved in a communications system. Figure 1.2 illustrates a three-layer model connecting two systems together.

A commonly used term in relation to communications models is that of an **entity**. An entity is anything capable of sending, or receiving, information. Examples of entities are user application programs, terminals and electronic mail facilities. Each layer of the model communicates using a layer–layer protocol between the two systems. This may be thought of as a communication at a particular layer between a pair of different programs, each operating at the same layer. Within a layered communication model, however, communication ultimately may only occur between the two systems via the physical connection. In order to support a protocol at a particular layer it must therefore operate via the lower layers of the model and then finally over the

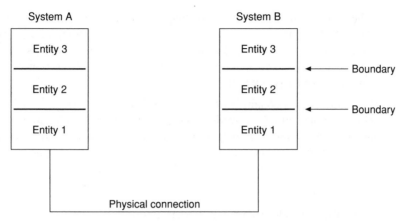

Figure 1.2 A layered communications model.

physical connection. The boundary between the lowest layer and the physical connection is a hardware interface. However, boundaries between the other layers are predominantly software in nature.

A well-constructed layered model enables complex systems to be specified, designed and implemented. This is achieved by the development of a model which splits these tasks into manageable layers and in such a way that the function of each layer is unique and can be implemented separately. Such a layered model then provides a framework for the development of protocols and standards to support information exchange between different systems. Although we have so far only considered layered models conceptually, later on in this chapter we shall look in detail at the dominant layered model which is shaping data communications today and in the future.

1.4　Standards

Standards are required to govern the physical, electrical and procedural characteristics of communications equipment. Standards attempt to ensure that communications equipment made by different manufacturers will satisfactorily interwork with each other. The principal advantages of standards are that they:

1. Ensure a large market for a particular product.
2. Allow products from multiple vendors to communicate with each other. This gives purchasers more flexibility in equipment selection and use. It also limits monopoly and enables healthy competition.

Disadvantages are:

1. A standard tends to lock or freeze technology at that point in time.
2. Standards take several years to become established via numerous discussions and committee meetings. Often, by the time they are in place more efficient techniques have appeared.

3. Multiple standards for the same thing often exist. This means that standards conversion is sometimes necessary. An example is the variety of TV standards existing throughout the world. In data communications an example is the USA's use of 1.5 Mbps digital cable transmission systems operated by PTTs compared with Europe's use of 2 Mbps systems.

The world of data communications is heavily regulated, legally and *de facto*. There exists a whole raft of standards bodies at international, regional and national level. Internationally, the two principal standards bodies concerned with standards for data communications are the International Telecommunications Union (ITU) and the International Organization for Standardization (ISO).

International Telecommunications Union

The ITU is based in Geneva and is a specialized agency of the UN. It comprises member countries, each with equal status and voting rights, as well as industrial companies and international organizations. On 1 July 1994 it was restructured. The Telecommunications Standardization Sector (ITU-T) is responsible for setting standards for public voice and data services (formerly the remit of the Consultative Committee on International Telegraphy and Telephony or CCITT). The Radio Communications Sector (ITU-R) is responsible for radio-frequency spectrum management for both space and terrestrial use. Both this and standards setting for radio used to be performed by the International Radio Consultative Committee (CCIR). The third sector of the ITU is the Development Sector (ITU-D), which is responsible for improving telecommunications equipment and systems in developing countries.

Each sector also organizes conferences on a world and/or regional basis and operates study groups. Standards eventually are produced as a result of such activity to govern interworking and data transfer between equipment at an international level, rather than within the confines of a single nation. ITU-T standards which have been produced for use in data communication are:

G-series – Transmission systems and media, digital systems and networks

H-series – Audiovisual and multimedia systems

I-series – Integrated Services Digital Network (ISDN) transmission

Q-series – Switching and signalling

V-series – Data communications over the telephone network

X-series – Data networks and open system communication

Later chapters will be exploring systems and make reference to the relevant standards as appropriate.

International Organization for Standardization

The ISO promotes the development of standards in the world with the view of facilitating the international exchange of goods and services. Its sphere of interest is not merely confined to data communications, as seen, for instance, in ISO specifications for photographic film. The organization is made up of members from most countries, each representing the standards bodies of their parent country, for example BSI for the UK and ANSI for the USA. The main implication of ISO in data communications has been its development of the reference model for OSI which, as already mentioned, is discussed later in this chapter. In the area of data communications, the ISO standards are developed in cooperation with another body, the International Electrotechnical Committee (IEC). Since the IEC is primarily interested in standards in electrical and electronic engineering, it tends to concentrate on hardware issues, whereas ISO is more concerned with software issues. In the area of data communications (and information technology), in which their interests overlap, they have formed a joint technical committee which is the prime mover in developing standards.

Other standards bodies

The European Telecommunications Standards Institute (ETSI) has 912 members drawn from 54 countries inside and outside Europe. It represents PTT administrations, network operators, manufacturers, service providers, research bodies and users. ETSI plays a major role in developing a wide range of standards and other technical documentation as Europe's contribution to worldwide standardization in telecommunications, broadcasting and information technology. Its prime objective is to support global harmonization by providing a forum in which all the key players can contribute actively and is officially recognized by the European Commission and EFTA secretariat.

1.5　Open Systems Interconnection

As computer networks have proliferated, so the need to communicate between users located on different networks has emerged. Such intercommunicating computer systems may be termed distributed computer systems and are required to process information and pass it between each other.

Historically, communication between groups of computers and DTEs was generally restricted to equipment from a single manufacturer. Many systems used either IBM's Systems Network Architecture (SNA) or DEC's Digital Network Architecture (DNA) which are not directly compatible with each other. ISO formulated its Open Systems Interconnection (OSI) reference model in the late 1970s specifically to address the problem of interconnectivity between different user systems.

OSI gives users of data networks the freedom and flexibility to choose equipment, software and systems from any vendor. It aims to sweep away proprietary systems which oblige a user to build a system with kit from a single vendor. It is a concept which relies upon the emergence of common standards to which components and systems must conform. In this way full interconnectivity will occur between users, each using equipment supplied by vendors of their choice.

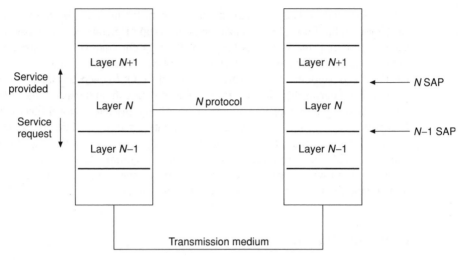

Figure 1.3   *N*-layer service.

N-layer service

The OSI reference model may be thought of as a series of conceptual layers. Such layers operate on the principle shown in Figure 1.3. Layer *N* provides service *N* to layer *N*+1. In order for layer *N* to fulfil its service to layer *N*+1, it in turn requests a service from layer *N*−1. The interfaces or boundaries between adjacent layers or services are known as *N*-layer service access points (SAPs).

Peer-to-peer protocols

The concept of an *N*-layer service is intended to break down the complex tasks of networking into a series of logical and ordered subtasks, each of which becomes relatively simple to design and implement. Another plank in this process of decomposition of the networking task is the concept of peer-to-peer communication protocols whereby any given layer 'talks' to its corresponding layer at the distant end.

Encapsulation

We have established that protocols are operating horizontally between layers in peer-to-peer fashion. However, in order to support such protocols, communication must in reality occur up and down through the layers. The question then arises: how are protocols implemented between layers and also across the network? The answer is illustrated in Figure 1.4. When an application has a message to send, data is sent to the application layer which appends an application layer **header** (H). The purpose of the header is to include the additional information required for peer-to-peer communication. The resultant header and data are termed a **protocol data unit** or PDU. Each PDU is said to **encapsulate** data by adding such a header. This process is repeated a

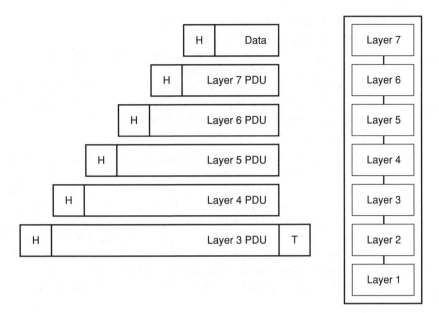

Figure 1.4 Encapsulation.

number of times and generates a PDU at each layer. The data link layer also adds a **trailer** to produce what is known as a **frame**. Finally the frame, with all of the encapsulated PDUs, is transmitted over the physical medium. The receiving station performs the reverse operation to encapsulation (known as **decapsulation**) as headers are stripped off at each layer to separate the respective communications protocols from the data units, the latter being successively passed up through the layers.

Primitives

The way in which a layer provides a service is by means of **primitives**. A primitive specifies an operation or action to occur. It may be a request for a certain service, or an indication that a certain action, or event, has happened. In general there are four types of primitives available, Table 1.1.

Table 1.1 Primitives.

Primitive	Meaning
Request	An entity requires a service
Indication	An entity is informed that an event or action is to take place
Response	Response by an entity when the event or action has occurred
Confirm	Acknowledgement that an earlier request has been granted

Let us examine primitives in an everyday example such as making a telephone call:

Caller lifts handset – *Request* a connection.

Dial tone, dialling and switching follow.

Ringing is applied to callee – *Indication*, ringing tone applied to callee to indicate that a connection is being requested.

Callee answers – *Response*. Caller responds by accepting a connection.

Caller advised of callee's response – *Confirmation* that call is accepted by callee.

Connection established – communication ensues.

Caller, or callee, hangs up to terminate connection.

In a similar way the communication, or in data communications terminology, the data transfer phase and the disconnection phase, may make use of primitives. The above example could therefore be further extended, and even shown diagrammatically, making use of various service primitives as shown in Figure 1.5. This figure also illustrates another point. The CONNECTION primitive uses a confirmed service whereas the DATA and DISCONNECT primitives are unconfirmed. Confirmed services have a response and confirmation, or acknowledgement, whereas unconfirmed services do not use an acknowledgement. Connections must be confirmed so that both parties are certain that a connection exists before transferring any information. Data may be

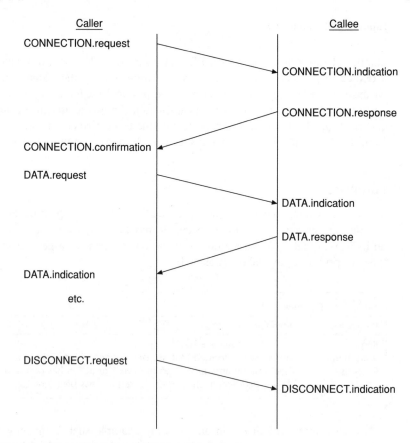

Figure 1.5 Connection-oriented data transfer sequence.

confirmed or unconfirmed, as in the above example, depending upon which service is required. If voice is being conveyed over the connection confirmation is not usually necessary. If some data is lost it may not even matter, or the receiving party could ask for some repetition. Where a data transfer is more critical, for example in transferring a webpage, any data loss could be of concern and therefore a confirmed service could be used. Disconnections are invariably unconfirmed since once one party has disconnected, the connection has ceased. In general either party may initiate a disconnection.

1.6 OSI Reference Model

The ISO's OSI seven-layer reference model is shown in Figure 1.6.

The reference model has been developed based upon some of the principles discussed in general terms in the previous section. In addition the choice of seven layers has sprung from the following:

1. Only sufficient layers have been agreed such that each layer represents a different and unique function within the model.

2. A layer may be thought of as the position of a related group of functions within the model which ranges from one specific to the user application at one end to one involving the transmission or data bits at the other. Layers between these two extremes

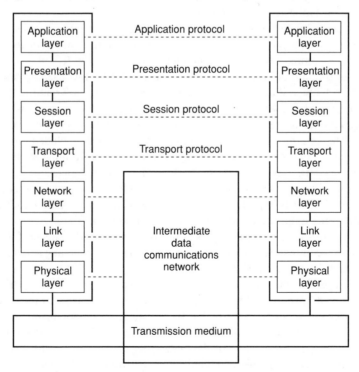

Figure 1.6 OSI Reference Model.

offer functions which include interaction with an intermediate network to establish a connection, error control and data format representation.

3. A layer should be so organized that it may be modified at a later date to enable new functions to be added and yet not require any changes within any other layer.

4. The seven layers and their boundaries have attempted to build upon other models which have proved successful and in such a way as to optimize the transfer of information between layers.

Layer 1, the physical layer, defines the electrical, mechanical and functional interface between a DCE and the transmission medium to enable bits to be transmitted successfully. The layer is always implemented in hardware. A common example used extensively in modems is the ITU-T's V.24 serial interface which will be discussed in detail in Chapter 6. No error control exists at layer 1 but line coding may be incorporated in order to match data signals to certain properties of the communication channel. An example might be to remove a dc component from the signal. Line coding is introduced in Chapter 2.

Layer 2 is the data link layer, the function of which is to perform error-free, reliable transmission of data over a link. Link management procedures allow for the setting up and disconnection of links as required for communication. Having established a connection, error detection, and optionally error correction, is implemented to ensure that the data transfer is reliable. Flow control is also performed to provide for the orderly flow of data (normally in the form of packets) and to ensure that it is not lost or duplicated during transmission.

Layer 3 is the network layer, whose principal task is to establish, maintain and terminate connections to support the transfer of information between end systems via one, or more, intermediate communication networks. It is the only layer concerned with routing, offering addressing schemes which allow users to refer unambiguously to each other. Apart from the control of connections and routing, the layer, by engaging in a dialogue with the network, offers other services such as a user requesting a certain quality of service or reset and synchronization procedures.

The intermediate data communications network included in Figure 1.5 is not strictly a part of the reference model. It is included to draw attention to the fact that the network may be regarded as a black box. What happens *within* it does not necessarily have to conform to any standards, although in practice this is rarely the case. Rather, what is important is that interfaces and protocols are fully supported between networks to ensure compatibility and interworking.

All of the lower three layers are heavily network dependent, for example ITU-T's X.25 recommendation for gaining access to packet-switching networks specifies operation at layers 1, 2 and 3 only.

Layer 4 is the transport layer and separates the function of the higher layers, layers 5, 6 and 7, from the lower layers already discussed. It hides the complexities of data communications from the higher layers which are predominantly concerned with supporting applications. The layer provides a reliable end-to-end service for the transfer of messages irrespective of the underlying network. To fulfil this role, the transport layer selects a suitable communications network which provides the required quality of service. Some of the factors which the layer would consider in such selection are throughput, error rate and delay. Furthermore, the layer is responsible for splitting up messages into a series of packets of suitable size for onward transmission through the selected communications network.

Layer 5, the session layer, is responsible for establishing and maintaining a logical connection. This may include access controls such as log-on and password protection. Secondly, the session layer performs a function known as **dialogue management**. This is merely a protocol used to order communication between each party during a session. It may be best explained by way of an example. Consider an enquiry/response application such as is used for airline ticket booking systems. Although two-way communication is necessary for such an interactive application it need not be simultaneous. Suppose that the connection only provides communication in one direction at a time. The protocol must therefore regulate the direction of communication at any one instant. If, however, full simultaneous two-way communication is available then little dialogue management is required save some negotiation at set-up time. The third, and most important, function of the session layer is that of recovery (or synchronization). Synchronizing points are marked periodically throughout the period of dialogue. In the event of a failure, dialogue can return to a synchronizing point, restart and continue from that point (using back-up facilities) as though no failure had occurred.

Layer 6 is the presentation layer and presents data to the application layer in a form which it is able to understand. To that end, it performs any necessary code and/or data format conversion. In this way there is no necessity for the application layer to be aware of the code used in the peer-to-peer communication at the presentation layer. This means that in practice, users may operate with entirely different codes at each end and which may in turn be different again from the code used across the network for intercommunication. Encryption may also be added at layer 6 for security of messages. Encryption converts the original data into a form which ideally should be unintelligible to any unauthorized third party. Such messages may usually only be decrypted by knowledge of a **key** which of course must be kept secure.

Layer 7, the application layer, gives the end-user access to the OSI environment. This means that the layer provides the necessary software to offer the user's application programs a set of network services, for example an e-mail service. It is effectively the junction between the user's operating system and the OSI network software. In addition, layer 7 may include network management, diagnostics and statistics gathering, and other monitoring facilities.

Most standards activity has centred on the lower layers to support communications networks and their interfaces, for example ITU-T's X.25 recommendation for packet-switched network operation addresses layers 1, 2 and 3, only. ISO standards have more recently addressed this imbalance with standards for some applications being available at all seven layers to support a truly open system interconnection.

1.7 Institute of Electrical and Electronic Engineers 802 standards

The Institute of Electrical and Electronic Engineers (IEEE) is a US professional society and is not a standards body in its own right. Its major influence on international standards is through its IEEE 802 project which produced recommendations, initially for use with LANs, in 1985 and which were adopted as standards by ISO in 1987. Since then further standards have been developed for MANs. Work continues in the development of new standards via technical advisory groups. The current activities of the IEEE 802 Committee are shown below:

802. 1 Overview of 802 standards
802. 2 Logical Link Control
802. 3 Carrier Sense Multiple Access/Collision Detection CSMA/CD
802. 4 Token Bus
802. 5 Token Ring
802. 6 MANs
802. 7 Broadband LANs
802. 9 LAN Integration
802.10 LAN Security
802.11 Wireless LANs
802.12 100VG AnyLAN
802.17 Resilient Packet Ring

Logical Link Control (802.2) specifies the link control procedures for the correct flow and interchange of frames for use with the three basic LAN types. These are distinguished by the way in which a user gains access to the physical medium of the LAN, a process known as **medium access control** (MAC), and are known as CSMA/CD, Token Bus and Token Ring (802.3, 4 and 5 respectively). A number of differences exist between these types of LAN which relate fundamentally to network topology and access methods, signalling technique, transmission speed and media length. In Chapter 10 we shall examine MAC in some depth.

1.8 OSI Reference Model and other standards

Table 1.2 compares the OSI Reference Model and various other standards for a variety of applications. In many instances the other standards are comparable with and sometimes identical to those of ISO.

Table 1.2 Comparison of OSI with other standards.

OSI layers	OSI	ITU-T	IAB	IEEE
7. Application	CCR, FTAM, JTM, VT	X.500 (Directory Services) X.400 (Message Handling Services)		
6. Presentation	Presentation	ACSE, ROSE, RTSE		
5. Session	Session			
4. Transport	Transport		TCP	
3. Network	IP	I-series (ISDN)	IP	
2. Data Link	8802.2	X.25 (Packet Switching) X.21 (Circuit Switching)		802.2 Logical Link Control
1. Physical	8802.3/4.5			802.3/4/5

Some texts also include DNA and SNA in comparisons with ISO but as they are not standards they are omitted here. ISO itself has standards to support applications at the application layer such as:

FTAM – File Transfer & Access Management
VTs – Virtual Terminals
CCR – Commitment, Concurrency & Recovery
JTM – Job Transfer, Access & Management

ISO also has standards to implement the remaining protocol layer functions. The LAN standards 802.2–802.5 have been adopted by ISO as 8802.2–8802.5 respectively. The data link layer standard is 8802.2. Similarly at the physical layer, MAC procedures and physical interconnection are offered as ISO 8802.3–8802.5.

ITU-T supports a number of application layer services including:

X.500 – Directory Services
X.400 – Message Handling Services
RTSE – Reliable Transfer
ROSE – Remote Operations
ACSE – Association Control

ITU-T also has standards defining operation at the lower three layers for ISDN, packet switching and circuit switching.

The OSI Reference Model seeks to set out a method of developing intercommunication or internetworking via one or more, often different, computer communication networks. Additionally, having established the reference model, ISO is committed to developing a full range of standards to enable such internetworking to be established effectively and easily.

Finally, any discussion on OSI would be incomplete without reference to the Internet and the TCP/IP suite. The US Department of Defense (DoD) had already addressed and produced a solution to internetworking before ISO standardization occurred. The DoD's developments culminated in the Transmission Control Protocol/ Internet Protocol (TCP/IP), which is a suite of protocols used almost universally to interconnect computer networks. As explained in Chapter 15, the **Internet Architecture Board** (IAB) has taken over responsibility for Internet standards. The IAB publishes documents called **Request for Comments** (RFCs), which are now in fact *de facto* standards ratified by the ITU-T. Access is easily and inexpensively achieved by means of subscription to any of the networks which form the Internet.

TCP/IP assumes that the Internet, or some of the underlying networks, is unreliable. With reference to Figure 1.7, reliable operation on an end-to-end basis is achieved by

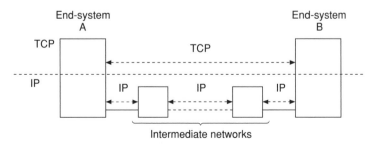

Figure 1.7   TCP/IP operation.

means of connection-oriented operation using TCP at layer 4. TCP is therefore only provided at the two end-systems rather than in any intermediate network forming part of the connection. The use of TCP means that lost packets can be retransmitted. IP is implemented at the network layer and is used for routing each packet in all intermediate networks and is a connectionless service.

Exercises

1.1 Suggest some alternative models to that of the OSI Reference Model. Compare and contrast them with that of the OSI Reference Model.

1.2 Are there any situations where a reduced version of the OSI Reference Model may be adequate? Draw such a model.

1.3 Explain the terms 'peer-to-peer communication' and 'encapsulation'. What advantage do these concepts offer designers of open systems?

1.4 Explain what is meant by 'service' and 'protocol' for a given layer of the OSI Reference Model.

1.5 Summarize the structure of the OSI Reference Model using a sketch and indicate where the following services are provided:
(a) distributed information services
(b) code-independent message interchange service
(c) network-independent message interchange service.

1.6 A relatively long file transfer is to be made between two stations connected to an open system. Assuming that some form of switched communications network is utilized, outline all of the stages that occur to accomplish the file transfer. You should make appropriate reference to each layer of the OSI Reference Model.

1.7 The OSI Reference Model is often drawn with the inclusion of an intermediate communications network at the lower three layers. This network does not necessarily have to conform to any particular set of standards, but what is obligatory for inclusion of such networks within an OSI-based design?

1.8 Compare the TCP/IP stack with that of the OSI Reference Model. Explain what implications exist concerning the TCP/IP stack since not all of the equivalent layers compared with that of the OSI Reference Model are implemented.

Chapter 2

Data communications

In Chapter 1 we discussed the nature of data and commonly found signal types that are conveyed by it. In this chapter we shall look at the transmission of the data over a transmission channel. We shall consider the techniques used to transmit the data, the different configurations in which communications networks can be arranged and the media over which the data may be transmitted; introduce one of the principal ways in which data may be signalled over the media; and finally examine the effect of practical channels upon signals.

2.1   Data transmission techniques

Probably the most fundamental aspect of a data communications system is the technique used to transmit the data between two points. The transmission path between the two points is known as a **link** and the portion of the link dedicated to a particular transmission of data is a **channel**. Within a data network, the two ends of the link are generally referred to as **nodes**. The term **station** has been used to mean node in the past, but the term more aptly describes **end-system** or **end-user** nowadays. In this way a clear distinction may be made between intermediate nodes within a network and end-systems, which occur at the periphery. Most data networks **multiplex** a number of different data sources over a link, in which case there would be a number of channels within the link. Multiplexing is dealt with in detail in Chapter 8.

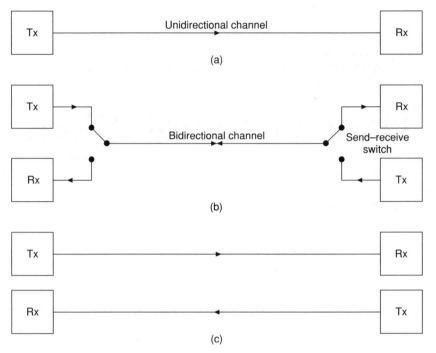

Figure 2.1   Communication modes: (a) simplex; (b) half duplex; (c) full duplex.

Communication modes

Communications systems may operate in either a one-way or a two-way mode. In the context of data communications, an example of one-way communication is a **broadcast system** in which data is transmitted from a central point to a number of receive-only stations; there is no requirement for a return channel and therefore no interaction exists. Teletex services are one-way transmission systems. Transmission which is confined to one direction is known as **simplex** operation and is illustrated in Figure 2.1(a).

Simplex operation is limited in terms of its operational capability but it is simple to implement since little is required by way of a protocol. It has a major limitation in that a receiver cannot directly indicate to a transmitter that it is experiencing any difficulty in reception.

Most data applications require a channel that allows for communication in both directions for either some form of dialogue or interaction, as is the case with Internet shopping or travel agent booking services. Two-way communication is also required if data is to be retransmitted when errors have been detected and some form of repeat request has been sent back to the transmitter. Two possibilities exist for two-way communication:

1. **Half-duplex** operation, as shown in Figure 2.1(b), can support two-way communication, but only one direction at a time. This is typical of many radio systems which, for simplicity and cheapness, employ a common channel for both directions of

transmission. If a node is transmitting it cannot receive from a distant node at the same time. Some form of protocol is therefore necessary to ensure that one node is in transmit mode and the other is in receive mode at any one time as well as to determine when stations should change state.

2. **Full-duplex** operation, as shown in Figure 2.1(c), can support simultaneous two-way communication by using two separate channels, one for each direction of transmission. This is clearly more costly but is simpler to operate. Although at first glance full-duplex operation appears to be an obvious choice, it must be remembered that two-way transmission is not always necessary. Furthermore, where transmission is predominantly in one direction, with little data traffic in the reverse direction of transmission, half-duplex operation may be quite adequate.

Parallel and serial transmission

Computer-based systems store and process data in the form of bits arranged in **words** of fixed size. A computer memory typically consists of a series of stores, each of which has a unique address. Computer systems may handle words of 8, 16, 32 or 64 bits. Within many sections of a system data exists and is passed around in parallel form, which means that each bit of a word has its own physical conducting path. Examples of **parallel transmission** may be found on printed circuit boards and in printer interface cables. Parallel interfaces, such as a computer interconnected to a printer, need to signal in some way when data is available from the computer and also when the printer is, or is not, ready to receive data. The main reason for such signalling is that very often there are appreciable differences in operating speeds between two interfaced devices. In the case of the computer–printer example, the computer is able to send data at a much faster rate than the printer is able to print. This facility of matching devices is achieved using an exchange of control signals known as **handshaking**.

Figure 2.2 shows an example of handshaking in a simple parallel interface. The computer first places data upon the parallel data bus. It then signals to the printer that new data is available by changing the state of the control signal DAV (Data AVailable) from low to high. The printer then accepts the data currently on the parallel data bus. When the printer is ready for the next character, it takes $\overline{\text{DAC}}$ low to indicate to the computer that the data was accepted. DAV and $\overline{\text{DAC}}$ are then returned to their normal states in readiness for signalling commencement of the next data transfer. Clearly the computer must change data on the bus only when DAV is low. Thereafter the sequence may be repeated to pass further characters to the printer.

Parallel transmission is a convenient method of interconnection or interfacing between devices that are situated very close together. However, if signals are to be transferred any distance, parallel transmission becomes impractical owing to the increased cabling and connector requirements.

The alternative approach is to use **serial transmission** where only a *single* data line exists and the data bits are sent one after the other along the line. Although serial transmission is inherently slower than parallel transmission, the reduced cabling arrangements enable longer connections and this is the usual method of sending data over any distance. Figure 2.3(a) shows a basic serial interface arrangement. Figure 2.3(b)

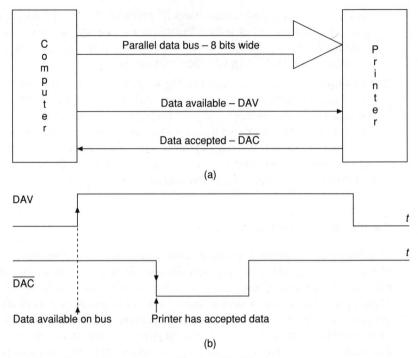

(a)

(b)

Figure 2.2 (a) Parallel transmission and (b) handshaking.

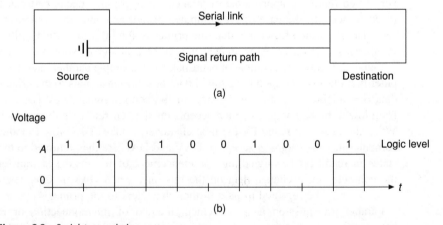

Figure 2.3 Serial transmission.

shows data in the form of a serial bit stream. Each bit, or **signal element**, of this serial data stream occupies the same interval of time. Signals may be represented by positive or negative logic. In Figure 2.3(b) positive logic is employed and where the amplitude of logic 1 is A Volts in this case.

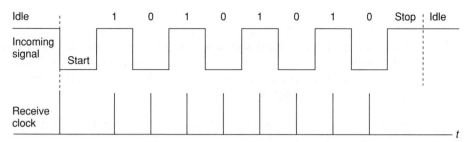

Figure 2.4   Start–stop operation.

Asynchronous and synchronous operation

Any data communications system comprises, as a minimum, a transmitter, a receiver and some form of communication channel. The transmitter produces a data stream, the timing of each bit being generated under the control of a local **clock** (alternate logic ones and zeros).

Asynchronous transmission is where a transmitter may generate bits at any moment in time. Transmission does not necessarily communicate any knowledge of the transmitter clock, or bit, timing to the receiver. For the receiver to interpret incoming signals it must produce a local clock of its own which is of the correct frequency and is positioned at, or near, the centre of each received bit in order to interpret each received bit correctly. Transmitter and receiver use separate independent clocks which are of similar frequency to support a particular nominal bit transmission rate. To position the receiver clock correctly a method of working over short point-to-point links known as **start–stop** operation may be employed. An example of data transmitted using such a system is shown in Figure 2.4.

When there is no data to send the line remains in an **idle** state. The data is preceded by a start signal which is normally of one signal element duration and must be of opposite polarity to that of the idle state. This is followed by several data bits, typically eight. Finally a stop signal is appended which has the same polarity as the idle state. Stop elements have a time period equal to 1, $1\frac{1}{2}$ or 2 signal elements. A stop bit is included to ensure that the start bit is clearly distinguishable from the last bit of a preceding, contiguous, character. When the receiver detects the leading edge of the start bit it starts the production of its receive clock. The first appearance of the clock is so timed to fall at, or near, the centre of the first data bit and is used to strobe the bit into a register. Subsequent clock pulses repeat the process for the remainder of the data bits. Clearly, if the arrival rate of the received signal and the local clock are identical, strobing will occur precisely at the centre of the bit durations. In practice, this may not be the case for, as the number of data bits increases, the coincidence of clock pulses and data bit centres progressively deteriorates. This limits the length of asynchronous bit streams to a maximum of about 12 bits for reliable detection, rendering asynchronous operation unsuitable for most data communications networks.

(**Example 2.1**)

Data is transmitted asynchronously using bits of 20 ms duration. Ignoring any constraints on the number of data bits which may be accommodated between start and
stop bits, estimate the maximum number of bits which may be reliably received if the
receiver clock is operating at 48 Hz.

Assume that the start bit arranges that the receiver clock starts exactly in the centre
of the first received bit period:

Receiver bit duration   = 20 ms
Receiver clock period = 1/48 Hz
                                 $\approx$ 20.83 ms

It is clear from Figure 2.5(a) that after the first bit is received, the receiver clock slips
by approximately 0.83 ms on each successive bit. The problem therefore resolves into
finding how many such slips are necessary to slide beyond half of one received bit
period, or 10 ms:

10/0.83 = 12

Therefore the 12th clock pulse after the first one which was perfectly centred on bit 1,
that is the 13th actual clock pulse, occurs just on the trailing edge of the 13th bit as
may be seen in Figure 2.5(b). This means that bit 13 may or may not be successfully
received. The 14th receiver clock pulse occurs 20.83 ms after the 13th clock pulse
and is in fact 0.83 ms into the 15th bit. Hence the 14th bit is completely missed. As
a result the receiver outputs all of the bits up to and including the 12th correctly, may
or may not correctly interpret bit 13 and outputs the 15th bit received as the 14th bit.
Hence only 12 bits may be reliably received in this example.

A more efficient means of receiver clock synchronization is offered by **synchronous transmission**. Data appears at a receiver as a continuous stream of regularly timed data bits. Transmitter and receiver operate in exact synchronism. The
transmitter generates a clock which can be either transmitted to the receiver over a
separate channel or regenerated at the receiver directly from the transmitted data.
For the latter, sufficient timing information must be contained within the transmitted
signal to enable a component of the transmitter clock frequency to be recovered at
the receiver. This clock recovery process is shown in Figure 2.6.

Effective clock synchronization is an important factor in the design of data communications networks, particularly if traffic which is sensitive to variations in time
delays, such as multimedia traffic, is to be transmitted over the network. An important factor in ensuring that timing information is contained in transmitted data signals
is the choice of signalling technique. This issue is explored further in section 2.4. In
contrast to asynchronous operation, synchronous operation requires a continuous signal to be transmitted, even if no data is present, to ensure that the receiver clock remains
in synchronism with that of the transmitter. Furthermore, for a receiver to interpret
the incoming bit stream correctly, some **framing** of bits into identifiable fixed-length
blocks or **frames** is necessary at the transmitter. Also, at start-up, it takes some time

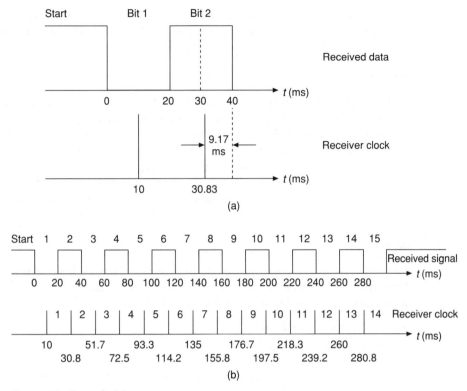

Figure 2.5 Example 2.1.

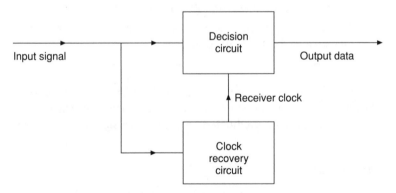

Figure 2.6 Synchronous receiver.

before a stable clock appears at the receiver. In the meantime, no data signals may be reliably output by the receiver. Synchronism at the receiver is achieved by transmitting a special bit sequence (or pattern) known as a **preamble** to enable the receiver clock to be established. The additional circuitry at the transmitter and receiver to enable clock recovery adds a degree of complexity to synchronous transmission which is not required with asynchronous transmission. However, the framing bits in synchronous transmission are relatively few compared with start and stop signalling elements in asynchronous operation. In consequence, the increased efficiency of synchronous transmission allows much higher data transmission speeds than asynchronous transmission.

Signalling rate

Transmission rate, also known as data rate, is the number of bits transmitted during a period of time divided by that time and is measured in bits per second (bps). It is important to distinguish between the transmission rate measured in bps and the **signalling rate** or **baud rate** measured in **baud**. The signalling rate is the rate at which an individual signalling element is transmitted and is probably best defined as the inverse of the duration of the shortest signalling element in a transmission. The difference between these two rates is not immediately obvious and is probably best explained by an example.

Example 2.2

Asynchronous data is transmitted in the form of characters made up as follows: five information bits each of duration 20 ms, a start bit of the same duration as the information bits and a stop bit of duration 30 ms. Determine:

(a) The transmission rate in bps.

(b) The signalling rate in baud.

(a) The time taken to transmit a single character = $(6 \times 20) + 30 = 150$ ms.

   The number of bits transmitted during this time is 7.

   The transmission rate = $7/(150 \times 10^{-3}) = 46.67$ bps.

(b) The shortest signalling element has a duration of 20 ms, therefore the signalling rate = $1/(20 \times 10^{-3}) = 50$ baud.

The difference between the bit rate and the baud rate arises because not all of the bits are of the same duration. Another circumstance in which such a difference can arise is if signals are **modulated** onto a **carrier signal** as outlined in Chapter 6.

ASCII code

So far, we have looked at the different techniques used to transmit data but not at the way in which the data is represented. Text **characters** are normally represented as fixed-length bit sequences. A number of characters are then grouped together in what is, strictly speaking, an **alphabet** but which is more commonly called a **code**. The alphabet most often used in data communications is the ITU-T alphabet number 5, or more commonly the US national version of this, known as the American Standard Code for Information Interchange (ASCII). Each character in this alphabet is represented by a 7-bit pattern, leading to the 2^7 different characters which are listed in Table 2.1.

Table 2.1 ASCII code.

Bit			7	0	0	0	0	1	1	1	1
positions			6	0	0	1	1	0	0	1	1
			5	0	1	0	1	0	1	0	1
4	3	2	1								
0	0	0	0	NUL	DLE	SP	0	@	P	\	p
0	0	0	1	SOH	DC1	!	1	A	Q	a	q
0	0	1	0	STX	DC2	"	2	B	R	b	r
0	0	1	1	ETX	DC3	#	3	C	S	c	s
0	1	0	0	EOT	DC4	$	4	D	T	d	t
0	1	0	1	ENQ	NAK	%	5	E	U	e	u
0	1	1	0	ACK	SYN	&	6	F	V	f	v
0	1	1	1	BEL	ETB	'	7	G	W	g	w
1	0	0	0	BS	CAN	(	8	H	X	h	x
1	0	0	1	HT	EM	)	9	I	Y	i	y
1	0	1	0	LF	SUB	*	:	J	Z	j	z
1	0	1	1	VT	ESC	+	;	K	[	k	{
1	1	0	0	FF	FS	,	<	L	\	l	:
1	1	0	1	CR	GS	-	=	M	]	m	}
1	1	1	0	SO	RS	.	>	N	^	n	~
1	1	1	1	SI	US	/	?	O	-	o	DEL

The alphabet consists of 96 print characters including both upper- and lower-case letters and digits 0 to 9 ('space' and 'delete' are often included in this grouping) and 32 other characters which cannot be printed but which are associated with control functions. This latter grouping includes 'backspace' and 'carriage return'. A full list of the ASCII control characters is provided in Table 2.2.

Table 2.2 ASCII control characters.

Character	Meaning	Character	Meaning
NUL	No character	DLE	Data link escape
SOH	Start of heading	DC1	Device control 1
STX	Start of text	DC2	Device control 2
ETX	End of text	DC3	Device control 3
EOT	End of transmission	DC4	Device control 4
ENQ	Enquiry	NAK	Negative acknowledgement
ACK	Acknowledgement	SYN	Synchronous/idle
BEL	Bell	ETB	End of transmission block
BS	Backspace	CAN	Cancel
HT	Horizontal tabs	EM	End of medium
LF	Line feed	SUB	Substitute
VT	Vertical tabs	ESC	Escape
FF	Form feed	FS	File separator
CR	Carriage return	GS	Group separator
SO	Shift out	RS	Record separator
SI	Shift in	US	Unit separator

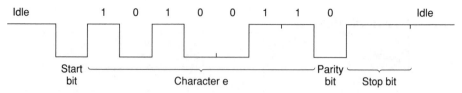

Figure 2.7   ASCII character 'e'.

If ASCII characters are transmitted asynchronously, start and stop bits are added along with an additional eighth bit which is known as a **parity bit** and is used as a rudimentary check for errors. The parity bit is added so that the transmitted 8-bit sequences contain only an even number of ones (even parity) or only an odd number of ones (odd parity). Figure 2.7 shows the ASCII character 'e' as it would typically be transmitted asynchronously using even parity. Note that the stop bit is twice as long as the other bits.

At the receiver a check is made to determine whether the 8-bit sequences still have the same parity. Any character which has not retained its parity is assumed to have been received erroneously. If ASCII characters are transmitted synchronously, a number of characters are normally made into frames.

Errors

In practice, transmission impairments result in data sometimes appearing in error at the receiver. Thus a transmitted logic 0 may be output by a receiver as a logic 1 and vice versa. It is usual to express the number of errors that are likely to occur in a system as a **bit error rate** (BER). A BER of 10^{-5} means that the probability of a bit being received in error is 10^{-5}. Alternatively we can say that, on average, 1 bit in every 100 000 (10^5) will be in error. One of the major causes of error is noise, especially that introduced during transmission, which causes the receiver to interpret bits wrongly on occasion. Noise and other transmission impairments, errors and the techniques used to overcome them will be dealt with in detail in Chapter 4.

Many systems employ some form of error control to attempt to improve the overall BER. The simplest systems employ some form of **error detection**. In such a system, the receiver may be aware of an error within a group of bits but does not know which particular bit is in error. This system is therefore not able to correct errors. The parity check mentioned above is a simple form of error detection which can detect single errors. **Error correction** systems, however, attempt to identify the positions of the bits which are in error and hence correct them. In a binary system, correction is effected by a simple change of state of the offending bit (from 0 to 1 or from 1 to 0). No error control systems can guarantee to detect or correct 100% of errors; they are all probabilistic by nature and hence liable to miss some errors. The use of error control only ever serves to improve the BER, although the resulting improvement is often dramatic.

2.2 Network topology

Network topology is concerned with how communicating nodes are connected together. The physical arrangement which is used to interconnect nodes is known as the **network topology** and the process of determining a path between any two nodes over which traffic can pass is called **routing**. Various topologies are shown in Figure 2.8.

One such technology is a fully interconnected **mesh**, shown in Figure 2.8(a). Such a mesh might seem an obvious first approach to interconnecting nodes. If there are n nodes, each node requires $n - 1$ links to individually interconnect to each of the other nodes. If one assumes that each such link is bidirectional, then the total number of links required in the system may be halved and is given by:

$$\text{Total number of links} = \frac{n(n - 1)}{2}$$

A little investigation reveals that even for modest values of n, the number of links becomes excessive.

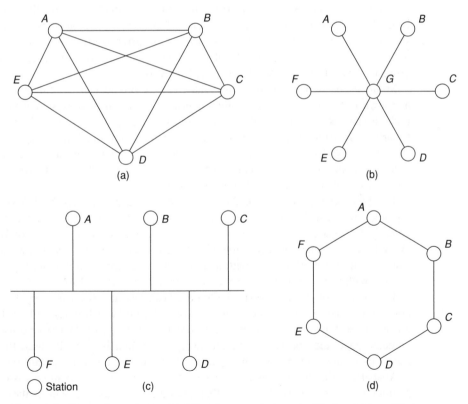

Figure 2.8 Network topologies: (a) fully interconnected mesh; (b) star; (c) bus; (d) ring.

(**Example 2.3**)

A network is to use a fully interconnected mesh topology to connect 10 nodes together. How many links are required?

Number of nodes, $n = 10$

$$\text{Total number of links} = \frac{n(n-1)}{2}$$

$$= \frac{10 \times 9}{2} = 45$$

Even though the size of the network is small, an excessive number of links is necessary. Furthermore, with 10 nodes the maximum number of links which can be in use simultaneously is only five. Thus, with 45 links, there is a nine-fold overprovision.

An attraction of a mesh-type configuration is that each node could have equal share in any control strategy. A node is able to control the selection of the route to another node directly, a process known as **fully distributed control**. Additionally, nodes may be made to perform an intermediate switching function to interconnect two other nodes should their direct link fail. This is known as **adaptive routing**. Example 2.3 highlights one of the disadvantages of fully interconnected networks, that is excessive link provision except in the case of very small networks.

Minimal connectivity, popular in LANs, can be provided by a **star** configuration as shown in Figure 2.8(b). For a small overhead in switching provision at the central node, a star network may make large savings in link provision, as in Example 2.3. Clearly, only 10 links are required, which is more than a four-fold saving. Nevertheless there is still an overprovision by a factor of 2 in that there are twice as many links as are strictly required. This control arrangement is called **centralized control**, a good example of which is a telephone exchange.

The **bus** topology of Figure 2.8(c) has been used extensively by LANs. A bus topology may also be thought of as a tree-like structure. Points to consider are the control of user access to the system and security, since every user potentially 'sees' every message transmitted. Multiple simultaneous accesses to a bus, known as **collisions**, are impossible to avoid with a simple bus and form an important topic of discussion within the section on LAN access control in Section 9.1.

The **ring** topology, as shown in Figure 2.8(d), has also been used by LANs and appears as either a true physical ring or a physical bus which is logically ordered as a ring (token bus). Logical rings simply order the passage of data around users in a predetermined and consistent circular manner. A **token** is normally used to control access to the medium in a ring arrangement, hopefully in a way that is fair to all users.

Apart from the differences in access control, a bus lends itself more easily to the addition (or subtraction) of stations than does a ring. In some instances these alterations may be done without interruption of service. This is clearly not the case with a ring.

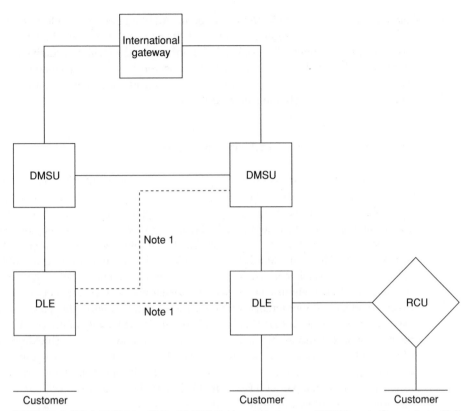

DMSU Digital Main Switching Unit   DLE Digital Local Exchange   RCU Remote Concentrator Unit
Note 1: Supplementary routes subject to demand

Figure 2.9   Telephone network topology.

In reality many networks are configured using a combination of both mesh and tree configurations and where only the network **core** is arranged as a full mesh. Figure 2.9 shows the broad framework for the interconnection of telephone exchanges typical of national telephone operators. Modern telephone exchanges, or switching centres, are effectively real-time digital computer systems. They are virtually a network of computer systems, or a data communications network in its own right. It should be noted in passing that, at the time of writing, considerable effort is being put into the convergence of telephone and data switching networks. The network shown contains a number of fully interconnected, or meshed, Digital Main Switching Units (DMSUs). A typical network may have 50 DMSUs and each serves a number of Digital Local Exchanges (DLEs) to which customers are connected in a star fashion.

Clearly, the choice of topology for a network depends upon factors such as the number of nodes, geographical location, traffic usage between node pairs and link capacities. Choice focuses upon optimization of the number of switching points and overall link provision in terms of both their number and capacity. A single star configuration, for instance, does not suit a national network since many of the more distant nodes require long links to connect to the star point. Additionally, in a single-star configuration, there may be an inordinate number of links to deal with at the hub as well as an overwhelming amount of associated terminating and patching equipment. An example is if the whole of the UK were to be served by a single telephone exchange! There are also reliability and security issues to consider and, indeed, duplicate provision may be deliberately built in to deal with these.

(2.3) Transmission media and characteristics

In addition to the transmission techniques used in a data communications system the different media over which the data is transmitted must also be considered. Media available for transmission of signals are twisted-pair and coaxial-pair metallic conductors and optical fibres. Additionally, signals may be transmitted using radio waves.

Twisted-pair cable is used for baseband communication over relatively short distances, typically in modern LAN installations. A twisted pair possesses low inductance but high capacitance which causes substantial attenuation of signals at higher frequencies. Some environments where twisted-pair cables are deployed contain excessive electrical interference which may easily ingress into cable pairs and lead to excessive signal degradation. This typically occurs in the vicinity of high-voltage equipment. In such situations shielded twisted-pair cable may be used. Shielding consists of a tube of metallic braid, or winding a strip of foil, around each pair within the cable to minimize the amount of interference. Twisted-pair cables are therefore described as unshielded twisted pair (UTP) or shielded twisted pair (STP) and examples of their construction are shown in Figure 2.10.

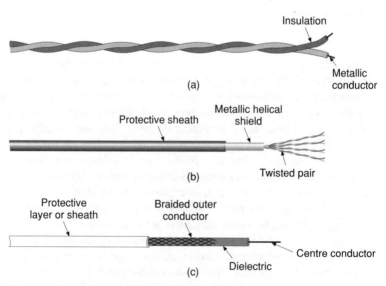

Figure 2.10 Metallic cable construction: (a) unshielded twisted pair; (b) shielded twisted pair; (c) coaxial pair.

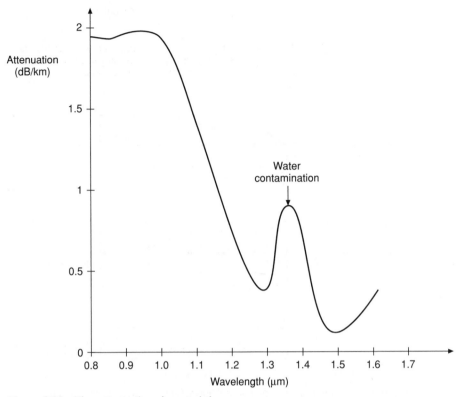

Figure 2.11   Fibre attenuation characteristics.

Coaxial-pair cable, Figure 2.10(c), was developed to overcome the deficiencies of twisted-pair conductors by enabling much higher frequencies of operation, typically up to hundreds of MHz. In addition, its construction produces very little electromagnetic radiation, thus limiting any unwanted emissions and reducing the possibility for eavesdropping. Conversely, very little interference may enter coaxial pairs, affording a high degree of immunity to external interference. Coaxial conductors may support data rates in excess of 100 Mbps making them suitable for use in both LANs and WANs. The velocity of propagation in metallic conductors, twisted-pair and coaxial, is about two-thirds that of the free space velocity of propagation of electromagnetic radiation and is about 200 000 km/s.

Optical fibre was specifically developed to handle even higher transmission rates with lower losses than are possible with coaxial conductors. Digital transmission is achieved by modulating data onto an optical carrier. There are two main wavelengths where transmission loss is extremely low and which are used with optical fibre systems. As Figure 2.11 shows, one occurs at a wavelength of 1.3 μm and the other at 1.5 μm, both of which are in the infrared region of the electromagnetic spectrum. The longer wavelength is used in submarine systems where it is important for losses to be as low as possible. In Figure 2.11, losses peak at about 1.4 μm owing to water

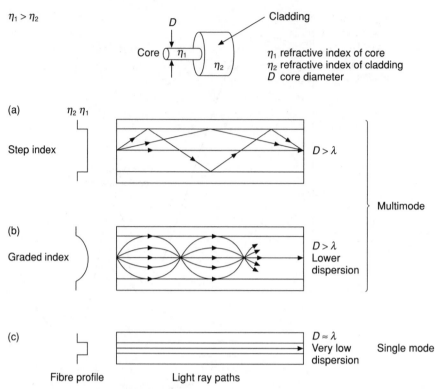

Figure 2.12   Light propagation in optical fibres: (a) step index; (b) graded index; (c) monomode.

contamination in the manufacturing process. At shorter wavelengths below 0.8 μm loss rises rapidly as a result of metallic impurities within the glass.

Fibres are constructed of glass or plastic and contain an inner core and an outer cladding. The refractive index of the core η_1 is slightly higher than that of the core's surrounding cladding, η_2, and, as a result, light is contained within the core due to multiple reflections caused by total internal reflection at the core–cladding boundary. Earlier optical communication systems predominantly used fibre with a relatively large core diameter. This permits light rays to follow a range of different paths within the core of the fibre. Such multipath propagation is known as **multimode** operation and is illustrated in Figure 2.12(a) and (b). As a result of multimode operation, rays arrive at the remote end of the fibre at slightly different times, leading to a spreading of the received signal pulses, a phenomenon known as **dispersion**. The earlier systems used a fibre with a **step index** profile in which the refractive index of the glass changed abruptly at the boundary between the core and cladding. The use of **graded index** fibre, in which the refractive index changes gradually, in multimode operation produces an improvement over step index fibre. Here the gradual variation of the refractive index of the core causes the rays of light to follow curved paths, as Figure 2.12(b) shows. Consequently, the range of path lengths is less than in a step index fibre thus reducing dispersion and allowing higher transmission rates to be used. Transmission rates of up to 155 Mbps and ranges of up to 10 km are possible using multimode, graded index fibre.

Although multimode operation is still used in short-haul systems and also in LANs, **monomode** or **single mode** (Figure 2.12(c)) operation is now dominant for higher speed operation such as high-speed trunk links operated by PTTs. Monomode operation uses a much smaller core diameter and eliminates all but the direct ray of light that can be thought of as passing down the centre of the core, thus greatly reducing dispersion and enabling current systems to operate at speeds of 10 Gbps and beyond.

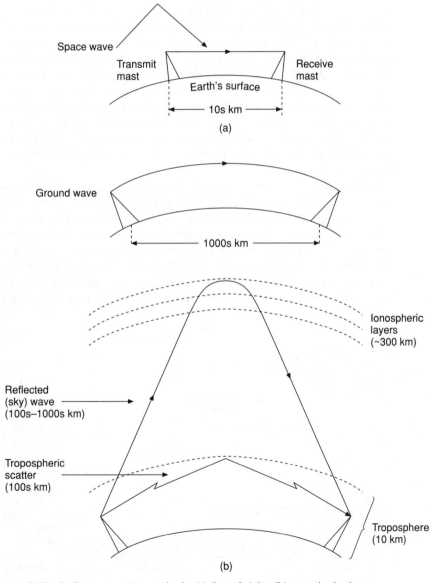

Figure 2.13   Radio propagation methods: (a) line of sight; (b) over the horizon.

Wireless operation, by means of radio propagation, is difficult to summarize simply within an introductory topic. Propagation is dependent upon the frequency of operation, geographical location and time, and is a complex subject for design engineers. Radio may be used to good effect in point-to-point operation, especially over difficult or hostile terrain, and is a natural choice in many broadcast applications, obviating the need to install many separate physical circuits. Radio communication is of course essential for most mobile networks.

Figure 2.13 illustrates the principal radio propagation methods and indicates approximate ranges. **Line of sight** (LOS) operation, as the name suggests, requires a clear unobstructed path between transmitter and receiver which can easily be arranged in point-to-point operation. Many mobile communication systems, such as GSM, operate on frequencies that operate in an LOS mode but cannot always ensure that this condition is satisfied. In such circumstances radio waves which reflect from man-made and natural obstacles provide alternative ray paths between transmitter and receiver and which for much of the time enable satisfactory communication. Telecommunication satellite communications is by means of LOS operation. At frequencies below about 100 MHz radio communication **over the horizon** (OTH) operation is possible using a variety of means. Radio waves at frequencies up to a few megahertz 'bend' and give rise to a **ground wave**. Such waves may travel tremendous distances if enough power is transmitted.

Radio waves at frequencies around 3 to 30 MHz, that is the **high-frequency** (HF) band, can be made to reflect from the ionosphere to a point some considerable distance from the transmitter, in which case they are known as **sky waves**. Although not apparent in Figure 2.13(b), sky wave propagation may traverse considerably greater distances – many thousands of km – than is indicated, as a result of multiple reflections of the wave from both the earth's surface and the ionosphere.

Figure 2.14 relates these propagation methods to the corresponding frequencies, and also compares those used for metallic and optical media. Frequencies in the **ultra high-**

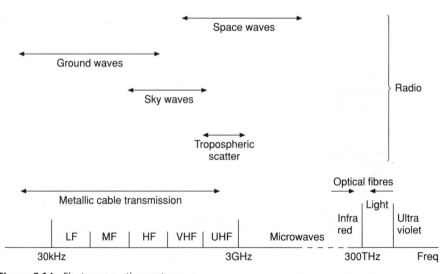

Figure 2.14 Electromagnetic spectrum.

frequency (UHF) band can make use of **scattering** within the troposphere to achieve similar range to that of HF communication.

Optical fibre is potentially much cheaper than coaxial conductors. Optical fibre's inherently low loss enables propagation over several tens of km without signals requiring any regeneration, which is an appreciably greater spacing than is possible using coaxial conductors. Coaxial-pair conductors (and twisted-pairs) suffer from varying degrees of interference, but this is non-existent in fibre systems.

For secure transmission, coaxial or optical media are preferred since they radiate very little, if at all. Radio is inherently insecure and twisted-pair is easily monitored. Where these latter media are unavoidable data encryption may be used.

2.4 Baseband signalling

In this section we shall firstly consider how data is represented as a digital signal and then outline why signals generally require to be encoded before being sent on a transmission line. Finally the effect of restricting the range of frequency of a signal transmitted over a channel and ways of mitigating the effect of any distortion which may result is examined.

Data is almost universally represented in binary form using two elements: logic 1 and logic 0. These elements are very often mapped into two signal elements but such mapping can occur in a number of ways:

- Unipolar, Figure 2.15(a):
  - All elements have the same polarity. Use of the word 'all' indicates that in some systems there may be more than simply two signal elements, or symbols, as we shall see.
  - Note that one element may be mapped to zero volts and therefore regarded as either positive or negative, and hence be consistent with the other signal element irrespective of its polarity.

- Bipolar, Figure 2.15(b):
  - Two (or more) signal elements have different polarity.

Now consider some ways in which data may be represented as an electrical signal. Only binary data is considered although all of the codes could be extended to signals containing more than two symbols.

- Non-return to zero level (NRZL), Figure 2.16(a):
  - High level represents logic 1.
  - Low level represents logic 0.
  - Note that NRZL does not of necessity define unipolar or bipolar operation; either may equally well be used.

- Non-return to zero-level inverted (NRZ-I), Figure 2.16(b):
  - Logic 0, no transition at commencement of signal. That is, the signal voltage remains the same as for the previous element.
  - Logic 1, transition at commencement of signal.

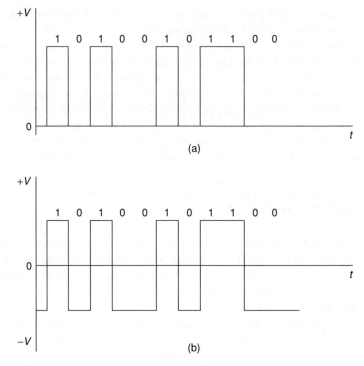

Figure 2.15   Signal representations: (a) unipolar; (b) bipolar.

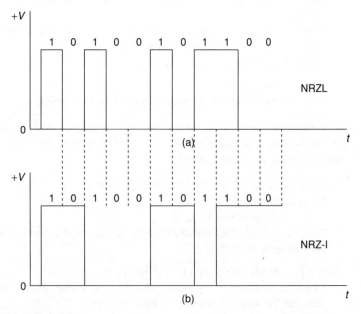

Figure 2.16   NRZ signals.

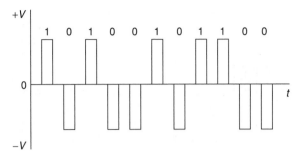

Figure 2.17　RZ signals.

It is evident from the figure that NRZ-I only has a transition for each logic 1, but no transition in the case of a zero. This means that the receiver clock must be accurately maintained in synchronism to ensure that strings of zeros are reliably received.

● Return to zero (RZ), Figure 2.17:
　－ Each bit, or symbol, is encoded into three distinct signal elements. The three signal elements available are 0 V, a positive voltage which we shall call +V and a negative voltage, −V.
　－ Any symbol to be transmitted starts and finishes with 0 V, which gives rise to the name of 'return to zero'.
　－ Binary 1 symbol is transmitted with a +V element in the centre of the symbol, and binary 0 a −V element.

RZ is an example of a binary code where one binary signal is encoded into three signal elements. Each signal element is selected from one of three states and for this reason RZ is an example of a **ternary** code. There is a generalized method of describing codes. RZ is classified as 1B3T, meaning that one binary signal is encoded into three signal elements, any one of which may have one of three (ternary) states.

Line coding

Most digital signals *within* electronic and computer systems are unipolar NRZL. Although binary data signals found in computer systems may be transmitted directly onto a transmission line, in practice it is usual for some form of encoding, called **line coding**, to be applied first to the signals.

　Transmitting signals either directly, or via line encoding, is known as **baseband transmission**. The corollary is where signal elements are impressed upon a carrier, a process known as **modulation** and discussed in detail in Chapter 6. Some form of modulation must be used over radio and optical transmission media but baseband transmission may be used over metallic cables.

　Line coding is almost invariably performed in baseband transmission systems longer than a few tens of metres. There are three principal reasons why line coding is used immediately prior to transmitting signals to a line:

1. Baseline wander: Systems interconnected by a transmission line each have their own power supplies. For reasons of safety and isolation of supplies, most lines are

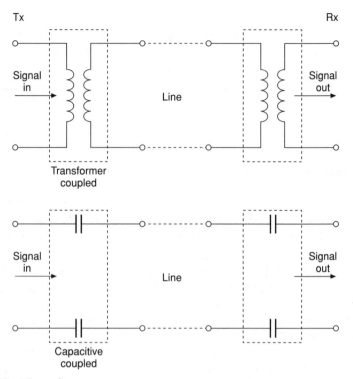

Figure 2.18   AC coupling.

ac coupled. This means that a line blocks dc and low frequencies due to either inductive, or capacitive, components at one, or both, ends of the line as shown in Figure 2.18.

DC blocking means that low-frequency elements of a signal are rejected, or severely attenuated. In particular, and most importantly, ac coupled lines are unable to pass a steady, or dc, voltage. If NRZ signals are applied to such a line an effect known as **baseline wander** may occur as shown in Figure 2.19. Here we may see that transitions successfully pass through the line. However, any constant dc voltage representing several similar bits in succession appears at the receiver as a voltage that steadily decays towards zero volts, the baseline about which signals are referenced. The problem caused by baseline wander is that signal element voltages may become too small to determine accurately if they are above, or below, the baseline and hence become misinterpreted. This is compounded by such weaker signals having reduced immunity to noise. Both of these effects lead to increased BER.

2. Receiver clock synchronism: Synchronous operation is usually employed in lines of any appreciable length (i.e. a hundred metres, or more). The absence of transitions in NRZ signals conveying long strings of logic 0, or logic 1, means that the receiver has insufficient transitions with which to synchronize. In consequence its clock will drift over time leading to errors due to making decisions at the wrong moment, for similar reasons to those discussed in Section 2.1, earlier.

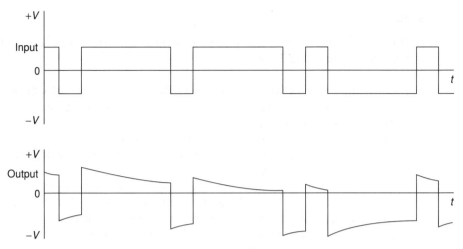

Figure 2.19 Baseline wander.

3. Bandwidth of the line: All transmission media have a limited bandwidth which places a constraint upon the maximum signalling rate. Optical and radio channels exhibit a bandpass response positioned at relatively high frequency and are therefore incapable of passing baseband signals directly. Metallic conductors intrinsically offer a low-pass response. In practice, as indicated earlier, line terminating equipment places dc blocking elements in circuit, which severely attenuates low frequencies. As a result metallic conductors usually also exhibit a bandpass response, except for very short cables. Accepting that virtually all transmission links are in effect bandpass means that transmitted signals must have a spectrum that matches such a response. In particular signals ideally must not contain dc and low-frequency components.

Over the years a variety of line codes have been devised to mitigate the band-limiting effect of practical lines. Their complexity and sophistication have increased as advances in electronic circuits have occurred. Many such codes have been devised and currently a variety of codes are used dependent upon the characteristics of a line in question and the features desired.

The principal design goals of a line code are:

● negligible baseline wander to avoid any appreciable deviation of signal voltage from the ideal at the receiver. This is normally achieved by arranging that over time a signal has no long strings of the same polarity. In addition there should be an equal number of positive and negative voltage signals over time, in which case the signal is said to exhibit a **zero balance** of voltage. That is, the long-term line voltage averages to zero.

● relatively frequent signal transitions sufficient to support reliable clock recovery at the receiver.

● matching the transmitted signal's spectrum to that of the line.

(**Example 2.4**)

How well does the RZ code satisfy the generalized design criteria of a line code? Contrast RZ coding with that of NRZ.

RZ offers no protection against baseline wander since sequences of successive ones, or zeros, are encoded into runs of same polarity. There is also no guarantee that sequences of symbols have zero balance.

RZ offers good clock recovery prospects. It is said to be 'clock rich'. Unlike NRZ, for instance, RZ coding produces two transitions for every symbol, making clock recovery at the receiver relatively trivial.

However, with two transitions per symbol, RZ results in double the spectrum that might reasonably be expected. What this means in practice is that for a given channel bandwidth, if RZ is to be used the effective data rate is halved.

In summary, RZ provides for reliable clock recovery at the receiver, cannot combat baseline wander and is rather inefficient spectrally.

RZ produces at least twice as many transitions as NRZ and so provides good prospects for clock recovery. This contrasts with NRZ coding which only produces one signal transition for one binary symbol and no transition for the other, which does not easily facilitate clock recovery. However, it does mean that RZ signals produce double the spectrum of NRZ signals. Therefore, for a given bandwidth, NRZ may operate at a higher data rate.

The above example serves to illustrate that NRZ and RZ codes are not suited as line codes for transmission lines. Appendix 2 explores a number of line codes used in practice.

Band-limited channels

A metallic transmission line may be represented by an equivalent electrical circuit (Dunlop and Smith 1994) which includes series inductance and shunt capacitance. This, in addition to any ac coupling elements which may also be present, means that transmission lines exhibit a low-pass filtering effect which gives rise to both attenuation and phase distortion.

Theoretically baseband signals, which are examples of digital signals, have an infinite spectrum which at face value implies that a band-limited channel is unable to handle such signals. However, the low-pass filtering effect of a transmission line, or indeed any practical channel, does not automatically mean that perfect recovery of a baseband signal at a receiver is not possible. Signalling rate R has the unit baud and equals the reciprocal of the duration of the shortest signalling element. Perfect recovery of digital signals is possible providing that the signalling rate does not exceed twice the available bandwidth, W. This rate is known as the **Nyquist rate** (Nyquist 1928, pp617–644):

$$R = 1/T \leq 2W \tag{2.1}$$

where T is the duration of one signalling element, or symbol. Alternatively the Nyquist limit, for baseband signals, may be regarded as transmission of a maximum of two symbols per hertz of bandwidth. (Note that for signalling over channels using modulation,

(a)

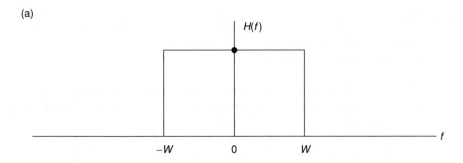

(b)

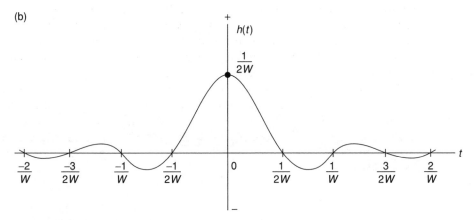

Figure 2.20 Ideal low-pass filter response to a pulse train: (a) ideal low-pass filter-transfer; (b) time domain response.

signalling is at best half the rate for baseband and, depending upon the type of modulation employed, generally less than this.) If signals are transmitted at a rate in excess of the Nyquist rate an effect known as **aliasing** (Read 1998, p48) occurs at the receiver.

Analysis of the practical aspects of the low-pass filtering effect of a transmission line upon a baseband signal requires exact knowledge of a transmission line's particular frequency response or **transfer function**. Consider the effect of a perfect filter upon a train of pulses where the line's frequency response is assumed to be ideal as shown in Figure 2.20(a). We shall assume a signalling rate equal to exactly twice the filter's bandwidth, W. That is:

$$\text{Signalling rate} = 1/T = 2W \tag{2.2}$$

The effect of such filtering upon the pulse train may be found by multiplying the signal, in the frequency domain, with that of the filter's frequency response. In practice it is easier to determine the effect of filtering by considering the time domain. Here the effect of the filter may be found by **convolving** the time domain response of the filter with that of the digital signal. It may be shown that the time domain response of an ideal low-pass filter is given by the expression shown in Equation (2.3) and is a so-called **sinc** function, Figure 2.20(b):

$$h(t) = \text{sinc}(2Wt) \tag{2.3}$$

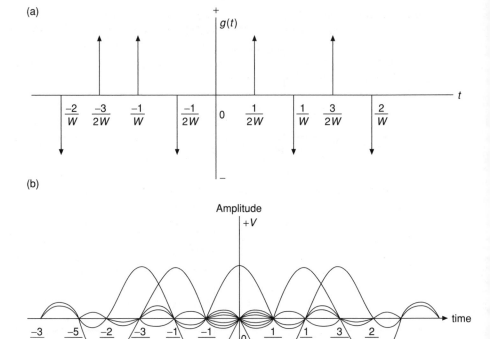

Figure 2.21 Transmission of a digital signal through ideal low-pass filter: (a) digital signal; (b) output signal components.

Determination of the effect of convolving a digital signal consisting of pulses with the above sinc pulse is not trivial. For simplicity we shall assume that each pulse is an impulse, or delta, function and that the signal is bipolar. Such a signal is shown in Figure 2.21(a).

Convolution of a single impulse function with the sinc function response of the filter, Figure 2.20(b), produces another sinc function, but centred upon the instant in time of the particular impulse function. Superposition may be brought to bear and hence the output response of the filter is the sum of the channel response to each individual impulse function. We may therefore conclude that the overall effect of the filter upon the train of impulse functions shown in Figure 2.21(a) is the sum of a series of sinc functions, each similar to that shown in Figure 2.20(b), each centred upon the time interval of their respective impulse function. The individual sinc functions for each impulse function are shown in Figure 2.21(b). This figure does not include the final output voltage, that is the sum of the series of time-shifted sinc functions. However, it is clear from the idealized channel output response shown that at the sampling intervals ($1/2W$, or multiples thereof) the amplitude is a peak and due entirely to the corresponding impulse pulse to the line. Secondly, the amplitude of all other sinc pulses at each sampling interval other than its own is zero. The receiver clock must be perfectly synchronized so that the decision regarding the signal's amplitude is made at the correct interval in time. Under this condition the only voltage present is that purely due to the desired received symbol, in which case no other symbols interfere. This condition means that there is no interference between different symbols, that is there is no **intersymbol interference** (ISI).

The above reveals that, even with a band-limited channel, each symbol may be correctly received. In practice baseband signals are broader than impulse functions leading to a 'smearing' of the received signal. Secondly the channel response is imperfect and introduces distortion effects, of which **phase distortion** is the most detrimental. Thirdly, clock timing, and hence decision timing of the received signal, is subject to variation or **jitter**. All three effects introduce ISI which, in the extreme, may completely change the meaning, or sense, of a received symbol at the moment of decision which in turn will give rise to an error.

In practice a transmission line, although possessing a low-pass filtering effect, does not have an abrupt cut-off frequency as considered earlier with the ideal low-pass filter response. A typical baseband signal received in practice might be as shown in Figure 2.22(a). In such cases the receiver must establish a **decision threshold**. A voltage which, at the decision moment, is above that of the threshold level is output as binary 1, and vice versa. In the case of two-level (binary) signalling the threshold is simply mid-way between the maximum range of voltage excursion of the received signal, or half the peak-to-peak amplitude. The receiver must also establish reliable timing of the moment at which the signal should be sampled. This should be as closely synchronized with that of the transmitter's data clock as possible.

A useful and simple test performed in practice to monitor the effect of a transmission link, and associated noise and interference, is that of an **eye diagram**. Consider again the received digital signal shown in Figure 2.22(a). If an oscilloscope is synchronized with the symbol rate such that each trace displays precisely one symbol, successive traces become superimposed as shown in Figure 2.22(b). For ease of illustration the symbols shown in Figure 2.22(a) have been numbered. Their corresponding appearances within the eye diagram of Figure 2.22(b) are indicated. The exact number of traces visible will depend upon the persistence capability of the cathode ray tube of the oscilloscope.

Figure 2.22(b) appears similar in shape to an eye, hence its name. The receiver samples the received signal periodically at the centre of each symbol, and hence eye. It may be clearly seen from the eye diagram that the signal amplitudes at the moment of decision vary. This is an indication that ISI is present and caused by distortion, noise, interference and band limiting of the channel.

Figure 2.23 shows a generalized eye diagram. The fuzzy bands are stylized lines and due to signal and ISI, as shown earlier in Figure 2.22, and accompanying variation due to noise. Noise increases the overall width of the bands and its effect is to reduce the open area of the eye. The eye diagram indicates the degree of immunity to noise, or noise margin. This is the amount by which noise may be further increased before complete closure of the eye occurs. If this occurs, no meaningful decision may be made and reception becomes impossible. In practice, the decision level itself has an associated tolerance which reduces the noise margin further. An eye which has a wide opening horizontally, or sides of small slope, is tolerant to timing error variation, or jitter, in regard to the moment of decision. Under this condition any jitter only

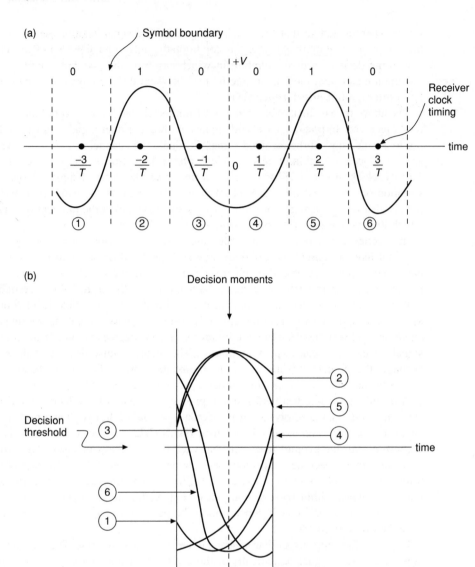

Figure 2.22 Eye diagram.

has a marginal effect upon noise margin and the error rate is substantially unaltered. Where the eye is narrow and the slope is steep, tolerance to jitter diminishes rapidly as the moment of decision moves from the optimum position. Thus eye slope indicates tolerance, or otherwise, to timing error or jitter.

In practice an **equalizer** may be used to compensate for a non-ideal channel response found in practice. An equalizer may be positioned either between the transmitter and line, or between the line and receiver. The aim of an equalizer is to reduce

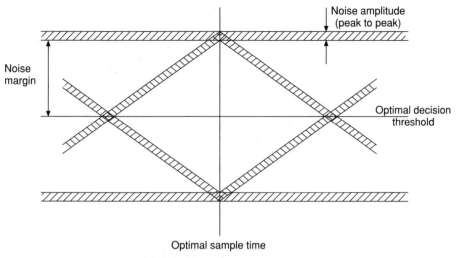

Noise amplitude
(peak to peak)

Noise
margin

Optimal decision
threshold

Optimal sample time

Figure 2.23   Generalized eye diagram.

the amplitude of oscillatory tails shown in Figure 2.20 and yet preserve the zero-crossing feature of sinc pulses. This would result in a more open eye and therefore reduced ISI and a commensurate reduction in BER. The combined response of channel and equalizer can be made equivalent to multiplication in time an of ideal low-pass filter response of bandwidth equivalent to the Nyquist minimum with a suitable frequency response to satisfy the above requirements.

A popular response sought in practice is equivalent to that produced by convolving the ideal rectangular response seen earlier with that of a truncated raised cosine with double the bandwidth of the filter. Figure 2.24(a) illustrates the ideal and truncated raised cosine frequency responses desired. The desired channel and equalizer response found by their convolution may be represented as $H(f)$. It may be shown that the time domain response (Read 1998, pp139–141) $h(t)$ is given by the expression:

$$h(t) = \text{sinc } 2Wt \cdot \frac{\text{sinc } 4W\pi t}{(1 - 4^2 W^2 t^2)} \tag{2.4}$$

Note that in practice the channel response is not rectangular and therefore the equalizer response differs from the truncated raised cosine form. The equalizer response is, as far as possible, such that when convolved with that of the channel it nevertheless produces the time domain response indicated in Equation (2.4).

The response to an impulse produces a time response at the equalizer output as shown in Figure 2.24(b) where we may see that, as with the sinc response of an ideal channel, there is zero ISI. Raised cosine pulse shaping is slightly less tolerant to timing jitter owing to the narrower pulse but the tails decay far more rapidly, which offers superior overall ISI performance. This improvement does mean that a channel must have a bandwidth at least twice that of the ideal value. A trade-off must therefore be made between reduced ISI, and hence improved BER performance, and transmission rate.

In practical transmission systems pulses are broader than impulses in order to provide greater energy and increase immunity to noise. The equalizer response is modified

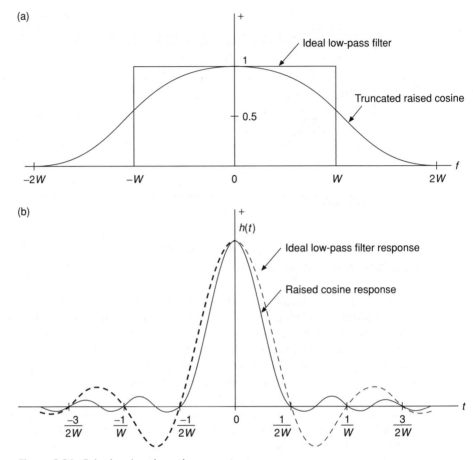

Figure 2.24 Raised cosine channel response.

to produce the same overall response as that required for an impulse. Hence the time domain response to a finite width pulse remains the same as for an impulse described above, but will result in improved BER performance.

In some cases baseband operation is not possible. This particularly applies to the use of RF channels and optical fibre cables. In such cases signals must be modulated to reposition them within a suitable spectral band to match that of the medium in use. Modulation is discussed in Chapter 6.

Exercises

2.1 For each of the services shown below, state whether a simplex, half-duplex or full-duplex form of communication is most suitable. Give reasons for your choices.
(a) Traditional terrestrial TV
(b) Cable TV
(c) Pay-TV

(d) Viewing webpages

(e) File transfers

(f) PC banking

(g) Telephone call

2.2   Compare serial and parallel transmission. Why is parallel transmission unsuited for communication over appreciable distance?

2.3   With reference to Example 2.1, explain what happens if the first appearance of the clock pulse at the receiver is not exactly in the centre of the first incoming bit.

2.4   Data is transmitted asynchronously at 50 bps. Ignoring any constraints on the number of data bits which may be accommodated between start and stop bits, estimate the maximum number of bits which may be reliably received if the receiver clock is operating at 52 Hz.

2.5   Data is transmitted asynchronously in the form of short blocks consisting of a start bit, seven information bits, a parity bit and a stop bit. All bits are of 9.09 ms duration apart from the stop bit which is of double length. Determine:

(a) the bit rate

(b) the baud rate

2.6   Compare synchronous and asynchronous transmission.

2.7   Explain why synchronous transmission has the potential to operate at higher transmission rates than asynchronous transmission.

2.8   A computer network is to consist of 20 stations.

(a) Determine the number of links required if:

(i) mesh topology is used;

(ii) star topology is used.

(b) Suppose that four stations are designated as hubs, each fully interconnected with the others. The remaining 16 stations are equally distributed to the hubs, any one station only being connected to one hub. Sketch the topology and determine the number of links.

(c) Compare all three topologies from (a) and (b).

2.9   Compare the relative merits of transmitting data over copper conductors, optical fibre and radio.

2.10 Briefly outline and explain the functions of line coding.

2.11 (a) Compare the following types of encoding:

(i)   NRZL

(ii) NRZ-I

(iii) RZ

(b) Comment upon their relative advantages for transmission over appreciable distance.

2.12 Explain what is meant by the term 'intersymbol interference' (ISI). How in practice may ISI be reduced in a baseband channel?

Chapter 3

Information theory

··

In Chapter 2 we discussed how information such as alphanumeric symbols may be source encoded into data representations. The purpose of a communications system is not fundamentally to send data but primarily to convey information between two, or more, parties. This raises the twin questions of what is information and how may we represent it in a communications system?

In data communications we are not fundamentally concerned with data but with information. For instance, a message could simply consist of the word 'cat'. A person may receive the word 'cat' but, from an information viewpoint, receive much more in terms of a perception of a cat with all of its general attributes such as physical form, capabilities and so on. In most circumstances communications systems are rather devoid of such deep-level views of information, and perhaps perception, too. Rather information sources are only considered later in the communication process where their input is almost invariably alphabetical and/or numerical in nature, speech or image. The underlying information in pure form is not directly considered. Instead it is mapped (encoded) into more tangible terms which a machine is able to deal with, for example by means of a computer keyboard.

This chapter will explore some of the more theoretical aspects of information, hopefully in a manageable and relevant manner to the reader. Specifically, topics such as where information comes from and how it may be measured are addressed. This leads naturally into the topic of source coding, which is concerned with how information from a source may be usefully represented in an appropriate coded form for transmission through communications systems. Many source codes are somewhat cumbersome inasmuch that they cater for more information than they are actually required to handle. This represents an inefficiency which may appear as using too many bits in source code representations and leads to additional cost and/or delay in a communications system. The chapter then addresses these problems by looking at data and examining ways in which the number of bits transmitted can be reduced, where possible, without loss of information delivered to a receiver. This process is known as data compression. In particular, current data compression techniques for image, video and speech are examined. The chapter concludes with a brief discussion of a recent ISO standard, MPEG-7, to consider how the vast array of multimedia information available may be categorized in an attempt to make its management and access as simple and easy as possible for users and distributors alike.

3.1 Information source

One standard method of defining an information source is based upon indicating the number, and identity, of each possible symbol as well as their associated frequency of occurrence, each of which is expressed as a probability. Consider the following received message:

THA CIT SAT ON THA MIT

A person receiving such a message, armed with prior knowledge that most characters received in fact form words in English, may reasonably suppose that this forms a sentence in which some words have been corrupted, perhaps due to errors in transmission. Not unreasonably the message might fairly readily be interpreted as:

THE CAT SAT ON THE MAT

The reason that such a correct interpretation may be made is that the English language contains a degree of **redundancy**. That is, the information that the symbols used to encode the information produce more than is strictly required, as seen in the above trivial example. This example illustrates that the **information content** of the original message is not necessarily the same as the original set of symbols used to convey the message.

The information content of a message may be quantified. An information source may be modelled by a repertoire of messages from which that desired may be selected. Suppose a source contains a set of symbols denoted by:

$(x_1, x_2, x_3, \ldots, x_n)$

In this model of an information source the output consists of a sequence of symbols in time, each symbol being random and statistically independent of any other symbol. The probability of any one symbol n appearing at any moment in the sequence may be known and denoted by $P(x_n)$ and where we may express a source by the following parameters:

- the number of symbols in the repertoire, or alphabet, denoted by n;
- the symbols themselves are denoted by $x_1, \ldots, x_n$;
- the probabilities of occurrence of each of the symbols, denoted by $P(x_1), \ldots, P(x_n)$.

Such a source is called **discrete memory-less source**. By memory-less we mean that the probability of a symbol occurring is independent of any other symbol. In practice the model is simplistic inasmuch that symbols are often not statistically independent and therefore not memory-less. A good example is English where there are correlations between adjacent letters. For instance, the probability of a 'c' occurring directly after another 'c' is higher than the general probability of a 'c' occurring. The word 'accelerate' illustrates the point, as with many other words, that adjacent 'c's are common. Many letters in the English language are therefore not statistically independent and therefore not memory-less. Nevertheless for a general introduction to information theory we shall assume discrete memory-less sources since the mathematics becomes appreciably more complex where this is not the case.

As an example let us model a source based upon binary signals:

● The number of symbols n is two. That is, one of two possible voltage levels may be transmitted.

● Symbols are denoted as x_0 representing binary 0 and x_1 representing binary 1.

● Finally, the probability of occurrence of these symbols is denoted:

$$P(x_0) = P(x_1) = 0.5$$

that is they are equiprobable.

Similarly a simple telegraphic code comprising 26 letters and a space character may be modelled:

$$n = 27$$
$$x_1 = A, x_2 = B, \ldots, x_{26} = Z, x_{27} = \text{space}$$

Symbols are unlikely to be equiprobable and would depend upon the type of English in use, for example legal documents, scientific reports and so on. Frequencies of occurrence for English symbols (Beker and Piper 1982, pp396–397) have been published and are widely available.

3.2 Information measure

Having established a formal method of defining, or modelling, sources of information it is now possible to establish a technique to measure information. Information received in the form of a message may be thought of as uncertainty that existed in the mind of the recipient but that the arrival of the message removed some of the uncertainty. Hence receipt of a message should, in general, remove some uncertainty. Therefore a measure of the information content of a message can be based on the amount of uncertainty it removes. This may be illustrated by the following three examples:

1. An information source consists of the outcomes of tossing a fair coin. The source can be modelled as follows:
    The number of symbols $n = 2$.
    The symbols represent the outcome of tossing a fair coin so that x_1 represents heads and x_2 tails.

The probabilities of occurrence of the symbols are, assuming that it is a fair coin:

$$P(x_1) = P(x_2) = 0.5$$

Hence there is equal uncertainty with regard to the outcome of a single toss, so that either outcome removes the same amount of uncertainty and therefore contains the same amount of information.

2. However, when the symbols represent the answers to the question 'Did you watch television last night?', then the source may be modelled as follows:

The number of symbols $n = 2$.

The symbols are then $x_1 =$ Yes, $x_2 =$ No.

On the assumption that 80% of the population watched television last night, the probabilities of occurrence of the symbols are:

$$P(x_1) = 0.8 \text{ and } P(x_2) = 0.2$$

Hence the receipt of x_1 removes little uncertainty and therefore conveys little information, but receipt of x_2 contains a considerable amount of information. It may therefore be deduced that receipt of a high-probability symbol contains little information but receipt of a low-probability symbol contains a lot more information.

3. Consider the source where the number of symbols is $n = 2$:

The symbols are a binary source with $x_1 = 1$, $x_2 = 0$.

The probabilities of occurrence are:

$$P(x_1) = 1 \text{ and } P(x_2) = 0$$

The receipt of x_1 is certain and therefore there is no uncertainty and hence no information; x_2 of course will never be received.

We are now in a position to establish the relationship between the probability of a source symbol and the information content of a message.

Let the information content conveyed by x_i be denoted by $I(x_i)$. Then from the relationships established above we can say that:

1. If $P(x_i) = P(x_j)$ then $I(x_i) = I(x_j)$
2. If $P(x_i) < P(x_j)$ then $I(x_i) > I(x_j)$
3. If $P(x_i) = 1$ then $I(x_i) = 0$

A mathematical function that will satisfy the above constraints is given by:

$$I(x_i) = \log_b(1/P(x_i)) = -\log_b(P(x_i))$$

The choice of the logarithmic base b is equivalent to selecting the unit of information. The standard convention in information theory is for b to be numerically equal to two, in which case the unit of information is called a **bit**. The choice of two assumes two equiprobable messages, as in the case of binary 1 and binary 0, and is known as an unbiased binary choice. The information unit is therefore normalized to this lowest order situation and 1 bit of information is the amount required or conveyed by the choice between two equally likely possibilities. That is:

If $P(x_i) = P(x_j) = 0.5$

then $I(x_i) = I(x_j) = \log_2(2) = 1$ bit

Hence in general:

$$I(x_i) = \log_2(1/P(x_i)) = -\log_2(P(x_i))$$

Example 3.1

A source consisting of four symbols has the following probabilities of occurrence:

$$P(x_1) = 1/4, \quad P(x_2) = 1/8,$$
$$P(x_3) = 1/8, \quad P(x_4) = 1/2$$

Find the information contained by receipt of the symbol (a) x_1, (b) x_2, (c) x_3, (d) x_4.

Now the number of symbols $n = 4$:

(a) $I(x_1) = -\log_2(1/4) = 2$ bits
(b) $I(x_2) = -\log_2(1/8) = 3$ bits
(c) $I(x_3) = -\log_2(1/8) = 3$ bits
(d) $I(x_4) = -\log_2(1/2) = 1$ bits

In this example, evaluation of the log to base two was trivial for the case of 0.5. Unfortunately, finding a logarithm to base two of any general number is not so easy. Logarithms to base two are not readily to hand. In order to work out information content it is often necessary to change the base of the log from 2 in order to make use of logarithms which are readily to hand. This may be achieved as follows:

$$\log_2(a) = \frac{\log_x(a)}{\log_x(2)}$$

Base x may conveniently be either e or 10, the logarithms for which are widely available.

Example 3.2

A source consisting of four symbols $x_1, \ldots, x_4$, has respective probabilities of occurrence:

$$P(x_1) = 1/9$$
$$P(x_2) = 2/9$$
$$P(x_3) = 1/3$$
$$P(x_4) = 1/3$$

Find the information contained by receipt of each of the four symbols:

Now the number of symbols $n = 4$:

(a) $I(x_1) = -\log_2(1/9) = \log_2(9)$

$$= \frac{\log_e 9}{\log_e 2} = 3.17 \text{ bits}$$

(b) $I(x_2) = -\log_2(2/9) = \log_2(4.5)$

$$= \frac{\log_e 4.5}{\log_e 2} = 2.17 \text{ bits}$$

(c) $I(x_3) = -\log_2(1/3) = \log_2(3)$

$$= \frac{\log_e 3}{\log_e 2} = 1.585 \text{ bits}$$

(d) $I(x_4) = 1.585$ bits

using the same computation as for (c) above.

The term bit can lead to some confusion as it is used on one hand by the communications engineer to represent information content, and on the other hand by the computer scientist to indicate the number of binary digits. There is only one condition where the information content of a source in bits is equal to the number of digits in a binary sequence and that is the condition where all the sequences are of equal length and all the symbols are equally probable. This is shown below for a binary sequence of length m.

As the symbols are all binary, the number of symbols is specified as $n = 2^m$.

Let there be x_i symbols for $i = 1, 2, \ldots, n$.

The probability of occurrence $P(x_i) = 1/2^m$ or 2^{-m}. Therefore:

$$I(x_i) = \log_2(1/P(x_i)) = \log_2 2^m = m \text{ bits}$$

This indicates that the information of each symbol is identical and equal to m. Hence we have proved that a sequence of m binary digits can convey m bits of information.

For an information source that has symbols x_i, x_j, x_k, etc., and where the probability of occurrence of the symbols is $P(x_i)$, $P(x_j)$, $P(x_k)$, etc., the information content of receiving a message made up of a number of symbols is simply the sum of the information content of the individual symbols. This may be shown as follows.

When a message comprising three symbols $x_i x_j x_k$ is received its probability of occurrence will be $P(x_i)P(x_j)P(x_k)$. Hence the information content $I(X)$ will be:

$$I(X) = \log_2 \frac{1}{P(x_i)P(x_j)P(x_k)}$$
$$= \log_2(1/P(x_i)) + \log_2(1/P(x_j)) + \log_2(1/P(x_k))$$
$$= I(x_i) + I(x_j) + I(x_k)$$

3.3 Entropy

We have just determined the information content, in bits, of a message. **Entropy** (H) expresses the average amount of information conveyed by a single symbol within a set of codewords and may be determind as follows:

$$H(X) = \sum_{i=1}^{i=n} P(x_i)\log_2(1/P(x_i)) \text{ bits/symbol}$$

and where:

$$\log_2(1/P(x_i))$$

is, as we have seen, simply the information content of the ith symbol. The formula for entropy shown above is therefore simply averaging each of the products of a symbol's probability and length, in bits, for all of the symbols or codewords in the codeword set.

In designing source codes it is the *average* information content of the code that is of interest rather than the information content of particular symbols. Entropy effectively provides the average content and this may be used to estimate the bandwidth of a channel required to transmit a particular code, or the size of memory to store a certain number of symbols within a code.

Example 3.3

A weather information source transmits visibility information with the probabilities given in Table 3.1.

Evaluate the entropy of the source code.

Table 3.1 Example 3.3.

Visibility	Probability
Very poor	1/4
Poor	1/8
Moderate	1/8
Good	1/2

Now, with $n = 4$:

$$P(x_1) = 1/4$$

$$P(x_2) = 1/8$$

$$P(x_3) = 1/8$$

$$P(x_4) = 1/2$$

the entropy can be found:

$$H(X) = \sum_{i=1}^{i=n} P(x_i)\log_2(1/P(x_i))$$

$$= P(x_1)\log_2(1/P(x_1)) + P(x_2)\log_2(1/P(x_2)) + P(x_3)\log_2(1/P(x_3))$$
$$+ P(x_4)\log_2(1/P(x_4))$$

$$= (1/4) \times 2 + (1/8) \times 3 + (1/8) \times 3 + (1/2) \times 1$$

$$= 1.75 \text{ bits/symbol}$$

In general, if sources with the same number of symbols have different symbol probabilities, then their entropies will also be different. For a source of n symbols maximum uncertainty must exist when all the symbols are equally likely. Hence the maximum information content of a code must occur when all the symbols are equally likely. For n equally likely symbols, the probability of the occurrence of any one symbol will be $1/n$. Therefore the entropy is given by:

$$H(X) = \sum_{i=1}^{i=n} \frac{1}{n} \log_2(n)$$

Therefore $H(X) = \log_2 n$ and this will be the maximum value of entropy possible.

Log$_2 n$ therefore represents an upper bound upon entropy for a code comprising n symbols. That is, a code comprising n symbols cannot have an entropy greater than its logarithm to the base 2. In practice, dependent upon the individual probabilities of each symbol contained by a code, entropy may be equal to or less than this maximum value of entropy.

Hence, for any codeword set:

$$H(X) \le \log_2 n$$

3.4   Source codes

As indicated earlier, the aim of source coding is to produce a code which, on average, requires the transmission of the maximum amount of information for the fewest binary digits. This can be quantified by calculating the **efficiency** η of the code. However before calculating efficiency we need to establish the length of the code. The length of a code is the average length of its codewords and is obtained by:

$$L = \sum_{i=1}^{i=n} P(x_i) l_i$$

where l_i is the number of digits in the ith symbol and n is the number of symbols the code contains.

The efficiency of a code is obtained by dividing the entropy by the average code length:

$$\eta = \frac{H(X)}{L} \times 100\%$$

Example 3.4

Evaluate the efficiency of the source code containing the following symbols:

x_1 is encoded as 1
x_2 is encoded as 10
x_3 is encoded as 100
x_4 is encoded as 1000

There probabilities of occurrence are given by:

$P(x_1) = 1/4$

$P(x_2) = 1/8$

$P(x_3) = 1/8$

$P(x_4) = 1/2$

The efficiency is:

$$\eta = \frac{H(X)}{L} \times 100\%$$

The length of this code is obtained as follows:

$$L = \sum_{i=1}^{i=n} P(x_i)l_i$$

$$= \frac{1}{4} \times 1 + \frac{1}{8} \times 2 + \frac{1}{8} \times 3 + \frac{1}{2} \times 4$$

$$= 2.875 \text{ digits}$$

The entropy of the source code was previously evaluated in Example 3.3 as 1.75 bits/symbol. Therefore:

$$\eta = \frac{1.75}{2.875} \times 100 = 60.9\%$$

Analysis and design of source codes

Where messages consisting of sequences of symbols from an n-symbol source have to be transmitted to their destination via a binary data transmission channel, each symbol must be coded into a sequence of binary digits at the transmitter to produce a suitable input to the channel.

In order to design suitable source codes some descriptors for classifying source codes have been produced, as follows:

- A **codeword** is a sequence of binary digits.
- A **code** is a mapping of source symbols into codewords.
- A code is **distinct** if all its codewords are different, or unique.
- A distinct code is **uniquely decodable** if all its codewords are identifiable when embedded in any sequence of codewords from the code. A code must have this property if its codewords are to be uniquely decoded to its original message symbols.
- A uniquely decodable code is **instantaneously decodable** if all its codewords are identifiable as soon as their final binary digit is received.

A **prefix** of a codeword is a binary sequence obtained by truncating the codeword. For example, the codeword 1010 has the following prefixes:

1, 10, 101 and 1010

Clearly, each of the first three codewords are prefixes of later codewords. A uniquely decodable codeword is instantaneously decodable if no codeword is a prefix of another codeword. It is not absolutely necessary for the code to be instantaneously decodable, but in a real-time system or any system where speed of operation is vital such a code enables communication to proceed as quickly as possible.

Example 3.5

For the source given in Table 3.2, classify each code in the table according to the above definitions and evaluate the length for each instantaneously decodable code.

Table 3.2   Examples of source codes.

Source symbol	$P(x)$	Code 1	Code 2	Code 3	Code 4	Code 5	Code 6
x_1	5/8	0	0	00	0	0	0
x_2	1/4	1	1	01	01	10	10
x_3	1/16	11	00	11	011	110	110
x_4	1/16	11	10	10	0111	1110	111

Code 1: Not distinct, x_3 and x_4 are both coded 11.

Code 2: Is distinct but not uniquely decodable, that is $x_3 x_4$ is coded 0010 so this could be $x_3 x_4$, or $x_3 x_2 x_1$, $x_1 x_1 x_4$ or $x_1 x_1 x_2 x_1$.

Code 3: Instantaneously decodable, each codeword being of length 2. Thus $L = 2$ binary digits/codeword.

Code 4: Uniquely decodable since receipt of zero always indicates the start of a new codeword. However, it is not instantaneously decodable because the end of the codeword cannot be recognized instantaneously.

Code 5: Instantaneously decodable as receipt of logic 0 always indicates the end of the codeword. Thus $L = 1\frac{9}{16}$ binary digits/codeword.

Code 6: Instantaneously decodable. Thus $L = 1\frac{1}{2}$ binary digits/codeword.

The entropy of the source may be determined and is 1.42 bits/symbol. No uniquely decodable code in the table has a length shorter than this value.

Instantaneous codewords may be generated and decoded by using a **code tree** or **decision tree**, which is rather like a family tree. The root is at the top of the tree and the branches are at the bottom. The tree is read from root to branch. As the binary code is received the digits are followed from the root until the branch is reached when the codeword can be read. A code tree is shown in Figure 3.1 for a three-digit binary code. When the codeword 101 is received, take the right-hand branch to junction (a),

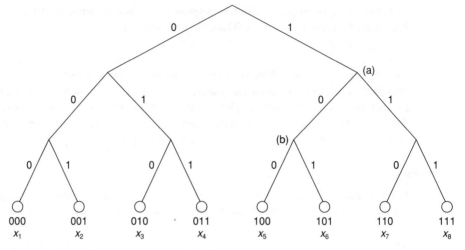

Figure 3.1 Decision tree for a three-digit binary code.

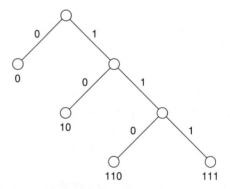

Figure 3.2 Decision (code) tree for a weather information system.

then from there the left-hand branch to junction (b), then the right-hand branch to the end of the branch to read off the codeword x_6. In the case of an instantaneous code, the codewords used to represent the possible states of the source must all correspond to the ends of a branch.

Table 3.3 Weather information system source code.

Visibility	Probability	Code
Very poor	0.1	111
Poor	0.2	10
Moderate	0.6	0
Good	0.1	110

A code tree, Figure 3.2, could be used to describe the source code of a weather information system shown in Table 3.3.

Code trees in themselves are very useful for describing a source code once it has been designed but they are difficult to use in the original design of a code.

If messages are selected from a message set where all messages are equiprobable, then every message carries the same information and direct coding into binary digits is all that is required. For example, if the message set consists of eight symbols all equally likely then just a 3-bit binary code could be used such that:

$$x_1 = 000 \quad x_2 = 001$$

$$x_3 = 010 \quad x_4 = 011$$

$$x_5 = 100 \quad x_6 = 101$$

$$x_7 = 110 \quad x_8 = 111$$

However, if the messages have widely different probabilities, then the information associated with the least probable messages is greater than that associated with the most probable messages. Since the least probable messages also occur less frequently, it is sensible that they should be associated with larger groups of binary digits than the most frequent highly probable messages which should be associated with the smaller group of binary digits. In this way it is possible to minimize the number of digits required to transmit a message sequence to somewhere near the actual information content of the message. This does, however, mean that variable length codes will be used but this is not a problem in most communications systems. A well-known low-redundancy source coding technique is that of Huffman coding. This code is *optimal* in the sense that it produces the most efficient code possible.

Huffman code

Codewords are listed vertically and to the left in descending order of probability. The lowest two probabilities are then combined to give a new, intermediate, probability which is simply the sum of their probabilities. The procedure of combining the lowest pair of probabilities is iteratively repeated until a final sum of probability 1 is reached. An important point to note in deciding which two probabilities to sum next is that once intermediate probabilities appear, the lowest two probabilities available, including intermediate probabilities, are chosen. Where there are three, or more, equal probabilities available, any one of them may be selected.

At each combination point the binary symbols 0 and 1 are allocated. Which way round symbols are assigned does not effect the outcome of the Huffman coding. However, for ease and consistency, binary 0 may be assigned to the upper division and binary 1 to the lower one, or vice versa. (Another approach is to assign one binary symbol to the highest probability, and vice versa.)

Finally codewords are deduced from the diagram by reading the binary symbols assigned from right to left.

Huffman coding is best explained using an example.

Example 3.6

Deduce a suitable Huffman code if there are eight symbols, each of probability shown:

$P(x_1) = 0.25$ $P(x_2) = 0.25$

$P(x_3) = 0.15$ $P(x_4) = 0.1$

$P(x_5) = 0.1$ $P(x_6) = 0.08$

$P(x_7) = 0.06$ $P(x_8) = 0.01$

The probabilities are ranked in descending order, x_1 at the top and x_8 at the bottom, see Figure 3.3. The two lowest probabilities $P(x_8)$ and $P(x_7)$ are combined to give an intermediate probability $P(x_7') = 0.07$. The two lowest probabilities $P(x_6)$ and $P(x_7')$ are then combined to give a new probability $P(x_6') = 0.15$. The two lowest probabilities $P(x_4)$ and $P(x_5)$ are then combined to give a new probability $P(x_4') = 0.2$. The two lowest probabilities $P(x_3)$ and $P(x_6')$ are then combined to give a new probability $P(x_3') = 0.3$. The two lowest probabilities $P(x_2)$ and $P(x_4')$ are then combined to give a new probability $P(x_2') = 0.45$. The two lowest probabilities $P(x_1)$ and $P(x_3')$ are then combined to give a new probability $P(x_1') = 0.55$. The final two probabilities $P(x_1')$ and $P(x_2')$ are combined to give the resultant overall probability of 1. Binary 1 and binary 0 are then allocated at every junction, working from right to left.

The resulting codewords are:

$x_1 = 00$, $x_2 = 10$, $x_3 = 010$, $x_4 = 110$,

$x_5 = 111$, $x_6 = 0110$, $x_7 = 01110$, $x_8 = 01111$

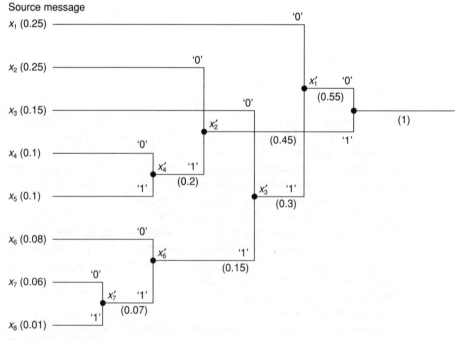

Figure 3.3 Example 3.6.

Note that the mapping produced here is not unique. Other mappings could have been produced, as indicated above. The only effect would be to change the binary patterns assigned to a codeword, but the important point to note is that the *number* of bits assigned to each codeword would be unchanged. This means that the coding efficiency and entropy would remain the same.

3.5 Data compression

Source encoding maps the information to be communicated into suitable signals to form what we call data. We have seen earlier in this chapter how source encoding may not always be optimal in that the number of bits in the data used to convey a message may exceed the number of bits necessary to convey the information.

Data **compression** seeks to reduce the data transmitted by reducing, or eliminating, any redundancy in the data. One of the prime reasons for this is that some messages which contain large amounts of data often require high-bandwidth communication links in order to transmit a message within a reasonable amount of time. This is particularly true of many Internet connections to an ISP over dial-up modems. Compression and source encoding, although strictly speaking separate operations, are in many cases integrated and not readily separated out as two distinct operations.

Compression is said to be **lossless** if all of the information at the transmitter prior to compression is preserved after decompression at the receiver. Alternatively, compression may be **lossy** if some information is lost in the compression–decompression processes. The advantage of lossy compression is that compression ratios may be substantially increased and yet retain an acceptable reproduction of information at the receiver. However, lossy compression is not suited to all forms of information. It is mainly suitable for speech and image communication where a small degree of error may be acceptable, unlike, say, financial data where errors are intolerable.

We have seen in Chapter 2 how information may be mapped, or encoded, into data representations, or codewords. For example, the alphabet contains 26 characters and, if binary encoded, requires 5 bits per character. This example highlights a problem in encoding which is that of redundancy. Strictly mathematically, 26 codewords only require about 4.7 bits, but this is a nonsense since the number of bits must be integer and so in this example we round to 5. Intuitively a bit stream which assigns 5 bits per character must have some redundancy. Now let us examine the 26 characters from an information point of view, as considered earlier in the chapter:

$$I(x_i) = \log_2(1/P(x_i))$$

And if we assume (although not true in practice) that each character is equiprobable:

$$I(x) = \log_2\left(\frac{1}{1/26}\right)$$

which, as stated earlier, is 4.7 bits.

In practice some characters are more likely, or probable, than others. Therefore, if we knew the probabilities of each character we could calculate the number of bits needed to encode each one, and of course the least probable characters would have less than

4.7 bits, and vice versa. This probabilistic approach, if used, would lead to a net reduction in the total number of bits required to transmit a message compared with our initial simplistic 5-bit/character approach to encoding. Huffman illustrated one way of achieving this. Huffman coding is also an example of the notion that data encoding and data compression are not always separate operations in data communications. Certainly Huffman coding combines the two operations as a single process.

As might be expected, there are a number of different compression techniques. **Difference compression**, also known as relative encoding, is where instead of transmitting consecutive data, only the difference between current data and last data is sent. It is only effective where there are only small differences between successive data. For example, a telemetry system may monitor flow rate or pressure in a process control system and which, by and large, only varies in the main by small degrees over time. This form of compression works on the basis that the number of bits to represent change are fewer than the number of bits to represent an absolute value, otherwise there is no coding gain. Difference compression is well suited to digitized speech and sensor measurements but unsuitable for documents and moving and still images.

Another compression technique is that of **run-length encoding**. Again, instead of transmitting absolute values, repeated patterns or **runs** are detected. The repeated value itself is then sent, and the number of times that it is repeated.

Example 3.7

Consider the expression aaargh! This could be compressed using run-length encoding and sent as:

a × 3, r × 1, g × 1, h × 1, ! × 1

Because the number of runs in each case is so short, the overhead in compressing means that no compression would result. In fact, it would be better not to compress since the opposite would happen. The example nevertheless illustrates the mechanism of run-length encoding.

Run-length encoding is suitable for data containing long runs as may be found in still and many moving images, but is unsuitable for text-based sources where runs are generally very short.

Another compression technique that identifies runs is **index compression**. Repeated patterns are placed in a table and both transmitter and receiver hold a copy of the table. In order to transmit a run an index is used at the transmitter to point to the entry of the run in the table. It is this index which is then transmitted and which the receiver uses to extract the run in question. This is widely used with zip compression techniques and is suitable for text and images, but not for speech. A commonly used code is Lempel–Ziv (LZ) code.

Although, in the above, compression generally appears to be advantageous, other factors must be considered before going down this route. In order to compress it is clear, and further examples will underline this, that modern approaches can be quite complex. This means that a high degree of processing power may be required and that the time to compress and decompress may be significant. Compression only becomes attractive where the bandwidth of uncompressed data exceeds that of compressed data several fold.

Facsimile compression

Fax, as in television, is based upon scanning a document line by line but differs inasmuch that only monochrome is provided. Operation is by means of a sharply focused light source scanned across the document in a series of closely spaced lines. An optical detector detects the reflected light from the scanned area which is encoded as either binary 0 for a 'white' area or binary 1 for 'dark'. The receiver then interprets the data as a black dot for 1 or 'no printing' for 0. The identical dots described are termed **picture elements**, or **pels**.

The ITU has produced a number of fax standards, namely T2 (Group 1), T3 (Group 2), T4 (Group 3) and T6 (Group 4). Only Group 3 and Group 4 are commonly used. Group 3 is intended to operate over analogue PSTN lines using modulation and operating at 14.4 kbps. Group 4 operates digitally at 64 kbps by means of baseband transmission over ISDN lines.

Group 3 scans an A4 sheet of information from the top left-hand corner to the bottom right-hand corner. Each line is subdivided into 1728 picture elements (pels). Each pel is quantized into either black or white. In the vertical direction the page is scanned to give approximately 1145 lines. Hence the total number of pels per page is just under 2 million.

Example 3.8

Estimate the time to transmit an A4 document without the use of compression. Assume Group 3 scanning.

$$\text{Number of pels} = 1728 \times 1145$$
$$= 1\ 978\ 560$$

The data rate specified for Group 3 terminals is 4800 bps. Hence:

$$\text{Transmission time} = \frac{1\ 978\ 560}{4800} = 412.2 \text{ s}$$

which is approximately 7 minutes.

In practice the scanned data contains considerable redundancy and by means of compression Group 3 manages to reduce the transmission speed by a factor of about 10. Group 3 can transmit a typical A4 document in less than 1 minute, and Group 4, with its superior data rate, perhaps in only a few seconds.

The Group 3 standard is based upon extensive analysis of a number of representative documents. The analysis uses Huffman coding to produce tables of codewords for black, and white, runs of differing lengths. The length of each codeword was

Table 3.4 ITU-T Groups 3 and 4.
(a) Termination codes

White run length	Codeword	Black run length	Codeword	White run length	Codeword	Black run length	Codeword
0	00110101	0	0000110111	32	00011011	32	000001101010
1	000111	1	010	33	0010010	33	000001101011
2	0111	2	11	34	00010011	34	000011010010
3	1000	3	10	35	00010100	35	000011010011
4	1011	4	011	36	00010101	36	000011010100
5	1100	5	0011	37	00010110	37	000011010101
6	1110	6	0010	38	00010111	38	000011010110
7	1111	7	00011	39	00101000	39	000011010111
8	10011	8	000101	40	00101001	40	000001101100
9	10100	9	000100	41	00101010	41	000001101101
10	00111	10	0000100	42	00101011	42	000011011010
11	01000	11	0000101	43	00101100	43	000011011011
12	001000	12	0000111	44	00101101	44	000001010100
13	000011	13	00000100	45	00000100	45	000001010101
14	110100	14	00000111	46	00000101	46	000001010110
15	110101	15	000011000	47	00001010	47	000001010111
16	101010	16	0000010111	48	00001011	48	000001100100
17	101011	17	0000011000	49	01010010	49	000001100101
18	0100111	18	0000001000	50	01010011	50	000001010010
19	0001100	19	00001100111	51	01010100	51	000001010011
20	0001000	20	00001101000	52	01010101	52	000000100100
21	0010111	21	00001101100	53	00100100	53	000000110111
22	0000011	22	00000110111	54	00100101	54	000000111000
23	0000100	23	00000101000	55	01011000	55	000000100111
24	0101000	24	00000010111	56	01011001	56	000000101000
25	0101011	25	00000011000	57	01011010	57	000001011000
26	0010011	26	000011001010	58	01011011	58	000001011001
27	0100100	27	000011001011	59	01001010	59	000000101011
28	0011000	28	000011001100	60	01001011	60	000000101100
29	00000010	29	000011001101	61	00110010	61	000001011010
30	00000011	30	000001101000	62	00110011	62	000001100110
31	00011010	31	000001101001	63	00110100	63	000001100111

determined by the relative frequency of occurrence of a run. The coding is in two parts, dependent upon how long a run is (Table 3.4(a)). **Termination codes** are merely white, or black, runs 0 to 63 pels long. **Make-up** codes (Table 3.4(b)) are multiples of 64 pels of the same colour. Coding is based on assuming that the first pel of a line is always white. Runs of less than 64 pels are simply encoded directly and the appropriate termination code selected. Runs of 64 pels or more are encoded using an appropriate make-up code and, if necessary, one or more termination codes. Runs in excess of 2623 pels make use of more than one make-up code. This use of Huffman coding whereby codewords may in some instances be selected from both tables, rather than directly encoding into a single codeword, is known as **modified Huffman coding**.

If a code suffers error in transmission the receiver will misinterpret the incoming bit stream such that it reads data as different codewords. At the end of each line scan

Table 3.4 (Cont'd)
(b) Make-up codes

White run length	Codeword	Black run length	Codeword
64	11011	64	0000001111
128	10010	128	000011001000
192	010111	192	000011001001
256	0110111	256	000001011011
320	00110110	320	000000110011
384	00110111	384	000000110100
448	01100100	448	000000110101
512	01100101	512	0000001101100
576	01101000	576	0000001101101
640	01100111	640	0000001001010
704	011001100	704	0000001001011
768	011001101	768	0000001001100
832	011010010	832	0000001001101
896	011010011	896	0000001110010
960	011010100	960	0000001110011
1024	011010101	1024	0000001110100
1088	011010110	1088	0000001110101
1152	011010111	1152	0000001110110
1216	011011000	1216	0000001110111
1280	011011001	1280	0000001010010
1344	011011010	1344	0000001010011
1408	011011011	1408	0000001010100
1472	010011000	1472	0000001010101
1536	010011001	1536	0000001011010
1600	010011010	1600	0000001011011
1664	011000	1664	0000001100100
1728	010011011	1728	0000001100101
1792	00000001000	1792	00000001000
1856	00000001100	1856	00000001100
1920	00000001101	1920	00000001101
1984	000000010010	1984	000000010010
2048	000000010011	2048	000000010011
2112	000000010100	2112	000000010100
2176	000000010101	2176	000000010101
2240	000000010110	2240	000000010110
2304	000000010111	2304	000000010111
2368	000000011100	2368	000000011100
2432	000000011101	2432	000000011101
2496	000000011110	2496	000000011110
2560	000000011111	2560	000000011111
EOL	000000000001	EOL	000000000001

an end-of-line (EOL) code is inserted. When a receiver is reading in erroneous data it may count the number of bits from the last correctly received EOL and, given that the number of bits in a line is known, eventually realize that an error has occurred. This may be because the next EOL is in error and therefore not detected. Alternatively, the errored bit stream could indicate a line that is either too long, or too short. Once the receiver detects an error has occurred as described, it commences a search for an

EOL. Once an EOL is then found transmission may continue as normal from that point. Providing errors are few only one, or just a few, lines may be corrupted and have little effect upon the overall document reproduced. If the number of lines in error exceeds a predetermined number, reception is aborted and the transmitter informed.

Although run-length encoding used by Group 3 works satisfactorily with text and line drawings leading to compression ratios of up to 10:1, it is not ideally suited to images. Documents such as photographs and images contain large degrees of shades of grey which do not compress well. Images attempt to produce **half tones** by blending very short runs of black and white. Inspection of the termination codes reveals that short runs of alternate black and white patterns are encoded into relatively long codewords compared with a run of an equivalent number of bits of a single colour. In consequence images may result in the opposite to compression, or negative compression where more than 1 bit per pel on average is produced.

Group 4 specifies a different coding strategy to that of modified Huffman in order to cope with images. Although photographs and images may contain large degrees of shades in one line, there is often only a very small change between *adjacent* lines. Much better compression may therefore be achieved if difference encoding across adjacent lines is used. Group 4 uses a code known as **modified relative element address designate**, or **modified READ** code, which is also optionally specified for Group 3. (The term modified is to indicate that it is a variant of an earlier READ code.)

Modified Huffman coding only encodes a single line at a time and is referred to as a **one-dimensional code**. Modified READ coding is known as a **two-dimensional code** because the encoding is based upon a pair of lines.

Modified READ coding is achieved as follows. The first line to be scanned is assumed to consist of white pels only and is referred to as the **reference line**, Figure 3.4. Coding proper starts on the second line and is here referred to as the **coding line**. Compression is achieved on the basis that in general a run on one line will appear in the second line and only differ in length by a few pels, either way. Once the second line has been encoded, it then becomes the reference line when the third line is being encoded, and so on. A pel type marked a_0 is the first pel of the next run to be encoded and may be black or white. Note that to the left of each line is an imaginary white pel which is taken as a_0 and from which the length of the first run on a line is determined. In order to code a line four other pels must be identified:

- a_1 is simply the first pel to the right of a_0 which has opposite colour, that is the first pel of the next run.

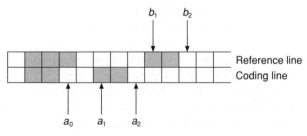

Figure 3.4 Modified READ coding.

● a_2 is similar to a_1 and denotes the start of the next run after that defined by a_1.

● b_1 is the first pel on the reference line to the right of a_0 whose colour differs from the pel immediately to its left and *also* that of a_0.

● b_2 is the start of the next run after b_1.

A run to be encoded may be in one of three different modes:

1. **Pass mode**: This occurs when a run in the reference line is no longer present in the succeeding coding line, Figure 3.5(a).

   The run that has 'disappeared', $b_1 b_2$, is represented by the codeword 0001. The next codeword to be produced will be based upon the run starting at a_1, and which is in this case a run of only 1 pel. The significance of a_1', which corresponds to b_2 in the reference line above, is that this position in the coding line will be regarded as a_0 of the next run to be encoded. Note that this run, which is the next to be encoded after the run that disappeared, has the same colour.

2. **Vertical mode**: This in fact applies to most runs and is where a black run in the coding line is within ±3 pels of the start of a corresponding black run in the reference line. The two extreme cases are shown in Figure 3.5(b).

   There are five other possibilities, namely ±1 pel or ±2 different, or the commencement of the two runs coincides.

3. **Horizontal mode**: This mode is similar to the vertical mode but where the degree of overlap is in excess of ±3 pels. Two examples are shown in Figure 3.5(c). Encoding uses the codeword 001 to indicate that it is horizontal mode followed by codewords for the run length $a_0 a_1$ and $a_1 a_2$. In the case of the upper example, the coding line commences with the disappearance of a run of two black pels and would be encoded as pass mode. This is followed by two white pels, $a_0 a_1$, which do not fall within the category of pass or vertical mode and must therefore be in horizontal mode. To complete horizontal coding, the next black run, $a_1 a_2$, is also encoded. Hence the horizontal mode is encoded 001 0111 00011. Similarly it is left to readers to satisfy themselves that the lower example is encoded 001 00111 11.

Table 3.5 indicates the codewords for each of the three modified READ modes.

Modified READ encoding is summarized as a flowchart in Figure 3.6.

Table 3.5 Summary of modified READ encoding.

Mode	Run length	Abbreviation	Codeword
Pass	$b_1 b_2$	P	$0001 + b_1 b_2$
Vertical	$a_1 b_1 = 0$	V(0)	1
	$a_1 b_1 = -1$	$V_R(1)$	011
	$a_1 b_1 = -2$	$V_R(2)$	000011
	$a_1 b_1 = -3$	$V_R(3)$	0000011
	$a_1 b_1 = +1$	$V_L(1)$	010
	$a_1 b_1 = +2$	$V_L(2)$	000010
	$a_1 b_1 = +3$	$V_L(3)$	0000010
			0000001000
Horizontal	$a_0 a_1,\ a_1 a_2$	H	001 followed by codes for $a_0 a_1$ and $a_1 a_2$

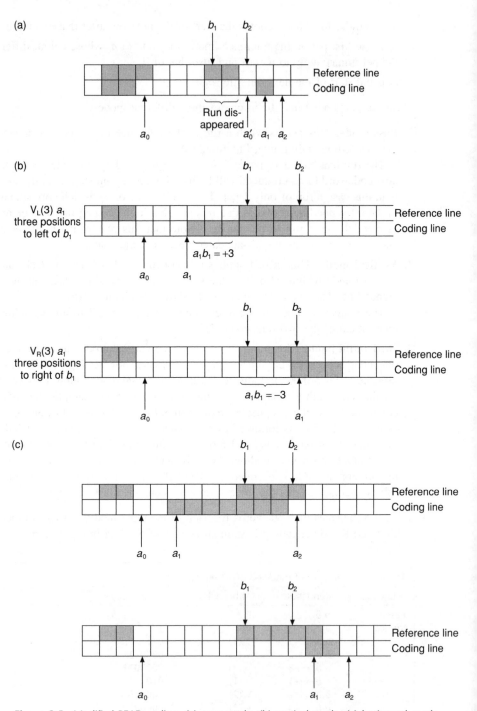

Figure 3.5 Modified READ coding: (a) pass mode; (b) vertical mode; (c) horizontal mode.

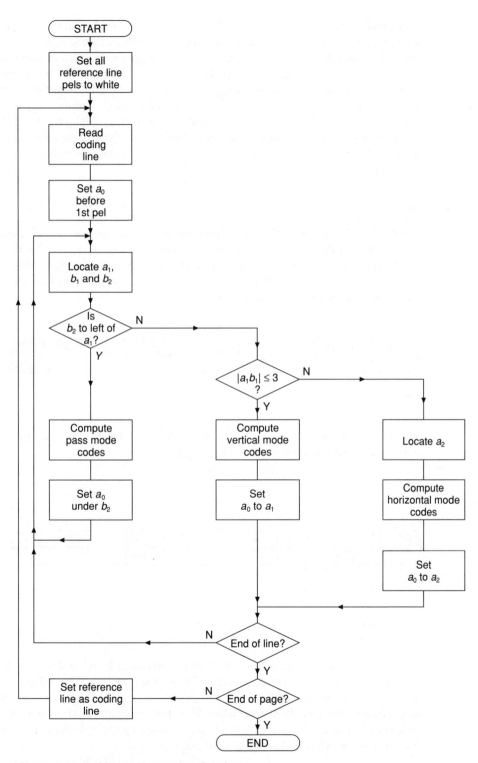

Figure 3.6 Modified READ encoding flowchart.

A problem in all differential techniques is that if an error occurs at any point its effect may propagate much further into successive points in the process. In Group 4 fax coding an error in one coding line received becomes the reference line in considering the next coding line received. This will in turn lead to errors being produced when decoding this subsequent coding line, and so on. To limit this effect, Group 3 reverts to one-dimensional encoding using modified Huffman coding every other line standard, or every fourth line where higher resolution is deployed (the ITU has specified two levels of resolution known as standard or high). In the case of Group 4 modified READ coding is used on all lines, but error correction coding is additionally employed.

Example 3.9

Figure 3.7 shows a section of a pair of lines within a pair of adjacent lines to be encoded in black and white format using modified READ encoding. Assuming that the lower line is the current coding line, derive the codes for the first four runs of this section of the coding line. Assume that the first and last complete pel shown on the coding line is the start and end of a run, respectively.

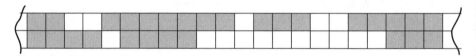

Figure 3.7

The first run, Figure 3.7(a), comprises four black pels and is in vertical mode with a_1b_1 equal to -2. This run is encoded as $V_R(2)$.

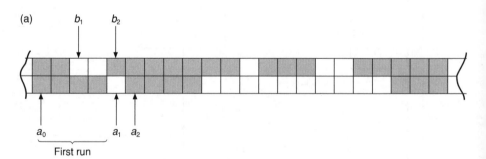

The second run comprises a single white pel, indicated by a_0, and which takes the position marked as a_1 when considering the previous, first, run. In addition the run also contains the following four black pels, Figure 3.7(b). The reasoning is as follows: a_1 and b_1 are more than three pels distant. Therefore horizontal mode is indicated. The codeword 001 is used to indicate the mode followed by the codewords for a_0a_1 and a_1a_2, that is one white and four black, respectively,

(b)

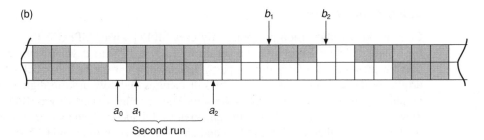

Second run

The third run, Figure 3.7(c), comprises six white pels. The run b_1b_2 in the reference line has disappeared indicating pass mode. This is encoded by the codeword 0001. Note that it is not possible to show a_2. The receiving facsimile machine knows the start of the run (which is from the end of the second run) and notes the disappearance of the run of three black pels. It is then able to deduce it is receiving a run of six white pels.

(c)

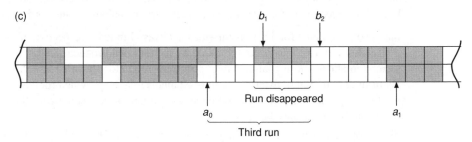

Run disappeared

Third run

The fourth run consists of four white pels, Figure 3.7(d), and commences from a_0 being positioned directly under b_2 used in determining the third run. It is not possible to determine the position of a_2 or b_2. Here a_1 and b_1 are within three pels of each other indicating vertical mode, $V_R(2)$.

(d)

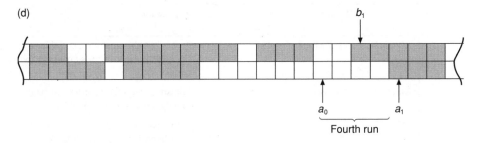

Fourth run

Hence the four runs are encoded as follows:

000011	to indicate $V_R(2)$
001	to indicate horizontal mode
000111	to indicate one white pel
011	to indicate four black pels
0001	to indicate pass mode
000011	to indicate $V_R(2)$

Video compression

Current video compression predominantly uses MPEG where MPEG is the acronym for Moving Picture Experts Group set up by ISO in 1990 to develop standards for moving pictures. MPEG in turn is partly based upon the use of a parallel standard originally devised for digital coding of still pictures and now used in digital photographic equipment. This standard is the Joint Photographic Expert Group (JPEG) and drew upon experts from industry, the universities, broadcasters and so on. The group worked with the then CCITT and ISO and commenced work in the mid-1980s. JPEG compresses single still images by means of **spatial compression**. This is based upon the fact that most images there is considerable similarity between neighbouring areas within an image. This, from an information point of view, indicates redundancy for which various compression techniques exist and of course have been capitalized upon with JPEG.

MPEG combines source encoding with compression to support the applications in Table 3.6. MPEG also includes audio compression, which is described shortly.

The advantages of digital transmission over earlier analogue transmission are:

- bandwidth available for TV transmissions is always limited, irrespective of the delivery medium in use. This is compounded by the fact that broadcasters have in recent years demanded more channels than spectrum regulators have been able to grant. By turning to digital transmissions more channels may be provided for a given bandwidth compared with analogue predecessors, enabling an increase in the number of channels which may be supported.

- digital operation has the advantage of generally providing high-quality transmission and recording capabilities. In addition it is more flexible, for instance providing subtitles in different languages is more readily accommodated.

Table 3.6   MPEG standards.

	Data rate	Year of introduction	Application
MPEG-1	~1.5 Mbps,	1992	Primarily VCR-quality video storage, or very short-distance transmission using twisted-pair conductors
MPEG-2	4/6 Mbps	1995	Transmission and recording of broadcast-quality signals, e.g. digital TV
MPEG-3	–	N/A	Originally planned for HDTV but this has now been included in MPEG-2
MPEG-4	–	1999	Initially for medium resolution, e.g. video conferencing and telephony, over an N-ISDN (64 kbps) connection. Later extended to develop interactive applications in entertainment, or via the Internet
MPEG-7	–	2001	Provides an indexing system for mutlimedia to describe audiovisual material. This enables users to search for sound and video clips as well as still images and graphics

Video signals are based upon a series of still pictures, or **frames**, which are obtained at a constant rate using a scanning technique. Very often interleaved scanning is used, as in public broadcast transmissions, where on one cycle of scanning, odd lines of the picture are produced, and even lines, the next. These 'half frames' are known as **fields**. This means that a complete image requires two such fields and the image rate is half that of the field rate. Scanning rate is normally related to the frequency of the mains in use. For example, in the USA fields are generated at 60 Hz whereas in Europe it is 50 Hz.

Frames may be regarded as a succession of stills each of which may therefore be digitally compressed using JPEG. However, as in all compression techniques, the aim is to minimize redundancy. MPEG takes advantage of the fact that many images contain very little change when compared with their immediate predecessor, or successor. For most of the time, unless a complete scene change occurs, any two successive frames are almost identical. The difference between their information content and the actual content of either frame is therefore considerable. This feature is exploited in encoding moving images using **temporal compression** which only transmits information relating to changes between images. Much greater compression ratios may be achieved than if only JPEG were to be used on a frame-by-frame basis. For instance, raw broadcast-quality TV may require a bandwidth of hundreds of Mbps but MPEG-2 may compress the signal to only 4 or 6 Mbps.

MPEG-1 produces four types of frame:

1. **I-frames** (intrapicture) which are free-standing JPEG encoded images.
2. **P-frames** (predictive) which, as with B-frames next, are not free standing. A P-frame specifies the differences compared with the last I-frame or P-frame.
3. **B-frames** (bidirectional) which specify the difference between the immediately preceding/succeeding I- and/or P-frames.
4. **D-frames** (dc-coded) which use low-level compression and are optionally inserted at regular intervals in order to facilitate display of low-resolution images during fast forward, or rewind, of a VCR or Video-on-Demand video source. Like I-frames, they are free standing and not used in P- or B-frame compression. D-frames are based upon an average (hence dc, meaning direct current) of many small areas within a frame, each called a macroblock (macroblocks are explained shortly).

I-frames, as stated earlier, are free standing and fully compressed using JPEG (Halsall 2001, pp150–168) and typically have compression ratios of 10:1 or 20:1. They are required for a number of reasons, one being that P-frames are in effect referenced to I-frames and therefore utilize differential coding. Therefore the first frame of a transmission must be an I-frame. Furthermore I-frames must also be interspersed throughout a transmission at regular intervals, perhaps every second or fraction thereof, in order that P-frames can be decoded by a viewer commencing reception part way through a transmission. Another reason for their periodic insertion is that P- and B-frames are using differential coding based upon them and if an error in transmission occurred, it would no longer be possible to decode such frames at the receiver.

Figure 3.8 shows an example of a series of frames. The distance between successive I-frames is known as a **group of pictures** (GOP) and labelled as *N*, and is in fact

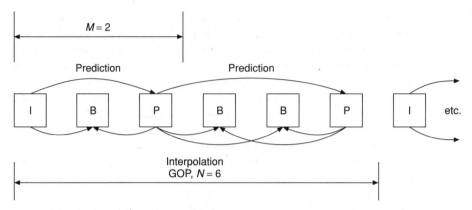

Figure 3.8   Example of a sequence of frames.

6 in this example. N generally ranges between 3 and 12. M is the **prediction span** and defines the number of frames between a P-frame and an immediately preceding/ succeeding I- or P-frame. The decision of what mix of N and M to use is a trade-off between degree of compression and resultant bandwidth requirement and quality, and would be influenced by the subject matter.

P-frames exploit the fact that much of the background in consecutive images does not change greatly, if at all. Rather the objects within the scene move. Where there is change, many of the objects, although moving, do not in themselves actually change very much. A good example to illustrate this point is a static video camera viewing a snooker match. The table, background, most of the audience and many of the balls remain stationary. The only motion is one or two people and a single cue, although the cue as an object hardly changes, only its position. Motion may be compared between either a P-frame and the preceding I- or P-frame, or between a B-frame and the preceding and succeeding I- or P-frames.

P-frames use a combination of **motion estimation** and **motion compensation** leading to approximately double the compression ratio achieved within an I-frame. Motion estimation is based upon the principle of dividing the image to be compressed into a number of smaller rectangular areas, or **macroblocks**. A macroblock in one frame, and regarded as a reference, Figure 3.9(a), is compared with macroblocks in the same region in a subsequent frame on a pixel-by-pixel basis. This process is called **block matching**. The block most like that of the reference block is chosen, Figure 3.9(b), and from this the motion of the object may be estimated. Where a match cannot be found the macroblock is encoded independently, as if it were an I-frame. Actual movement of the object between the two frames is defined by the parameters Δx and Δy which, in combination, are known as the **motion vector**, and effectively indicate an object offset between frames. Motion estimation is not made between adjacent images, partly because the processing required, especially at the receiver, would prove excessive. The other reason is that motion estimation would in any case, except for very fast motion, be unnecessary given the small time interval between adjacent images. Instead, to improve overall compression, motion estimation is made between a pair of frames several frames distant.

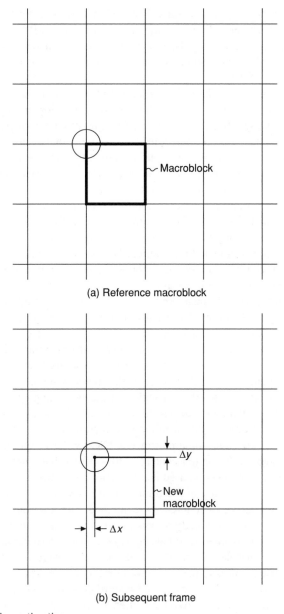

(a) Reference macroblock

(b) Subsequent frame

Figure 3.9 Motion estimation.

Motion estimation is not sufficiently precise and hence motion compensation must also be employed. In the encoder the image predicted using motion estimation is compared with the actual image to be encoded. Any differences are also transmitted, along with the motion estimation information, to the receiver. A parameter known as the **prediction error** is calculated for each macroblock, which indicates the difference, on a pixel-by-pixel basis, between the target macroblock and that found in the search area. The motion vector is suitably encoded as well as the prediction error which uses the same JPEG encoding technique used for I-frames. P-frames are decoded using the received information for the target frame in conjunction with that of the preceding I- or P-frame. These techniques enable P-frames to be substantially compressed compared with I-frames.

B-frames, as with I-frames, make use of prediction but additionally employ **interpolation** by estimating the target frames' motion vectors from preceding and succeeding P- or I-frames. P-frames are suitable for slow-motion images. Where motion becomes sufficiently fast a target object may move completely outside of a preceding, or succeeding, search area. B-frames are designed to cater for this situation.

Motion vectors and predication errors for the target frame are initially computed using the preceding frame (forward interpolation) and also the succeeding frame (backward interpolation) as references, in turn. The average of these two sets is then found. The set which yields the lowest error is chosen from the two interpolations and that of the average. Only the difference, or prediction, errors are then encoded in the same manner to a P-frame and transmitted. B-frames gain a further compression advantage compared with P-frames because motion vectors are not transmitted. Compression ratios of the order of 50:1 are possible.

D-frames, like I-frames, are free standing and not used in P- or B-frame compression. They are based upon averages (hence dc, meaning direct current) of each macroblock contained within a frame.

The degree of compression for each type of frame has only been loosely specified. It is not possible to state compression ratios exactly because they vary from frame to frame, depending upon the nature of the image being compressed. Recalling the discussion on the nature of information at the beginning of the chapter, the degree of information contained in an image which is blank and of uniform colour will be relatively small. Compare this with the information in an image portraying a close-up of a variety of different coloured flowers. Clearly the image of the flowers would have a much larger information content. Although we have not gone into specific details of the spatial compression used in JPEG and in I-frames, for instance, clearly the degree of compression for any of the frames encoded is in part a function of the information content and degree of redundancy contained within an image.

One factor which directly affects the compression ratio is the degree of granularity in terms of the number of pixels considered per macroblock. In MPEG this is one of the system variables which affects not only the resolution of the decoded image and hence quality, but also the degree of compression produced in an image.

Another factor which affects the overall compression of a transmission is the precise sequence of frames. We have already seen that different types of frame produce differing degrees of compression. A transmitting source could elect to transmit only successive I-frames, in which case the overall compression would be the least possible. To reduce this P- and B-frames are interspersed but the question arises, bearing in mind that one of the principal aims in MPEG is compression: how many such frames should one intersperse before returning to an I-frame? Obviously, from a purely compression-based view, as many as possible. But, as we have already indicated, there are other system considerations that require reasonably frequent interspersion of I-frames. MPEG leaves the precise decision on the mix of frames up to the operator. The deci-

Table 3.7   MPEG-2 resolutions.

Level	Resolution
Low	352 × 240
Main	720 × 480
High-1440	1440 × 1152
High	1920 × 1080

Data: Tanenbaum (1996) p. 742.

sion is a trade-off between degree of compression and resultant bandwidth requirement and quality and would be influenced by the subject matter.

Compression ratios for MPEG have been quoted up to 90:1, or even as high as 150:1.
More generally, I-frames can provide compression of the order of 30:1. P- and B-frames
provide greater compression with typical rates of 100:1 to 150:1.

MPEG-2 uses the compression techniques of MPEG-1 described above but, because
it was developed for broadcast transmissions, also supports interlaced scanning though
D-frames are not used. MPEG-2 has been adopted for use in Digital Video Broadcasting (DVB) for broadcast digital TV. Higher bit rates and resolution demanded by
broadcast TV are available. Four different resolutions (Tanenbaum 2003, p704) are
offered, see Table 3.7.

Low resolution is only suitable for video players and to provide backward compatibility with MPEG-1 and does not use B frames in order to make encoders and
decoders less complex. Main uses I-, B- and P-frames and is for traditional broadcast
TV; it is the main resolution used in practice. High has been specified for HDTV,
with the second variant shown for wide-screen operation. HDTV seems unlikely to
appear in the near future.

In addition to various resolutions, five profiles are specified for use with each level:
simple, main, spatial resolution, quantization accuracy and high. These, in combination with the four resolutions, offer a framework of 20 possible realizations of MPEG-
2 to support existing standards, and new ones to be developed.

MPEG-4 differs from MPEG-2 in that, with interactive TV and multimedia applications in mind, it enables users to interact with objects within a scene. That is, a
user may add, remove, reposition or modify, or manipulate an object in some way.
For instance, an object's shape could be changed, or it may be moved to a different
position on the screen. MPEG-4 moves away from the passive delivery of image and
TV found in MPEG-1 and 2 to a dynamic mode of operation required to fully exploit
emerging multimedia applications. MPEG-4 supports streaming, both video and audio,
whereby signals may be delivered and accessed, perhaps via the Internet, without any
need to download first, and then move into a 'playback' mode. The compression offers
a wide range of transmission rates so that MPEG-4 is compatible with almost any transmission medium/service currently available. Speeds available vary from a few kbps
to tens of Mbps. The compression technique is adapted to the transmission speed to
be used in an attempt to provide adequate quality whatever speed is used. A version
2 of MPEG-4 is currently being developed.

MPEG-7 provides an indexing system for multimedia to describe audiovisual material. This enables users to search for sound and video clips as well as still images and graphics. MPEG-7 continues to be developed to provide the specification of description tools in terms of both **descriptors** to describe material and **description schemes** for referencing and to support searching strategies. With this in mind standards are developing for referencing software called **Description Definition Language** (DDL). Such development is undertaken by working groups of which there are three main ones. One group is dealing with *audio* information, where information such as waveforms, spectra, frequency, content and timbre are under consideration. Another group is concerned with *visual* information, that is image, graphic and video information. Description and searching may be done by colour or texture, for instance, and a whole image or frame may be searched, or simply a user-specified region within a picture. Motion description tools enable a sequence to be searched for. For example, a particular dance sequence may be required in order to examine the step sequence of dancers. The third group deals with **multimedia description schemes**. This group's work is concerned with content management description tools to allow searches based around a number of parameters, such as how the subject is stored, its title, creator and so forth. Content description is used to describe both spatial and temporal aspects in order to search for certain regions or segments of the material. In addition, conceptual description tools describe the material in terms of object, event, language, etc. The group's work also considers other aspects such as navigating and filtering.

MPEG-2 and 4 are mainly concerned with coding of audiovisual information. MPEG-7 concentrates upon standardizing classification, and facilitating searching, of multimedia material. That is, information *about* the content rather than the content itself. It is not intended to replace earlier versions of MPEG. In consequence MPEG-7 may be used in conjunction with MPEG-2 and 4 to make use of its content description features. Equally, MPEG-7 is free standing and may also be used independently of earlier versions of MPEG for use with other audiovisual material represented in a different form.

Audio compression

MPEG also includes compression of audio to accompany moving images or for standalone purposes such as audio compact discs (CD). MPEG-1 supports two audio channels and is therefore suitable for normal stereophonic use. The main difference with MPEG-2 is that multiple channels are supported making it suitable for applications such as surround sound.

Standard CD audio recording is based upon a sampling rate of 44.1 kHz and 16 bits per sample. Additional bits are also required to provide synchronization and error correction, which results in 49 bits being produced per 16-bit sample.

Example 3.10

Calculate the raw data rate required to support a CD used for recording stereophonic quality music assumed to have a bandwidth which extends to 20 kHz. Assume 16 bits per sample are used.

The Nyquist limit suggests that the sampling frequency must be at least twice 20 kHz, or 40 kHz. In practice 44.1 kHz is used. Therefore the raw data rate is given by:

Data rate = 44.1 kHz $\times$ n $\times$ 16 bps

where n is the number of channels, and is 2 in this example:

$\approx$ 1.41 Mbps

Clearly this is a relatively high data rate to have to transmit. In consequence MPEG offers three different levels of compression shown in Table 3.8.

Layer I produces hi-fi quality and layer II near-CD quality. The most commonly used level of compression is that of layer III, known as MP3, which is widely used to distribute popular music over the Internet and offers CD quality.

MPEG actually allows three different sampling frequencies: 32, 44.1 (that used for CDs) and 48 kHz. Audio compression techniques are complex and beyond the scope of this text but are not in principal dissimilar from those employed in encoding video using MPEG. In essence the audio stream spectrum is divided into a number of frequency sub-bands (Halsall 2001, pp185–189). Each sub-band is sampled and encoded, but the number of bits per sample, and hence sub-band, is variable and under the control of a **psycho-acoustic** model. The quantized outputs of the encoder for each sub-band are finally mixed together and transmitted along with parameters of the compression generated by the model and the layer concerned.

The output of both video encoding and audio encoding must finally be combined into a single signal. Each individual output is first separately packetized. The two packetized sources are then multiplexed into the final signal to be transmitted.

Table 3.8 MPEG audio compression.

Coding layer	Data rate/channel kbps (encoder output)	Typical compression ratio*
I	32–448	4
II	64–192	7
III	64	11

* Encoder output rates compared with raw data rate of disk.

Exercises

3.1 State the maximum entropy of a 16-symbol source.

3.2 Determine which of the following codes are distinct, uniquely decodable and instantaneously decodable.
(a) $x_1 = 0$, $x_2 = 11$, $x_3 = 111$
(b) $x_1 = 0$, $x_2 = 10$, $x_3 = 111$, $x_4 = 110$
(c) $x_1 = 11$, $x_2 = 10$, $x_3 = 01$, $x_4 = 001$, $x_5 = 000$

3.3 Briefly outline and explain the functions of source coding.

3.4 For each of the following sources obtain an optimum source code, then calculate its entropy, length and efficiency.
(a) $n = 5$: $P(x_1) = 0.5$, $P(x_2) = P(x_3) = P(x_4) = P(x_5) = 0.125$
(b) $n = 4$: $P(x_1) = 0.35$, $P(x_2) = 0.3$, $P(x_3) = 0.2$, $P(x_4) = 0.15$
(c) $n = 4$: $P(x_1) = 0.5$, $P(x_2) = 0.25$, $P(x_3) = 0.1875$, $P(x_4) = 0.0625$

3.5 A code contains the following symbols, each shown with their associated probability:
A, $P(A) = 5/16$
B, $P(B) = 1/4$
C, $P(C) = 1/8$
D, $P(D) = 1/8$
E, $P(E) = 1/8$
F, $P(F) = 1/16$

Encode the symbol set using Huffman coding and calculate the efficiency of the code.

3.6 Explain the purpose of compression and how, in principle, it is achieved.

3.7 Figure 3.10 shows the start of two consecutive lines. Encode the lower line using modified READ encoding.

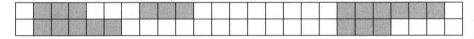

Figure 3.10 Exercise 3.7.

3.8 Briefly explain the video coding technique employed by MPEG-2.

3.9 Explain what I-, P- and B-frames are and compare them.

3.10 Explain the major difference between MPEG-2 and MPEG-7.

Error control

In Chapter 3 we saw how information theory and source coding allow us to optimize the information content of transmitted data and thus increase the efficiency of the transmission. However, once the data is dispatched over the transmission medium the characteristics of the medium normally conspire to alter the transmitted data in various ways so that the signals received at the remote end of a link differ from the transmitted signals. The effects of these adverse characteristics of a medium are known as **transmission impairments** and they often reduce transmission efficiency. In the case of binary data they may lead to errors, in that some binary zeros are transformed into binary ones and vice versa. To overcome the effects of such impairments it is necessary to introduce some form of error control. The first step in any form of error control is to detect whether any errors are present in the received data, a process which will be explored in some detail in Section 4.2. Having detected the presence of errors there are two strategies commonly used to correct them: either further computations are carried out at the receiver to correct the errors, a process known as **forward error control**; or a message is returned to the transmitter indicating that errors have occurred and requesting a retransmission of the data, which is known as **feedback error control**. Error control is a function of the data link layer of the OSI reference model.

4.1 Transmission impairments

A signal which is received at the remote end of a link will differ from the transmitted signal as a result of transmission impairments introduced by the transmission medium. The three main impairments are **attenuation**, **distortion** and **noise**.

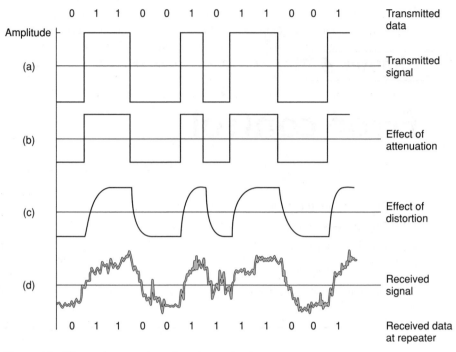

Figure 4.1   Effects of attenuation, distortion and noise.

Attenuation

As a signal is transmitted over a transmission medium its amplitude decreases, a phenomenon known as attenuation. The effect of attenuation, distortion and noise on data signals is shown in Figure 4.1(d). If an electrical signal is transmitted over a distance of more than a few kilometres then the attenuation and distortion are such that noise might cause erroneous reception of data.

Thus, metallic data circuits have repeaters spaced at regular intervals which take attenuated (and distorted) signals, such as those in Figure 4.1(d), and repeat them as perfect signals, as in Figure 4.1(a). Note, however, that in this instance, the repeater will retransmit an erroneous bit in position 7 as a result of the transmission impairments. A major advantage of optical circuits is that attenuation is dramatically less than in other media, resulting in links of 100 km or more without repeaters. Attenuation in electrical circuits is a function of frequency, which introduces further distortion in a received signal as some frequency components within a signal are attenuated more than others. This problem can be overcome by the use of **equalizers** which equalize the amount of attenuation across the range of frequencies used.

Distortion

Signals transmitted along a transmission line suffer various kinds of distortion. In an electrical circuit the inherent capacitance produces the familiar changes of shape in a signal illustrated in Figure 4.1(c). A further type of distortion occurs in all guided transmission circuits, including optical fibres, because different signal frequencies travel at different velocities within a waveguide and hence arrive at a receiver at slightly different times. This effect is known as **delay distortion** in electrical circuits and **dispersion** in optical circuits. If distortion is severe enough, received bits can spread into adjacent bit positions, an effect known as **intersymbol interference**.

Noise

The main factor which constrains the operation of any communications system is the presence in a communications channel of random, unwanted signals, known as noise. One form of noise, **thermal noise**, is present in all electronic devices and metallic transmission media, as a result of the thermal agitation of electrons within the material. It can never be eliminated and places an upper limit on the performance of a communications system. Probably the most troublesome form of noise in a data link is **impulse noise**. This consists of electrical impulses in a communications channel which are picked up from external sources such as lightning or noisy electromechanical equipment. The problem with impulse noise is that, although normally infrequent, it can have a fairly high amplitude and can be of a relatively long duration thus corrupting substantial numbers of bits. Although it is, strictly speaking, an example of **interference**, **crosstalk** produces similar problems to noise. It arises from unwanted electrical coupling between adjacent communications channels. Its most obvious manifestation is when some other conversation can be heard in the background of a telephone call. The effect of noise on data signals is illustrated in Figure 4.1(d).

4.2 Forward error control

The need to detect and correct errors was mentioned in Section 4.1, but not the means by which the detection process can be carried out. Error detection (and correction) is also known as **channel coding**. Channel coding is the process of coding data prior to transmission over a communications channel so that if errors do occur during transmission it is possible to detect and possibly even to correct those errors once the data has been received. In order to achieve this error detection/correction some bit patterns need to be identified as error free at the receiver, whereas other bit patterns will be identified as erroneous. To increase the number of identifiable bit patterns at the receiver above the bare minimum required to represent the data, additional bits, known as **redundant bits**, are added to the data or information bits prior to transmission. Various different types of code are available for use in channel coding but the most commonly used are called **linear block codes**.

4.3 Linear block codes

These constitute the simplest and most commonly used type of channel code. Data is transmitted as a fixed-length block. Prior to transmission the data is treated as a binary number and some form of linear mathematical process is carried out on a group of information bits so as to generate additional redundant bits which are known as **check bits**.

The check bits are transmitted along with the information bits, normally at the end of the block. At the receiver, a similar mathematical process is used to determine whether there are errors or not. Typical mathematical processes used are addition and division. A study of these codes inevitably requires some knowledge of mathematics but although the theory underlying the codes is complex, the following treatment has been kept fairly straightforward without being too simplistic.

Hamming codes

This is an important group of early error-correcting codes pioneered by R.W. Hamming in the 1950s. They involve the production of check bits by adding together different groups of information bits. The type of addition used is known as modulo-2 addition and is equivalent to normal binary addition without any carries. The best way to see how the check bits are obtained is to consider a particular code as an example. We shall consider a Hamming (7,4) code, in which three check bits (c_1, c_2 and c_3) are combined with four information bits (k_1, k_2, k_3 and k_4) to produce a block of data of length $n = 7$. This block of data is known as a **codeword**. A block of data of length 7 is too short to be appropriate for a practical data communications system, but the mathematics involved in longer blocks would become tedious. Three check equations are used to obtain the three check bits of this Hamming (7,4) code as follows:

$$c_1 = k_1 \oplus k_2 \oplus k_4$$
$$c_2 = k_1 \oplus k_3 \oplus k_4$$
$$c_3 = k_2 \oplus k_3 \oplus k_4$$

where $\oplus$ represents modulo-2 addition. The rules of modulo-2 addition are:

$$0 \oplus 0 = 0$$
$$0 \oplus 1 = 1$$
$$1 \oplus 1 = 0 \text{ (no carry)}$$

If we choose the information bits 1010 as an example then $k_1 = 1$, $k_2 = 0$, $k_3 = 1$ and $k_4 = 0$ and the check bits obtained from the three check equations above are as follows:

$$c_1 = k_1 \oplus k_2 \oplus k_4 = 1 \oplus 0 \oplus 0 = 1$$
$$c_2 = k_1 \oplus k_3 \oplus k_4 = 1 \oplus 1 \oplus 0 = 0$$
$$c_3 = k_2 \oplus k_3 \oplus k_4 = 0 \oplus 1 \oplus 0 = 1$$

The codeword is obtained by adding the check bits to the end of the information bits and therefore the data 1010101 will be transmitted (information bits first).

A complete set of codewords can be obtained in a similar way:

Codeword no.	$k_1\ k_2\ k_3\ k_4\ c_1\ c_2\ c_3$	Codeword no.	$k_1\ k_2\ k_3\ k_4\ c_1\ c_2\ c_3$
0	0 0 0 0 0 0 0	8	1 0 0 0 1 1 0
1	0 0 0 1 1 1 1	9	1 0 0 1 0 0 1
2	0 0 1 0 0 1 1	10	1 0 1 0 1 0 1
3	0 0 1 1 1 0 0	11	1 0 1 1 0 1 0
4	0 1 0 0 1 0 1	12	1 1 0 0 0 1 1
5	0 1 0 1 0 1 0	13	1 1 0 1 1 0 0
4	0 1 1 0 1 1 0	14	1 1 1 0 0 0 0
7	0 1 1 1 0 0 1	15	1 1 1 1 1 1 1

An error that occurs in a transmitted codeword can be detected only if the error changes the codeword into some other bit pattern that does not appear in the code. This means that the codewords transmitted over a channel must differ from each other in at least two bit positions. If two codewords differ in only one position and an error occurs in that position then one codeword will be changed into another codeword and there will be no way of knowing that an error has occurred. Inspection of the set of codewords of the Hamming (7,4) code reveals that they all differ from each other in at least three places. Taking codewords 3 and 8 as an example, we have:

    Codeword 3   0 0 1 1 1 0 0
    Codeword 8   1 0 0 0 1 1 0

These two codewords differ in positions 1, 3, 4 and 4 (counting from the left). The number of positions by which any two codewords in a code differ is known as the **Hamming distance** or just the distance, so that the distance between these two words is four. Since all linear block codes contain the all-zeros codeword, then an easy way to find the **minimum distance** of a code is to compare a non-zero codeword which has the minimum number of ones with the all-zeros codeword. Thus the minimum distance of a code is equal to the smallest number of ones in any non-zero codeword, which in the case of this Hamming (7,4) code is three. If the codewords of a code differ in three or more positions then error correction is possible since an erroneous bit pattern will be 'closer' to one codeword than another (this assumes that one error is more likely than two, two more likely than three, and so on). If we take codewords 8 and 10 as an example, we have:

    Codeword 8   1 0 0 0 1 1 0
    Codeword 10   1 0 1 0 1 0 1

The distance between these two codewords is three. If codeword 8 is transmitted and an error occurs in bit 3 then the received data will be:

    1 0 1 0 1 1 0

This is not one of the other 15 Hamming (7,4) codewords since an error has occurred. Furthermore, the most likely codeword to have been transmitted is codeword 8 since this is the nearest to the received bit pattern. Thus, it should also be possible to correct the received data by making the assumption that the transmitted codeword was number 8. If, however, a second error occurs in bit 7 then the received bit pattern will be:

1 0 1 0 1 1 1

It should still be possible to detect that an error has occurred since this is not one of the 16 codewords. However, it is no longer possible to correct the errors since the received bit pattern has changed in two places and is no longer closer to codeword 8 than any other (it is, in fact, now closer to codeword 10). Thus, this Hamming (7,4) code is able to detect two errors but correct only one error. In general, if the minimum distance of a code is d, then $d - 1$ errors can normally be detected using a linear block code and mod$(d - 1)/2$ can be corrected.

A feature of all linear block codes which arises out of the mathematical rules used to determine the check bits is that all the codewords are related by these rules. Received data which contains errors no longer conforms to the mathematical rules, and it is this fact that is used to carry out the detection and correction processes at the receiver. If we take the example of the Hamming (7,4) code then the encoding process will restrict the number of different codewords that can be transmitted to the 16 listed above. As a result of errors that may occur in the transmission process, the data arriving at a receiver in 7-bit blocks can have any one of $2^7 = 128$ different 7-bit patterns. This allows the receiver to detect whether errors have occurred since it is aware of the rules used in the encoding process and can apply them to see whether the received data is one of the 14 'legal' codewords or not. Furthermore, it is the case that all Hamming codes (indeed, all linear block codes) possess the mathematical property that if we add any two codewords together (modulo-2 addition) then the resulting sum is also a codeword. For example, if we add codewords 1 and 2 from the earlier list we obtain:

$$
\begin{array}{c}
0\ 0\ 0\ 1\ 1\ 1 \\
\oplus\ 0\ 0\ 1\ 0\ 0\ 1 \\
\hline
0\ 0\ 1\ 1\ 1\ 0
\end{array} \quad \text{which is codeword 3}
$$

This allows us to represent a whole code by means of a small 'subset' of codewords, since further codewords can simply be obtained by modulo-2 addition. In the case of the Hamming (7,4) code this is not important, since there are only 14 codewords. However, with longer block lengths the number of codewords becomes unmanageable. For example, a short block of 32 bits involves $2^{32} = 4\ 294\ 967\ 296$ different codewords. The subset of codewords is often expressed as a matrix known as a **generator matrix**, G. The codewords chosen are normally powers of 2, that is codewords 1, 2, 4, 8, ... A suitable generator matrix for the Hamming (7,4) code consists of the following four codewords:

$$
G = \begin{bmatrix}
1\ 0\ 0\ 0\ 1\ 1\ 0 \\
0\ 1\ 0\ 0\ 1\ 0\ 1 \\
0\ 0\ 1\ 0\ 0\ 1\ 1 \\
0\ 0\ 0\ 1\ 1\ 1\ 1
\end{bmatrix}
$$

The matrix has four rows and seven columns, that is it has dimensions 4×7 ($k \times n$). The whole code can be generated from this matrix just by adding together rows, and it is for this reason that it is called a generator matrix. A further reason for the generator matrix being so named is that it can be used to generate codewords directly from the information bits without using the check equations. This is achieved by multiplying the information bits by the generator matrix using matrix multiplication, as Example 4.1 shows.

Example 4.1

Information consisting of the bits 1010 is to be encoded using the Hamming (7,4) code. Use the generator matrix to obtain the codeword to be transmitted.

The codeword is obtained by multiplying the four information bits (expressed as a row vector) by the generator matrix as follows:

$$[1\ 0\ 1\ 0] \times \begin{bmatrix} 1\ 0\ 0\ 0\ 1\ 1\ 0 \\ 0\ 1\ 0\ 0\ 1\ 0\ 1 \\ 0\ 0\ 1\ 0\ 0\ 1\ 1 \\ 0\ 0\ 0\ 1\ 1\ 1\ 1 \end{bmatrix}$$

The multiplication is achieved by multiplying each column of the generator matrix in turn by the row vector as follows:

$$[(1 \times 1 \oplus 0 \times 0 \oplus 1 \times 0 \oplus 0 \times 0),(1 \times 0 \oplus 0 \times 1 \oplus 1 \times 0 \oplus 0 \times 0),(1 \times 0 \oplus 0 \times 0 \oplus 0 \times 0$$
$$\oplus 1 \times 1 \oplus 0 \times 0),(1 \times 0 \oplus 0 \times 0 \oplus 1 \times 0 \oplus 0 \times 1),(1 \times 1 \oplus 0 \times 1 \oplus 1 \times 0 \oplus 0 \times 1),$$
$$(1 \times 1 \oplus 0 \times 0 \oplus 1 \times 1 \oplus 0 \times 1),(1 \times 0 \oplus 0 \times 1 \oplus 1 \times 1 \oplus 0 \times 1)] = 1\ 0\ 1\ 0\ 1\ 0\ 1$$

Note that this process is, in fact, the same as adding together the first and third rows of the matrix. There are thus three different ways in which encoding may be carried out in a Hamming code:

1. Use the check equations to obtain the check bits and then add the check bits to the end of the information bits.

2. Add together appropriate rows from the generator matrix.

3. Multiply the information bits by the generator matrix.

It is also possible to express the three check equations of the Hamming (7,4) code in the form of a matrix known as the check matrix H, as follows:

Check equations   *Check matrix*

$$c_1 = k_1 \oplus k_2 \oplus k_4$$
$$c_2 = k_1 \oplus k_3 \oplus k_4$$
$$c_3 = k_2 \oplus k_3 \oplus k_4$$

$$\begin{bmatrix} 1\ 1\ 0\ 1\ 1\ 0\ 0 \\ 1\ 0\ 1\ 1\ 0\ 1\ 0 \\ 0\ 1\ 1\ 1\ 0\ 0\ 1 \end{bmatrix} = H$$

$$k_1\ k_2\ k_3\ k_4\ c_1\ c_2\ c_3$$

The check matrix is obtained by having each row of the matrix correspond to one of the check equations in that if a particular bit is present in an equation, then that bit is marked by a one in the matrix. This results in a matrix with dimensions 3×7 ($c \times n$). If we now compare the two types of matrix we note that the generator matrix has an **identity** matrix consisting of a diagonal or **echelon** of ones to its left and the check matrix has this echelon to its right. When a generator or check matrix conforms to this pattern, it is in **standard echelon form**. In the case of single error-correcting codes such as the Hamming codes it usually makes calculations easier if the matrices are in this form. A further point to note is that if the echelons are removed from the two matrices, then what remains is the transpose of each other. In the case of the Hamming (7,4) code:

$$
\begin{bmatrix} 1 & 1 & 0 & 1 \\ 1 & 0 & 1 & 1 \\ 0 & 1 & 1 & 1 \end{bmatrix} \text{ is the transpose of } \begin{bmatrix} 1 & 1 & 0 \\ 1 & 0 & 1 \\ 0 & 1 & 1 \\ 1 & 1 & 1 \end{bmatrix}
$$

Example 4.2

The generator matrix for a Hamming (15,11) code is as follows:

$$
G = \begin{bmatrix}
1 & 0 & 0 & 0 & 0 & 0 & 0 & 0 & 0 & 0 & 0 & 1 & 1 & 0 & 0 \\
0 & 1 & 0 & 0 & 0 & 0 & 0 & 0 & 0 & 0 & 0 & 0 & 1 & 1 & 0 \\
0 & 0 & 1 & 0 & 0 & 0 & 0 & 0 & 0 & 0 & 0 & 0 & 0 & 1 & 1 \\
0 & 0 & 0 & 1 & 0 & 0 & 0 & 0 & 0 & 0 & 1 & 1 & 0 & 1 \\
0 & 0 & 0 & 0 & 1 & 0 & 0 & 0 & 0 & 0 & 1 & 0 & 1 & 0 \\
0 & 0 & 0 & 0 & 0 & 1 & 0 & 0 & 0 & 0 & 0 & 1 & 0 & 1 \\
0 & 0 & 0 & 0 & 0 & 0 & 1 & 0 & 0 & 0 & 1 & 1 & 1 & 0 \\
0 & 0 & 0 & 0 & 0 & 0 & 0 & 1 & 0 & 0 & 0 & 1 & 1 & 1 \\
0 & 0 & 0 & 0 & 0 & 0 & 0 & 0 & 1 & 0 & 0 & 1 & 1 & 1 & 1 \\
0 & 0 & 0 & 0 & 0 & 0 & 0 & 0 & 0 & 1 & 0 & 1 & 0 & 1 & 1 \\
0 & 0 & 0 & 0 & 0 & 0 & 0 & 0 & 0 & 0 & 1 & 1 & 0 & 0 & 1
\end{bmatrix}
$$

Obtain the check matrix of this code.

The code has a block length $n = 15$, consisting of $k = 11$ information bits and $c = 4$ check bits. The generator matrix has dimensions 11×15, and includes an 11×11 identity matrix (an echelon) to the left. The check matrix has dimensions 4×15 and contains a 4×4 identity matrix to its right-hand side. The rest of the check matrix is obtained by removing the identity matrix from the generator matrix and transposing what is left. This results in the last 4 bits of the first row of the generator matrix becoming the first column of the check matrix and the last 4 bits of the last row of the generator matrix becoming the 11th column of the check matrix. The check matrix is as follows:

$$
H = \begin{bmatrix}
1 & 0 & 0 & 1 & 1 & 0 & 1 & 0 & 1 & 1 & 1 & 1 & 0 & 0 & 0 \\
1 & 1 & 0 & 1 & 0 & 1 & 1 & 1 & 1 & 0 & 0 & 0 & 1 & 0 & 0 \\
0 & 1 & 1 & 0 & 1 & 0 & 1 & 1 & 1 & 1 & 0 & 0 & 0 & 1 & 0 \\
0 & 0 & 1 & 1 & 0 & 1 & 0 & 1 & 1 & 1 & 1 & 0 & 0 & 0 & 1
\end{bmatrix}
$$

Having looked in some detail at several ways of encoding information bits, we shall turn our attention to the decoding process which takes place at the remote end of a channel. To determine whether received data is error free or not, it is necessary for all of the check equations to be verified. This can be done by recalculating the check bits from the received data or, alternatively, received data can be checked by using the check matrix. As its name implies, the check matrix can be used to check the received data for errors in a similar way to using the generator matrix to generate a codeword. The check matrix, H, is multiplied by the received data expressed as a column vector:

$$\begin{bmatrix} 1 & 1 & 0 & 1 & 1 & 0 & 0 \\ 1 & 0 & 1 & 1 & 0 & 1 & 0 \\ 0 & 1 & 1 & 1 & 0 & 0 & 1 \end{bmatrix} \times \begin{bmatrix} 1 \\ 0 \\ 0 \\ 0 \\ 1 \\ 1 \\ 0 \end{bmatrix}$$

H matrix

Data vector

This time the multiplication is achieved by multiplying each row of the check matrix in turn by the received data vector, as follows:

$$\begin{matrix} (1 \times 1 \oplus 1 \times 0 \oplus 0 \times 0 \oplus 1 \times 0 \oplus 1 \times 1 \oplus 0 \times 1 \oplus 0 \times 0) \\ (1 \times 1 \oplus 0 \times 0 \oplus 1 \times 0 \oplus 1 \times 0 \oplus 0 \times 1 \oplus 1 \times 1 \oplus 0 \times 0) = \\ (0 \times 1 \oplus 1 \times 0 \oplus 1 \times 0 \oplus 1 \times 0 \oplus 1 \times 0 \oplus 0 \times 1 \oplus 1 \times 0) \end{matrix} \begin{bmatrix} 0 \\ 0 \\ 0 \end{bmatrix}$$

If, as is the case here, the received data is error free then the result of this multiplication is zero. This result, which in this case is a 3-bit vector, is known as the **syndrome**. 'Syndrome' is a medical term, and its use in this context seems a bit idiosyncratic. The word 'diagnosis' seems more appropriate as what we are referring to is something that gives us information on the nature of a problem that we wish to cure. (The problem is the presence of an error.) We can now ask the question: what will the syndrome tell us if an error occurs during the data transmission? Suppose that coded data is transmitted as a 7-bit codeword $[t]$ and an erroneous 7-bit stream $[r]$ is received. The error that caused the erroneous received data can also be expressed as a vector $[e]$ which contains zeros apart from the error position in which there is a one.

Then the received data can be thought of as the transmitted codeword plus an error vector:

$$[r] = [t] + [e]$$

These vectors can be multiplied by the check matrix H, as follows:

$$[H][r] = [H][t] + [H][e]$$

But $[H][t]$ is the check matrix multiplied by an error-free codeword which, by definition, is equal to zero so that:

$$[H][r] = [H][e]$$

Thus $[H][r]$, which is the check matrix multiplied by the received data (i.e. the syndrome), will give some indication as to the nature of the error. It is this basic assumption which forms the basis of error correction. This may seem a bit complicated at first sight but Example 4.3 shows that, in practice, it is not too difficult.

Example 4.3

Information consisting of four ones is to be transmitted using the Hamming (7,4) code.

(a) Determine the transmitted codeword.

(b) If an error occurs in bit 4 during transmission, determine the syndrome.

(c) Show how the syndrome can be used to correct the error.

(a) To determine the transmitted codeword we can use the three check equations to determine the check bits:

$$c_1 = k_1 \oplus k_2 \oplus k_4 = 1 \oplus 1 \oplus 1 = 1$$
$$c_2 = k_1 \oplus k_3 \oplus k_4 = 1 \oplus 1 \oplus 1 = 1$$
$$c_3 = k_2 \oplus k_3 \oplus k_4 = 1 \oplus 1 \oplus 1 = 1$$

The transmitted codeword is therefore seven ones as follows:

$$k_1\ k_2\ k_3\ k_4\ c_1\ c_2\ c_3$$
$$1\ \ 1\ \ 1\ \ 1\ \ 1\ \ 1\ \ 1$$

(b) If an error occurs in bit 4 then the received data is 1110111. To check whether there is an error in the received data, we multiply by the check matrix:

$$\begin{bmatrix} 1\ 1\ 0\ 1\ 1\ 0\ 0 \\ 1\ 0\ 1\ 1\ 0\ 1\ 0 \\ 0\ 1\ 1\ 1\ 0\ 0\ 1 \end{bmatrix} \times \begin{bmatrix} 1 \\ 1 \\ 1 \\ 0 \\ 1 \\ 1 \\ 1 \end{bmatrix} = \begin{bmatrix} 1 \\ 1 \\ 1 \end{bmatrix} \quad \text{Syndrome}$$

$$\uparrow$$
$$\text{Column 4}$$

(c) The fact that an error has occurred has caused the syndrome to be non-zero. Furthermore the position of the error can be located by comparing the syndrome with the columns of the check matrix. In this case the syndrome provides us with all we need to know about the error since its numerical value equates with column 4 of the check matrix, thus indicating an error in bit 4.

Thus all of the mathematics that we have used so far proves to be worthwhile since Hamming codes provide an easily implemented way not only of detecting an error but also of locating its position.

Encoding and decoding circuits

An attractive feature of Hamming codes in the early days of error correction was that they could be easily implemented in hardware circuits, particularly if the block length was fairly short. Since modulo-2 addition is identical to an exclusive-or (EX-OR) function, a number of multiple input EX-OR gates can be used to determine the check bits, as in the circuit for a Hamming (7,4) encoder shown in Figure 4.2.

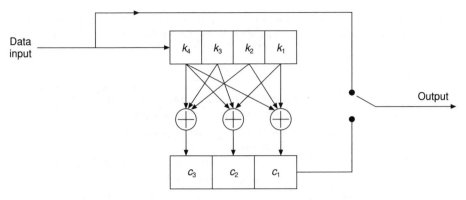

Figure 4.2 Hamming (7,4) encoder.

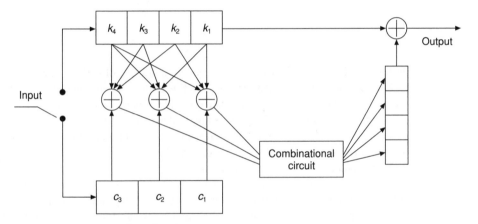

Figure 4.3 Hamming (7,4) decoder.

The information bits are fed into a 4-bit shift register and the check bits are calcu-lated by the EX-OR circuits and are held in a 3-bit shift register. The switch is in the up position to transmit the information bits and down for the check bits. Figure 4.3 shows a corresponding decoder.

With the receive switch up the information bits are received into a 4-bit shift register and with it down the check bits flow into a 3-bit shift register. The left-hand EX-OR gate works out the modulo-2 sum $k_2 \oplus k_3 \oplus k_4 \oplus c_3$. This equals zero if no errors have occurred during transmission. The output from the three EX-OR gates thus represents the syndrome which is fed into a combinational logic circuit to deter-mine the position of any error. The error is corrected by means of a k-stage shift register at the output of the combinational logic circuit. This will contain all zeros apart from any erroneous position which will contain a one. The output from the shift register is added (modulo-2) serially to the received information bits and any bit position within the received data which gets added to a one will change from 0 to 1 (or 1 to 0), thus correcting the error. Unfortunately, circuits such as these, although simple in the case of the Hamming (7,4) code, become excessively complicated for the longer block lengths used in data communications networks. Hamming codes do, however, find uses in situations which do not require large block lengths, such as remote control of robotic systems.

Cyclic codes

As mentioned above, simple linear codes such as the Hamming code have a limitation in that if large block lengths are used, for example in data communications, then the encoding and decoding circuitry becomes very complex. Paradoxically, the circuitry can be made simpler if the mathematical structure of the code is made more complex. A cyclic code is one in which all the codewords are related by the fact that if a codeword is rotated, it becomes another codeword. The following code is obtained from the single check equation $c_1 = k_1 \oplus k_2$ and, although trivial, is cyclic:

$$
\begin{array}{ccc}
k_1 & k_2 & c_1 \\
0 & 0 & 0 \\
0 & 1 & 1 \\
1 & 0 & 1 \\
1 & 1 & 0
\end{array}
$$

All four of these codewords can be rotated in either direction and will result in another codeword. Consequently, to define this code, it is only necessary to have one non-zero codeword, since all the other codewords can be obtained from it (the all-zeros codeword is obtained by adding any codeword to itself). Cyclic codes are usually defined by a single codeword expressed as a polynomial, known as a **generator polynomial**. For example, the cyclic code used in the High-Level Data Link Control (HDLC) protocol has a generator polynomial $x^{16} + x^{12} + x^5 + 1$, where $x = 2$ since the code is binary. This is expressed as a polynomial rather than the binary number 10001000000100001 because the latter is rather unmanageable. The highest power of a generator polynomial is called its **degree** and is always equal to the number of check bits in the code. Since cyclic codes are invariably linear block codes, they can also be described by a generator matrix, which can be readily obtained from the generator polynomial as Example 4.4 shows.

Example 4.4

A cyclic block code with block length $n = 7$ has a generator polynomial $x^3 + x + 1$. Determine the generator matrix, and the full set of codewords.

The codewords have three check bits since the degree of the polynomial is 3 and the number of information bits, $k = 7 - 3 = 4$. The generator polynomial $G(x) = x^3 + x + 1$ = 1011 in binary. To make this into a 7-bit codeword, three insignificant zeros are added to give 0001011. This codeword is made the bottom row of the generator matrix and the other rows are obtained by rotating this codeword to the left. The generator matrix is of size $k \times n = 4 \times 7$ as follows:

$$
G = \begin{bmatrix}
1 & 0 & 1 & 1 & 0 & 0 & 0 \\
0 & 1 & 0 & 1 & 1 & 0 & 0 \\
0 & 0 & 1 & 0 & 1 & 1 & 0 \\
0 & 0 & 0 & 1 & 0 & 1 & 1
\end{bmatrix}
\begin{matrix}
a \\ b \\ c \\ d
\end{matrix}
$$

However, as we saw with Hamming codes, it is convenient if a generator matrix has an echelon to the left, when it is in standard echelon form. Rows c and d fit this pattern, but the top two rows need to be changed by means of modulo-2 addition as follows:

$$G = \begin{bmatrix} 1\ 0\ 0\ 0\ 1\ 0\ 1 \\ 0\ 1\ 0\ 0\ 1\ 1\ 1 \\ 0\ 0\ 1\ 0\ 1\ 1\ 0 \\ 0\ 0\ 0\ 1\ 0\ 1\ 1 \end{bmatrix} \begin{matrix} a \oplus c \oplus d \\ b \oplus d \\ c \\ d \end{matrix}$$

Further codewords can be obtained by further left rotations as follows:

0001011	0110001
0010110	1100010
0101100	1000101
1011000	

To obtain further codewords it is necessary to add two together; choosing the last two above gives $1100010 + 1000101 = 0100111$. Shifting of this codeword provides the following:

0100111	1110100
1001110	1101001
0011101	1010011
0111010	

Two further codewords are required to make a total of 16; one is the all-zeros codeword 0000000 and the other is obtained by adding two codewords as follows:

```
   0100111
⊕ 1011000
   1111111
```

The fact that the codewords of a cyclic code are obtained by shifting and adding the generator polynomial leads to the important characteristic that all codewords are a multiple of the generator polynomial. To encode incoming information bits, a cyclic encoder must therefore generate check bits which, when added to the information bits, will produce a codeword which is a multiple of $G(x)$, the generator polynomial. This is achieved as follows: firstly, the information bits, normally a lengthy bit pattern, are represented as a polynomial $K(x)$, where x is, in practice, 2. Secondly, let the information bits $K(x)$, followed by c zeros (i.e. a codeword with all the check bits set to zero), be represented by the polynomial $F(x)$ which is in fact $K(x)$ shifted by c places, that is $x^c K(x)$. If $F(x)$ is now divided by the generator polynomial $G(x)$ then:

$$\frac{F(x)}{G(x)} = Q(x) + \frac{R(x)}{G(x)}$$

where $Q(x)$ is the quotient and $R(x)$ the remainder, that is:

$$F(x) = Q(x)G(x) + R(x)$$

If the remainder $R(x)$ is now added (modulo-2) to $F(x)$, we obtain:

$$F(x) + R(x) = Q(x)G(x)$$

since addition and subtraction will give the same result in modulo-2. It is this bit sequence, $F(x) + R(x)$, which is transmitted, since it is always a multiple of the generator polynomial $G(x)$ and is therefore always a legal codeword. Thus, encoding for a cyclic code consists of adding c zeros to the end of the information bits and dividing by the generator polynomial to find the remainder. (Note that modulo-2 division is used.) The remainder is added to the information bits in place of the c zeros and the resulting codeword transmitted. At the receiver, a decoder tests to see whether the received bit sequence is error free by dividing again by the generator polynomial. An error-free transmission results in a zero remainder. Such a process is also known as a **cyclic redundancy check** (CRC). The process is illustrated by Example 4.5.

Example 4.5

A (7,4) cyclic code has a generator polynomial $x^3 + x + 1$. Information bits consisting of 1100 (most significant bit on the left) are to be coded and transmitted. Determine:

(a) the transmitted codeword,

(b) the remainder obtained at the receiver if the transmission is error free,

(c) the remainder obtained at the receiver if an error occurs in bit 4.

(a) The generator polynomial $x^3 + x + 1$ expressed as a binary number is 1011. Firstly, three zeros are added to the information bits to produce $F(x) = 1100000$. Dividing $F(x)$ by the generator polynomial $G(x)$ using modulo-2 division gives:

```
            1110        Quotient
    1011)1100000
         1011
         1110
         1011
         1010
         1011
          010        Remainder
```

Thus the remainder = 010 and this is added to the information bits in place of the three zeros to give the transmitted codeword 1100010.

(b) If the transmission is error free, we divide the received data by $G(x)$ and obtain:

```
            1110
    1011)1100010
         1011
         1110
         1011
         1011
         1011
          000        Zero remainder
```

(c) If an error occurs in bit 4, the received bit pattern is 1101010, resulting in:

```
              1111
      1011)1101010
           1011
           1100
           1011
           1111
           1011
           1000
           1011
            011          Remainder
```

The fact that this remainder in (c) is non-zero indicates that an error has occurred. Note that the division used is modulo-2 division and no 'carries' or 'borrows' can be used. In this example, the numbers that are used within the division process are restricted to 4 bits.

What if we now use a check matrix to determine the syndrome? A cyclic code is a linear block code and so it should be possible to do this. The check matrix for this code can be obtained from the generator matrix of Example 4.4 in exactly the same way as the check matrix was obtained in Example 4.2, as follows:

$$
G = \begin{bmatrix} 1\,0\,0\,0\,1\,0\,1 \\ 0\,1\,0\,0\,1\,1\,1 \\ 0\,0\,1\,0\,1\,1\,0 \\ 0\,0\,0\,1\,0\,1\,1 \end{bmatrix} \quad \text{and} \quad H = \begin{bmatrix} 1\,1\,1\,0\,1\,0\,0 \\ 0\,1\,1\,1\,0\,1\,0 \\ 1\,1\,0\,1\,0\,0\,1 \end{bmatrix}
$$

and the syndrome is obtained by multiplying the check matrix by the received data:

$$
\begin{bmatrix} 1\,1\,1\,0\,1\,0\,0 \\ 0\,1\,1\,1\,0\,1\,0 \\ 1\,1\,0\,1\,0\,0\,1 \end{bmatrix} \times \begin{bmatrix} 1 \\ 1 \\ 0 \\ 1 \\ 0 \\ 1 \\ 0 \end{bmatrix} = \begin{bmatrix} 0 \\ 1 \\ 1 \end{bmatrix}
$$

which gives the same result as the remainder obtained from the division. Although the two mathematical processes appear to be different, they produce the same result.

Modulo-2 division circuits

Modulo-2 division is achieved in an electronic circuit by repeated shifting and subtraction. This can be very easily implemented using shift registers and, bearing in mind that modulo-2 subtraction is identical to addition, EX-OR gates. A circuit that will divide by $1 + x + x^3$ is given in Figure 4.4.

The best way to understand the working of this circuit is to analyse its step-by-step operation. Firstly we choose an input bit pattern which will give a known remainder.

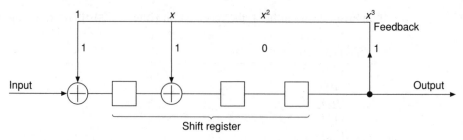

Figure 4.4   Modulo-2 division circuit.

Table 4.1   Modulo-2 division.

Step J	Input on Jth shift	Feedback on Jth shift	Shift register after Jth shift	Output after Jth shift
0	–	–	0 0 0	0
1	1	0	1 0 0	0
2	1	0	1 1 0	0
3	0	0	0 1 1	1
4	0	1	1 1 1	1
5	0	1	1 0 1	1
4	1	1	0 0 0	0
7	0	0	0 0 0	

In Table 4.1, the input 1100010 is used. We already know from Example 4.5 that this is divisible by 1011 ($x^3 + x + 1$) and should therefore produce a remainder of zero. Note that after six shifts, the shift register contains the required remainder of 000. The quotient will appear at the output of the circuit. However, in coding circuits, it is only the remainder that is of significance.

Cyclic encoding and decoding circuits

Encoding for a cyclic code consists of dividing the polynomial $F(x)$ (incoming information bits with zeros in the check bit positions) by the generator polynomial $G(x)$ to find a remainder $R(x)$ which is then added to $F(x)$ to give the codeword $F(x) + R(x)$. To obtain the zero check bits, the information bits $K(x)$ are shifted c places prior to the division process. An encoding circuit, known as a Meggitt encoder, that achieves this for $G(x) = 1 + x + x^3$ is shown in Figure 4.5.

Bringing the input information bits $K(x)$ into the circuit at the point shown rather than to the left of the circuit as in the division circuit of Figure 4.4 is equivalent to shifting c places ($c = 3$ in this case). Initially S_1 is in the up position and S_2 is closed, while $F(x)$ is simultaneously transmitted and processed in the division circuit. After k shifts, the shift register will contain the remainder $R(x)$. S_1 then moves to the down position and S_2 opens so that the remainder is then transmitted.

A similar arrangement is shown in the decoder circuit of Figure 4.6. Initially the information bits are received into a k-stage shift register with S_1 and S_2 closed. At the same time, the check bits are recalculated by the division circuit and then fed into a

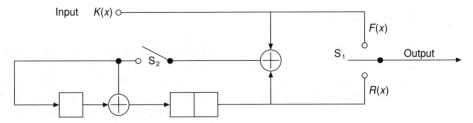

Figure 4.5   Cyclic encoding circuit.

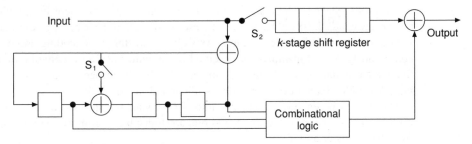

Figure 4.6   Cyclic decoding circuit.

combinational logic circuit. The check bits are received with S_1 and S_2 open and are fed straight into the combinational logic circuit where they are compared with the recalculated check bits to determine a syndrome. S_1 and S_2 are then closed again and the syndrome is used by the combinational circuit to correct the data at the output of the decoding circuit.

Practical cyclic redundancy checks

Although the material in this section appears quite theoretical, it is of great practical importance to most data communications networks. This is because most networks use a cyclic redundancy check as part of the level 2 protocol error checking. Table 4.2 shows some commonly used generator polynomials.

Table 4.2   Commonly used generator protocols.

Protocol(s)	Generator polynomial
ATM (Header error check)	$x^8 + x^2 + x + 1$
ATM (OAM cells)	$x^{10} + x^9 + x^5 + x^4 + x + 1$
ATM adaptation layer 1	$x^3 + x + 1$
ATM adaptation layer 2	$x^5 + x^2 + x + 1$
Ethernet (and FDDI)	$x^{32} + x^{24} + x^{23} + x^{22} + x^{14} + x^{12} + x^{11} + x^{10} + x^8$ $+ x^7 + x^5 + x^4 + x^2 + x + 1$
X.25 (HDLC)	$x^{16} + x^{12} + x^5 + 1$

4.4 Convolutional codes

In order to carry out a cyclic redundancy check on a block of data, it is necessary for the complete block of data to be received into an input buffer at a network node within a data communications network. This is convenient for most data communications protocols, including IP, which transmit data in the form of blocks known as packets or frames. Convolutional codes work in a fundamentally different manner in that they operate on data continuously as it is received (or transmitted) by a network node. Consequently, convolutional encoders and decoders can be constructed with a minimum of circuitry. This has meant that they have proved particularly popular in mobile communications systems where a minimum of circuitry and consequent light weight are a great advantage. It should be noted that these considerations have become less significant with advances in electronic circuitry. As well as carrying out encoding and decoding continuously on a transmitted or received bit stream, the way a convolutional code treats a particular group of bits depends on what has happened to previous groups of bits. A simple convolutional encoder is illustrated in Figure 4.7.

The data to be encoded is entered into a 3-bit shift register one bit at a time. For each bit that is fed in at the input two bits are transmitted from the output, one each from terminals X and Y.

Table 4.3 shows the outputs that will appear as a result of different combinations of existing shift register contents and new input values.

This table is of limited usefulness since it does not give any indication of the output resulting from a prolonged stream of bits at the input. In order to observe this a slightly more complicated representation, called a **Trellis diagram**, is used. There are two branches from every point in a Trellis diagram. The upper branch represents 0 input, and the lower branch represents 1 input, and the resulting output is written alongside each branch. This is illustrated in Figure 4.8 that represents the first row of Table 4.3.

At point A, it is assumed that the contents of the shift register are 000. Thus, the branch AB that represents a 0 input has an output of 00 alongside it since that is the output indicated in Table 4.3 for these values. Similarly, the lower branch AC that

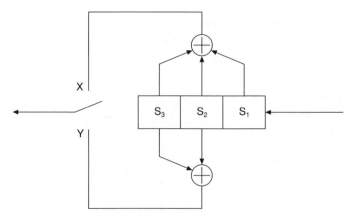

Figure 4.7 Simple convolutional encoder.

Table 4.3 Convolutional encoder output values.

Shift register S3 S2 S1	New input	Output X Y	Shift register S3 S2 S1	New input	Output X Y
0 0 0	0	0 0	0 0 0	1	1 0
0 0 1	0	1 1	0 0 1	1	0 1
0 1 0	0	1 1	0 1 0	1	0 1
0 1 1	0	0 0	0 1 1	1	1 0
1 0 0	0	0 0	1 0 0	1	1 0
1 0 1	0	1 1	1 0 1	1	0 1
1 1 0	0	1 1	1 1 0	1	0 1
1 1 1	0	0 0	1 1 1	1	1 0

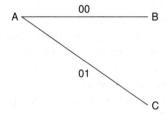

Figure 4.8 Initial part of a Trellis diagram.

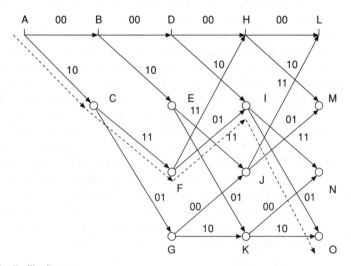

Figure 4.9 Trellis diagram.

represents a 1 input has a value 01 alongside it. A full Trellis diagram, so called because it resembles a garden trellis, for the above encoder is illustrated in Figure 4.9.

Note that the pattern of branches AB and AC is repeated all along the top of the trellis diagram with branches BE and BD and so on. This is because the pair of output bits will always be 00 as long as the shift register contains 000 and a zero arrives at the input. Branches CF and CG represent the second row of Table 4.3 where the contents of the shift register are 001; branches FH and FI represent the third row where the contents of the shift register are 010. The Trellis diagram can be used to indicate the output produced by a particular input bit stream by drawing a line through the trellis to represent the input bit stream. This is illustrated by the line in Figure 4.9 that follows the path ACFIO representing an input of 1011. To obtain the resulting output, we note the pairs of digits along path ACFIO, namely 10110101.

Decoding and error correction

The principle involved in decoding convolutional codes and subsequently correcting errors is the same as that involved in linear block codes; that is, error-free transmission will produce certain received bit patterns (codewords in the terminology of linear block codes) and errors are likely to produce different bit patterns that cannot possibly be received in error-free transmissions. An inspection of Figure 4.9 immediately reveals that certain bit patterns are not possible. For example, consider the bit pattern of 11111110 that cannot be obtained from any of the paths through the trellis. If such a pattern is received in a system using the decoder of Figure 4.7 then it is assumed that an error (or errors) has occurred in transmission.

If no errors occur during transmission, the path taken through the trellis diagram will be the same at the receiver as at the transmitter. Errors that occur during transmission will cause the path taken at the receiver to be different, and will eventually result in an impossible path. At this point, the receiver can notify the transmitter of an error and it may be able to correct the error by deducing the path that would have been the most likely in the absence of errors. In order to do this we need to have a measure of the different paths through the trellis. In the linear block codes of Section 4.3, we used the concept of Hamming distance, which was defined as the number of positions in which two codewords differ and the minimum distance, that is the number of positions that a codeword differs from the all-zero codeword. In convolutional codes, we retain the term **distance** to indicate the number of positions in which two paths differ and we define the **weight** as the number of bit positions in which a path differs from the all-zero path, that is the number of logical ones that appear in a particular path. Thus, in Figure 4.9, path ACFIN is defined by the output sequence 10110111 and therefore possesses a weight of 6 since it contains six logical ones. We can also define the **free distance**, d_{free}, as the smallest weight of any path that diverges from the all-zero path and subsequently returns to it. This will be comparable with the minimum Hamming distance of a linear block code and is used to define the error-detecting/correcting capabilities of the code as follows:

$d_{free} - 1$ errors can be detected

$mod(d_{free} - 1)/2$ errors can be corrected

(**Example 4.6**)

For the code illustrated by the trellis diagram of Figure 4.10, determine:

(a) The free distance of the code.

(b) The number of bits in error that can be corrected.

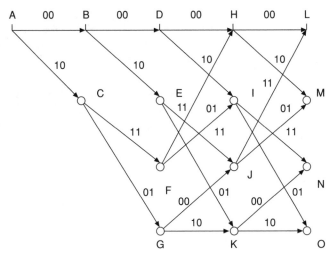

Figure 4.10 Example 4.6.

(a) In order to determine the free distance, we must examine all paths that diverge from and then return to the all-zero path ABDHL. There are three such paths, namely ACFHL, ACGJL and ABEJL. The weights of these paths is given below

Path	Output sequence	Weight
ACFHL	10111100	5
ACGJL	10010011	4
ABEJL	00011111	5

It can be seen that path ACGJL has the smallest weight and that the free distance of this code is 4.

(b) The number of bits that can be corrected is:

$$\mathrm{mod}(d_{\mathrm{free}} - 1)/2 = \mathrm{mod}(4 - 1)/2 = 1$$

An algorithm for decoding convolutional codes was developed by Viterbi (1967). In order to understand the algorithm, let us consider the received bit pattern 11111110 mentioned earlier. It is immediately obvious that this is an erroneously received bit pattern as the first two bits are not compatible with the trellis diagram. The Viterbi algorithm takes the received bit stream, compares it with the trellis diagram and calculates the distance between each line in the trellis diagram and the received bit pattern. This is illustrated in Figure 4.11.

If we look at the first stage of the trellis we note that AB is marked 2 and AC is marked 1. This is because AB represents the output 00 which is a distance of 2 from the first two received bits (11) and AC represents 10 which is a distance of 1 from the first two received bits. The other stages of the trellis are marked in the same way. The Viterbi algorithm now computes the minimal path through this trellis. It does this in a step-by-step fashion, the details of which are beyond the scope of this text.

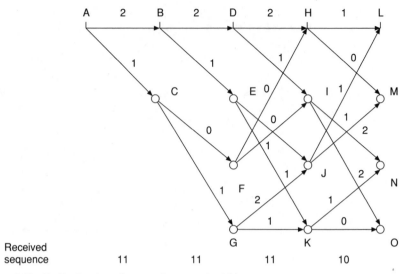

Received
sequence   11   11   11   10

Figure 4.11   Trellis showing distances from received bits.

In this particular case, the minimal path is ACFHM which should have a distance of 1 from the received bit sequence of 11111110. It can be seen from Figure 4.9 that path ACFHM represents an output of 10111110, which is indeed a distance of 1 from the received bit sequence. A convolutional code receiver using the Viterbi algorithm would therefore assume that the error-free received data was 10111110 and decode it accordingly as 1001. It is worth noting that, like most other error-correcting systems, the algorithm relies on the fact that one error is more likely than two, two errors are more likely than three, and so on.

Example 4.7

A trellis for a convolutional encoder/decoder is shown in Figure 4.12:

(a) Determine the output of the encoder for an input bit stream of 1101.

(b) Determine the free distance of the code.

(c) A bit sequence of 11101010 is received at the decoder. Use the trellis to correct the received data.

(a) The output is obtained from the trellis. Upper branches represent 0 inputs and lower branches represent 1 inputs so that an input bit stream of 1101 will produce an output of 11010100.

(b) The free distance of the code is the smallest weight of any path that diverges from the all-zero path and subsequently returns to it. There are two such paths in this trellis, namely 11101100 and 00111011. Both of these have a weight of 5, giving a free distance of 5.

(c) The path of bit sequence 11101010 is shown superimposed on the trellis in Figure 4.13.

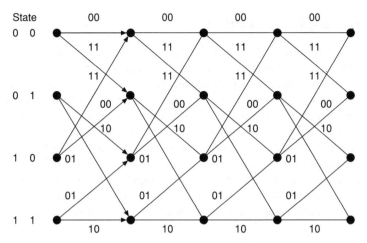

Figure 4.12 Example 4.7.

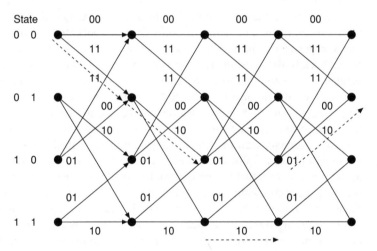

Figure 4.13 Example 4.7(c).

It is immediately obvious that this is not a valid sequence since it is does not form a continuous path. Rather than going through the steps of the Viterbi algorithm, we can observe the trellis and decide which is the most likely valid path. We note that it is the third pair of the received bits (11) that stands out as not conforming to a continuous path through the trellis. On the basis that one error is more likely than two, we can assume that it is here that an error has occurred and that if this pair of bits were 00 then a valid, continuous path of 11100010 would exist through the trellis. We therefore assume that the correct received bits sequence is 11100010. The distance between this sequence and the received sequence of 11101010 is 1 since they differ only in the fifth bit from the left. We are therefore safe in assuming 11100010 to be the transmitted bit stream since, even if there are other possible valid paths through the trellis, they cannot have a distance from the received bit stream that is less than 1.

(4.5) Feedback error control

Even very powerful error-correcting codes may not be able to correct all errors that arise in a communications channel. Consequently, many data communications links provide a further error control mechanism, in which errors in data are detected and the data is retransmitted. This procedure is known as **feedback error control** and it involves using a channel code to detect errors at the receive end of a link and then returning a message to the transmitter requesting the retransmission of a block (or blocks) of data. Alternatively, errors in received data can be detected and corrected up to a certain number of errors and a retransmission requested only if more than this number of errors occurs. The process of retransmitting the data has traditionally been known as **Automatic Repeat Request** (ARQ). There are three types of ARQ that have been used: namely, **stop-and-wait**, **go-back-*n*** and **selective-repeat**.

Stop-and-wait ARQ

This technique is the simplest method of operating ARQ and ensures that each transmitted block of data or **frame** is correctly received before sending the next. At the receiver, the data is checked for errors and if it is error free an acknowledgement (ACK) is sent back to the transmitter. If errors are detected at the receiver a negative acknowledgement (NAK) is returned. Since errors could equally occur in the ACK or NAK signals, they should also be checked for errors. Thus, only if each frame is received error free and an ACK is returned error free can the next frame be transmitted. If, however, errors are detected either in the transmitted frame or in the returned acknowledgement, then the frame is retransmitted. A further (and hopefully remote) possibility is that a frame or acknowledgement becomes lost for some reason. To take account of this eventuality, the transmitter should retransmit if it does not receive an acknowledgement within a certain time period known as the **timeout interval**. Finally, a frame may be received correctly but the resulting ACK may be lost, resulting in the same frame being transmitted a second time. This problem can be overcome by numbering frames and discarding any correctly received duplicates at the receiver. Although stop-and-wait offers a simple implementation of an ARQ system it can be inefficient in its utilization of the transmission link since time is spent in acknowledging each frame. Efficiency of utilization of a link is an important consideration in the design of a communications link which will be explored in Section 5.1.

Go-back-*n* ARQ

If the error rate on a link is relatively low, then the link efficiency can be increased by transmitting a number of frames continuously without waiting for an immediate acknowledgement. This strategy is used in go-back-*n* ARQ which is used in a number of standard protocols including HDLC (High-level Data Link Control) and, in modified form, TCP (Transmission Control Protocol), both of which are dealt with later in the text. The go-back number *n* determines how many frames can be transmitted without an acknowledgement having been received and is often referred to as a transmission **window**.

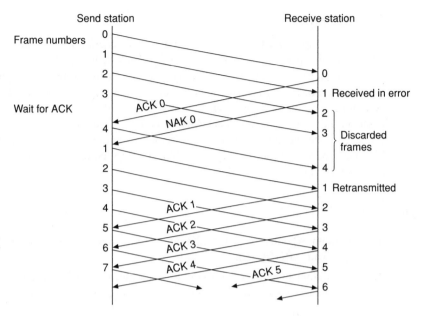

Figure 4.14   Frame transfer go-back-*n*.

Frame *i* + *n* cannot be transmitted until frame *i* has been acknowledged. Figure 4.14 shows a typical transfer of frames for a go-back-4 ARQ system over a full-duplex link.

Note that the send node transmits four frames (numbered 0, 1, 2, 3) without receiving an acknowledgement. There then follows a short wait before receipt of the first ACK which contains the number of the last correctly received frame (0 in this case). Although this acknowledgement is returned immediately after the correct receipt of frame 0, transmission delays mean that it does not reach the send node until after frame 3 has been transmitted (the send node having carried on transmitting as a result of the go-back-4 strategy). If we now assume that an error occurs in frame 1, the receive node will reply with NAK 0, indicating that an error has been detected and that the last correctly received frame was frame 0. The send node will now *go back* and retransmit the frame after the last correctly received frame, which in this case is frame 1. Meanwhile the receive node will have received frames 2, 3 and 4 which, since they have not been acknowledged, need to be discarded. In the absence of further errors, the transmit node continues transmitting frames 2, 3, 4, 5, . . . for as long as ACK signals continue to be returned. A go-back-*n* strategy allows for the efficient transfer of frames without the need for any substantial buffer storage by receive equipment as long as error rates are low. However, if errors occur during transmission then frames that have already been received correctly need to be retransmitted along with erroneous frames. If buffer storage is available at the receive equipment then it seems reasonable that some form of selective retransmission strategy would be more efficient than go-back-*n* in the presence of errors.

Selective-repeat ARQ

In selective-repeat ARQ only those frames that generate a NAK are retransmitted. Although this appears more efficient than go-back-n, it requires sufficient storage at the transmitter to save all frames that have been transmitted but not acknowledged in case a frame proves to be erroneous. In this system a go-back number is still used to determine how many frames can be transmitted without receiving an acknowledgement. In the past, selective-repeat ARQ was not a particularly popular ARQ strategy because of the increased memory requirements mentioned, but, as memory capabilities have become more readily available, it offers potential efficiency gains in the presence of high error rates.

Exercises

4.1 Explain whether or not ACKs and NAKs need to be numbered in a stop-and-wait ARQ system.

4.2 By adding together rows (modulo-2 addition), rearrange the following generator matrix so that it is in standard echelon form:

$$G = \begin{bmatrix} 1 & 0 & 0 & 1 & 1 \\ 1 & 1 & 0 & 0 & 1 \\ 1 & 1 & 1 & 0 & 0 \end{bmatrix}$$

4.3 Information consisting of the bits 1100 is to be encoded into the Hamming (7,4) code. Use the generator matrix to obtain the codeword to be transmitted.

4.4 An (8,4) linear block code has the following check equations:

$$c_1 = k_2 \oplus k_3 \oplus k_4$$
$$c_2 = k_1 \oplus k_2 \oplus k_3$$
$$c_3 = k_1 \oplus k_2 \oplus k_4$$
$$c_4 = k_1 \oplus k_3 \oplus k_4$$

(a) Determine the check and generator matrices.
(b) What is the minimum distance of this code?
(c) Sketch an encoding circuit for this code.

4.5 By adding a fourth check bit to the Hamming (7,4) code of Section 4.3, devise an (8,4) code. For this code, determine:

(a) the check matrix,
(b) the generator matrix,
(c) the minimum distance of the code,
(d) the numbers of errors that can be detected and that can be corrected.

4.6 Divide the polynomial $x^7 + 1$ by $x^3 + x + 1$ (modulo-2 division) and hence determine the factors of $x^7 + 1$.

4.7 Devise a circuit that will divide by $x^3 + x + 1$ (modulo-2 division). If data consisting of the polynomial $x^4 + x^5 + x + 1$ is fed into the circuit (most significant bit first), determine the contents of the circuit shift register after the seventh shift.

4.8   A (7,3) cyclic code has a generator polynomial $x^4 + x^2 + x + 1$.

(a) Determine the generator and check matrices of this code.
(b) Sketch circuits of a Meggitt encoder and decoder for this code.
(c) Obtain the complete code set.

4.9   A cyclic code with block length 7 has the generator polynomial
$G(x) = x^3 + x^2 + 1$.
Determine:

(a) the number of information and check bits in a codeword,
(b) the number of codewords in the code,
(c) the generator and check matrices of the code,
(d) the minimum distance of the code.

4.10 Data consisting of the sequence 10101010101 is to be encoded and transmitted
using a cyclic (15,11) code with generator polynomial $x^4 + x^2 + x + 1$. Using
modulo-2 division, determine the four check bits that need to be added before
transmission. The encoded data is transmitted and an error occurs in bit 8.
Determine the syndrome (remainder).

4.11 A trellis for a convolutional code encoder is shown in Figure 4.15.

(a) Determine the output for the encoder for a bit stream of 100110.
(b) Determine the free distance of the code.
(c) A bit sequence of 111011101111100101 is received at the decoder. Use the
trellis to correct the received data.

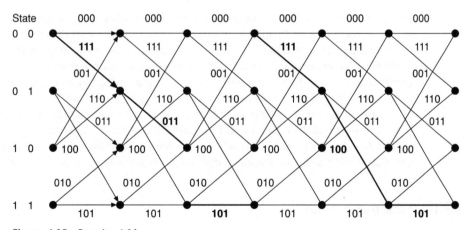

Figure 4.15   Exercise 4.11.

Chapter 5

Data link control

....

The topic of error control is covered by level 2, the data link layer, of the OSI reference model. As mentioned in Chapter 1, this layer is also concerned with the control of a data communications link and has two further functions, namely link management and flow control. Link management involves the setting up and disconnecting of a link. Flow control ensures that data in the form of frames is transmitted in an orderly fashion so that, for example, a send node does not transmit frames faster than a receive node can accept them. Before discussing these topics, this chapter takes a look at the measurement of the flow of data over a link. The chapter concludes by examining a commonly used data link layer protocol, namely the High-level Data Link Control (HDLC) protocol, and a further protocol developed from it known as the Point-to-Point Protocol (PPP).

5.1 Link throughput

The transmission rate of a data link, once established, represents an upper limit for the transfer of information over the link. In practice, a variety of factors cause the useful information transfer rate to be reduced to a value below that of the transmission rate. As mentioned in Section 2.1, most data communications systems divide data into fixed-length blocks or frames. We can define throughput as the number of information bits in a frame (or frames) divided by the total time taken to transmit and acknowledge the frame (or frames). The major factors that cause throughput to be less than the transmission rate are listed below as follows:

● Frame overheads: Not all of the contents of a frame are information bits. Typically, in addition to information bits, a frame also contains a **header** and a **trailer**. The header contains control information such as an address and sequence numbers. The trailer normally contains error-checking bits which are often called a **frame check sequence**. A frame might typically contain 256 bytes of which 251 are information bits, thus leading to a 2% reduction in potential throughput even before the frame is transmitted.

● Propagation delay: This is the time that it takes for a frame to propagate from one end of a link to the other; that is, the difference in time between the first bit of a frame leaving the send node and arriving at the receive node. Propagation delay must not be confused with the frame transmission time, which is the difference in time between the first bit and the last bit of a frame leaving the send node. Propagation delay often has only a small effect on throughput but in some situations, such as long-distance wireless links and especially satellite links, it can be a major factor in reducing the throughput if acknowledgements are used.

● Acknowledgements: Normally, some form of ARQ is used and time may be spent waiting for acknowledgements to reach the send node, particularly if there is a half-duplex link. Since the acknowledgements will normally be much shorter than the information frames, the transmission time of the acknowledgements can often be ignored. However, the propagation delay of an acknowledgement will be the same as that of an information frame providing they take the same transmission path.

● Retransmissions: Frames may need to be retransmitted as a result of errors or frames being discarded for whatever reason. The retransmission is accompanied by acknowledgements if ARQ is being used. If the error rate or discard rate is high then this is the most serious cause of reduction in throughput.

● Processing time: Time is spent at the send and receive nodes in processing the data. This includes detecting (and possibly correcting) errors and also the implementation of flow control. If wireless links are used there will be further processing delays associated with the modulation and demodulation process.

Link utilization and efficiency

The best way to illustrate the concept of throughput is by way of an example. However, before we look at an example, it is useful to define two further terms, **link utilization** and **link efficiency**. Link utilization is simply the average traffic over a particular link expressed as a percentage of the total link capacity. It is a term that is used extensively in the design process of a network. Links in a network might typically be designed to have a utilization of only 50% so as to allow for increased link traffic in the event of link failure elsewhere in the network. Link efficiency is a less commonly used term that is defined as the ratio of the time taken to transmit a frame (or frames) of data to the total time it takes to transmit and acknowledge the frame or frames:

$$\text{Efficiency}, U = \frac{\text{time taken to transmit frame}}{\text{total transmission time}}$$

Note that link efficiency applies only to a single data transfer over a link whereas link utilization applies to the total traffic over a link which may well include a number of data transfers multiplexed together. It is for this reason that utilization is a more commonly used term in network design. Link efficiency will depend on the type of ARQ used. The efficiency of a link with stop-and-wait ARQ can be determined as follows. If the time taken to transmit a frame or block of data is t_f, the propagation delay for both frame and acknowledgement is t_d, the time taken to transmit an acknowledgement is t_a and the total processing time is t_p, then:

$$U = \frac{t_f}{t_f + t_a + t_p + 2t_d}$$

In many situations the acknowledgement transmission time and processing times can be ignored, giving:

$$U = \frac{t_f}{t_f + 2t_d} = \frac{1}{1 + 2a}$$

The concept of efficiency is often used in the analysis of LANs and is also explored in some detail in Section 9.2.

Example 5.1

A point-to-point satellite transmission link connecting two computers uses a stop-and-wait ARQ strategy and has the following characteristics:

Data transmission rate = 64 kbps

Frame size, n = 2048 bytes

Information bytes per frame, k = 2043 bytes

Propagation delay, t_d = 180 ms

Acknowledgement size, t_a = 10 bytes

Round-trip processing delay, t_p = 25 ms

Determine the throughput and link efficiency.

$$\text{Frame transmission time, } t_f = \frac{2048 \times 8}{64\ 000} = 0.256 \text{ s}$$

$$\text{Acknowledgement transmission time, } t_a = \frac{10 \times 8}{64\ 000} = 1.25 \text{ ms}$$

Total time to transmit frame and receive an acknowledgement is:

$$t_f + t_a + t_p + 2t_d = 0.256 + 0.0012 + 0.05 + 0.36 = 0.667 \text{ s}$$

$$\text{Throughput } k = \frac{2043 \times 8}{0.667} = 24.5 \text{ kbps}$$

Note that the resulting throughput is considerably less than the transmission rate of 64 kbps.

The link efficiency can now be calculated, neglecting t_a and t_p, as follows:

$$a = t_d/t_f = 0.18/0.256 = 0.7$$

$$\frac{1}{1+2a} = \frac{1}{1+1.4} = 41.67\%$$

This example is instructive. The throughput of 26.28 kbps is substantially less than the data transmission rate and the link efficiency is under 42%. The conclusion to be drawn from this is that link-by-link error-checking strategies like ARQ are inherently inefficient, particularly over a satellite link. Early data communications protocols such as the ITU-T X.25 protocol used link-by-link error checking. However, improvements in link BERs led to later protocols such as Frame Relay and ATM dispensing with link-by-link error checking.

Effect of errors on throughput

As mentioned in Section 4.1, the effect of transmission impairments on a data communications link is to introduce errors. As mentioned in Section 2.1 the number of errors present in a link is expressed as a BER. If a link has a BER of 0.000 001 (10^{-6}), this means that there is a probability of 0.000 001 that any bit is in error. Alternatively, we can say that, on average, one in every 1 000 000 bits will be in error. This may seem a very low error rate but if bits are transmitted as a block in a frame then the probability of the frame being in error will be much greater. The frame error rate, P, can be obtained from the bit error rate, E, as follows. The probability of a bit being error free is $1 - E$ and the probability of a block of length n being error free is $(1 - E)^n$. The frame error probability is therefore:

$$P = 1 - (1 - E)^n$$

Example 5.2

A frame of data of length 2048 bits is transmitted over a link with a BER of 10^{-4}. Determine the probability that a frame will be received erroneously.

BER, $E = 0.0001$. Probability of a bit being error free $= 1 - 0.0001 = 0.9999$. If the frame length, n, is 2048 bits then the probability of the frame being error free is $(0.9999)^{2048} = 0.815$.

The probability of a frame being in error is given by:

$$P = 1 - 0.815 = 0.185$$

so that even though only one in every 10 000 bits is, on average, in error there is an almost 20% chance of a frame being received in error and almost 1 in every 5 frames will need to be either corrected at the receiver or retransmitted.

Effect of ARQ on throughput

The situation illustrated in Example 5.2 is compounded if ARQ is used since retransmitted frames are equally likely to contain errors (errors in acknowledgements are much less likely since they normally are of very short length). Thus a frame may need to be retransmitted a number of times and the probability of retransmission will be equal to the probability of a frame containing errors since only erroneous frames are retransmitted. If a frame is transmitted m times then the probability of this occurring is the probability of transmitting $m - 1$ consecutive erroneous frames followed by a single correctly received frame. This is given by:

$$P^{m-1}(1 - P)$$

A problem which arises is that the number of times, m, that a frame is transmitted will vary according to some form of probability distribution. Since the determination of the value of m is not particularly simple, the value is just presented here without any analysis. For a full analysis see Bertsekas and Gallager (1992). If stop-and-wait ARQ is used then the average number of times that a frame is transmitted is given by:

$$m = 1 + \frac{P}{(1 - P)} = \frac{1}{(1 - P)}$$

If go-back-n ARQ is used then an error detected in a frame causes that frame, along with all other unacknowledged frames, to be retransmitted. Since this situation is more complicated than with a stop-and-wait strategy, we shall make the following assumptions to simplify the calculation:

1. Frames are retransmitted only when a frame is rejected at the receiver for being erroneous. In practice, there may be other reasons for frames being retransmitted.

2. The rejection of frame i by the receiver is followed by the transmitter sending frames $i + 1, i + 2, \ldots, i + n - 1$ and then retransmitting the original frame i. This may not always be the case since there may be fewer than $n - 1$ frames waiting to be transmitted after frame i.

The resulting analysis, which is also carried out in Bertsekas and Gallager (1992), gives the number of times that a frame is likely to be transmitted as:

$$m = 1 + \frac{nP}{(1 - P)}$$

This result will be used in Example 5.5. Selective-repeat will produce the same result as stop-and-wait in respect of the number of times that a frame is transmitted. However, selective-repeat normally outperforms stop-and-wait significantly in terms of the throughput. To appreciate the effect of ARQ on throughput consider Example 5.3.

Example 5.3

A wireless link uses a stop-and-wait ARQ strategy with half-duplex transmission and has the following characteristics:

Data transmission rate = 19.2 kbps

Frame size, n = 512 bytes

Information bits per frame, k = 506 bytes

Propagation delay, t_d = 10 ms

If processing delays and acknowledgement transmission time can be neglected, determine the throughput: (a) in the absence of errors and (b) in the presence of a BER of 10^{-4}.

(a) Frame transmission time:

$$t_f = \frac{512 \times 8}{19\ 200} = 0.213 \text{ s}$$

Throughput in the absence of errors:

$$\frac{k}{t_f + 2t_d} = \frac{506 \times 8}{0.213 + 0.02} = 17\ 373 \text{ bps}$$

(b) Frame error rate:

$$P = 1 - (1 - E)^n = 1 - (1 - 0.0001)^{512 \times 8} = 0.664$$

Average number of times a frame is transmitted:

$$1 + \frac{P}{1 - P} = 1 + \frac{0.664}{0.336} = 2.98$$

The transmission and delay times will be increased by this amount, giving a throughput:

$$\frac{k}{2.44(t_f + 2t_d)} = \frac{506 \times 8}{2.98(0.213 + 0.02)} = 5829 \text{ bps}$$

The effect of the errors in part (b) of Example 5.3 is to reduce the throughput to less than one-third of the data transmission rate. This reduction in throughput is fairly excessive and is a result of the high BER of 10^{-4}. A good-quality data communications link is more likely to have a BER of at most 10^{-8}.

Optimum block length

What is the effect of altering the length of a frame in Example 5.3? If the frame length is increased in an error-free situation then the throughput increases since the value of k is greater and the value of t_d remains the same. However, in the presence of errors the situation is more complicated. An increased block size still produces a larger number of information bits transmitted in each block but a point will be reached at which throughput falls as a result of having to retransmit a large block of data each time an error is detected. This leads us to consider an optimum length of block. Figure 5.1

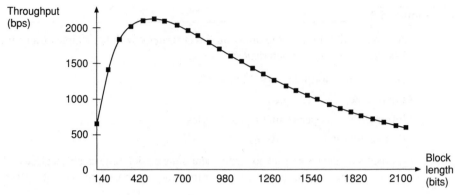

Figure 5.1   Throughput for BER of 10^{-3}.

shows a plot of throughput against block length for a system similar to that described in part (b) of Example 5.3 but with a BER of 10^{-3}.

Note that there is a maximum value of throughput of about 2130 bps which occurs at a block length of 490 bits.

The choice of block length is particularly important if data is being transmitted long distances in the presence of a high BER. A typical application in which it is crucial to choose an appropriate block length is radio-frequency modems operating over long distances.

5.2   Flow control

Whichever form of ARQ is used over a data communications link, a certain amount of buffer storage is required at both ends of a link to allow for the processing of data. Flow control involves the control of the data transmission so that transmitters and receivers have sufficient buffer space to process each frame or character as and when it arrives. Two flow control schemes are in common use depending on the type of link and these are described in the next sections.

Window mechanisms

If a frame-oriented system uses a continuous form of ARQ such as go-back-n or selective-repeat then, as long as information is available for transmission, a send node can continue sending information frames before receiving an acknowledgement. The send node will be provided with a predetermined amount of buffer storage and it is important that this storage does not become overloaded. It is common, therefore, for an additional flow control mechanism to be used with these systems that limits the number of information frames that can be transmitted before receiving an acknowledgement. The send node keeps a copy of those frames transmitted but not acknowledged so that it can retransmit if necessary. A maximum limit is set on the number of copies that are being held at the send node which is known as the **send window**. If the send node reaches its maximum window size it stops transmitting and, in the absence of any acknowledgements, it does not transmit any more frames. When the

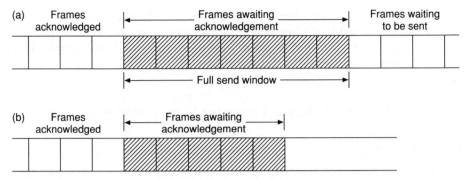

Figure 5.2 Operation of send window: (a) window full; (b) continuous flow possible.

send node finally receives an acknowledgement it can start transmitting again. The window size is chosen so that it does not impede the flow of frames. As well as the amount of send buffer storage available, the frame size and transmission rate are also taken into account in determining the window size. The operation of a send window is illustrated in Figure 5.2.

A list of information frames transmitted but, as yet, unacknowledged is kept at the send node. Each time an information frame is transmitted the list is increased by one and each time an acknowledgement is received it is reduced by one.

Effect of windows on throughput

As we saw in Example 5.1, the throughput of a frame-oriented link using stop-and-wait ARQ depends upon the number of information bits, k, the frame transmission time, t_f, and the propagation delay, t_d, according to the expression:

$$\text{Throughput} = \frac{k}{t_f + 2t_d} \qquad \text{where } a = \frac{t_d}{t_f}$$

This assumes that, as in Example 5.3, both the processing delays and acknowledgement transmission times can be neglected. Now, if a send window of size N is used, this will clearly have some effect on the throughput. Consider a send node commencing transmission of a stream of data at time t_o. The leading edge of the first data bit will reach the receive node at time $t_o + t_d$ and the trailing edge of the last data bit will reach the receive node at time $t_o + t_d + t_f$. Neglecting the processing time means that we can assume that the receive node responds immediately by transmitting an acknowledgement. The acknowledgement (which we have already assumed to be of negligible length) will reach the send node at time $t_o + 2t_d + t_f$. There are now two possible scenarios depending on the window size N:

1. The acknowledgement transmitted by the receive node reaches the send node before the send window is full. This can be represented by the expression:

$$Nt_f > 2t_d + t_f$$

In this case the send node is able to transmit continuously without having to stop as a result of the send window becoming full. In the absence of errors, throughput is optimal.

2. The send window becomes full at time $t_o + Nt_f$. The send node then stops transmitting until an acknowledgement is returned that reaches the send node at time $t_o + 2t_d + t_f$, at which point the send node may resume transmission. This situation can be represented by the expression:

$$Nt_f < 2t_d + t_f$$

Clearly, the throughput is reduced under these circumstances.

Example 5.4

A frame-oriented data communications system operates at a transmission rate of 512 kbps with a frame length of 512 bytes over a long-distance link which produces a propagation delay of 20 ms. A flow control system is required using a window mechanism. Determine the minimum window size which allows for optimum throughput.

Optimum throughput cannot be achieved unless the expression of scenario 1 above is satisfied as follows:

$$Nt_f > 2t_d + t_f$$

$$N > \frac{2t_d}{t_f} + 1$$

The delay time, $t_d = 20$ ms.
    The frame transmission time:

$$t_f = \frac{\text{frame length}}{\text{bit rate}} = \frac{512 \times 8}{512\ 000} = 8 \text{ ms}$$

Substituting these times gives a value for N:

$$N > \frac{(2 \times 20)}{8} + 1 = 6$$

Thus the minimum window size for efficient operation of the link is 6 and a window size of 5 would be adequate, requiring 3 bits to specify a frame within the window at any time.

It is useful at this stage to determine the efficiency of a link that uses windows in conjunction with some form of continuous ARQ (go-back-n or selective-repeat). If N frames are transmitted continuously then the time spent in transmitting data will be Nt_f. The value of the efficiency in the absence of errors will depend on which of the two scenarios mentioned above applies, as follows:

1. If the send node is able to transmit continuously, the efficiency is given by:

$$U = \frac{\text{time spent transmitting frames}}{\text{total time}} = \frac{Nt_f}{Nt_f} = 1$$

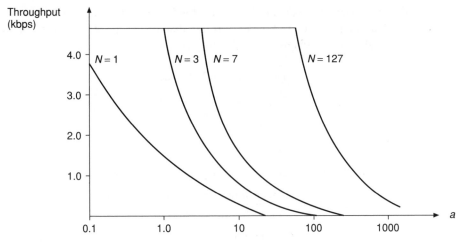

Figure 5.3   Effect of window size on throughput.

2. If the send window becomes full after a time Nt_f, when transmission stops until an acknowledgement is received after time $t_f + 2t_d$, the expression becomes:

$$U = \frac{\text{time spent transmitting frames}}{\text{total time}} = \frac{Nt_f}{t_f + 2t_d}$$

The effect of window size on efficiency is shown in Figure 5.3. Throughput is plotted against $a = t_d/t_f$ for different values of window size, N.

A window size of $N = 1$ corresponds to a stop-and-wait ARQ strategy which, although it never provides an optimum value of throughput, is adequate for relatively short transmission links in which the propagation delay is short. A window size of 5 is adequate for most terrestrial links but in the case of links which have large propagation delays, such as satellite systems, a large window size is required to produce a satisfactory throughput (127 being a typical window size for such systems).

Example 5.5

If the data communications system of Example 5.4 operates using a go-back-3 ARQ system (with a window size of 3) and 506 information bytes in each frame, determine:

(a) the efficiency,

(b) the throughput obtained on an error-free link,

(c) the throughput for a BER of 0.00003.

Frame length, $n = 512$ bytes

Information bits, $k = 506$ bytes

Bit rate $= 512$ kbps

Delay time, $t_d = 20$ ms

Frame transmission time, $t_f = 8$ ms

Window size, $N = 3$

(a) We know from Example 5.4 that the send window becomes full before an acknowledgement is received (since N is less than 6) and the efficiency is not optimized. Under these circumstances, the efficiency is given by:

$$U = \frac{N}{1 + 2a} \quad \text{where } a = t_\text{d}/t_\text{f} = 20/8 = 2.5$$

Therefore:

Efficiency, $U = \dfrac{3}{6} = 0.5$

(b) In the absence of errors, the throughput is given by:

$$\text{Throughput} = \frac{\text{number of information bits transmitted}}{\text{total time taken}}$$

$$= \frac{Nk}{t_\text{f} + 2t_\text{d}} = \frac{3 \times 506 \times 8}{(8 + 40) \times 10^{-3}} = 253 \text{ kbps}$$

(c) Bit error rate, $E = 10^{-4} = 0.00003$.

Frame error probability is given by:

$$P = 1 - (1 - E)^n = 1 - (1 - 0.00003)^{4096} = 0.11$$

The effect of errors and the go-back-3 ARQ strategy will be for frames to be retransmitted. The average number of transmissions, m, is given in Section 5.1 as:

$$m = \frac{1 + NP}{1 - P} = \frac{1 + (3 \times 0.11)}{0.9} = 1.48$$

The total time taken by the data transfer will be increased by this amount, giving a value for throughput as follows:

$$\text{Throughput} = \frac{Nk}{m(t_\text{f} + 2t_\text{d})} = \frac{253}{1.33} = 171.2 \text{ kbps}$$

The throughput has been reduced to under half the transmission rate. This is partly due to the presence of errors, but more important is the fact that an inappropriate window size has been chosen. If a window size of, for example, 5 had been chosen then the throughput would have been optimized. Many systems allow for the window size to be configured in software and an appropriate choice of window size is an important consideration for network design.

The discussion above concerns data transmission in one direction only. If two-way data transmission is used then a window is required at each end of the link. In this case a technique known as **piggybacking** is often used, in which an acknowledgement signal is returned inside an information frame. In links in which propagation delay is high, piggybacking improves the link throughput considerably since separate acknowledgements can be dispensed with.

5.3 Link management

The flow control that has been discussed so far and the error control techniques of Chapter 4 are both concerned with the transfer of data across a link. Flow control ensures that the data is in the correct sequence and error control that the data is received correctly without errors. However, before either of these functions can take place the link needs to be set up and after the data transfer has taken place it needs to be disconnected. These two functions are known as **link management**. In the case of a physically short link these functions can be carried out by using separate control lines over which handshaking signals can be exchanged. An example of such a procedure is the ITU-T V.24 protocol, described in Chapter 6. In frame-oriented links, which are normally established over longer distances, it is common to exchange separate **supervisory** frames over the same channel as the information frames. Clearly, these frames, as in the case of acknowledgements, need only be of a short length compared with the information frames. Figure 5.4 shows the signal flow diagram of a typical link set-up and disconnection procedure. As can be seen, two supervisory frames are used, namely a SETUP-frame and a DISC-frame. On the transmission of the SETUP-frame, frame numbers are set to zero and send and receive windows are initialized. Note that the supervisory frames need to be acknowledged since they may be corrupted by errors. Once the link is established, information frames and acknowledgements can be exchanged. Once the data transfer has ended a DISC-frame is used to terminate the logical connection between the two nodes.

This process seems almost trivial at first sight but the situation becomes more complex if a failure occurs on a link or at a node. A problem arises when frames have

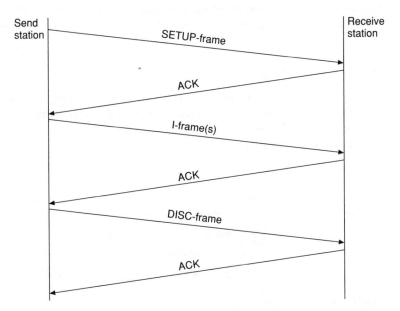

Figure 5.4 Link set-up and disconnection.

been accepted for transmission over a link but have not reached a receive node before a failure occurs. Link management procedures need to be able to cope with such failures.

5.4 High-level Data Link Control (HDLC) protocol

HDLC is a commonly used protocol developed by the ISO and used to control data transfer over a link. It includes not only the functions of flow control and link management already referred to in this chapter and in previous sections but also error control. It thus serves as a good practical illustration of the principles discussed in this chapter. The protocol allows for a variety of different types of link, the two nodes at either end of the link being referred to as **stations**. To satisfy the requirements of different types of link the protocol distinguishes between three modes of operation (although only two of them are normally used) and two types of link configuration:

1. Unbalanced configuration: This is the situation in which a single **primary station** has control over the operation of one or more **secondary stations**. Frames transmitted by the primary are called **commands** and those by the secondary **responses**. A typical example of this type of configuration is a **multidrop link** in which a single computer is connected to a number of DTEs which are under its control. This mode of working is called **normal response mode** (NRM). HDLC also specifies an alternative mode, called asynchronous response mode, for use within unbalanced configurations which, since it is rarely used, is not explained here.

2. Balanced configuration: This refers to a point-to-point link in which the nodes at each end of the link have equal status, each capable of issuing a command. HDLC calls these **combined stations** and they can transmit both commands and responses. This mode of working is called **asynchronous balanced mode** (ABM).

HDLC frame structure

HDLC uses synchronous transmission with data being transmitted in frames. All frames have the common format shown in Figure 5.5. The address and control fields are known collectively as a **header** and the error-checking bits are called the frame check sequence (FCS) or **trailer**.

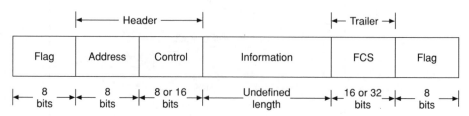

Figure 5.5 HDLC frame structure.

Flag fields

These two fields mark the start and finish of the frame with the bit sequence 01111110. A single flag field may be used to mark the end of one frame and the start of another if one frame follows immediately after another. Since receive nodes are continuously looking for the flag sequence of six consecutive binary 1 bits to indicate the start or finish of a frame, it is essential that this sequence is prevented from occurring elsewhere in the frame. This is achieved by a process known as **bit stuffing** which takes place at the send node. When the frame is being assembled, if a sequence of five consecutive ones appears within a frame then an extra zero is inserted (stuffed) immediately after the sequence. At the receive node, when a sequence of five ones is received, the next bit is examined. If this bit is a zero it is removed. If the sequence is followed by the two bits 10 then the combination is accepted as a flag. If the sequence is followed by two more ones it is assumed that some form of error has occurred.

Address field

The contents of the address field depend on the mode of operation being used. In an unbalanced configuration it contains an 8-bit address which always identifies the secondary station, whether it is the primary or secondary that is transmitting. Alternatively, a group of secondary stations may have the same address, known as a **group address**, in which case a frame is transmitted from the primary station to all secondary stations in the group. The unique address containing all ones is used to allow a primary to broadcast a frame to all the secondary stations connected to it. The protocol also allows for the length of the address field to be extended in the event of the number of secondaries being too large to be addressed by an 8-bit address. In a balanced configuration the address field always contains the address of the destination. Since a balanced configuration involves a point-to-point link, the destination address is not strictly required but is included for consistency. Note that the address is not used for any routing purposes since routing is a function of the network level of the ISO model and HDLC is primarily a link-level protocol.

Control field

The control field distinguishes between the three different types of frame used in HDLC, namely information, control and unnumbered frames. The first one or two bits of the field determine the type of frame. The field also contains control information which is used for flow control and link management.

Information field

The information field does not have a length specified by HDLC. In practice, it normally has a maximum length determined by a particular implementation. Information frames (also known as I-frames) are the only frames that carry information bits which are normally in the form of a fixed-length block of data of several kilobytes in length. All other types of frame normally have an empty information field.

Frame check sequence

The FCS field contains error-checking bits, normally 16 but with a provision for increasing this to 32 in the event of systems operating in an unreliable environment or with particularly long I-frames. The details of the error-checking code used are covered later in this chapter.

Frame types

The different types of frame are distinguished by the contents of the control field. The structure of all three types of control field is shown in Figure 5.6.

Information frames

An I-frame is distinguished by the first bit of the control field being a binary 0. Note also that the control field of an I-frame contains both a send sequence number, N(S), and a receive sequence number, N(R), which are used to facilitate flow control. N(S) is the sequence number of frames sent and N(R) the sequence number of frames successfully received by the sending node prior to the present frame being sent. Thus the first frame transmitted in a data transfer has send and receive sequence numbers 0,0. Since 3 bits are available for each of the sequence numbers N(S) and N(R), they can have values only between 0 and 7, that is they use modulo-8 numbering. This imposes a limit on the size of the windows used for flow control. I-frames also contain a poll/final (P/F) bit (as do other frames). This acts as a poll bit when used by a primary station and a final bit by a secondary. A poll bit is set when a primary is transmitting to a secondary and requires a frame or frames to be returned in response, and the final bit is set in the final frame of a response. Since there are no primaries or secondaries in asynchronous balanced mode, the P/F bit is used differently in this mode as we shall see later.

Supervisory frames

Supervisory frames are distinguished by the first 2 bits of the control field being 10. These frames are used as acknowledgements for flow and error control. HDLC allows for both go-back-*n* and selective-repeat ARQ. Note that the supervisory frames

Frame type	1	2	3	4	5	6	7	8	Bits
Information	0		N(S)		P		N(R)		
Supervisory	1	0	F		P		N(R)		
Unnumbered	1	1	F		P		F		

N(S) = send sequence number, N(R) = receive sequence number, F = function bits,
P = poll/final bit used for polling in normal response mode

Figure 5.6 Control field structure.

Table 5.1 Supervisory commands and responses.

Name	Function
Receive Ready (RR)	Positive acknowledgement (ACK), ready to receive I-frame
Receive Not Ready (RNR)	Positive acknowledgement, not ready to receive I-frame
Reject (REJ)	Negative acknowledgement (NAK), go-back-*n*
Selective Reject (SREJ)	Negative acknowledgement, selective-repeat

contain only a receive sequence number since they relate to the acknowledgement of I-frames and not to their transmission. They also contain two function bits which allow for four functions as shown in Table 5.1 which lists the supervisory commands/ responses.

Unnumbered frames

Unnumbered frames do not contain any sequence numbers (hence their name) and are used for various control functions. They have five function bits which allow for the fairly large number of commands and responses listed in Table 5.2.

The first five commands are used to initialize, change or terminate modes and are known as **mode-setting commands**. A node receiving such a command normally acknowledges its receipt with the UA response. A change of mode causes the I-frame sequence numbers to be reset to zero. Other responses that may result from a mode-setting command are RIM, RD and DM. The UI and UP frames are used to exchange control information between nodes. The response FRMR is returned when an error occurs in a received frame. It is normally followed by a RSET command, resulting in send and receive sequence numbers being reset.

Table 5.2 Unnumbered commands and responses.

Name	Function
Set Normal Response Mode (SNRM)	
Set Asynchronous Response Mode (SARM)	Used to initialize or change modes
Set Asynchronous Balanced Mode (SABM)	
Set Initialization Mode (SIM)	Used to initialize a link
Disconnect (DISC)	Causes the link connection to be terminated
Unnumbered Acknowledgement (UA)	Acknowledges the above mode-setting commands
Request Initialization Mode (RIM)	Requests SIM command when initialization required
Request Disconnect (RD)	Requests a disconnection of a link
Disconnected Mode (DM)	Indicates responding station disconnected
Unnumbered Poll (UP)	Used to request control information
Unnumbered Information (UI)	Used to exchange control information
Frame Reject (FRMR)	Reports that unacceptable frame has been received
Reset (RSET)	Resets sequence numbers
Test (TEST)	Used to exchange test signals
Exchange Identification (XID)	Used to exchange identity and status

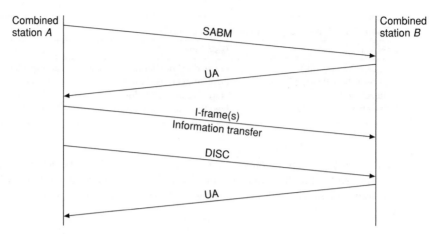

Figure 5.7 Frame transfer in an ABM link.

Link management

For data to be exchanged over an HDLC link, a connection must first be set up. Normally, this is achieved by the transfer of either an SNRM or an SABM command, depending on whether normal response or asynchronous balanced mode is being established. The receive node will respond with a UA frame if it is in a position to set up the link. A typical transfer of frames illustrating the link management aspects of an ABM link is shown in the signal flow diagram of Figure 5.7.

In this mode, the setting up or clearing of a link may be initiated by either node. The link is set up by an SABM command and cleared by a DISC command. The UA response is used in both cases to acknowledge the successful acceptance of the commands.

Error control

This is achieved in HDLC by the use of ARQ and a cyclic error-detecting code. Prior to transmission the block of data consisting of address, control and information fields is treated as a single binary number and modulo-2 divided by a generator polynomial which is specified by the ITU-T as $x^{16} + x^{12} + x^5 + 1$ (10001000000100001 in binary). The remainder of this division constitutes the FCS. The flags are then added and the frame transmitted. At the receive node the received frame is stripped of the flags and divided by the same generator polynomial. The remainder of this division provides a syndrome which is zero if no errors have occurred. In the event of a non-zero syndrome, an REJ frame is returned if go-back-n ARQ is being used and an SREJ frame is returned if selective-repeat ARQ is being used.

Flow control

The flow control aspects of HDLC vary slightly depending on whether NRM or ABM is being used. In NRM, data flow is carried out under the control of the primary

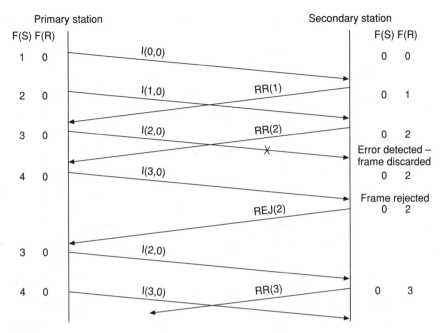

Figure 5.8 NRM data transfer.

station. A typical NRM data transfer between primary and secondary stations using a go-back-n ARQ strategy is shown in Figure 5.8.

In this figure, data flow is from the primary to the secondary only, so that the I-frames are acknowledged by supervisory frames. Each node keeps a count of the send sequence number, F(S), of the next I-frame to be sent and a count of the receive sequence number, F(R), of the next I-frame to be received and it is these counts, along with the sequence numbers inside frames, that allow the flow control to function. When a node receives a frame it compares its own receive sequence number, F(R), with the frame's send sequence number, N(S). If these two numbers are equal then the frame is accepted; if they are not equal the frame is rejected. The receive node then uses the value of its receive sequence number in the resulting acknowledgement. Thus I-frame (0,0) in this example is accepted because F(R) = N(S) = 0 and the frame is positively acknowledged by the supervisory frame RR(1) which has a receive sequence number of 1, indicating that one frame has been received correctly. Remember, as above, that supervisory frames contain only a receive sequence number whereas I-frames contain both send and receive sequence numbers. The orderly flow of I-frames from the primary is disrupted in this case by the detection at the secondary of an error in I-frame (2,0) which is immediately discarded. When I-frame (3,0) arrives at the secondary there is now a sequence mismatch between the frame, which has a send sequence number of 3, and the secondary, which has a receive count of 2 and is therefore expecting to receive a frame with a send sequence number of 2. This causes I-frame (3,0) to be rejected and a negative acknowledgement of REJ(2) to be returned indicating that the primary should retransmit I-frame (2,0). The primary will now go back and transmit this frame and the subsequent I-frame (3,0) again.

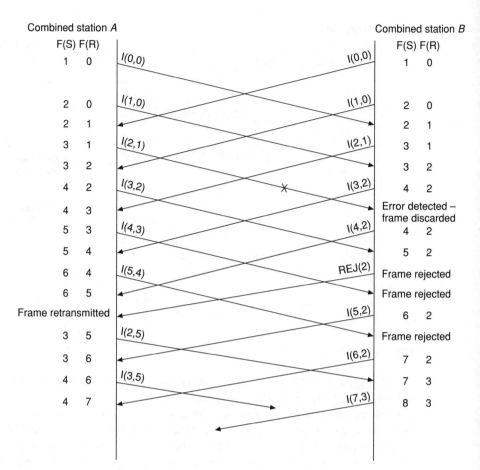

Figure 5.9 ABM data transfer using go-back-n ARQ.

In the case of the ABM, both nodes can transmit I-frames independently, that is there is full-duplex transmission. Once again the best way to understand the flow control procedure is by means of a flow diagram. A typical ABM data transfer between two nodes using a go-back-n ARQ strategy is shown in Figure 5.9. The link employs a window mechanism which, since 3 bits are allocated for a frame's send and receive sequence numbers, operates with modulo-8 numbers. This means that the window size is restricted to 7; that is, the maximum number of frames that can be transmitted without receiving an acknowledgement is 7. Since I-frames are flowing in each direction and each frame contains both send and receive sequence numbers, these sequence numbers can be used to acknowledge the correct receipt of a frame rather than using separate acknowledgement frames as in the case of NRM operation. This type of acknowledgement process, as was explained in Section 5.2, is known as piggybacking. The flow control procedure operates in a similar way to NRM. As each frame is received, the frame send sequence number, N(S), is compared with the receive count of the receive node, F(R). If these two are the same then the frame is accepted; if they are not the same the frame is rejected. The frame receive sequence number, N(R), is then used as an acknowledgement that the frame has been successfully received at the remote end as shown. Thus, the first frame to be received by node B, node A's frame I(0,0), is acknowledged by the next I-frame to be sent from node B which carries the sequence numbers (2,1) indicating that, at this point, node B has sent two previous frames and has successfully received one frame. Likewise, the receipt by node A of frame I(3,2) from node B is an acknowledgement that frame I(1,0) from node A has been correctly received at node B. This is because frame I(3,2) has a receive count equal to 2 and node B has correctly received two I-frames (I(0,0) and I(1,0)).

The procedure for dealing with erroneously received frames is the same as in NRM. Frame I(2,1) from node A in Figure 5.9 is received erroneously at node B and is discarded. The next frame transmitted by node B is frame I(4,2) indicating that only two frames have been received successfully. The next frame to arrive at node B (frame I(3,2) from node A) is rejected because its send sequence number of 3 does not match node B's receive sequence number which has remained at 2, and the negative acknowledgement REJ(2) is sent by node B. The effect of full-duplex working in this example is such that, by the time the REJ(2) frame reaches node A, it has transmitted two further frames (I(4,3) and I(,4)), both of which are rejected at node B because their frame send sequence numbers do not match the receive count at node B. Once node A receives the frame REJ(2) it retransmits its original frame I(2,1) which is now renumbered I(2,5) as a result of further frames having been successfully received by node A. It can be seen from this example that, for a go-back-n strategy to work successfully, there needs to be a manageable level of errors or there will be a loss of throughput due to the retransmission of frames. ABM allows for efficient full-duplex transmission on a point-to-point link and this mode of operation is incorporated in the link level of the ITU-T X.2 protocol for packet-switched networks.

5.5   Point-to-Point Protocol

A further protocol, defined in RFC 1661 and known as the Point-to-Point Protocol (PPP), has been developed from HDLC and has been used extensively for transporting IP traffic over point-to-point links. PPP encapsulates IP packets inside the data field of a modified HDLC frame, as illustrated in Figure 5.10.

Note that, as with HDLC, the frame header contains 1-byte address and control fields along with an additional 2-byte protocol field. PPP does not assign individual station addresses and the address field contains the binary sequence 11111111. The control field contains the binary sequence 00000011. The protocol field contains 2 bytes that

	1	1	1	2	Variable	2 or 4
Field length in bytes	Flag	Address	Control	Protocol	Data	FCS

Figure 5.10   PPP frame structure.

identify the protocol encapsulated in the information field of the frame. In addition to IP, PPP supports other protocols, including Novell's Internetwork Packet Exchange (IPX) and IBM's Synchronous Network Architecture (SNA). The FCS performs an identical function to that in an HDLC frame.

PPP uses a **Link Control Protocol** (LCP) to establish, configure and test the data link connection that goes through four distinct phases: Firstly, link establishment and configuration negotiation occur. Before any network layer packets (e.g. IP) can be exchanged, LCP first must open the connection and negotiate configuration parameters. This phase is complete when a configuration–acknowledgement frame has been both sent and received. This is followed by an optional link-quality determination phase. In this phase, the link is tested to determine whether the link quality is sufficient to support the network layer protocols. Transmission of network layer protocol information is delayed until this phase is complete. At this point, a network layer protocol configuration negotiation occurs. PPP is designed to allow the simultaneous use of multiple network layer protocols and network layer protocols can be configured separately and can be brought into use and taken down at any time. If the LCP closes the link, it informs the network layer protocols so that they can take appropriate action. Finally, link termination can occur. This is usually carried out at the request of a user but can happen because of a physical event, such as the loss of line signals or the expiration of an idle-period timer.

Three classes of LCP frames exist. Link-establishment frames are used to establish and configure a link; link-termination frames are used to terminate a link; and link-maintenance frames are used to manage and debug a link.

Exercises

5.1   A point-to-point link operating at 6 kbps uses a stop-and-wait ARQ strategy. The link has a propagation delay of 20 ms and a total processing delay of 10 ms. Data is transmitted using a frame size of 896 bytes of which 868 bytes contain information. The acknowledgements contain 8 bytes. Determine the throughput and link efficiency.

5.2   A frame of data of length 1024 bytes is transmitted over a link with a bit error rate of 10^{-5}. Determine the probability that a frame will be received erroneously.

5.3   Data is transmitted over a half-duplex radio link at a rate of 28.8 kbps using a stop-and-wait ARQ strategy. Frames have a block length of 256 bytes of which 5 are non-information bytes. If the propagation delay is 1 ms and processing delays and acknowledgement transmission time can be neglected, determine:

(a) the throughput in the absence of errors,
(b) the throughput in the presence of a bit error rate of 10^{-4}.

5.4   Explain the meaning of the term 'send window', as used in a data communications network.

5.5   A frame-oriented data communications system operates at a bit rate of 2.048 Mbps with a frame length of 2048 bytes over a long-distance link which produces a propagation delay of 18 ms. A flow control system is required using a window mechanism. Determine the minimum window size which would allow for optimum throughput.

5.6   A long-distance half-duplex RF link uses go-back-3 ARQ and has the following characteristics:

Data transmission rate: 128 kbps
Frame size: 256 bytes
Information bytes per frame: 251
Propagation delay: 20 ms
Processing delay: 4 ms

Determine:

(a) the efficiency and throughput in the absence of errors,
(b) the throughput in the presence of a bit error rate of 0.00004.

Modems

Data is often transmitted using dc levels to represent binary ones and zeros using baseband transmission as discussed in Chapter 2. Such transmission of data ideally requires a channel with a frequency range from 0 Hz to a frequency equivalent to several times that of the signalling rate. Until digital services were offered by PTTs the predominant method available for data transmission was via an analogue telephone channel. Such a channel is characterized by a bandwidth of 300–3400 Hz and therefore precludes the transmission of dc, or baseband, signals. The physical characteristics of alternative transmission channels to metallic conductors, namely radio and optical links, require operation in a particular spectral range and thus preclude transmission of low-frequency and dc signals.

To overcome bandwidth and distance limitations of many channels, using any type of media, data may be **modulated** onto a suitable **carrier** which may then be readily transmitted over an analogue channel. We shall concentrate upon the use of analogue telephone channels in this chapter since, even today, they remain a very common means of gaining access to computer networks. Data is commonly communicated between networks and computers via a dial-up telephone network, access to which is widely available throughout much of the world. To this end **modems (modulator/demodulator)** were initially developed although now are also found in applications such as mobile phones, cable modems in CATV systems and satellite communication systems.

The chapter commences by explaining the principal methods of modulation used for transmission of digital signals and continues to examine the effect of noise upon such signals. Channel capacity is introduced where the effect of noise and bandwidth place an upper bound upon capacity. Practical modems are then discussed in terms of their principal elements and how they generally conform to internationally agreed standards to ensure that interoperating modems are compatible. Finally, some other types of modems for use with radio-based systems and cable TV are also considered.

6.1 Modulation

Before examining modems in detail, we shall first consider modulation techniques available for use in a modem. A sinusoidal carrier is described by its amplitude, frequency and phase, and each of these parameters may be modulated or **keyed** by a digital modulating signal. The term 'keyed' has its roots in telegraphy where signalling used to be performed manually by means of a Morse **key sender**. The three basic forms of modulation, namely amplitude modulation (AM), frequency modulation (FM) and phase modulation (PM), are, in the case of digital modulation, known as **amplitude shift keying**, **frequency shift keying** or **phase shift keying** or for short, ASK, FSK and PSK respectively.

Amplitude shift keying

AM may be accomplished by means of multiplying the carrier, which is usually sinusoidal, with that of the baseband digital signal. The time domain representation is illustrated in Figure 6.1 for the special case of ASK, where one symbol causes transmission of the carrier (binary 1, in this figure) and the other binary signal results in no transmission, and is known as **on–off keying** (OOK).

The spectrum of an ASK modulated signal cannot be precisely specified because the pattern of ones and zeros depends upon the nature of the particular signal being transmitted. Consider the case of a repeated 1010 binary signal. Fourier analysis (Read 1998, pp15–23) indicates that the spectrum of such a signal contains an infinite

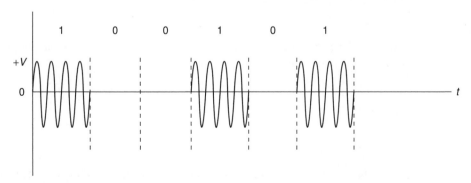

Figure 6.1 Amplitude shift keying.

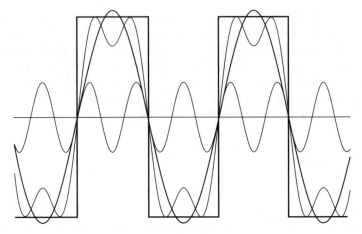

Figure 6.2 Spectral consideration for a square wave.

number of odd harmonics. This implies that the channel must have an infinite bandwidth, which is clearly impossible. However, satisfactory recovery at a receiver is
possible if the bandwidth is constrained such that only the fundamental and third
harmonic are accepted. Figure 6.2 shows the effect of restricting a square wave's spectrum to that of the third harmonic. The figure shows the fundamental frequency, third
harmonic and the sum of these two frequency components. The resultant complex wave
is then compared with a square wave where it may be seen that it has a broadly square
shape, albeit with some ripple within the mid-region of the 'pulse'. Note that there
are 2 bits/cycle of fundamental frequency and therefore the signalling rate R is twice
the fundamental frequency.

Now consider the bandwidth of an ASK signal, Figure 6.3. The modulating signal
has, as discussed above, frequency components at the fundamental frequency f_1 and
also at a multiple of three times that frequency. ASK modulation is equivalent to full
AM and therefore its spectrum contains both upper and lower sidebands, as shown. It
is now a relatively simple matter to estimate the bandwidth W of the modulated signal:

$$W = (f_c + 3f_1) - (f_c - 3f_1)$$

where f_c is the carrier frequency. Therefore:

$$W = 6f_1$$

And, since there are 2 bits/Hz of fundamental frequency f_1, we can relate the signalling
rate R to the bandwidth:

$$f_1 = R/2$$

Therefore:

$$W = 6R/2$$
$$= 3R$$

That is, the minimum bandwidth is three times that of the signalling rate. Although this
has been determined for the case of ASK it turns out to be an extremely important

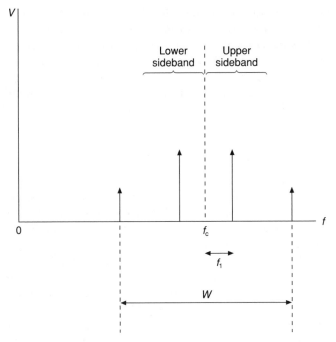

Figure 6.3   Bandwidth of an ASK signal.

result. This is because it represents an upper bound for AM and is also a useful basis with which other modulation techniques, discussed shortly, may be compared.

Example 6.1

A telephone channel has a frequency range from 300 to 3400 Hz. Estimate the maximum rate at which data may be transmitted over such a channel if ASK modulation is employed. State the carrier frequency that must be used.

ASK, as with nearly all modulation, has a symmetrical spectrum about a carrier frequency. Therefore the carrier frequency must be in the centre of the available bandwidth, that is 1850 Hz.

The bandwidth W has been indicated earlier as $3R$, where R in this case is the data rate. Therefore:

$R = W/3$
$\quad = (3400 - 300)/3$
$\quad = 1033$ bps

An ASK signal can be very simply and cheaply demodulated by means of an **envelope detector** (Read 1998, pp102–104). Alternatively, for increased cost and complexity, **coherent detection** may be used in which case the signal-to-noise (S/N) ratio may be reduced by 3 or 4 dB for the same error rate. Alternatively if the S/N ratio remained the same, the BER would the smaller. Since coherent detection is more expensive there is a trade-off to be made between performance and cost.

ASK is rarely found in practice. This is because distortion due to noise, or interference, results in disturbance of the signal's amplitude. This means that on occasion, where the disturbance is large enough, the receiver may misinterpret the amplitude giving rise to an error. However, knowledge of ASK is very useful as some other forms of shift keying may be likened to variations of ASK so forming a basis for comparison.

Frequency shift keying

FSK normally assigns two different frequencies to represent binary 1 and binary 0, so-called **binary FSK (BFSK)**. An FSK modulator may be thought of as consisting of two frequency sources, each of which is switched to the output under control of the binary modulating signal, as required. Figure 6.4(a) illustrates an FSK signal where the frequency for binary 0 is f_0, say, and that for binary 1 is f_1.

An advantage of FSK compared with ASK is that it is a constant amplitude signal. This means that much of the noise and interference, which appears predominantly as amplitude variation at the receiver input, may be removed by a simple amplitude-limiting circuit leading to improved BER performance.

FSK may be thought of as the sum of two separate OOK waveforms, Figure 6.4(b). One represents the occurrence of binary ones, the other binary zeros. The resulting spectrum is shown in Figure 6.5. The two separate carrier frequencies must be sufficiently widely spaced to avoid overlap of the individual OOK spectra. This places a

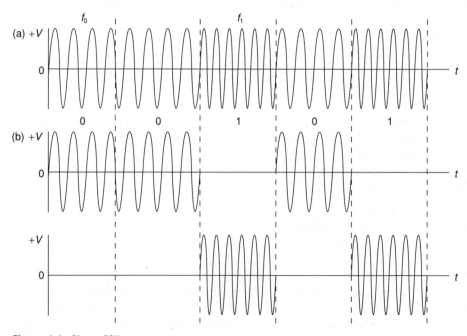

Figure 6.4 Binary FSK.

Amplitude

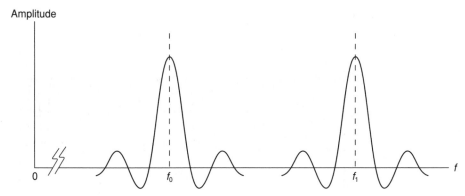

Figure 6.5 BFSK spectrum.

limit upon the maximum rate at which the carrier may be modulated for a given bandwidth order to constrain the spreading effect of modulation. This tends to limit FSK to lower speed modulation, especially compared with phase modulation techniques discussed next. Clearly, in comparing, the bandwidth required of FSK is at least double that of an equivalent ASK signal.

Detection of FSK may be performed by either coherent or non-coherent means. FSK may be detected non-coherently using simple envelope detection since FSK may be considered as two OOK signals, each with a different carrier frequency. Consider Figure 6.5 again. Each carrier frequency and associated OOK signal may be selected by means of a suitable bandpass filter, as shown in Figure 6.6. Each filter output is a single OOK signal centred upon its respective carrier frequency. A binary 0 OOK signal produces a one at the output of its corresponding filter and envelope detector. Similarly a binary 1 signal results in a one at the output of its associated detector. If the output of the binary 0 detector is inverted and summed with that of the binary 1 detector, the original binary signal may be recovered.

Improved noise performance may be achieved using coherent detection at additional cost and complexity. The complexity is exacerbated inasmuch that a BFSK signal comprises two carrier frequencies. Therefore two carrier recovery operations and demodulator stages are necessary. Just as in non-coherent detection, separate detec-

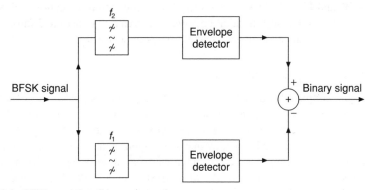

Figure 6.6 BFSK reception (Non-coherent).

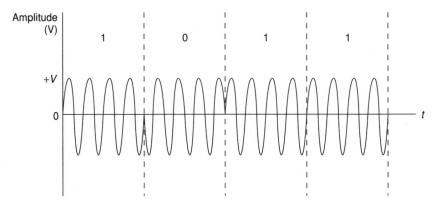

Figure 6.7 Binary phase shift keying.

tors are necessary for binary 1 and binary 0 signals, as we saw above. A coherent receiver is therefore similar to that shown in Figure 6.6 but where envelope detectors are replaced by multipliers and additional carrier recovery circuits.

Phase shift keying

We shall initially consider **binary phase shift keying**, or **BPSK**, where a binary digital signal causes one of two phases to be transmitted, usually spaced π radians (180°) apart, as shown in Figure 6.7. In this example binary 1 cause transmission of zero phase and binary 0 transmission of π phase.

BPSK may be regarded as switching between two *identical* frequency sources of opposite phase. Therefore a BPSK signal may be regarded as a pair of ASK signals, each with the same carrier frequency but opposite phase. Therefore the BPSK spectrum is similar to that of OOK.

BPSK, as too does BFSK, enjoys the advantage of a constant amplitude form of modulation and hence superior error rate performance for a given S/N ratio compared with ASK. In addition BPSK, as with ASK, has a narrower bandwidth than FSK. BPSK is therefore spectrally efficient and in fact performs better than both ASK and FSK in the presence of noise. The trade-off to be made when selecting BPSK is that, unlike ASK and FSK, it does not lend itself to non-coherent detection and is therefore more complex and costly. In addition, since the signal is transmitted through phase change, a channel with good phase characteristics is necessary.

Differential phase shift keying

In the simplest form of DPSK binary 1 may cause a phase shift of π radians whereas binary 0 causes no phase change, or vice versa. At the receiver the phase of each symbol is compared with that of the previous symbol, which means some method of delaying the received signal by one symbol length in time is necessary. A phase change indicates a one is received, no phase change a zero. Spectrally a binary-modulated DPSK signal is similar to that of a BPSK signal. DPSK may be employed to overcome the need for coherent detection necessary in BPSK systems.

A problem may arise when using differential techniques when a long string of identical symbols is transmitted in which there are no phase changes. Over time the absence of any symbol, or data signal boundaries, means that the receiver is unable to retrieve a clock signal from the incoming signal and the receiver data clock would then drift from its optimum position. When a change in data state does occur at the receiver some time may elapse before the clock is able to realign itself correctly, and only then ensure that the clock recovery circuit is reliably synchronized. During such periods the data output from the receiver may be incorrectly timed and lead to errors. To overcome this modems commonly randomize data before application to a modulator at the transmitter by using a **scrambler**. This ensures that no one symbol is transmitted continuously for any length of time and so overcomes the above difficulty.

Quadrature phase shift keying

All of the digital modulation methods, ASK, FSK, BPSK and DPSK, discussed so far are examples of binary keying. That is, the modulating signal has only two possible states resulting in modulation which consists of only two symbols. However, there is in principle no reason why the modulator may not output more than two symbols. Such modulation is called **m-ary** where m is the number of possible symbols.

Consider the PSK case of four phases each spaced $\pi/2$ radians apart. Such a system, consisting of four symbols, requires that binary data be taken 2 bits, called **dibits**, at a time to produce one of four possible symbols. That is, each symbol represents one of four possible dibits. This is known as **quadrature PSK**, or **QPSK**, modulation. The more complex modulation strategies of m-ary systems are often shown in more convenient form as a **signal constellation**, for example Figure 6.8. Instead of

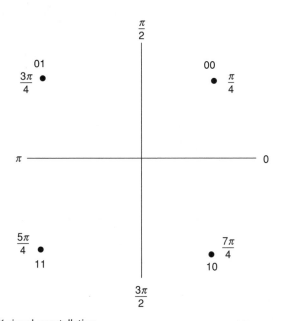

Figure 6.8 QPSK signal constellation.

illustrating QPSK as a time domain graph, a phasor diagram representation is used. Four different phases are available for the four different symbols which may be transmitted. For instance, if the dibit 01 is transmitted, the phase of the signal (with respect to a notional unmodulated carrier phase of 0 degrees or radians is $3\pi/4$ radians, or 135°. Note that, unlike a normal phasor diagram, a line is not drawn from the origin to the points shown for each of the four phases.

Figure 6.9(a) illustrates how the QPSK signal constellation of Figure 6.8 may be formed at a transmitter. The output of a 2-bit shift register is latched every 2 bits,

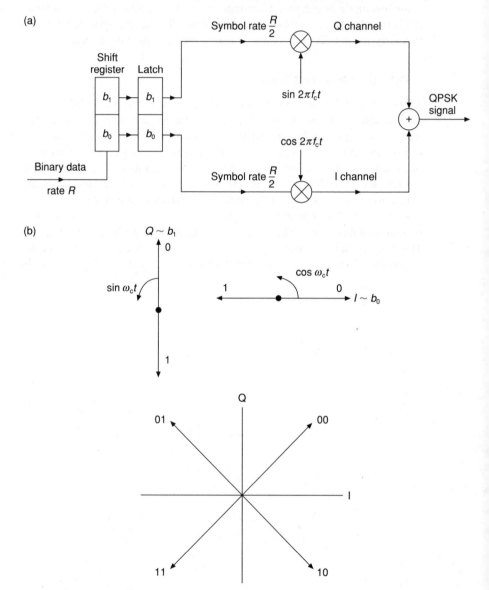

Figure 6.9   QPSK generation.

which means that a change in modulation, or new symbol, only occurs every 2 bits. Bits b_1 and b_0 act as modulating signals to multiply their respective carriers at a symbol rate which is half that of the transmission rate of the binary data. The two carriers are in quadrature phase, hence the use of the term 'quadrature' in describing this form of modulation. The cosine carrier is regarded as the in-phase (or I) carrier and the sine term the quadrature (or Q) carrier. The I and Q signals form a pair of ASK, or BPSK, signals which are in phase quadrature. Figure 6.9(b) illustrates both the signal constellations for the I and Q channels and the QPSK signal constellation as a whole. It is evident that the I and Q signals may be regarded as a BPSK signal. The I and Q signals are then summed to form the QPSK signal.

The use of quadrature carriers means that each BPSK signal is said to be **orthogonal**. A property of such signals is that they may coexist, by adding the two BPSK signals, and yet not interfere with each other. In consequence, providing the channel does not disturb the phase of each BPSK signal such as to upset orthogonality, each BPSK signal contained within the received QPSK signal may be recovered using coherent techniques by means of two quadrature carriers.

The attraction of QPSK is that, because two BPSK spectra are summed, its bandwidth is equal to that of a single BPSK signal. This means that a channel of given bandwidth may transmit data using QPSK at twice the rate compared with a single BPSK. Alternatively, for the same transmission rate, QPSK operates at half the modulation rate compared with BPSK signalling, and hence the bandwidth may be halved.

The above points serve to illustrate some of the advantages of m-ary systems. However, in practice some deterioration in BER results when compared with BPSK and DPSK for the same data rate and signal power. This is because points within a signal constellation of a QPSK signal are relatively closer together and therefore a smaller noise voltage disturbance is able to change a point from one symbol to that of another and so give rise to an error. QPSK, as with BPSK, may also employ differential operation, obviating any need for carrier recovery at the receiver.

Example 6.2

Derive the relationship between data transmission rate D, symbol rate R and the number of symbols m for an m-ary system.

Transmission rate $D = R \times n$

where n is the number of bits per symbol.
Now:

$$m = 2^n$$

Therefore:

$$n = \log_2 m$$

Thus:

$$D = R \times \log_2 m$$

Clearly modulation of phase need not be constrained to a four-point system. Since m must be integer, it follows from the above example that 8, 16, or more, phases may be employed, each symbol carrying 3, 4, etc., bits respectively. Irrespective of the size of m, a PSK signal constellation consists of points equally distributed around a circle (since all symbols have the same amplitude). For example, an eight-phase system has eight points, each spaced $\pi/4$ radians apart. If the signal power is not increased with the number of points in the signal constellation, the amplitude of each symbol (the radius of the circle upon which the points are positioned) also remains the same. This means that the minimum spacing between two adjacent points progressively decreases with m. In consequence higher order PSK systems are more vulnerable to noise, distortion and interference.

Example 6.3

A modem transmits using an eight-level signalling technique. If each signalling element has a duration of 0.8333 ms, determine:

(a) the baud rate,

(b) the bit rate.

(a) The baud rate is defined as the inverse of the shortest signalling element:

$$\text{Baud rate} = \frac{1}{0.8333 \times 10^{-3}}$$

$$= 1200 \text{ baud}$$

(b) If there are eight possible levels for each signal then each signalling element represents 3 bits (i.e. the eight levels are represented by 000 to 111). Thus 3 bits are transmitted every 0.8333 ms.

$$\text{Bit rate} = \frac{\text{no. of bits}}{\text{duration of one symbol}}$$

$$= 3/(0.8333 \text{ ms}) = 3600 \text{ bps}$$

Quadrature amplitude modulation

QAM, as its name suggests, also makes use of quadrature carriers to support a pair of orthogonal signals. Unlike QPSK where each quadrature channel is modulated with a binary signal, QAM modulates I and Q channels using m-ary, rather than binary, signalling. QAM is best illustrated by an example. Consider a 16-point QAM constellation. This may be achieved by means of two four-point ASK signals as shown in Figure 6.10(a) by taking data two pairs at a time. That is, dibits b_1 and b_0 modulate the in-phase carrier and b_3 and b_2 the quadrature carrier. Note that each dibit must be converted into one of four possible voltages, each of which effectively ASK modulates its respective carrier. The resulting signal constellation is shown in Figure 6.10(b).

QAM uses signal space more efficiently than PSK. Instead of only assigning signal points onto the circumference of a circle, points may be positioned more generally

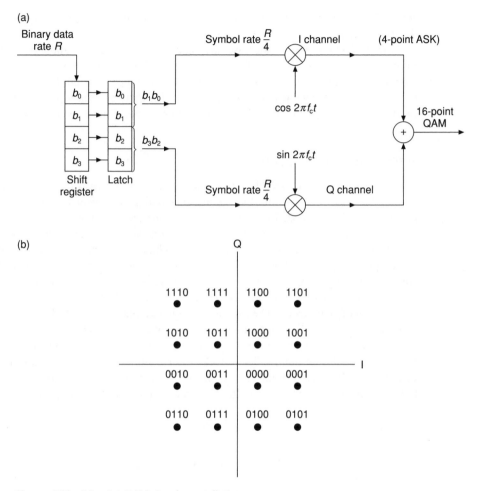

Figure 6.10   16-point QAM signal constellation.

throughout the *area* of the circle. This enables more points to be used, leading to increased signalling rate. The aim in designing signal constellations is to arrange that spacing between neighbouring points closest together remains comparable with that of BPSK. Therefore no increase in signal level is required and a similar S/N ratio is achieved.

The orthogonal nature of QAM is equivalent to two orthogonal ASK signals, each centred upon a carrier of identical frequency, but which are in phase quadrature. Their orthogonal nature means that their spectra coexist, without mutual interference, within the same spectral range. The sum of their spectra has a bandwidth equal to that of a single ASK signal. This is equivalent to a doubling of signalling rate for a given bandwidth compared with a single ASK signal.

In the case of a 16-point QAM constellation there are 4 bits per symbol and therefore the signalling, or symbol, rate is one-quarter that of the data rate. Higher order signal constellations may be used with QAM. For instance, a 32-bit constellation may carry 5 bits per symbol and the signalling rate reduced by a factor of 5 compared with the data rate.

Overall QAM seeks to increase the data rate that may be supported through improved noise immunity by efficient use of signal space without increase in system complexity. In practice a variety of signal constellation patterns are found rather than the rectangular arrangement shown in Figure 6.10. Patterns seek to match the modulated signal to the phase and S/N characteristics of the channel to be employed.

Trellis-coded modulation

At data rates in excess of 9600 bps it becomes difficult using QAM to produce sufficient spacing between points within the signal constellation consistent with adequate BER performance. Trellis-coded modulation (TCM) attempts to improve upon QAM and is based upon convolutional coding discussed in Chapter 4 and may be modelled by a trellis diagram. TCM goes beyond simple modulation whereby bits, or codewords, are simply mapped to signals. Rather redundancy is built in to provide forward error correction coding to improve BER performance. Hence this form of modulation, based upon both a trellis diagram and error coding, is termed TCM.

TCM usually employs a QAM signal constellation but for ease of illustration a PSK constellation is used here. Consider an eight-point PSK signal constellation, Figure 6.11. For each transmitted signal point, the receiver has to reliably discriminate each point against all other points. The effect of noise and impairments in transmission is generally to dislodge a point and the most likely point/s that any particular transmitted point may be confused with at the receiver are, in this case, the two nearest

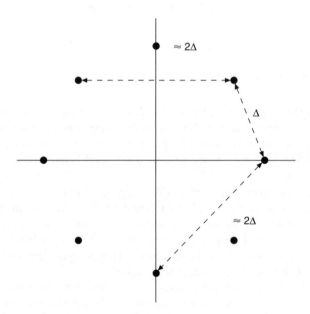

Figure 6.11 Eight-point PSK signal constellation.

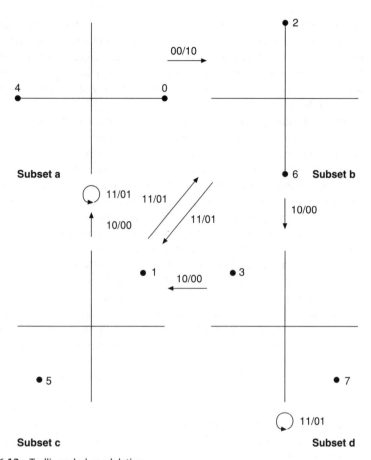

Figure 6.12 Trellis-coded modulation.

neighbour signal points. Providing the noise amplitude is less than half the distance between nearest neighbours, that is $\Delta/2$, an error will not occur at the receiver.

TCM employs a convolution encoder which adds a redundant bit in forming transmitted codewords. Figure 6.11 may be redrawn as four signal constellation subsets, Figure 6.12. In this example only 4 dibits, or codewords, exist but eight possible signal points may be transmitted due to the redundancy introduced by the encoder prior to modulation. In effect the receiver has prior knowledge about an incoming signal point based upon where the last signal point appeared within the constellation.

The operation of TCM may be explained using a trellis diagram but a simpler way of considering it is through the subsets shown in Figure 6.12. If the last signal point was in a particular subset, TCM, in this example, is such that the current signal point may only now be in one of two possible subsets. The arrows in Figure 6.12 show how movement occurs between subsets. For example, if a signal is received that falls within subset a, the next signal to be received is either 0, 2, 4 or 6. This means that the receiver knows that the next signal point to be received is either in subset a or subset b. Note that, because only data dibits (00, 01, 10 and 11) produce modulation, movement from any one signal point may only occur to one of three possible alternative signal points in this case. Obviously a received signal point could be confused, and the nearest neighbours are as a minimum between two points in different subsets, for example 0 and 6. This means that the minimum distance between any pair of signal points if TCM is being used is approximately 2Δ, or double that of the eight-point PSK case shown in Figure 6.11.

Note that although there are eight signal points only 4 dibits of data are encoded. This means that when moving from one signal point to another, there are only three possible codewords and hence signal points that may be moved to. A move is either to the other point within a subset, or to one of two signal points in another subset. Furthermore, any signal point no longer represents any particular data. Rather the way movement occurs between signal points indicates codewords to a receiver. This idea is similar in concept to differential encoding techniques.

Now if we compare this state of affairs with the normal eight-point PSK of Figure 6.11, clearly there is a much greater noise margin which leads to a reduced error rate. The TCM constellation shown can only operate at a data rate which is two-thirds that of the PSK equivalent. In practice TCM is only used with relatively larger QAM constellations to reduce the speed penalty introduced by trellis coding; for example, a 32-point TCM system maps four data bits to 5-bit codewords and therefore only experiences a speed penalty of four-fifths that of uncoded QAM. This small price in speed is more than offset by the greatly improved error performance of TCM where BER can be improved by as much as an order of 3. As has been illustrated in Chapter 4, one may engineer a situation using error coding where, although signalling rate is reduced owing to the redundancy introduced, the improved error performance more than compensates for this and leads to improved throughput compared with uncoded modulation. This is because the need for retransmissions is reduced because of the error protection afforded and hence there is an overall increase in data throughput.

6.2 Effect of noise upon digitally modulated signals

We saw in Chapter 2 that for the case of baseband digital signals the occurrence of noise in transmission gives rise to the probability of an error at the receiver. Similarly, in transmitting digitally modulated signals, noise again gives rise to errors in detection at the receiver.

A full analysis of the performance of the various modulation schemes described is beyond the scope of this text but may be found in advanced texts on communications theory (Roden 1996, pp507–512). Figure 6.13 compares BER against S/N ratio for the three basic keying methods used in digital modulation for the case of coherent detection. The graphs indicate that for a given BER, FSK requires an additional 3 dB in S/N ratio compared with PSK. Similarly ASK requires a further 3 dB to match the BER performance of FSK. Clearly PSK provides the lowest BER for a given S/N ratio. QAM and TCM, although not shown, are only extensions of ASK and may be further inferred from the graphs by knowledge of the number of signalling points in the particular signal constellation concerned, and number of data bits/symbol.

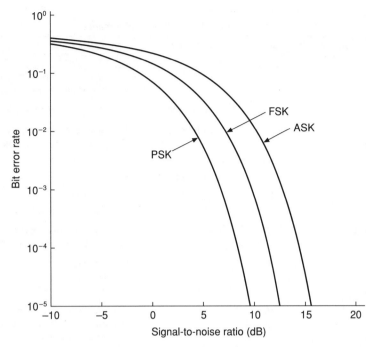

Figure 6.13 Bit error rate v. S/N ratio (coherent detection).

In the case of non-coherent reception an increase in S/N ratio of several dB is required for the same BER compared with coherent operation. There is thus a trade-off to be made between transmitted power and receiver complexity, in particular the added complexity of carrier recovery, between non-coherent and coherent operation.

PSK almost invariably operates coherently because of its complexity in requiring a phase reference at the receiver, which is only justified when BER is to be maximized. The exception is DPSK, a non-coherent technique, which has a poorer BER for a given S/N ratio compared with an equivalent coherent PSK modulation.

m-ary BPSK is similar to PSK but the energy is uniformly distributed among m symbols, rather than two. This means that the signal power available per symbol is reduced by the factor $\log_2 m$. To a close approximation the BER equation for PSK may be modified by this factor. That is, a given BER may only be achieved by raising the S/N ratio by the factor $\log_2 m$. For example, for the same BER as for BPSK, S/N ratio is required to be increased by 3 dB per doubling of the number of symbols in the signal constellation.

QAM, as already mentioned, may be regarded as two coherent ASK signals each transmitted on quadrature carriers. In the case of a four-point signal constellation it is similar to a pair of binary ASK signals and therefore would require an additional 3 dB in S/N ratio for similar BER performance. Where m is larger than 4, as is more usual, improved BER performance becomes possible compared with equivalent m-ary PSK transmission. This is because for the same number of signal points the separation between 'nearest neighbour' points is increased in QAM compared

Table 6.1 Comparison of digital modulation performance.

Modulation technique	Bandwidth	Detection	Performance
ASK	$\approx 3R$	Coherent	Similar to coherent PSK which has superior BER performance. Hence seldom employed
		Non-coherent	Poor BER performance. Simple detector
FSK	$> 3R$	Coherent	Similar to coherent PSK which has superior BER performance. Spectrally less efficient. Rarely employed
		Non-coherent	Improved BER performance, cf. ASK
PSK	$\approx 3R$	Coherent	Improved BER performance, cf. ASK and FSK. Spectrally efficient
DPSK	$\approx 3R$	–	Less complex detector, cf. PSK for small loss in BER performance
QAM	$\approx 3R$	–	More efficient signal constellations provide improved noise immunity. Improved BER performance, cf. PSK
TCM	$\approx 3R$	–	Generally uses QAM with FEC. Although spectrally less efficient net improvement in throughput leads to enhanced data rate

with PSK. In consequence a larger noise amplitude must occur to cause a symbol (and its associated bits) to be misinterpreted at the receiver. As a result increasingly larger sized QAM constellations show decreased BER performance compared with PSK.

Table 6.1 summarizes the performance of common digital modulation techniques.

6.3 Equalizers

All received signals experience distortion along their path from the transmitter. There are two prevalent forms of distortion: **amplitude distortion** is where the gain, or attenuation, varies over a channel's frequency spectrum, which means that the individual frequency components of a signal arrive at a receiver with different relative levels leading to distortion of signal shape. An ideal channel response is one where the phase shift is proportional to frequency. This means that if frequency is doubled, its phase shift is doubled. **Phase distortion**, the second form, occurs when a channel exhibits a non-linear phase–frequency response, in which case the relative phase shifts, and therefore time delays, experienced by different frequency components within a signal cause their relative positions in time to change and hence results again in distortion. This effect is known as **group delay** and is equivalent to different frequencies travelling at slightly different speeds. Its effect is to broaden the received binary pulses at the receiver and is an example of ISI and a major cause of error.

Amplitude distortion presents problems to both audio and data signals and is therefore closely controlled. Phase distortion has little effect on the intelligibility of speech and historically phase distortion has been of little interest in voice communication. However, where modems are used to transmit data over telephone channels, the effects of phase distortion can lead to significant degradation in BER.

A device known as an **equalizer** is commonly used in a modem and its purpose is to cancel out both phase and amplitude distortion introduced by a channel. They operate by arranging that the overall effect of channel and equalizer produces an approximately 'flat' amplitude response and linear phase response. In order to achieve this situation, the modem must know the channel response. Unfortunately each time a modem is used, especially in a dial-up scenario, the physical path is likely to be different, and have a correspondingly different channel response.

Lower data rates exhibit fairly broad pulses and have relatively low harmonic frequency responses. Modems for such rates use a **fixed compromise equalizer**, which optimizes for a typical channel and maintains an acceptable BER. They are generally located at the transmitter. At higher data rates an **adaptive equalizer** must be used which, as its name implies, adapts for the particular channel in use. Such an equalizer is in effect a controlled digital filter and implemented using digital signal processing (DSP). There are two methods of adaption: upon commencement of transmission a short training signal is transmitted of known pattern. Since the receiver knows what the pattern is it adjusts its equalizer until an optimum response appears at the receiver. Channel response may vary with time for a number of reasons (e.g. temperature variation) and lead to significant errors. Alternatively, some equalizers continually monitor and adjust throughout transmission in order to alleviate the last problem.

6.4 Channel capacity

The question arises: is there a limit to how fast a modem may operate? We have already seen how the available bandwidth has a profound effect upon the maximum signalling rate and hence speed. m-ary forms of modulation may be employed to gain an increase in data rate for the same signalling rate by simply mapping more and more bits onto a single symbol, and of course increase the number of symbols within a signal constellation. It became apparent that m-ary operation is ultimately limited by the available signal power and degree of noise encountered, or S/N ratio, in transmission. Eventually a point is reached where data rate becomes so fast that the error rate takes over and the effective data rate ultimately cannot be further increased without unacceptable degradation of the BER.

The above is all rather intuitive. Shannon (1948, pp379–423, 623–656) has formalized the determination of maximum data rate. He stated that the maximum rate at which data may be transmitted, irrespective of the modulation technique employed, over a channel C is given by:

$$C = W \log_2(1 + S/N) \text{ bps}$$

where W is the channel bandwidth.

Example 6.4

Determine the channel capacity of a telephone line if it has an S/N ratio of 30 dB.

S/N as a ratio is found as follows:

$$(S/N) \text{ dB} = 10 \log_{10}(S/N)$$

$$\therefore S/N = a \log_{10}\left(\frac{(S/N) \text{ dB}}{10}\right) = 1000$$

Hence, assuming a bandwidth of 3100 Hz:

$$C = 3100 \log_2(1 + 1000)$$
$$= 30.894 \text{ kbps}$$

The actual S/N ratio of a telephone line varies; 30 dB is fairly typical of a 'good' line. Many of the earlier multistate modems have data rates that fall far short of the theoretical value because lines often had poorer S/N ratios and signal processing was less advanced and unable to capitalize fully upon the available S/N ratio.

6.5 Generalized modem

Figure 6.14 shows the principal components found within a modem. It is assumed, as is the case in most modems, that it is operating synchronously.

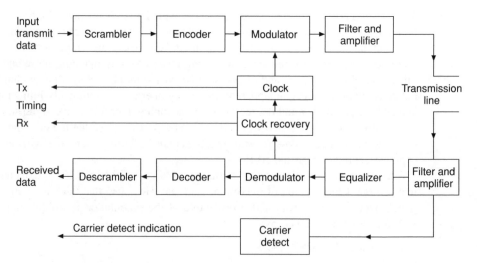

Figure 6.14 Generalized modem.

In the transmitter path, the following elements appear:

- *Scrambler* to randomize the input data stream to prevent long strings of either binary 1 or 0. This aids both modulation and clock recovery processes.
- *Encoder*. Many modems additionally, or in the case of TCM automatically, provide for some form of error control.
- *Modulator* to convert data signals, which are in digital form, into analogue form.
- *Filter and amplifier* limit the bandwidth of the signal's output from the modulator to match that permitted by the line. The amplifier enables the signal power to be adjusted to optimal level for the line.

And in the receiver path:

- *Filter and amplifier* ensure that the received signal bandwidth remains within limit to ensure that no unnecessary noise power appears at the demodulator input in order to minimize errors. Similarly the amplifier ensures, irrespective of line length, that the correct signal strength is applied to the modulator input.
- *Equalizer*.
- *Demodulator* performs the inverse operation to that of the transmitter's modulator.
- *Decoder* attempts to remove any errors and strips off redundant bits introduced by the error coding process at the transmitter.
- *Descrambler* performs the complementary process to that of the scrambler to yield the original data that was transmitted.
- *Clock* provides a reference clock which regulates the data rate at the transmitter.
- *Clock recovery* ensures that timing of transmitted and received data is consistent.

6.6   ITU-T V standards

Table 6.2 summarizes the recommendations for modems produced by the ITU. Note that *bis* indicates a second version and *ter* a third. Although date of introduction is not shown for each modem, they are effectively listed in date order. It may be seen that a spectacular increase in speed has appeared over the years. This is in part due to the fact that the quality of telephone connections, including bandwidth, has in general increased. Another major factor in modem development is the use of DSP and increased processing power, in the form of a CPU, which may be embedded within a modem. Indeed early modems had no processing power but were built around simple digital electronics. Over time, dedicated VLSI modem chips have appeared enabling powerful processing and DSP leading to improvements in combating noise and its effects upon error rate in the received signal. This in turn has led to increased speed and yet retains acceptable levels of error.

Table 6.2 also indicates how equalization has been introduced. Early modems using FSK had no need of equalizers. The introduction of phase modulation meant that they became necessary to overcome phase errors. Equalizers were originally pre-set and not able to be changed. Later they became **adaptive**, especially for use in dial-up connections where line performance will vary on each connection. The receiver within a

Table 6.2 ITU-T V standards.

V-series	Data rate (bps)	Modulation	Equalization
V.21	300	FSK (two carrier frequencies)	–
V.23	1200/1600	FSK (two carrier frequencies)	–
V.26*bis*	2400/1200	Four-phase DPSK	Fixed compromise
V.27	4800	Eight-phase DPSK	Manually adjusted
V.27*ter*	4800/2400	Eight-phase DPSK	Automatic adaptive
V.29	≤ 9600	16-point QAM	Automatic adaptive
V.32	≤ 9600	16-point QAM or 32-point TCM	Automatic adaptive
V.32*bis*	≤ 14 400	≤ 128-point TCM	Adaptive with echo cancellation
V.34	n × 2400 to ≤ 28 800 and 33 600 May be increased three-fold using V.42 compression	TCM	Adaptive bandwidth
V.90	≤ 33 600 upstream ≤ 56 000 downstream		TCM
V.92	Similar to V.90 but ≤ 48 000 upstream possible using V.44 compression		TCM

modem uses a training sequence to sense the line performance and optimally adapt the equalizer settings for maximum speed.

V.34 has largely superseded earlier modems. It not only gains benefit from employing DSP but also takes advantage of improved quality of analogue telephone lines where the bandwidth is often satisfactory over a slightly greater range than before. Signalling rate could then be adjusted, up or down, according to the bandwidth 'sensed' to be available to the modem. V.34 may also employ data compression and, in many connections, enable operation at speeds in excess of 33.6 kbps.

V.34 operates near to the theoretical maximum speed of 35.5 kbps for an analogue connection. ISPs, and some organizations, are connected to the PSTN via a digital connection and yet are required to operate with a distant user who only has an analogue connection with the local telephone exchange. V.90 has capitalized upon this when a digitally connected ISP, say, may operate with a distant user connected to an analogue local end. In comparing this with a traditional V.34 arrangement, only one local end means that the overall S/N ratio is better as less noise is introduced within the connection. In consequence channel capacity is increased and it is possible to operate up to 56 kbps. (This speed is not noise limited but is governed by the use of 64 kbps digital links where in some territories only 7 of each 8 bits are unavailable for data.) In practice transmission is asymmetrical in that the higher speed is only available downstream, that is from the ISP. Upstream transmissions are limited to 33.6

kbps and employ V.34-like modulation. Such asymmetrical operation is aimed at Internet applications (e.g. web browsing) where there is customarily more downstream traffic.

Subsequent to V.90, V.92 has appeared and is based upon V.90 technology. However, it uses the recently introduced V.44 data compression standard which can increase upstream speeds by about a third and double downstream rates. In addition V.92 uses superior initialization enabling adaptive equalization to occur much more rapidly, typically 15 s rather than 30 s. This is especially attractive where only small data transfers are necessary since connection time can be significantly reduced. This can result in cost savings and an increase in the effective data transfer rate.

Increasingly, data communications over analogue telephone lines are giving way to **cable modems** offered by CATV companies and discussed shortly, and higher speed digital connections via ISDN and ADSL technologies, both of which are explored in the next chapter.

V.24/V.28 standard

A modem is regarded as a DCE and typically interconnects a DTE, as shown in Figure 6.15. In order to regulate the interface between DCE and DTE a number of standard specifications have been produced. The Electronics Industries Association (EIA) produced the EIA 232D serial interface standard, better known as RS-232C. The ITU-T has defined a serial interface for use with modems for DCE–DTE interconnection, namely the V.24/V.28 interface, which is similar to that of the RS-232C. Both asynchonrous and synchronous DTEs may be supported.

V.24 states the functional and procedural arrangements while V.28 specifies the mechanical and electrical characteristics. A DTE uses a 25-pin D-type male connector and a DCE uses a female connector. Pin connections are as shown in Figure 6.16 and their pin assignations as in Table 6.3. Note that the signal names attached to each pin are as viewed from the DTE. In particular a DTE transmits data on pin 2 and receives on pin 3. The DCE, on the other hand, transmits on pin 2 and receives on 3.

The function of each line shown in Table 6.3 is as follows:

- Pins 1 and 7: Pin 1 is connected to the chassis of the equipment and is intended to be connected to one end of a shield if shielded cable is used. Such a cable may be used to minimize interference in high-noise environments. Pin 7 is the signal ground and is the common reference for all signals. The interface will not work without this pin being connected. It must be connected at both the DTE and the DCE end. The use of two separate ground connections can cause earth loops to occur and it is better to leave pin 1 unconnected in most systems.

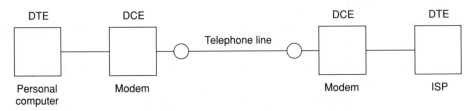

Figure 6.15 Typical modem arrangement.

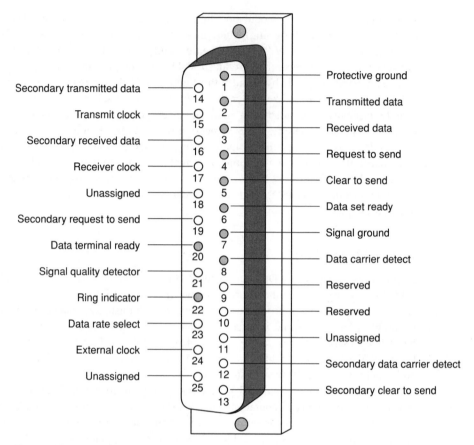

Figure 6.16 Typical D-type V.24/V.28 connector.

- Pins 2 and 3: The DTE transmits data on pin 2 and receives on pin 3.
- Pins 4 and 5: The DTE asserts RTS to indicate to the DCE that it is ready for use. Similarly, when the DCE is ready to accept data from the DTE, it asserts CTS.
- Pin 6, 20 and 22: DSR indicates to the DTE that the DCE is switched on, not in a test mode and ready for use. If an incoming call occurs at a DCE, RI indicates the presence of ringing current to the DTE to alert the DTE to the call. The DTE responds by asserting DTR to instruct the DCE to answer the incoming call.
- Pin 8: This indicates when the DCE is receiving a signal, providing it is of acceptable quality.

The above pin connections are by far the most often used in V.24 applications and little use is made of the following pin connections:

- Pins 15, 17, 21 and 24: These connections are used by synchronous DCEs to control bit timing.
- Pin 23: This is used in applications where a DCE can operate at two different data rates and the signal on this pin determines whether high or low speed is used.

Table 6.3   V.24/V.28 pin designations.

Pin no.	Signal description	Abbreviation	From DCE	To DCE
1	Chassis ground	GND		Yes
2	Transmitted data	TxD		Yes
3	Received data	RxD	Yes	
4	Request to send	RTS		Yes
5	Clear to send	CTS	Yes	
6	Data set ready	DSR	Yes	
7	Signal ground	SG	Yes	Yes
8	Data carrier detect	CD	Yes	
9	Reserved			
10	Reserved			
11	Unassigned			
12	Secondary data carrier detect	SEC RLSD	Yes	
13	Secondary clear to send	SEC RxD	Yes	
14	Secondary transmitted data	SEC TxD		Yes
15	Transmit clock	Tx TIMING	Yes	
16	Secondary received data	SEC RD	Yes	
17	Receiver clock	Rx TIMING		
18	Unassigned			
19	Secondary request to send	SEC CTS		Yes
20	Data terminal ready	DTR		Yes
21	Signal quality detector	SQ	Yes	
22	Ring indicator	RI	Yes	
23	Data rate detect		Yes	Yes
24	External clock		Yes	
25	Unassigned			

- Pins 12, 13, 14, 16 and 19: Some DCEs are equipped with both primary and secondary channels. All these pins are associated with the secondary channel operation. In these applications the primary channel usually has the higher data rate, and the secondary channel transmits in the reverse direction at a much lower data rate (e.g. 75 bps).

The electrical characteristics specify the method of signalling between DTE and DCE. Signal source circuitry may use signal voltages between +5 V and +25 V for a binary 0, and −5 V and −25 V for a binary 1. Signal sink circuitry recognizes voltages of above +3 V as being binary 0 and voltages below −3 V as binary 1. The data rate should be less than 20 kbps and the distance between a DTE and a DCE should be less than 15 m. In practice the actual voltage levels used are determined by the supply voltages and ±12 V, or ±15 V, are typical.

As an example we shall consider how the V.24 interface operates when two DTEs are interconnected via a pair of modems (DCEs) using a dial-up PSTN connection, and operating in half-duplex mode, Figure 6.17.

When DTE and DCE are ready for use, Data Terminal Ready (DTR) and Data Set Ready (DSR), respectively, are asserted, or on. The calling DTE transmits the telephone number of the called DTE over its Transmitted Data (TxD) line to the modem which in turn establishes a dial-up connection over the PSTN. Upon receipt

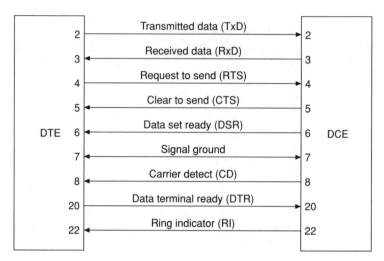

Figure 6.17 V.24 connections for half-duplex dial-up connection.

of ringing current at the called modem, Ringing Indication (RI) is set to on and the called DTE responds and sets Request to Send (RTS) to on. The called modem then returns a tone to the calling modem and also sets its Clear to Send (CTS) to on to indicate to the called DTE that it may transmit data. The calling modem, upon receipt of a tone, sets Carrier Detect (CD) to on to indicate to the calling DTE that a dial-up connection to the called DTE is now established. The **connection phase** is now complete.

Both modems now enter the **data transfer** phase. Currently, only the called modem has CTS on which, since half-duplex operation is in force, means that the called DTE may send data over its Transmitted Data (TxD) line, for example an invitation by an ISP DTE for the callee to enter their username and password. The data is modulated into tones by the modem. At the receiver the tones are demodulated and appear as data on the calling modem's Received Data (RxD) line.

Once the called DTE has finished sending data, RTS is set to off, which results in cessation of transmission of any further tones to the calling modem. The calling modem senses loss of tones and the following sequence ensues: CD is set to off, to which the calling DTE responds by setting RTS to on, which in turn leads to setting CTS to on. The calling DTE is then cleared to transmit data using TxD. In a similar way to the called DTE relinquishing transmission to the called DTE, the calling DTE may indicate to its modem when it has finished sending its data by setting RTS to off. The calling modem then suspends transmission of tones, which the called modem detects and sets RTS to on. The called DTE may then respond by setting CTS to on and commence transmission of data over TxD. This process of alternate phases of data transfer may continue.

Eventually, the **disconnection phase** is reached when neither modem has any further data to transmit and the connection is required to be cleared down. This is indicated by both modems ceasing to transmit tones, and both CD lines become set to off. When a DTE has no further data to send it sets DTR to off and the modem

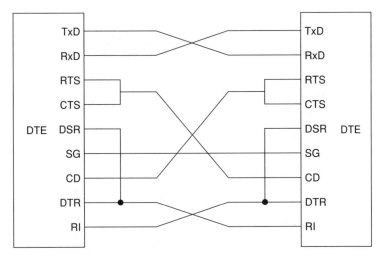

Figure 6.18 Null modem connections.

disconnects from the line thus clearing down the telephone connection. In addition the modem sets DSR to off.

In some instances two DTEs required to be interconnected via a V.24 interface may be close enough together that no communications network and attendant DCE equipment are necessary. A pair of DTEs may be directly connected using a **null modem** interconnection, Figure 6.18. Clearly the TxD and RxD connections must be crossed over in the connection. In addition, for the various control lines to operate correctly, as illustrated in the figure, other lines must also be crossed and in some cases jump connected to other lines as well.

6.7 Other types of modem

So far in this chapter discussion has been limited to modems for use over standard telephone channels. However, modems are by no means limited to such applications. In fact wherever there is a requirement to send data over a carrier of some description, a modem is used.

One area of increasing interest in recent years has been in cable TV (CATV) networks. TV channels are sent over the cable using frequency division multiplexing (FDM) whereby each channel is allocated a unique portion of the available spectrum. (In principle, this is identical to terrestrial TV delivered by means of radio signals to residential premises. Tens, or even hundreds, of channels may be transmitted by means of radio operation in the UHF band.) Each TV channel has a bandwidth of 6 MHz. One, or more, 6 MHz channels may be allocated, instead of to TV transmission, to data transmission. Just as in the case of telephone circuits, a modem known as a **cable modem** is necessary to convert binary data signals to RF signals and vice versa. A splitter is used at the residential premises (Figure 6.19) to split the data and TV channels and direct the respective signals to either computer equipment or TV.

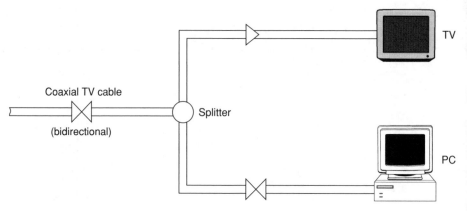

Figure 6.19   Cable modem.

Typically data is transmitted in the downstream direction to the home over a single 6 MHz channel using a 64-point (or 256-point) QAM constellation. In the upstream direction a lower frequency TV channel is used than for downstream and is more susceptible to noise and interference from home appliances. To combat this only a QPSK, or 16-point QAM, constellation is deployed and therefore upstream data rates are correspondingly lower. A number of different combinations of downstream and upstream data rates are offered. Typically 10 Mbps may be offered downstream with perhaps 500–1000 kbps upstream. (Downstream rates may be as much as 30 Mbps and upstream rates 2.5 Mbps.) Although these rates may sound a lot, they are often shared by a number of homes and the true bandwidth to an individual user is dependent upon the number of simultaneous users. This asymmetric data rate nevertheless is suitable for many emerging home applications such as web browsing and streaming where the majority of the data is flowing in the downstream direction.

Another important area where modems are needed is in situations where data is to be transmitted by means of a radio signal. Microwave terrestrial point-to-point and satellite radio links, mobile applications and wireless LANs (discussed in Chapter 10) are all examples of where modems are also found. Table 6.4 illustrates some examples of modulation schemes and associated data rates that have been employed for digital operation over terrestrial microwave radio point-to-point links.

Table 6.4   Terrestrial microwave radio point-to-point link modulation schemes.

Bit rate (Mbps)	Channel bandwidth (MHz)		
	20	30	40
34	4-PSK	4-PSK	4-PSK
68	16-QAM	8-PSK	4-PSK
140	256-QAM	64-QAM	16-QAM
280	–	1024-QAM	256-QAM

The Global System for Mobile Communications (GSM), or second-generation mobile network, operates around the 900 MHz portion of the RF spectrum. A pair of channels are required to link a handset with a base station, one channel in each direction of transmission. Each channel uses a bandwidth-efficient form of FSK known as minimum shift keying (MSK) (Dunlop and Smith 1994, pp549–550) operating at a data rate of 270.832 kps (note that because channels also operate with an eight slot TDM structure only a much lower true data rate is available to each handset). Each RF channel can support eight simultaneous handsets by assigning one TDM time slot to each user. This form of access is known is time division multiple access (TDMA). Any one handset effectively transmits data in bursts cyclically each time its assigned time slot occurs.

Exercises

6.1   Why are modems necessary?

6.2   Compare the relative merits of ASK, FSK and PSK.

6.3   Explain why ASK is seldom used in data communications.

6.4   Explain why QAM is able to transmit data over a given channel at higher speed compared with FSK and PSK.

6.5   A phase modulation system, where a binary 1 is transmitted directly and a binary 0 has a 180° phase shift inserted, has the following binary sequence applied to it:

101100101

Sketch the modulated waveform clearly showing the phase changes.

6.6   A DPSK system advances the phase shift by 90° for a binary 0 and 270° for a binary 1. Assuming that the previous bit had a phase of −90°, evaluate the phase for the last bit in the data stream 101100101.

6.7   If the number of points in a QAM signal constellation is increased, the data rate may also be increased. Can data rate be so increased without limit? Explain your reasoning.

6.8   A modem operates at a signalling rate of 1200 baud using a 16-point signal constellation. Calculate the rate at which data may be transmitted in bits per second.

6.9   Develop an expression to relate the number of bits per symbol to the number of symbols employed in a modulation strategy. Hence relate symbol rate, number of symbols and data rate.

6.10 A QAM modem transmits data over a standard telephone channel at 9600 bps. Estimate the signalling rate on the line and the number of points in the signal constellation.

6.11 A telephone channel has a bandwidth of 3400 Hz and S/N ratio of 27 dB. Determine the channel capacity. Can data be transmitted at this rate in practice? State your reasoning.

6.12 Shannon's Channel Capacity suggests a standard telephone channel may operate at up to 35 kbps. Explain why this is so. Modern modems commonly offer data rates up to 56 kbps. How do such modems appear to exceed Shannon's theoretical limit?

6.13 Explain why cable modems are able to operate at higher speed than those used on a typical dial-up telephone line.

Chapter 7

Access networks

This chapter commences with the development of the PSTN to that of an all-digital network capable of supporting a range of integrated services and known as an ISDN. The supporting technology is then examined followed by a discussion of the enhanced types of services and applications ISDN is able to offer compared with PSTN. We shall then look at how ISDN may support a number of different types of service. Next we consider a development of ISDN, namely Broadband ISDN, for which many standards have been defined by the ITU. Broadband ISDN was conceived to support very high-speed transmission for data and video-based services to customers. Finally a number of high-speed digital services, generically known as xDSL, are described whereby high-speed digital access may be delivered over standard telephone lines to customer premises. These are especially attractive for high-speed Internet and video services and form part of the broadband revolution now featuring prominently in the residential marketplace.

7.1 Integrated Services Digital Network

Digitalization of PSTN customer equipment and its exchange connections has lead to the integration of a variety of non-telephony-based services with those of more traditional telephone services. Such integrated services are carried over an enhanced PSTN network known as an **Integrated Services Digital Network** (ISDN).

Figure 7.1 shows a typical interconnection arrangement for telephone exchanges. Depending upon the size of the network there may be hundreds, or even thousands, of local telephone exchanges (LEs). Within a small geographical locality, a number of local exchanges are interconnected by local junctions. Calls between them are connected and generally charged at local rate, or are toll-free. Calls further afield

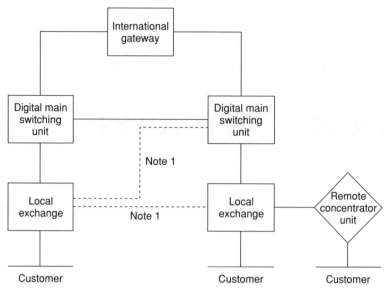

Note 1: Alternative routes where traffic usage is economic

Figure 7.1   Telephone network topology.

are generally regarded as trunk calls and are connected via one or two Digital Main Switching Units (DMSUs). The topology illustrated in Figure 7.1 contains a mixture of star and mesh configurations. There may be some tens of DMSUs and they are fully interconnected, or meshed, each serving a number of LEs connected in star fashion. Dialling of the international prefix automatically routes a call to the parent DMSU and on to its associated International Gateway Exchange, although, as indicated, an alternative route to an international exchange is possible via an intermediate DMSU. In general, the provision of alternative routes within a network provides resilience in the event of failure of either a route or a switching centre. In areas where telephone penetration is very sparse or line lengths extraordinarily long, predominantly rural areas, a saving in line plant may be achieved by using a Remote Concentrator Unit (RCU). A number of nearby customers may be connected in star fashion to an RCU and a single multiplexed connection employed to interconnect with the LE.

An Integrated Digital Network (IDN) is one in which all of the exchanges and their interconnections are digital. The term commonly used to describe the local line connection between exchange and customer is the **local end**. An IDN may accept analogue signals from customers over the local ends, in which case signals are immediately digitized before processing at the exchange.

ISDN is achieved by extending the IDN to provide end-to-end **digital** connectivity between customers which may then offer a wide range of services. Such digitization of the local end, or access network, is referred to as Integrated Digital Access (IDA). Figure 7.2 illustrates the relationship between IDN, IDA and ISDN. Once signals are digitized, then in principle a variety of additional services may then be offered, either on a dial-up basis, point-to-point or by further networking to other systems, for example by gaining access to a packet data network by means of a gateway.

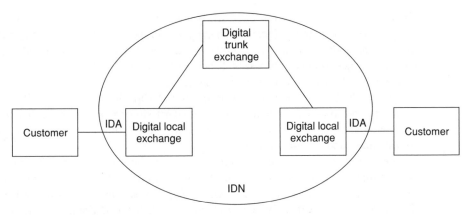

Figure 7.2 ISDN.

ISDN is reliant upon digital telephone exchanges and transport networks. The degree of ISDN service availability depends upon the particular territory within the world. Some countries now have all-digital networks. Others have yet to complete conversion from earlier analogue networks into fully digital networks.

ISDN technology

From the outset, ISDN has sought to offer a unified approach to customers to enable simple connection of equipment to the network. This desire is borne out of early experiences of the computer industry in attempting to use the PSTN for transmission of data.

ISDN was conceived to support a wide range of services, both voice and non-voice, to which users have access by means of a limited set of standard multipurpose customer interfaces. To support this aim a number of 'building blocks' exist:

1. transparent 64 kbps channels via a universal IDN;
2. control signalling external to the 64 kbps message channels (known as Common Channel Signalling);
3. standard protocols and interfaces which are, as far as is possible, independent of technology and common to many services;
4. a variety of terminals which interwork with the standard network.

Customer access

ISDN offers a **basic access** to customers over a single telephone. Basic access offers 2 B channels, each of 64 kbps, and a D channel at 16 kbps. This is known as a 2B+D service. Each B channel is full-duplex and can be used to carry a single digitized voice channel or transmit data. B channels may also be multiplexed, for example to carry two 32 kbps digitally compressed voice signals. The D channel may carry data at

16 kbps. However, it is not exclusively available for data because it also acts as the out-of-band common signalling channel for normal telephony operation on B channels to pass call set-up and clear down signals etc. between customer and exchange. However, once a connection is established, little further signalling occurs during a call, leaving the D channel available for customer use.

Clearly the total bit rate of basic access is 144 kbps in each direction. Basic access supports end-to-end operation using a standard single-pair telephone line between exchange and customer. Two alternative line transmission techniques exist, namely **burst-mode** and **echo-cancellation**.

Burst-mode operation and its frame structure are shown in Figure 7.3. Frames consist of forming a number of bits into bursts or frames. The D channel rate is only a quarter that of a B channel, hence each frame carries four times as many B channel bits compared with that for the D channel in each burst. Frames are generated at a rate of 8 kHz and sent alternately over the line, one frame for each direction in turn, a technique also known as **ping-pong**. Burst-mode activity has a duty cycle of 125 μs. This time is divided equally for a frame to be transmitted in each direction.

Transmission over the exchange connection is in fact half-duplex. Buffers are therefore required in both the transmitter and receiver because there is no longer continuous transmission in each direction of transmission.

In order for continuous end-to-end transmission to occur in each direction using burst-mode operation, then the burst for each direction must operate at least twice the end-to-end data rate, that is at least 288 kbps. Unfortunately, because propagation time increases with line length, the instantaneous line rate must be further increased with

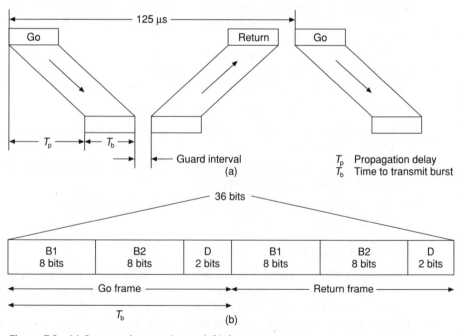

Figure 7.3 (a) Burst-mode operation and (b) frame structure.

distance. In practice there are limits to the maximum bit rate that simple telephone conductor pairs may support, hence burst-mode is restricted to lines of a few kilometres.

Example 7.1

Estimate the rate at which data must be transmitted over a line 4 km long using burst-mode operation. Ignore the guard interval.

Firstly we will assume a typical velocity of propagation in cable of 2×10^8 m/s. Therefore the propagation delay T_p is:

$$T_p = \frac{d}{v} = \frac{4000 \text{ m}}{2 \times 10^8 \text{ m/s}} = 20 \text{ μs}$$

From Figure 7.3 it is clear that the transmission time for one frame is 62.5 μs during which all 18 bits must be transmitted. Allowing for a propagation delay T_p of 20 μs, the time available to transmit the 18 bits contained in one-burst T_b is only 42.5 μs. Therefore:

$$\text{Transmission rate} = \frac{\text{number of bits}}{T_b}$$

$$= \frac{18 \text{ bits}}{42.5 \text{ μs}} = 424 \text{ kbps}$$

In practice, as indicated in Figure 7.3, a guard interval exists between consecutive bursts. This further reduces the time available to transmit a burst leading to an increase in transmission rate. Typical line signalling rates found in practice exceed 200 kbaud. Such rates are lower than Example 7.1 would suggest and are only made possible by the use of multilevel coding.

Alternatively the echo-cancellation technique, illustrated in Figure 7.4, may be used. Here full-duplex transmission is used between exchange and customer. This is achieved by means of a hybrid termination at each end to combine and split the Go and Return signals. Transmission theory suggests that a line can support two signals propagating simultaneously in opposite directions without interfering with each other. However, the possibility exists for a station's received signal to be accompanied by echo due to its transmitted signal. A major cause of such interference is **near-end crosstalk** (NEXT) where the relatively weak signal at a station's receiver is accompanied by some of the relatively strong signal output by its transmitter. Interfering echoes that are received are of course directly related to, or correlated with, the transmitted signal. Echo cancellation uses knowledge of the transmitted signal and appropriate subtraction from the received signal to cancel echoes.

The echo-cancellation technique is more complex than the burst-mode technique owing to its requirement of sophisticated DSP. However, the line signalling rate is less than half that for burst-mode operation and therefore longer lines may be supported so extending the geographical penetration of ISDN into the access network. Echo cancellation enables satisfactory operation on lines in excess of 10 km. A three-symbol or ternary line code is typically employed enabling the line signalling rate to

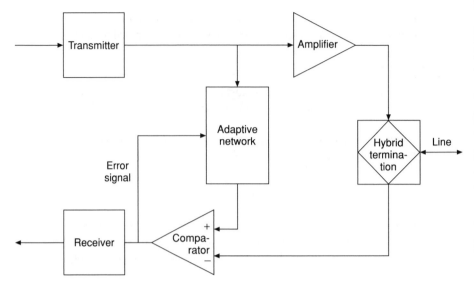

Figure 7.4 Echo-cancellation technique.

be reduced to 240 kbaud. Nearly all lines are therefore able to be successfully converted to basic access, if required.

Alternatively a **primary rate access** aimed at PABX customers is available based upon 2 Mbps pulse code modulation (PCM) digital line systems (discussed in Chapter 8). PCM uses two cable pairs, one for each direction of transmission, and offers up to 30 independent B channels and one D channel known as 30B+D. The D channel, unlike basic access, is not available for data. Rather it operates at 64 kbps, the higher rate being necessary because it is the common signalling channel for all 30 B channels between line and exchange. Provision of a separate pair for each direction of transmission obviates the need for burst-mode or echo-cancellation techniques.

The D channel used with both basic and primary rates is used as a common signalling channel. The protocol used with the channel is based upon HDLC and adheres to ITU I-series recommendations.

Customer installations

In the previous section we established the arrangements for the provision of basic and primary ISDN access from the LE to the customer. Now we shall consider how customers are able to interconnect their equipment to the PTT lines.

CCITT defined the I-series standards in its Blue Book for the interconnection of customer equipment to exchange lines. Figure 7.5 indicates that a number of **reference points** have been defined, that is R, S, T and U. Most PTTs terminate the exchange line in the customers' premises using a Network Terminating Unit No. 1 (NT1). This unit is owned by the PTT and prevents customers directly connecting their equipment to exchange lines at the U reference point. An NT1 for basic access provides services to the customer at the T reference point broadly equivalent to layer 1 of the OSI Reference

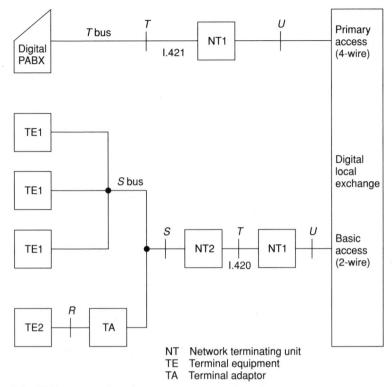

Figure 7.5 ISDN customer interface.

Model, that is simple physical and electrical connection to the line. It also includes performance monitoring and maintenance (e.g. loop-back test facilities), bit timing, multiplexing of B and D channels and multidrop facilities.

Customer access at the T reference point, as has already been explained, conforms to the I.420 standard for basic access and I.421 for primary access. Within customers' premises T and S busses are eight-wire passive busses. Two pairs are used for transmit and receive and the other four wires for power feeding of terminals.

NT2s are optional devices for use with basic access only. They are intelligent devices and available with various levels of functionality at layers 1 to 3 of the OSI Reference Model. An NT2 in its simplest form extends the I.420 interface from the T reference point to a number of S bus interfaces. Up to eight terminals may be multiplexed onto the S bus. An NT2 can provide switched voice and/or data facilities. Examples of NT2s are Terminal Controllers which offer multiplexing/concentration, or PABXs which provide switching facilities. NT2s are also available which offer a LAN capability. PABXs perform NT2 functions and may therefore be directly connected to a primary access via an NT1 at the T reference point.

A Terminating Equipment No. 1 (TE1) is an ISDN-compatible terminal, for example a videophone, and may be directly connected to the S bus using a standard RJ45 connector. Provision also exists to connect non-ISDN terminals using a Terminal Adapter (TA) providing a suitable adapter is available. A maximum of eight TAs and/or TEs may be connected to the bus. Non-ISDN terminals are called TE2s and are connected to a TA at the R reference point by one of a number of interfaces, for example V.24 or X.21.

ISDN applications

ISDN was originally conceived in the late 1970s. Early realizations in the 1980s resulted in a 'technology in search of an application'. At that time there was little requirement of anything more than simple POTS. The 1980s saw a change in this situation, firstly with the advent of PCs, and later as standalone PCs began to be replaced by networks of PCs. The demand for networking was in part addressed by using the existing telephone network in conjunction with a modem. The advent of ISDN opened up the possibility of dispensing with modems and directly interfacing computer equipment to a network able to support at least 64 kbps and often much higher rates.

Apart from standard telephone provision, ISDN also offers arrangements of other services:

- Switched data: Modems have been the traditional means of data transfer over analogue telephone dial-up networks. Even today the highest data rate possible on an analogue dial-up connection is 35 kbps with a modem. ISDN offers a convenient and widely available switched facility for interconnecting computer and other digital equipment at a data rate of 64 kbps, or multiples thereof. ISDN may also be economic for internetworking small computer networks together compared with the more traditional approach based upon forming a computer network using leased lines. An example might be where there are only a small number of nodes and the traffic between them is relatively low. ISDN lines are also extensively used in computer networks as secondary, or back-up, links to maintain some level of service should primary links fail.

- Fax: ISDN supports Group 4 Fax and because of the relatively high data rate offered, faxes may be sent much more quickly than over the PSTN. Typically a full A4 sheet may be sent in a matter of seconds.

- Slow-scan TV: A normal domestic TV generally uses either 625 or 525 picture lines and requires appreciable bandwidth to produce moving images. ISDN offers slow-scan TV using a single 64 kbps channel by means of a series of images which are gradually overwritten, line by line. A complete picture change may take place as quickly as 1 second. Applications are the connection of remote video surveillance camera signals to a central monitoring site, or remote monitoring of hazardous areas.

- Video phone: With advances in the capabilities and speed of signal processing techniques, by means of data compression techniques using DSP, and the advent of MPEG standards, real-time video signals of adequate quality may be transmitted over a basic access connection to support video phone applications.

- Video conferencing: An extension of the video phone is video conferencing where three or more parties, each with a video phone, may be interconnected. Video conferencing using an ISDN connection employs the same basic technology as that of a video phone. Typically a multimedia PC and camera are required. In addition the technology will support multiple connections if necessary and is readily available within ISDN.

- Fast file transfer: As already indicated, a dial-up connection may operate downstream at speeds up to 56 kbps over the PSTN, although such high rates cannot be guaranteed on every connection. ISDN offers full-duplex 64 kbps, or multiples thereof, enabling reliable fast file transfer and is attractive for home-based PC file transfers.

ISDN operation

We have discussed the general concept of ISDN, examined its underpinning technology and considered a range of services that it may support. Now we shall consider the operation of ISDN.

The following modes of operation are supported:

1. Circuit-switched connections
2. Semi-permanent connections
3. Packet-switched connections
4. Frame relay
5. Frame connection

A circuit-switched connection requires the establishment of a circuit, or virtual path, between the two users via the network. This is achieved using signalling messages over the D channel to the LE using layers 1, 2 and 3 of the OSI Reference Model. The telephone network then uses these signals to set up suitable connections to route the call to the intended destination. It does this using a separate signalling network which operates in accordance with ISDN Q series Switching and Signalling Systems standards. One of the key elements of these standards is known as Signalling System No. 7 (SS7). As its name suggests, it is based upon common channel signalling principles associated with the various switches within the network. The standard conforms to OSI principles and makes use of all seven layers of the Reference Model. Upon establishment of a circuit-switched connection, each B channel offers a transparent 64 kbps transmission path which the user may use for whatever purpose s/he chooses, for example one speech path or a number of lower speed data streams multiplexed together.

Semi-permanent connections are an extension of circuit-switched connections. They may be private circuits, in which case a permanent connection is established between two users. Alternatively, infrequent connections may be provided by the PTT operator for a period of time in accordance with a predetermined pattern, for example 2 hours one day per week. Because the connection is already established when it is required, only layer 1 functionality is necessary.

Packet-switched connections are supported using a three-layer protocol similar to X.25 described in Chapter 12. However, many Public Data Networks (PDNs) now offer a gateway to interconnect ISDN traffic. ITU-T defines X.31 and I.462 standards for interconnection of packet-switched ISDN connections via the PDN. Initially a circuit connection is established between user and gateway as for a normal circuit-switched call already described. Having established a connection to the PDN gateway a 64 kbps circuit now exists over which data packets may flow. In order to make packet-switched connections through the PDN the users packet-mode terminal uses the X.25 protocol at layer 3 whereas layers 1 and 2 use I.4240/421. As an alternative X.25 packets may also be routed through the ISDN to the gateway over the D channel.

The concept of frame relay and its relative merits compared with X.25 packet switching are discussed in Chapter 12. ISDN supports a frame relay service which is defined in the I.233/Q.922 recommendations. It allows several circuits, each to different locations, to be in existence simultaneously. This is achieved by assigning each circuit a virtual connection. ISDN is also able to support a service known as **Frame Switching**. However, Frame Relay dominates and is also being used widely in private networks. Both services use the same signalling procedures.

(7.2) Broadband ISDN

Broadband ISDN (B-ISDN) is a further development from ISDN. B-ISDN is envisaged to support services requiring transmission speeds far in excess of those used for basic telephony and lower speed data transmission. B-ISDN, unlike ISDN, is able to support multimedia applications such as cooperative computer working via voice and video accompanied by high-speed file transfers.

B-ISDN may be contrasted with ISDN or Narrowband ISDN (N-ISDN) in terms of the data rates that each is designed for. N-ISDN, as we have already seen, caters for a range of speeds from 16 kbps, through 64 kbps and multiples thereof, up to about 2 Mbps. Although the ITU-T recommendations have a variety of data rates assigned for B-ISDN operation, the principal rates are 155 Mbps and 622 Mbps which are able to be supported by ATM and which may be carried by the SONET transport networks (SONET is described in the next chapter). Lower rates of 34 Mbps and 45 Mbps are also used.

When B-ISDN was being standardized in the early 1990s voice and data requirements were then largely catered for by existing transport networks. B-ISDN's higher rates were driven by the need to support the very high data rates required of image communication, and especially the then envisaged uncompressed high-definition TV (HDTV). As the last decade witnessed rapid and advanced developments in the arena of data compression, MPEG developments have led to a dramatic decrease in the anticipated data rates needed for image communication, and MPEG-2 in particular makes provision for HDTV. In addition the roll-out of fibre to the home needed to fully realize B-ISDN for customers has been exceedingly small. In consequence the envisaged implementation of B-ISDN, even though the high-speed ATM networks exist to underpin it, is not going to occur overnight, if at all.

Both ISDN and B-ISDN services have been developed as access network technologies for delivery over the last mile to customers' premises. As already seen earlier in this chapter, traditional metallic conductors installed in the local-end network can support ISDN with its attendant data rate of up to 2 Mbps. However B-ISDN, with its relatively high transmission rates, has until recently only been supported within the environment of a PTT's domain in the form of an asynchronous transfer mode (ATM) network. ATM is a high-speed, packet-based, network switching technology able to transport any type of service, be it voice, data or video, and is dealt with in some detail in Chapter 13.

Some lower speed B-ISDN services only demand speeds of the order of tens of Mbps and may be supported by metallic transmission media. However, higher rates of the order of hundreds of Mbps will only be possible to customers using fibre technology. Clearly the delivery of such rates for broadband services to customers is gradually emerging but is rather patchy and generally not yet widely available.

Possible services, both now and envisaged, may be listed, the number only depending upon one's imagination! ITU-T has classified services as **interactive**, where information is two way, and **distribution**, where information is primarily one way and which may, or may not, allow a user **presentation control**. A distribution service with user presentation control cycles information repetitively, enabling a user to select the start or order of presentation. An example of such a service is Teletext. An example of where there is no user presentation control is that of national TV distribution.

Services may also be categorized as **conversational**, for example a telephone connection; **messaging** where there is no necessity for real-time activity between communicating parties, for example X.400 e-mail; **retrieval services** where a user may select information under his/her own control. Distribution (or broadcast) services provide a continuous flow of information to a user. Such services may or may not offer user presentation control.

A selection of interactive services is shown in Table 7.1, which represents something of the scope or range that could be reasonably envisaged. The list has been classified to some extent in order of bit rate, slowest first.

A list of possible distribution services, again ranked in approximate order of bit rate, is given in Table 7.2.

Table 7.1 Interactive services.

Message services	Retrieval services	Conversational services
Document mail	Data retrieval	High-speed information services
Video mail	Document retrieval	High-volume file transfer
	Broadband Videotex	High-speed telefax
	Video retrieval	Broadband video telephony
	High-resolution image retrieval	Broadband video conference
	Document retrieval	High-resolution images

Table 7.2 Distribution services.

Distribution services
Traditional TV distribution
Pay TV
Document distribution, e.g. electronic newspaper
Full-channel broadcast videography (text, graphics, sound, still images)
Video distribution
HDTV distribution

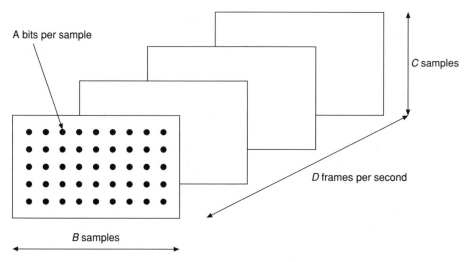

A bits per sample

C samples

D frames per second

B samples

Figure 7.6 Image bit rate requirement.

Let us now consider the general requirements of image communication with reference to Figure 7.6.

A digital signal may be considered as a succession of words, each of A bits, representing a single pixel. Frames consist of $B \times C$ such samples and the frame rate is D frames per second. This results in a raw bit rate for image communication which is the product of A, B, C and D. Even with modest resolution and quality, the bit rate of image signals becomes relatively excessive at several hundred Mbps. (Note that if resolution is doubled the number of samples, and hence bit rate, is quadrupled.)

Traditionally, many channels have been assigned to image signals on a **constant bit rate** (CBR) basis. That is, the channel operates at a single transmission speed which is available throughout the connection. From an information point of view this may mean that the channel represents overprovision when transmitting still and slowly moving images. Where action is rapid, the channel may not offer sufficient capacity and distortion may occur at the receiver. One way of looking at this is shown in Figure 7.7 where channel capacity is static but picture quality varies over time. Ideally picture quality should remain constant irrespective of changes in the image, but this implies that the bit rate must now vary. For efficient and economic operation, what is required is a channel which can match the instantaneous bit rate required and of course the maximum for a specified quality. Figure 7.8 shows such a **variable bit rate** (VBR) arrangement. Note the 'symmetry' with the previous figure.

Video signals, as indicated above, have a high ratio of peak to mean bit rate. If channel capacity sought to support the peak demand it would only be fully utilized for a very small proportion of the time. For much of the time it represents an overprovision in channel capacity.

Consider N video sources, each of average bit rate R, sharing a network. If each video source is conveying a different signal (e.g. each one is a different channel or network broadcast) they may then be regarded in statistical terms as uncorrelated, or

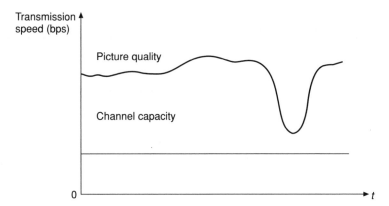

Figure 7.7   CBR transmission.

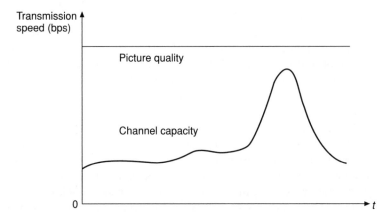

Figure 7.8   VBR transmission.

independent. Hence, irrespective of their peak bit rates, the average load presented to the network is given by:

Average load of N independent sources $= N \times R$ bps

$$\text{Utilization} = \frac{\text{average load}}{\text{network capacity}}$$

Utilization U is defined as the ratio of average load to network capacity C:

$$\text{Utilization } U = \frac{NR}{C}$$

Suppose that the network design only considered economic efficiency. Then network capacity C should be made equal to, or slightly greater than, NR to yield a utilization of about one. Statistically, however, it is the case that the sources will from time to time aggregate to a load in excess of NR. Clearly under these conditions overload and loss of signal (drop-out) results. There are a number of approaches to the solution of

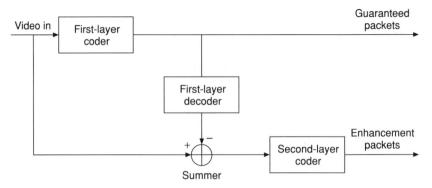

Figure 7.9 Two-layer video coder.

this problem. One is of course to increase the network capacity C, which increases the cost of the network. From a user's perspective, it increases the quality of service offered. In addition the time for which the network is underutilized is also increased. Such a solution is unattractive to PTTs. The main alternative is to use some form of coding of information signals to reduce their mean bit rate. Data compression is one such technique and whether B-ISDN or MPEG-based signals are to be transmitted, a feature of many bandwidth-hungry image services is to use some form of two-layer coding.

A generic example to illustrate two-layer video coding is shown in Figure 7.9. Once satisfactory communication is taking place, most packets are **guaranteed packets** which are produced by the first-layer coder. Very few **enhancement packets** then occur. The first-layer coder generates **essential packets** which are given priority and guaranteed transmission by the network, for example synchronization signals. Guaranteed packets also contain low-quality picture information essential to maintain a tolerable image at the receiver at all times. Enhancement packets are only generated when a change occurs in the picture, for example in colour or movement. If the image is constant, the output after first-layer coding and decoding is the same as the current video signal. In consequence no output occurs from the summer and thus no second-layer packets are produced. Such packets are in fact only generated when change occurs in the picture. Second-layer packets enhance picture quality but are not guaranteed transmission. If enhancement packets are not transmitted, picture change would, over time, appear at the receiver. The transitions between changes would simply be of inferior quality.

If the network is approaching congestion, it can reduce the load presented to it by only accepting priority packets. Under such circumstances, which, it must be stressed, may only occur very infrequently, and then only for a short duration, users experience some impairment. However, guaranteed packets ensure an acceptable quality. Two-layer coding therefore provides a good balance between quality and bandwidth and is an example of the use of VBR transmission.

MPEG is similar to two-layer coding in that I-frames contain all of the information to reproduce a frame, whereas P and B-frames contain a smaller amount of information so enabling the bandwidth of a connection to be reduced.

7.3 xDSL

Chapter 6 demonstrated the use of modems which are extensively used with PSTN lines to connect small business and residential premises to the Internet. The highest speed currently offered is 56 kbps, and whilst adequate for text-based transfers, it is rapidly becoming a bottleneck, especially for rapidly developing Internet applications. We then saw how ISDN and B-ISDN developed to deliver narrowband and broad-band digital access from the local exchange or central office (LE/CO) to customers. As has already been indicated, the ambitious plans for B-ISDN in terms of delivery of very high bit rates to the customer may only be realized via optical cable. Such a delivery system is not yet available to customers on a wholesale basis. In consequence a further evolution of digital subscriber line (DSL) to provide high-speed capacity has emerged during the last decade, predicated upon the notion of bringing the enormous advances in DSP and its capabilities to bear and to seek to improve the data rate that may be achieved over the standard PSTN cable infrastructure. There is an enormous investment in such cable plant, some of which has continued to operate reliably for decades and seems set so to continue. As a result a new family of relatively high-speed DSL services have emerged and which are grouped under the generic title of xDSL, where 'x' indicates that there are a variety of variants using a range of tech-nologies offering different speeds.

One thing that all xDSL services have in common is that they deliver their services to the customers using one, or more, unscreened twisted telephone pairs. xDSL has to address two major obstacles in its quest for speed:

1. Cable attenuation rises rapidly with increased frequency of operation. Cable attenuation–frequency characteristics are also non-linear and vary widely from line to line. They also determine geographical reach, which means that customers some distance from their LE/CO are either beyond the operational reach of the system, or endure slower speed operation.

2. The relatively high-speed signals used (cf. a few kilohertz for POTS) may cause interference with other systems and the ingress of RF signals may also pose significant interference problems.

Primary rate ISDN has evolved into what has come to be known as **High-speed DSL**, or HDSL, and provides data rates up to 2 Mbps, depending upon the length of line, simultaneously in each direction for transmission using two twisted pairs. HDSL is suitable for delivery of 1.5 or 2 Mbps data services (which, as may be seen in the next chapter, are T1 and E1 bearer circuits), or for pair gain, where 24 or 30 analogue circuits, each with their own pairs, can be replaced by a single HDSL arrangement. Pair gain may be used for growth within the access network as an alternative to installing more distribution cables. To maximize the reach of HDSL a spectrally efficient line code 2B1Q is used which enables unrepeatered operation over a local end up to 4 km long.

The need for two pairs in HDSL makes it less attractive for high-speed provision to customers who traditionally are only assigned a single pair. **Single Line DSL** (SDSL) has therefore also been developed and is similar to HDSL but, as its name suggests, only requires a single line. As a result its reach is slightly shorter than HDSL.

ISDN and HDSL are symmetric in that the same speed is offered in both directions of transmission. Coincidentally, in the early 1990s, a technology pull in the form of Video on Demand (VoD), which it was hoped would encourage a whole new market, led to the development of Asynchronous Digital Subscriber Line (ADSL) technology. This has a relatively high speed of up to 8 Mbps downstream from the LE/CO and a lower upstream rate up to 1 Mbps. ADSL, although asymmetrical, unlike ISDN and HDSL, is quite suitable for VoD since the major requirement is high-speed delivery of video downstream. In the upstream direction all that is transmitted is relatively low-speed data for channel selection, picture control (e.g. rewind) and administrative information regarding customer identity, charging and so forth.

VoD never really materialized, not because the technology did not work, but because of commercial reasons. Fortuitously, there has since been a rapid take-up of home PCs and increasingly user interests are moving into interactive and multimedia usage, such as gaming and video clips. These applications require much higher speeds than a few tens of kbps afforded by traditional modems and ADSL is therefore eminently suitable for modern-day Internet applications and provides a driver to take over from the failed VoD development.

ADSL makes use of a standard PSTN unscreened twisted pair for delivery to the customer. In addition it must coexist with the standard telephone service, or POTS. ADSL achieves this by signalling over frequencies that are above the 0–4 kHz assigned for POTS.

ADSL for VoD was standardized by ANSI in 1995 as T1.413 and subsequently adopted by the ITU in 1999 as G.992.1 based upon **discrete multitone transmission** (DMT; also known as G.dmt). G.992.2 has also appeared as a lighter weight (also known as G.lite or ADSL-Lite) version more suited to Internet applications and has lower quality of service (QoS) and bit rate requirements. We shall confine discussion of ADSL here to G.992.2 since this is far more commonplace and now proving extremely popular.

ADSL-Lite supports up to 1.5 Mbps downstream and up to several hundred kbps upstream. A bandwidth of 25 to 500 kHz is available for transmission and full-duplex transmission is employed using **frequency division duplex** (FDD) whereby the available spectrum is divided (asymmetrically) into an upstream and downstream portion.

The available spectrum is divided into 256 individual carriers, hence the description discrete multitone, and thus each subchannel has a bandwidth of 4 kHz. Data to be transmitted, which includes error control bits since FEC is employed to combat noise and interference, in a particular direction is split into a number of parallel streams, each of which modulates a subchannel using QAM, as shown systematically in Figure 7.10. Each transmitter only has a subset of a certain number, n, of subchannels. The rate at which each QAM modulator operates, $x_n R_n$ (where x_n is much less than 1), may be varied. In general the line characteristic has a non-linear attenuation–frequency characteristic where loss increases with frequency. Therefore the S/N ratio and noise performance of higher frequency subchannels are poorer. It would be inefficient therefore to modulate each subchannel at the lowest rate consistent with adequate performance for the worst-case subchannel. Rather, on initialization, the DMT modem effectively senses the signal transmission properties for each subchannel and makes an assessment of each rate. The coefficient x_n is determined to govern the corresponding rate at which the nth QAM modulator may be operated. In this way 'better' subchannels

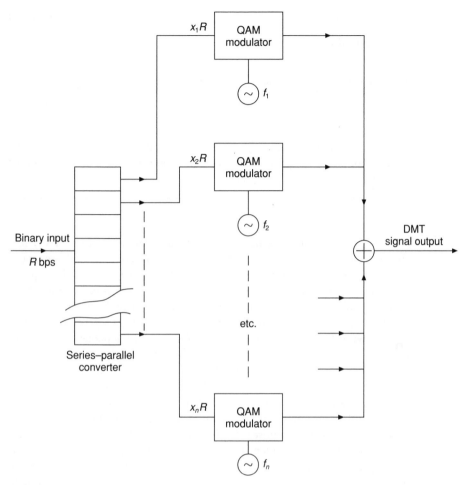

Figure 7.10 DMT transmitter.

operate at higher bit rates, and vice versa, and hopefully each subchannel will operate at its optimal speed.

Example 7.2

Estimate the total data rate that may be transmitted over an ADSL-Lite connection employing QAM.

There are 256×4 kHz channels. Each DMT channel employs QAM with variable options regarding the size of the signal constellation.

In Chapter 6 we stated that the bandwidth W for a binary ASK signal is $3R$ (where R is the signalling rate in baud).

A four-point QAM signal is equivalent to two orthogonal ASK channels and hence the data rate is double that for a single ASK signal.

Therefore the data rate for one 4 kHz subchannel is, for a 4-point constellation:

Data rate $R = 2W/3$
$= 2 \times 4000/3$

Therefore, for 256 channels:

Data rate $= 256 \times 2 \times 4000/3$
≈ 683 kbps

This rate could be extended by a factor 3/2 if, say, an eight-point constellation were used or doubled for a 16-point constellation, and of course more if even larger constellations were used.

Figure 7.11 indicates the network architecture for ADSL-Lite. A key feature, here shown in the LE/CO, is a **splitter**. This is used to combine and separate the POTS and ADSL signals. A low-pass filter is used to prevent any high-frequency signals which may accompany those of the POTS signals interfering with the ADSL signal. Similarly the ADSL signal enters the splitter via a high-pass filter to prevent any low-frequency signals interfering with those of the POTS. The splitter interconnects the line with that of the POTS line card for normal telephone operation and also to the ADSL modem for onward communication to a high-speed data network, typically the Internet. In order to ensure that the speed advantage of ADSL is realized, a PC may be interconnected to the ADSL modem at the customer's premises using an Ethernet card or, on occasion, via a universal serial bus (USB) port. Eventually connection will simply be by means of an ADSL card in the PC.

At the customer's premises the line, as with ISDN, terminates at the Network Termination (NT). A splitter is not necessarily required here as it is assumed that the respective telephone and ADSL equipment will deal with any issues of filtering of the signals. This low-cost approach, compared with G.992.1 where splitters are also installed at customers' premises, can lead to problems. The relatively high frequencies of ADSL signals can interfere with the telephone instrument. In some instances it may therefore be necessary to install low-pass filters in telephone sockets. In addition, external radio interference may ingress to adversely affect the ADSL service.

Figure 7.11 suggests that customers may be directly connected to the LE/CO by means of a metallic connection. ADSL has a reach of about 4 km which, although suitable for many customers, is by no means suitable for all. Concurrent with xDSL developments has been the introduction of optical fibre cable into the access network, which hitherto had only been used in transport networks.

There are a range of access network architectures, as Figure 7.12 illustrates. Note that the distances shown are maximum values. The figure effectively illustrates how in general optical fibre cable is being extended from the LE/CO towards the customer. It must be stressed that the particular model applying to a particular customer could be any one of those shown. Traditionally customers have been connected by a purely metallic path. A number of large multipair cables radiate from the LE/CO to a number of **cross-connect points**, or **cabinets**. Each cross-connect point in turn has

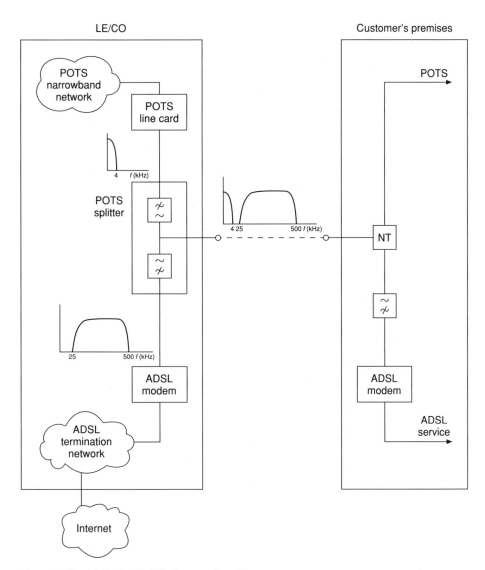

Figure 7.11   ADSL-Lite (G.992.2) network architecture.

a number of smaller sized multipair cables radiating within the particular physical area that the cross-connect serves. Each of these smaller cables terminates in a **footway junction box** from which distribution cables run to each customer's premises, possibly via an overhead cable. This arrangement, as already indicated, can support ADSL providing the customer is within about 4 km of the LE/CO.

A first development for optical cable is to link the cabinets back to the LE/CO by means of fibre – so-called **Fibre to the Cabinet** (FTTCab). An **Optical Network Unit** (ONU) terminates fibres, performs the necessary interface with copper conductors and provides the necessary optoelectronic conversions. The principal advantage of

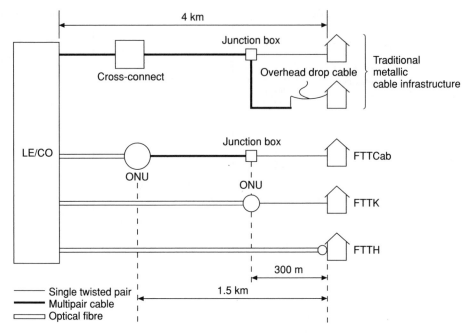

Figure 7.12 Access network architecture.

FTTCab is that customers may still fall within the ADSL service area, even if they are appreciably more than 4 km distant from the LE/CO, providing that they are within only 1.5 km of the ONU. Optical fibre may, as Figure 7.12 also shows, be extended even nearer to the home. **Fibre to the Kerb** (FTTK) places the ONU at the junction box position and enables customers to be reached providing they are only 300 m from the ONU. **Fibre to the Home** (FTTH) represents the ultimate where optical fibre is extended from the LE/CO right to the customer and provides maximum reach from the LE/CO, enabling even more premises to be reached by ADSL and, as we shall see shortly, pave the way for even higher speed services to be delivered.

The advantages of optical penetration towards the customer are obvious. Then why not simply deliver FFTH and enable broadband access for all? The answer is cost. Optical fibre installations are expensive and, if xDSL can bring a new lease of life to the existing PSTN, why spend any more than is necessary? Cost of optical cable is in fact rather subtle. Clearly the nearer fibre is to the home, the shorter the copper drop, and hence the faster the data rate possible. However, ONUs are relatively expensive, and the nearer they are placed to the customer, the fewer customers there are per ONU, meaning that the financial justification of the ONU is less attractive. This trade-off ultimately governs how far optical cable penetrates towards the home.

A further development of xDSL is that of Very High Digital Subscriber Line (VDSL) which may offer symmetrical and asymmetrical operation. At the time of writing, standards are under development. In principle VDSL is a higher speed version of ADSL. Increased speed is achieved by arranging subscribers to be within a few hundred metres of an optical connection, or ONU, leaving a relatively short metallic cable drop. Similar technologies to DMT and FDD are under consideration as well as sophisticated control of transmitter power levels to minimize the effect of crosstalk between VDSL connections. Various transmission speeds have been cited. Asymmetric operation at 1 or 2 Mbps upstream and several tens of Mbps downstream (e.g. 50 Mbps) is envisaged. Applications may include simultaneous delivery of two or three TV programmes, high-quality video conferencing as well as high-speed data services.

Exercises

7.1 Explain the differences between a PSTN and ISDN.

7.2 Compare the relative merits of burst-mode and echo-cancellation techniques used in ISDN local ends.

7.3 State the line transmission rate of a 2B+D line which uses echo cancellation. Assume binary data signals.

7.4 Estimate the rate at which data must be transmitted over a line 6 km long using burst-mode operation.

7.5 A 2B+D line is to use burst-mode transmission. If the maximum signalling rate is not to exceed 500 kbps (assuming binary coding), calculate the maximum length of line which may be supported.

7.6 Define the terms ISDN and B-ISDN and draw a distinction between them.

7.7 Discuss the services which B-ISDN has the potential to offer.

7.8 Distinguish between CBR and VBR transmission.

7.9 Explain clearly why constant bit rate networks are unsuitable for communication of image signals with high peak to mean bit rates.

7.10 Coding is seen as a way of reducing the capacity that a network is required to offer its customers and yet still provide adequate transmission quality. Discuss how such coding enables the above two conflicting parameters to be reconciled.

7.11 Explain the general principles which enable high-speed digital services to be delivered to residential customers.

7.12 Explain the terms FDD and DMT.

Transport networks

In the previous chapter we saw the principal ways in which customers may access telephone and computer networks. In later chapters we shall explore how computer networks operate in some detail. This chapter is concerned with how voice and data services may be carried, or transported, between different telephone and computer networks largely on a point-to-point basis. The main elements of such networks explored here are the specific elements used to convey signals across the network which in total are known as a **transport network**.

The chapter introduces the general concept used extensively to combine a number of channels which are usually, although not always, digital. This is followed by a practical example in the form of pulse code modulation (PCM) originally developed to enable a couple of dozen, or so, telephone circuits to be transmitted over only two cable pairs to exploit a saving in line plant provision. PCM was touched upon in the previous chapter on access technologies where it has been adapted for basic and primary rate ISDN provision to customers.

The two dominant topics contained within this chapter concern a natural extension of PCM to high-speed digital links used to connect towns, cities and countries together. The first topic covers a 'first-generation' plesiochronous digital hierarchy followed by a 'second-generation' synchronous digital hierarchy which, during the 1990s, has provided a gradual replacement. Synchronous digital hierarchy not only offers improved performance and is a superior system to operate, but is also able to support all of the former digital links and is designed to accommodate further, and higher speed, developments of transport networks.

8.1 Time division multiplexing

Figure 8.1 illustrates the principle of time division multiplexing (TDM). In pure form TDM is the process of switching a number of signal sources, or channels, in strict rotation on a one-at-a-time basis to a single output. Three channels are shown in the figure. A device which performs this function is known as a **multiplexer**. Providing

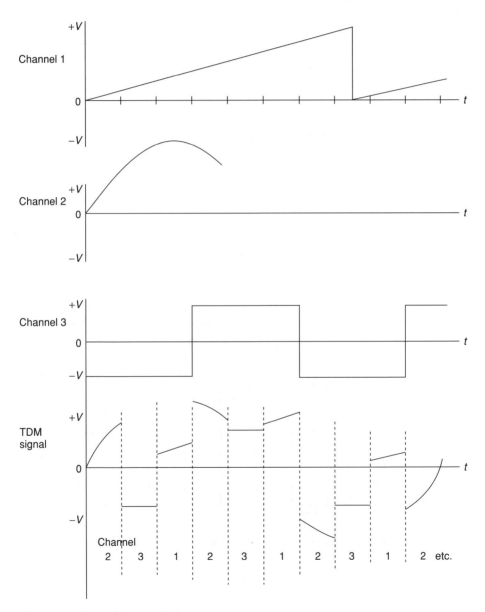

Figure 8.1 Time division multiplexing.

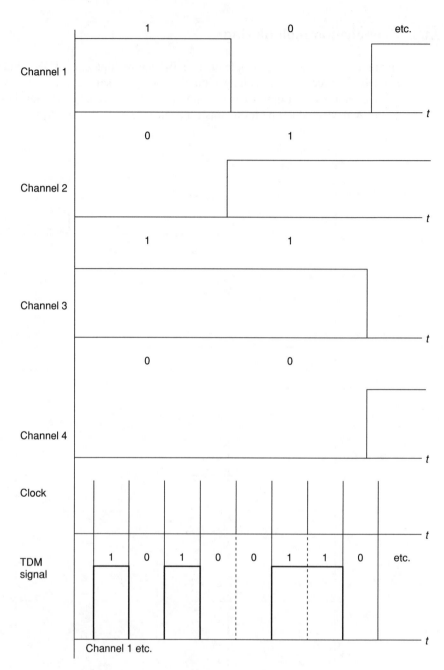

Figure 8.2 Multiplexing of four PCM signals.

each input channel is sampled sufficiently rapidly, each individual signal is perfectly recoverable at a receiver. In practice such an analogue-based TDM system as shown would suffer considerable distortion during transmission and the figure is only for purposes of illustration. Such a system would not be used in practice.

Modern TDM systems are digital and multiplex binary signals such as data and digitized voice. Such multiplexers often have four input channels in order to efficiently use two control lines which govern which particular input is to be switched to the output at any particular instant in time. A four-channel digital multiplex system is illustrated in Figure 8.2. It is assumed that each input channel, or **tributary**, is of the same transmission rate. In the case of a four-channel mutliplexer, during each input bit period, the multiplexer must output 4 bits, 1 bit for each of the input channels.

A receiver must perform the complementary function to that of the multiplexer, known as **demultiplexing**. The receiver clock controlling the demultiplexer operation must be very carefully synchronized with that of the incoming TDM signal to ensure that switching occurs exactly on the transition between received signal elements to avoid signals, or fragments of them, passing from one channel into another and producing a form of crosstalk.

8.2 Pulse code modulation

One of the earliest commercial applications of TDM was **pulse code modulation** (PCM). This is either a 24-, or 30-, channel line system initially used to multiplex speech signals using only two pairs, each operating in simplex mode to permit the use of regenerators. PCM appeared at a time of rapid growth in telephone penetration. Such high demand outstripped cable pair capacity between local telephone exchanges and PCM was a solution by providing **pair gain** whereby 24 (or 30) channels, which normally require 48 audio pairs, could be transmitted using only two audio pairs. That is, pair gain by a factor of 24.

Figure 8.3 illustrates a 30-channel PCM system and is also known as an **E1** bearer circuit. Each telephone or speech channel is sampled at 8 kHz. Samples are encoded into an 8-bit word, or **pulse code**. There are thus 256 different discrete sample values, or **quantization** levels. Each 8-bit pulse code is then time division multiplexed. There are a total of 32 time slots numbered 0 to 31, although in practice only 30 time slots are allocated for speech channels. The remaining two time slots are time slot 0 (TS 0) and TS 16. TS 0 is used for **frame alignment** to enable the receiver to align correctly with the incoming 32 time slot sequence. This ensures that the output time slots at the receiver are synchronized with those being received. TS 16 is assigned for signalling purposes (common channel signalling, e.g. dial code information, clearing signals, etc.). Each channel's pulse code is transmitted serially over the line system, each channel in turn. A complete system comprises sampling, encoding and multiplexing plus the converse functions for reception. A 24-channel system, widely used in North America, is very similar but only has 24 channels. It is called a **T1** or DS-1 bearer circuit.

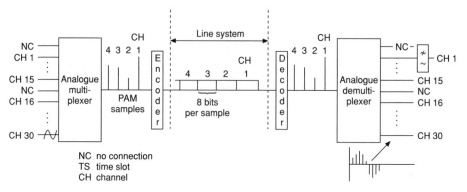

Figure 8.3 Pulse code modulation.

Example 8.1

Calculate the line rate of a 30-channel PCM system.

Line rate = sampling rate × bits/sample × no. of time slots
= 8 kHz × 8 × 32 bps
= 2.048 Mbps

In practice line encoding is applied to the multiplexed binary signals prior to application to the line (e.g. HDB3). Therefore the signalling rate upon the line usually differs from the value calculated in the above example.

PCM first appeared in the early 1960s originally as a 24-channel system. The USA, Canada and Japan continue to operate 24-channel systems but Europe has gravitated to 30 channels. The ITU-T I-series recommendations have adapted the 30-channel PCM system to provide Primary ISDN access, as seen in Chapter 7. Thirty 64 kbps PCM channels form the 30 B channels and the D channel uses one additional time slot. The remaining time slot is used for correct system operation by providing frame alignment between sending and receiving stations.

8.3 Plesiochronous Digital Hierarchy

It was not long before PCM systems, although TDM systems in their own right, became further multiplexed. Four PCM signals, **level 1** or **primary signals**, may be multiplexed together to form a level 2 signal, Figure 8.4. The resultant level 2 **Plesiochronous Digital Hierarchy** (PDH) signal has a transmission rate of 8 Mbps. Similarly level 2 signals may be further multiplexed with three other such signals. At level 2 four 8 Mbps streams can form a 34 Mbps stream, and so on, until a 140 Mbps stream may be produced, level 4. Signals at this speed are predominantly transmitted over optical links. Finally, four level 4 signals may be multiplexed to form a level 5 signal at a speed of 565 Mbps.

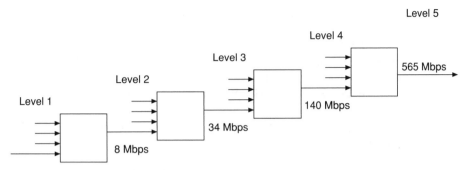

Figure 8.4 Plesiochronous Digital Trunk Hierarchy.

Inspection of Figure 8.4 reveals that signals at the output of a multiplexer are of higher rate than the sum of each of its input channels. This is because multiplexers introduce some additional bits for housekeeping purposes, and in particular to assist in the synchronism of receivers to ensure that they demultiplex the incoming bit stream correctly. Synchronism is needed with regard to both bit and frame.

The advantage of multiplexing a number of PCM systems was initially to make efficient use of existing coaxial cable systems originally laid between towns and cities for analogue trunk telephony traffic using frequency division multiplexing. The conversion of such coaxial links from analogue to digital operation led to cost reductions and the opportunity to exploit the improved transmission quality of digital operation. Further multiplexing may be performed to utilize the even higher bandwidth offered by optical fibre links. Such high transmission rates enable large numbers of separate signals to be carried over the same physical medium, rather than a plethora of separate physical paths. This in turn leads to savings in space, and cost, of transmission media.

PDH, as a term, was coined after TDM systems first appeared to distinguish them from later TDM developments known as the Synchronous Digital Hierarchy (SDH) and which is discussed in the next section. 'Plesiochronous' means that the system clocks at each end of a link are very nearly, but not quite, in synchronism. This lack of absolute synchronism does mean that occasional bit errors are inevitable. Such errors are minimized by using a mechanism known as **justification** which seeks to detect clock slips (see Example 2.1) due to difference in clock speeds and signal bits to a receiver which would otherwise have been lost.

Table 8.1 indicates PDH rates which are used in both national and international links. Unfortunately there is no universal system of PDH throughout the world. Europe for

Table 8.1 PDH data rates.

	Europe		USA, Canada and Japan	
Level	Designation	Data rate (Mbps)	Designation	Data rate (Mbps)
1	E1	2.048	DS-1	1.544
2	E2	8.448	DS-2 or T2	6.312
3	E3	34.368	DS-3 or T3	44.736
4	E4	139.264	DS-4 or T4	274.176
5	E5	565.158		

instance uses the speeds developed from 30-channel 2 Mbps PCM systems whereas the USA, Canada and Japan have built theirs around 24-channel PCM systems operating at 1.5 Mbps. This poses problems in marrying up different systems for international communication. The European rates are classified by ITU using the letter 'E' and where a level 1 signal is known as E1, level 2 as E2 and so on. Similarly the US signals, termed **Digital Carrier System** (DS), are classified as T1 to T4.

We saw earlier that in PCM bytes for each channel are transmitted in sequence. For this reason PCM is said to be a **byte-interleaved** system. However, PDH is **bit-interleaved** where 1 bit of each of the four tributaries is transmitted by the multiplexer at a time.

A disadvantage of PDH in the way in which justification operates is that in order to obtain a tributary from a higher order multiplex stream, it is only possible to do so by reversing any multiplexing that the tributary experiences. For instance, suppose an 8 Mbps signal is further multiplexed through 34 and 140 Mbps and then transmitted to Chicago. It is not possible at Chicago to extract the 8 Mbps signal directly from the 140 Mbps signal. Rather the 140 Mbps signal would have to be demultiplexed to 34, and then 8 Mbps to obtain the required level 2 signal. This is a major disadvantage of PDH in that full multiplexing equipment must be provided even though there may only be one, or a few, tributaries required to be extracted from a high-order multiplexed signal. This problem is often referred to as the **multiplex mountain**, so called because the raft of multiplexers and demultiplexers appears as a mountain pictorially, Figure 8.5, and also technically, physically in terms of the quantity of equipment necessary and economically.

8.4 Synchronous Digital Hierarchy

In the previous section on PDH we saw how 1.5 and 2 Mbps systems may be multiplexed into higher order systems operating at rates up to 565 Mbps. We saw also how two different sets of rates evolved from these two different primary rates, dependent largely upon region of operation within the world. These rates are embedded within ITU's various recommendations.

There is a problem of interoperability between different rates on an international basis. In parallel with the evolution of TDM rates there have been economic globalization and the breakdown of many national PTT monopolies to the point where there are now many TDM network operators. This in turn has led to far greater demands upon network management which now needs to deal with complex and long TDM paths crossing national borders and traversing many differently owned and operated networks. Network management support is required to locate and repair faults, for instance, as well as setting up and breaking down long international TDM links. The introduction of high-speed optical links operating at 565 Mbps and more has meant that another round of standardization was required to produce compatible multiplex systems that may satisfactorily interwork.

The difficulties and drivers outlined above led the industry to conclude that only a completely fresh approach to TDM would ultimately suffice. As a result work began in the USA to develop a new TDM standard called **Synchronous Optical Network**

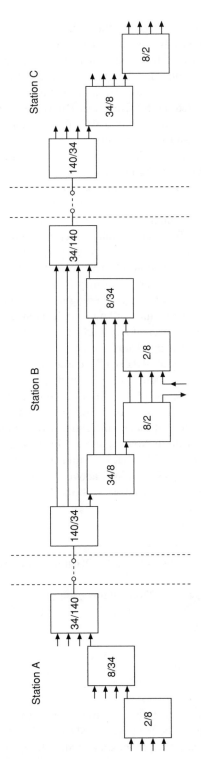

Figure 8.5 Multiplex mountain.

(SONET) that would not only resolve the earlier interoperating issues of PDH but also provide a suitable platform for further evolution of TDM systems to operate over high-speed fibre networks at 1 terabit per second, and beyond. Subsequently SONET became adopted by the ITU within G.700 series recommendations which govern PCM and TDM transmission systems. These recommendations are virtually identical to those of SONET and are called the **Synchronous Digital Hierarchy** (SDH).

A feature that is very attractive to a PTT for efficient operation and management of a network is a **drop and insert** facility, or add–drop. Add and drop is implemented in practice by means of a multiplexer, a so-called **add and drop multiplexer** (ADM). What this means is that any digital stream of the same, or lower, rate is able to be extracted from, or inserted into, a particular TDM system. As we saw earlier, the multiplex mountain problem of PDH precluded such direct operations. SDH contrasts with PDH inasmuch that very high-precision clock timing is employed with an accuracy between 1 in 10^{-9} and 10^{-11} and all equipment is synchronized to a master clock. As a result SDH is operating, for all practical purposes, as though transmitters and receivers are in perfect synchronism. This leads to one of SDH's great advantages over PDH, namely that drop and insert may be provided at any level directly. There is now no need to go through any intervening levels of multiplexing, or demultiplexing, and the multiplex mountain is eliminated. This affords appreciable cost savings because less equipment is needed and leads to a highly flexible system for the management of drop and insert provision.

The basic building block of SDH is a Synchronous Transport Module level 1 (STM-1) frame, Figure 8.6. SDH frames are generated at 8 kHz, with a duration of 125 μs, to match the standard rate used by PCM. The representation of the frame as a number of blocks (270 × 9) is merely conceptual. Each block represents 1 byte and they are numbered from the top left, along the entire row and then the leftmost position of row 2, and so on, until the bottom right-hand byte, byte 2430. A frame consists of nine rows and 270 columns. The bytes are transmitted as a bit stream in the order in which they are numbered, as described above. Frames are contiguous and therefore as soon as the last bit of byte 2430 is sent, the first bit of byte 1 of the next frame then follows immediately.

Example 8.2

Determine the rate at which an STM-1 SDH frame is transmitted.

An STM-1 frame consists of 270 columns each of nine rows of bytes.
The duration of an STM frame is 125 μs. Therefore the frequency of repetition of frames is 8 kHz. Hence:

data rate = 270 × 9 × 8 × 8 kbps
= 155.52 Mbps

The first nine columns of a frame are frame **overhead**, which means that the full 155.52 Mbps is not available for payload. SDH/SONET has a large number of overhead bytes used for a variety of purposes including frame alignment to enable the start

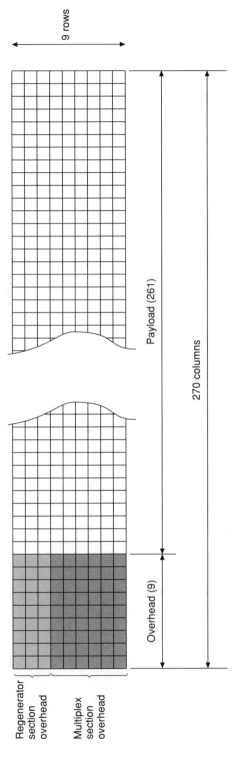

Figure 8.6 STM-1 frame structure.

of a frame to be distinguished, order wire (a dedicated speech channel for communication by technical personnel), error performance monitoring, data communications channels for network management purposes and a channel to facilitate switching to a reserve section connecting a pair of STM multiplexers in the case of failure.

The first three rows of the overhead are **regenerator section overhead** and relate to the link between two regenerators (there are usually a number of regenerator sections between a pair of multiplexers). The last six rows are **multiplex section overhead**. The multiplex section is the entire section between a pair of STM multiplexers. Halsall (1996, pp78–80) gives more detail about the organization of overhead bytes in an STM-1 frame.

Columns within an STM-1 frame enable drop and insert of lower bit rate PDH signals. For instance, a number of lower rate tributaries, for example three 34 Mbps streams, could be dropped into an STM-1 frame by allocating the requisite number of columns to each tributary.

(**Example 8.3**)
_____

Determine the number of columns required in an STM-1 frame to carry a level 4 signal which has a data rate of 139.264 Mbps.

Each column has 9 bytes. The column rate is the same as the frame rate which is 8 kHz. Therefore the data rate of one column is:

Column rate = $9 \times 8 \times 8000$ bps
              = 576 kbps

Hence number of columns = $139.264 \times 10^6/576$
                        = 241.78 columns

The payload area is 261 columns and therefore a level 4 signal can be accommodated.

In practice 242 columns would be assigned, although some bytes of one column would not be used since the data rate is not an exact multiple of the column rate.

SONET's basic frame structure is the synchronous transport signal (STS-1), as shown in Figure 8.7. Although, as with an STM-1 frame, it also has nine rows, it only has 90 columns and therefore is only a third of the size. In common with STM-1, there are some overhead bytes arranged as the leading three columns and also another column of **path overhead** within the payload area of the frame which is known as the **Synchronous Payload Environment** (SPE). The first three rows of the frame overhead are assigned as **section overhead**. The remaining six rows are for **line overhead**. (Section and line overhead are known as regenerator section and multiplex section overhead, respectively, in SDH.) In an STS-1 frame, the path overhead column does not have a fixed position within the SPE. Its precise purpose will be explained shortly. Stallings (2000a, pp256–257) presents more detail about the organization of STS-1 overhead bytes. Note that STS-1 applies to an electrical signal. The equivalent optical signal is designated optical carrier 1 (OC-1).

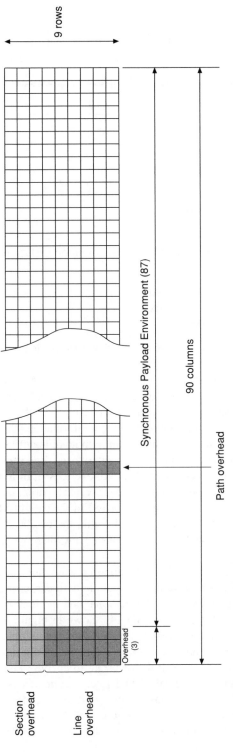

Figure 8.7 STS-1 frame structure.

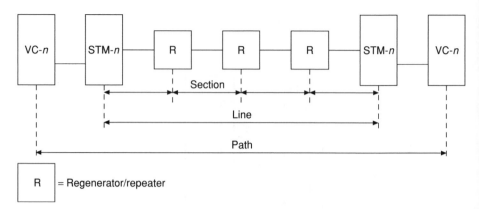

Figure 8.8 Sections, lines and paths.

An STS-1 frame, as with STM-1, has a duration of 125 μs. Therefore the data rate of the frame is:

Data rate = no. of bits/duration
= 90 × 9 × 8/125 μs
= 51.84 Mbps

and, of the 90 columns, only 86 are available for payload. Therefore a DS-3, operating at 44.736 Mbps, may readily be carried directly by an STS-1 frame. Alternatively, an STS-1 frame may carry seven DS-2 tributaries. An STM-1 frame corresponds to what SONET calls a Synchronous Transport Signal level 3 (STS-3). STM-1 and STS-3/OC-3 are designed to operate at a rate of 155 Mbps.

SDH/SONET frames contain management information relating to sections, lines and paths, Figure 8.8. A **section** is simply an individual length of transmission line and is normally connected at both ends to a regenerator. A **line** is one, or more, sections and describes the link between a pair of multiplexers. A **path** in general includes a number of lines and is the end-to-end path over which a particular **virtual container** (VC) passes. (VCs are described in detail shortly.) In the case of SDH and SONET section and line overhead bits are all contained within the overhead in the first few columns of a frame. The path overhead may be placed anywhere within the payload section of a frame.

Both STM-1 and STS-1/OC-1 can support a wide range of PDH data streams, making them flexible and backwardly compatible with earlier multiplex systems, as well as interwork successfully with other national and international networks.

The multiplexing hierarchy for SDH is shown in Figure 8.9. It may be seen that a wide range of PDH rates are supported and can be multiplexed together to form an STM-1. Each input stream is carried in a separate **container** (C) which may add bit stuffing (dummy bits) to match the data rate to enable satisfactory multiplexing as a suitable submultiple of the final STM-1 rate. A container is a payload carried over a particular path. The container has a path overhead added for end-to-end network management to form a **virtual container** (VC). In SDH the path overhead is therefore, like STS-1, also carried within the payload section of a frame. The VC is a key entity and

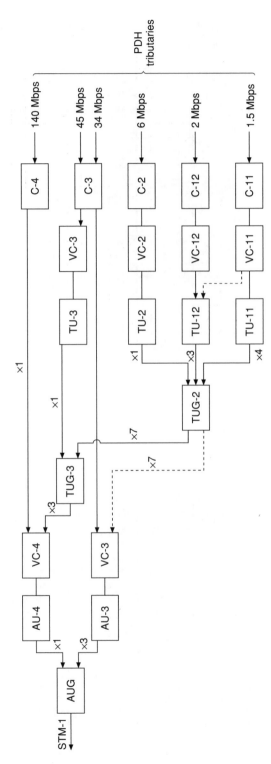

Figure 8.9 SDH multiplexing hierarchy.

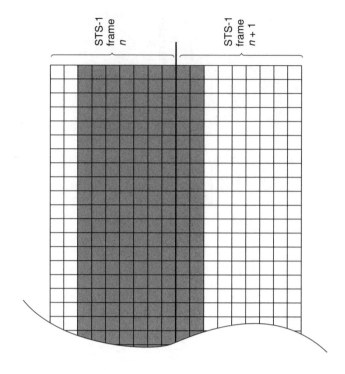

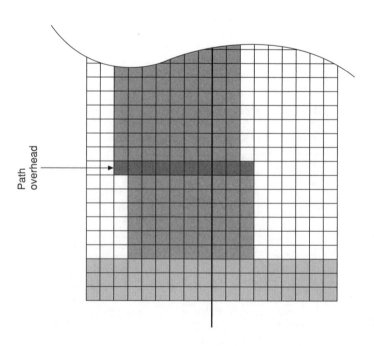

Figure 8.10 VC alignment (SONET).

is what is actually routed, transparently, through an SDH/SONET network. Containers, and VCs, have a certain logic in the way they are numbered: the first digit indicates the PDH level and the second, where present, which primary rate is contained; 2 indicates 2 Mpbs, and 1 is 1.5 Mbps.

VCs are then **aligned** into a **tributary unit** (TU) or, in the case of a VC-4, directly into an **administrative unit** (AU). Alignment simply positions the first byte of a VC frame at a convenient point within the TU/AU frame and sets a **pointer**, within the path overhead, to indicate the position of the first byte. The use of TU and AUs enable VCs to be aligned 'on the fly' immediately they appear without having to wait for the start of the next TU/AU to provide flexibility and reduce delay through multiplex stages. This does, however, mean that in general a VC will straddle two consecutive TU/AUs. The sizes of AUs and VCs, and TUs and VCs, are similar. AUs and TUs are slightly larger than their corresponding VCs since they also include a pointer.

Figure 8.10 shows how a VC-3 container might be aligned into an AU-3 in the case of SONET. The start position of the aligned payload is indicated by a **pointer** held in the line overhead portion of the frame. Note, too, how the column containing the first byte of the payload defines the column where the path overhead is located. Hence the position of the path overhead within the SPE is defined by where the next free byte happens to fall within a frame. The first three columns of each frame retain their significance, as indicated in Figure 8.7.

Returning to Figure 8.9, a number of TUs are, with the exception of a 140 Mbps tributary, multiplexed together to form a **tributary unit group** (TUG). A TUG-2 may consist of one C-2, or be formed by multiplexing a number of 2 Mbps, or 1.5 Mbps, tributaries together. A TUG-3 may comprise one 34, or 45, Mbps tributary, or seven TUG-2s multiplexed together. Similarly, three TUG-3s multiplexed together form a VC-4 which is aligned into an AU-4. Multiplexing of TUs into a TUG, and TUGs into a VC, is done in a cyclical, or round-robin, manner on a column-by-column basis. For instance, suppose four TU-11s are to be multiplexed into a TUG-2. One column of one tributary is placed into the TUG-2 structure, followed by one column from the next, and so on. After four columns have been assembled, the second column of the first tributary is then taken, and so on.

If, in Figure 8.9, one works out the final STM-1 rate it will of course be found to be approximately 155 Mbps. Therefore, working backwards, it is clear that an AU-3 has a rate which is approximately one-third of an STM-1 and therefore may be used to form one STS-1 frame. It is now possible to see, from Figure 8.9, how PDH tributaries up to 45 Mbps (DS-3) are multiplexed into an STS-1 frame. STM-1 and STS-1/OC-1 frames can be further multiplexed to form higher order SDH rates similar to those shown in Table 8.2. Higher order STMs and STSs/OCs are formed by interleaving on a column-by-column basis as was explained earlier for the case of TUs and TUGs. In practice STS-9, 18, 24, 36 and 96 are not usually implemented today.

Table 8.2   SONET and SDH classifications and data rates.

SONET	SDH	Data rate (Mbps)	Payload rate (Mbps)
STS-1		51.84	50.112
STS-3	STM-1	155.52	150.336
STS-9		466.56	451.008
STS-12	STM-4	622.08	601.344
STS-18		933.12	902.016
STS-24		1244.16	1202.688
STS-36		1866.24	1804.032
STS-48	STM-16	2488.32	2405.376
STS-96		4976.64	4810.752
STS-192	STM-64	9953.28	9621.504

Exercises

8.1   A four-way multiplexer has, over a period of time equal to four input bits, the following bit sequences on its input channels: Channel A, 1001; Channel B, 1100; Channel C, 0101; and Channel D, 0010. Sketch carefully to a common time axis, in a manner similar to Figure 8.2, the signals of each input channel and the associated multiplexed waveform.

8.2   Explain the term 'multiplex mountain' and discuss the problems that it creates.

8.3   In relation to SDH discuss the following terms and make clear the differences between them:
(a) section
(b) line
(c) path.

8.4   Describe in detail how sixty-three 2 Mbps PDH tributaries may be multiplexed into a single STM-1 frame.

Chapter 9

Introduction to local area networks

LANs generally encompass a small physical area, no more than a few kilometres in diameter, and are usually confined within a single site. There may be as many as several hundred stations. LANs use relatively high signalling rates, originally of the order of 10 Mbps, but now typically 100 Mbps, and even as high as 1 Gbps. This chapter is an introduction to LANs and reviews the mechanisms to control station access to the network and also makes some comparisons of their performance. The next chapter will examine the standards for lower speed LAN operation up to a few tens of Mbps. Higher speed LANs, operating at 100 Mbps and beyond, are discussed in Chapter 11.

Messages within a LAN are transmitted as a series of variable length frames using transmission media which introduce only relatively low error rates. Since the length of the medium in a LAN is, unlike in WANs, relatively short, propagation delay tends to be short. Athough real-time services such as voice and video are carried over LANs, their frame-based transmissions tend to be more suited to data applications. This is because delay may be unpredictable and hence, on occasion, excessive for real-time use. In addition, transmission capacity has tended to be insufficient to meet the high-data-rate demands of video. However, with the emergence of 100 Mbps operation and beyond, coupled with advances in compression, real-time and multimedia operation is now feasible in many LANs.

A LAN comprises three hardware elements, namely a transmission medium, a controlling mechanism or protocol to govern access to the transmission medium, and an interface between the station and transmission medium. A software element is required to implement the medium access protocol for intercommunication between stations and for preparation of frames for transmission, and vice versa. These hardware and software elements, all of which are implemented at the lowest two layers of the

OSI Reference Model, are usually combined into a **Network Interface Card** (NIC), also known as a **Network Adapter**. An NIC interfaces with a standard computer such as a PC and at the physical layer connects to the particular transmission media to be used. Another software element is therefore also required to regulate the interface between the computer system and NIC.

9.1 Medium Access Control

The media used in LANs generally convey frames from only one station at a time, although the media themselves are generally shared by a number of stations. In order to overcome the difficulties which may arise through sharing, a **Medium Access Control** (MAC) mechanism or protocol is necessary. A MAC protocol merely regulates how stations may access the medium in an orderly fashion for correct operation and also attempts to ensure that each station obtains a fair share of its use.

LAN networks usually have only a single medium over which all messages, represented over a series of frames, are transmitted. If the medium is not being used two, or more, stations may simultaneously attempt an access, leading to a collision. An MAC technique is therefore required to regulate access by stations to the medium and handle the effect of two, or more, stations simlultaneously attempting to acces the medium. There is also the danger that once a pair of stations have established communication, all other stations may be excluded, perhaps indefinitely, or at least for a considerable period of time.

A LAN does not usually have any separate network control function for operation. Nor is a separate control function required to detect abnormal network conditions, or to control recovery therefrom. Rather, each station is generally equally responsible in a LAN, in which case control is said to be **fully distributed**.

Three general MAC techniques exist for use within fully distributed networks:

1. Contention: Here there is no regulating mechanism directly to govern stations attempting to access a medium. Rather, two or more stations may contend for the medium and any multiple simultaneous accesses are resolved as they arise.

2. Token passing: A single **token** exists within the network and is passed between stations in turn. Only a station holding the token may use the medium for transmission. This eliminates multiple simultaneous accesses of the medium with the attendant risk of collision.

3. Slotted and register insertion rings: Similar in principle to token passing, but a unique time interval is granted to a station for transmission.

Carrier Sense Multiple Access

Many modern LANs evolved from a LAN known as **Aloha** which was one of the first primitive LANs to be developed. Aloha was packet based and used radio as its transmission medium. It was used by the University of Hawaii in the early 1970s to interconnect stations spread across a group of islands. When a station wished to transmit it did so immediately with no regard for whether, or not, another station was using the medium. Inevitably this lead on occasion to two, or more, simultaneous transmissions all of which would corrupt each other's transmissions and render communication useless. The effect of simultaneous transmission is to produce a **collision**. A flow control protocol was employed to identify any packets which become lost in the way described and arrange for their repeat transmission.

A simple improvement which could be made to Aloha is to 'listen' to activity, for example the presence of an RF carrier, prior to transmitting a frame. If there is no RF carrier present the medium may be assumed to be idle and a station may then make an access. This **carrier sense** strategy is also known as **Listen Before Talk** (LBT). If there is activity, a station may **defer** its transmission for a period of time and try again later. As there are usually a number of stations in a LAN, the possibility remains that several stations might access a single radio channel, or medium, simultaneously. Such multiple accesses will all fail and each station would have to attempt access again.

This improved scenario compared with Aloha is known as a **Carrier Sense Multiple Access** (CSMA) MAC protocol. Although not used on its own, CSMA nevertheless forms a part of some important MAC protocols in use today. In CSMA each station has equal status (fully distributed control) and follows a strict protocol for gaining access to the medium. It is assumed that only a single medium exists for access and hence the MAC protocol is contention based.

CSMA is not confined to networks using radio as the medium. Other early LANs which were cable based also made use of CSMA and behaved in a similar manner since a single medium was available to, and shared by, every station. The scenario described, coupled with a single medium for which stations contend for access, is conceptually akin to a bus topology, as described in Chapter 2.

LBT gives rise to two problems:

1. Two or more stations may listen to the bus at the same time, both detect absence of carrier, transmit simultaneously and a collision results.
2. Even if only one station makes an access then, because of the finite velocity of propagation of the signal, a second distant station may perceive the bus to be inactive for a very small interval of time after the first station commences transmission. If the second station transmits within this interval a collision will occur.

In the extreme case stations may be located at either end of the medium. When one station sends a frame the other is unaware of its presence until the frame has propagated the full length of the medium. Up until that moment the distant station may send a frame. The time interval between a station commencing transmission of a frame and the point in time whereafter a collision may no longer occur is known as the **vulnerable time** and is equivalent to the largest time interval between two stations (the two most distant) in the network.

The next section discusses various deferral strategies which, when used in an optimal manner, arrange for CSMA to have improved performance in terms of throughput compared with Aloha.

Persistence algorithms

There are a number of deferral strategies, or algorithms, used in CSMA for dealing with a station which discovers the medium to be busy.

1-persistent

A station wishing to transmit waits until the medium is free. When the medium is, or becomes, free any waiting station(s) transmit immediately. Waiting stations therefore have a probability of 1 of transmitting associated with them once the medium becomes free. This persistence algorithm means that where two or more stations are waiting, or deferring, a collision always results.

Non-persistent

Here, if the medium is busy, a station waits a period of time determined by a probability distribution and then re-examines the medium to see if it has become free. This deferral period is also called the **back-off time**. Two or more deferring stations are unlikely to be assigned the same back-off time. Hence the probability of two or more stations retrying simultaneously, with a resultant collision, is small. In general, such an approach means that when the medium becomes free, it often may not be used immediately because stations waiting to transmit may still be deferring.

P-persistent

This algorithm is a compromise between the previous two algorithms. It attempts to reduce collisions and also the time during which the medium is idle when stations are deferring. It generally offers improved performance.

Each station, upon detecting that the medium is free, transmits with a probability P. This, in comparison with the 1-persistent algorithm, reduces collisions due to two or more stations waiting for the medium to become idle. If the station fails to transmit, the probability of this occurring being $1-P$, it defers. Usually, deferral is for one time slot in a synchronous system, or at least twice the maximum propagation delay in an asynchronous system. If, after deferring, the medium is found to be busy again, the whole procedure is repeated. A number of probabilities are used in practice. In general, the lower the probability P, the lower the probability of collision and the greater the throughput attainable. Figure 9.1 compares the various CSMA protocols along with those for Aloha. Note that in the case of P-persistent algorithms, curves for $P = 0.5$, 0.1 and 0.01 are shown. Slotted Aloha is not discussed in this text.

Carrier Sense Multiple Access/Collision Detection

With CSMA, any collisions which occur are not immediately apparent to a station and the whole frame is transmitted. **Carrier Sense Multiple Access/Collision Detection** (CSMA/CD) MAC uses CSMA and a persistence strategy in the case of the medium being busy. However, with CSMA/CD, once a station commences transmission it

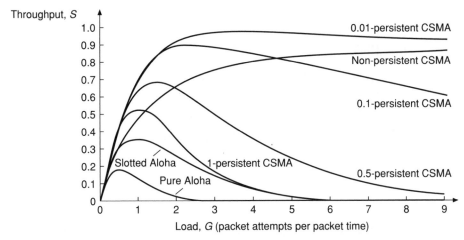

Figure 9.1 Comparison of Aloha and CSMA. Source: Stallings, William, *Data and Computer Communications*, 3rd edn, © 1991, p. 350. Reprinted by permission of Pearson Education, Inc. Upper Saddle River, NJ.

monitors its own transmissions on the medium and if it detects a collision, it ceases to transmit the remainder of its frame. Hence CSMA/CD releases the medium much earlier than is the case with Aloha and CSMA. Upon detection of a collision a **jamming signal** is transmitted immediately upon cessation of frame transmission. This ensures that all stations know that a collision has occurred; this is necessary because two colliding stations which are very close may both cease transmitting before either of their transmissions has fully propagated throughout the medium to other stations. Finally, stations perform a random back-off and then reattempt transmission using LBT.

The CSMA/CD algorithm may be summarized as follows:

1. Listen before talk.

2. If free, transmit and monitor transmission.

3. If busy, defer.

4. If a collision occurs during transmission, stop transmitting.

5. Send a jamming signal.

6. Random back-off.

7. Retry with LBT.

Consider the case shown in Figure 9.2 where station *A* is located at one end of the medium and station *B* at the opposite end. Suppose that station *A* sends a frame. Until the frame reaches station *B*, it too may send a frame. Suppose that station *B* chooses to send a frame at the exact moment that station *A*'s frame arrives at *B*. Station *A* will only become aware of a collision when station *B*'s frame has propagated the full length of the medium. The **collision window** is the interval in time between a station comencing frame transmission and the instant that it becomes aware that its frame has collided. This equals twice the propagation delay between stations *A* and *B* and is equal to twice the vulnerable time. The jamming signal must therefore be at least equal in

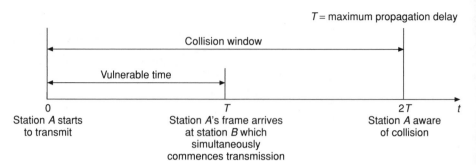

Figure 9.2   CSMA/CD collision mechanism.

time to the collision window in order to ensure correct operation of the deferral mechanism used by each station.

There is no reason why in CSMA frames need to be of fixed length. LANs, as we shall see, generally employ variable length frames. These have the advantage that their length may be adjusted to accommodate to an extent the length of the message, or data, that they have encapsulated within them. This can make for more efficient use of the network. Where only a small amount of data is to be transmitted, as in, say, an ACK, only a short frame may be necessary, in which case the medium occupancy is reduced and it is freed up as soon as possible for other stations to use, should they wish to. However, as with the jamming signal, frames are also arranged in time to be at least equal to the collision window.

LANs usually have frames of much greater duration than the collision window. In the worst case with CSMA/CD, the amount of time wasted in a collision equals the collision window interval plus the additional duration until the end of the jamming signal. This is appreciably less time than with CSMA where a complete frame is sent. It follows that the use of collision detection considerably reduces time wasted on the medium and so enables improved throughput compared with CSMA.

LAN performance will be examined in detail shortly. It will be seen that CSMA/CD throughput is similar to that of CSMA for networks which comprise a small number of stations. However, where more stations are connected to a network, CSMA/CD offers higher throughput.

Collision Avoidance

A network may have a central controller which governs (single) station access to the medium. Such a network is not contention based but is said to be **contention free**, in which case collisions may be prevented. In contention-based networks, where no such access central control exists, collisions are quite possible. However, collisions may be avoided if stations are constrained inasmuch that they cannot transmit at any time that the medium is free. Such a technique is known as **Collision Avoidance** (CA) and ensures that transmitting stations only transmit at optimal times when it is unlikely that other stations will commence transmission and hence avoid, or at least minimize, the risk

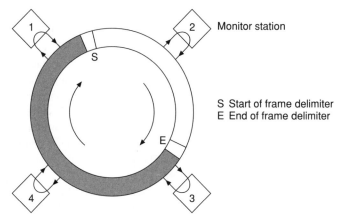

Figure 9.3   Token passing.

of a collision. In order for this to work stations understand the protocol in use and by monitoring activity on the medium may deduce suitable times to transmit when it is unlikely to cause a collision. In general, collisions are not completely eliminated, but can be considerably reduced. An example of the use of CA may be found in the next chapter where it is used in wireless LANs.

Control tokens

Token-based access strategies, Figure 9.3, rely upon the establishment of a physical or logical ring. A logical ring is a network which has a topology normally arranged as a bus. In such a situation frames, although broadcast to all stations, are only relayed by one station. It is then arranged that stations continue to relay frames in a pre-arranged sequence which gives the appearance that the stations are arranged as though they form a ring. Upon initialization of the network a single token is created and circulates around each station on the ring in turn. A station wishing to transmit a frame waits for the token to arrive at its node and then commences transmission. It should be pointed out that in practice rings additionally also employ a priority scheme whereby the token may have one of a number of priority levels assigned to it. Under these circumstances, a station may only seize a token if it has adequate priority. Stations are assigned priority as part of normal LAN management by a network administrator. When a station has finished transmitting, or if it is timed out, the token is reinserted and circulates the ring until seized by a station again.

The CSMA/CD MAC protocol is usually deployed in a bus or star-based network. In such networks the bus may be **passive** where each attached device is connected to the bus in such a way that it does not form part of the transmission path. Stations using token-based MACs can also be passive. However, in general, stations are usually **active**, as indicated in Figure 9.3, where they are inserted into the transmission medium and electronically **relay**, or repeat, signals received on their incoming port to their outgoing port.

The use of tokens introduces a high degree of control and order with regard to stations accessing the bus. They eliminate collisions and hence make for much higher throughput than contention-based networks. However, compared with contention-based networks, great care is needed to guard against a station which has obtained a token preventing any other stations transmitting by failing to release the token. It is for this reason that stations are usually individually assigned a **token holding time** (THT) which limits the maximum amount of time that a station may continue to transmit frames before it is obliged to release the token, even though it may still have further frames to transmit. Provision also has to be made to enable stations to be added to, or removed from, the network. The possibility also exists that the token may be lost or duplicated. In a well-designed token network, the MAC protocol needs to be quite sophisticated compared with contention-based protocols.

Another consideration is that of release of a token. A token may be released at the receiver or the transmitter. The former technique has the advantage that the medium is freed much earlier but an acknowledgement is required to confirm that the frame has been correctly received. Release at the transmitter can arrange for the recipient of frames to mark them to indicate that they have been successfully received. This may then be checked by the transmitter. The process eliminates any need for acknowledgement and is therefore simpler to implement.

Finally, one station may be designated a **monitor**, which has responsibility for functions such as ring management and operation. An example is the creation of a token upon initialization. Another function of a monitor is to guard against the endless circulation of a frame. Suppose a station seizes a token and then transmits a frame. If this frame is never removed by any station and in consequence a new token is not released, no other station is able to send any frames.

9.2 LAN performance

In Section 9.1 we discussed the two principal MAC protocols used within a LAN, namely CSMA/CD and token operation. As already indicated, LAN performance may vary according to the MAC protocol used, as well as other factors, such as transmission rate and number of stations. In this section we shall compare the performance of CSMA/CD and token passing. This comparison will conveniently conclude our general discussion on LANs and prepare the way for consideration of the specific details appertaining to LANs which conform to IEEE standards.

Firstly, we shall make a generalized analysis of both contention and token-type networks to enable a performance comparison to be made between CSMA/CD and token-based networks. In assessing network performance a number of factors may be regarded as independent of the attached devices and as purely attributable to network implementation. The following factors may be thought of as variables which affect performance:

- medium transmission speed, or capacity
- propagation delay
- length in bits

- MAC protocol
- load offered by stations
- number of stations
- error rate.

The first two variables have a profound effect upon performance in terms of maximum throughput. They characterize the network but, from a design consideration, can be thought of as constants as they are usually static for a particular network.

The frame length and MAC protocol are very much under the control, or at least selection, of a network designer. Load and number of stations are independent variables. This means that a system could be proposed and its performance analysed for varying load and number of stations to seek either the best network for given variables, or a limit to the variables. Errors may be controlled by overlaying protection or correction at the data link layer, or by employing retransmission techniques at the transport layer. In the absence of errors such protection inevitably leads to some reduction in throughput.

Measures of performance

Firstly, we must consider basic measures of performance. Two measures of performance commonly used are:

1. S, the throughput of the network. This was defined in Chapter 5. An alternative way of expressing S is as the effective (or mean) data transmission rate between stations. This often includes overheads in assembling frames such as headers and trailers but does not include retries. In consequence the effective data rate is lower when considering data throughput in practice.
2. D, delay – the time that elapses between a frame being assembled ready for transmission and the completion of successful transmission. It is caused by factors such as LBT, persistence algorithms and collisions which increase delay due to their attendant retransmission(s).

───────────────────────────

Example 9.1

Over a period of 1.8 s, 300 frames are transmitted over a 10 Mbps bus. Determine the effective throughput as a percentage of bus capacity. Assume that the average frame length is 782 bytes of which 750 convey data.

Throughput S in bps is obtained as follows:

$$\frac{\text{Number of frames} \times \text{average number of bits per frame}}{\text{transmission time}} = \frac{300 \times 782 \times 8 \text{ bits}}{1.8 \text{ s}}$$

$$= 1.042\ 67 \text{ Mps}$$

Normalizing S with respect to the bus capacity by expressing throughput against bus capacity gives:

$$S = \frac{1\ 042\ 670}{10 \times 10^6} = 0.1043$$

or approximately 10% of the potential medium capacity.

If the frame overhead bits are ignored, effective throughput in terms of actual data can be determined:

$$S = 0.010\ 43 \times 750/786$$
$$= 0.09\ 953$$

Frame overhead represents about 4.6% of the actual throughput.

A graph of throughput S may be plotted against the load (G) presented to a network. Ideally, as indicated in Figure 9.4, one might expect throughput to equal the load until throughput reaches a maximum of 1. Thereafter network throughput may not be increased any further and the network is now congested. In practice, under low utilization, S and G tend to be the same. S is ultimately limited, mainly by the medium capacity, but also by the MAC protocol used. In consequence, as a network becomes more heavily loaded throughput rises more slowly with load than in the ideal case, as demonstrated in Figure 9.1. Eventually a point occurs where any further rise in G causes no further increase in S and this often occurs at appreciably lower throughput than 1. Note that G would normally include repeat frames and any other non-data frames such as tokens.

Intuitively, we can expect delay D to increase with G. As load increases the mean time to gain access to the medium, or delay, rises. This is due to an increased

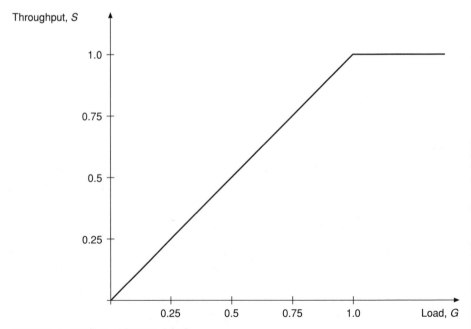

Figure 9.4 Medium utilization (ideal).

probability of a collision and attendant delay before retrying in contention-based networks. In token-based networks, the busier they become the longer a given station may have to wait for all stations ahead of it to gain a token, send their frame(s) and release the token. Hence mean token waiting time, or delay, is increased.

Propagation delay and frame transmission time

Another parameter which has a profound effect upon network performance is the ratio of propagation delay to that of frame size. We shall call this ratio the **transmission coefficient**, a:

$$a = \frac{\text{propagation delay}}{\text{frame transmission time}} \tag{9.1}$$

Propagation delay is simply the time it takes for a signal to propagate from a sending station to a receiver. Frame transmission time is the time it takes to transmit all of the bits of a frame, which equals the equivalent duration in time of a frame, onto the physical medium. As we shall see shortly, a is a useful parameter for analysing and comparing LANs.

Alternatively, and often more conveniently, a can be expressed as:

$$a = \frac{\text{length of medium}}{\text{length of frame}} \tag{9.2}$$

where frame transmission time is replaced by the equivalent physical distance occupied by the frame at one instant.

In analysing LAN performance it is assumed that the propagation delay is a maximum. This corresponds to the medium length being a maximum. Consider a perfectly efficient access mechanism that allows only one transmission at a time (no collisions). Additionally, as soon as one transmission finishes, the next commences immediately and frames contain data only, with no overhead. This idealistic model enables an upper bound on performance to be determined for varying medium lengths and hence different values of a.

To determine an upper bound for S as a function of a, some other terms must be introduced:

R, data rate of channel (bps)
d, maximum distance between any pair of stations
V, velocity of propagation (m/s)
L, frame length (assume an average if variable) (bits)

Throughput S may be expressed as:

$$S = \frac{\text{duration of one frame}}{\text{time occupied by medium for transmission of one frame}} \tag{9.3}$$

$$S = \frac{L/R}{d/V + L/R} \tag{9.4}$$

Similarly, a may be related to R, d, v and L thus:

$$a = \frac{\text{propagation time}}{\text{frame duration}} \qquad (9.5)$$

where propagation time is assumed to be the maximum possible. Therefore:

$$a = \frac{d/V}{L/R} \qquad (9.6)$$

$$a = \frac{Rd}{LV} \qquad (9.7)$$

Therefore:

$$L/R = d/aV \qquad (9.8)$$

and:

$$d/V = aL/R \qquad (9.9)$$

Substituting (9.8) and (9.9) into (9.4):

$$S = \frac{d/aV}{aL/R + d/aV} \qquad (9.10)$$

which simplifies to:

$$S = \frac{1}{1 + a} \qquad (9.11)$$

From (9.11) it is clear that throughput has a maximum value of 1 and is inversely proportional to a. Figure 9.5 illustrates the effect of a upon throughput, S. When $a = 0$, S increases in direct proportion to G until 100% utilization is achieved. Any further increase in G results in saturation. Any increase in a, as expected from (9.11), causes saturation to occur at a lower value of S. It is clear from the graphs that $1/(1 + a)$ forms an upper bound upon utilization or efficiency, irrespective of the access control mechanism used by the network.

Since an increase in a decreases network throughput, design should attempt to make a as small as possible. One method of achieving this is to keep the medium length as short as possible. There are clearly practical limits to this. Alternatively, the effect of a can be reduced by increasing the length of a frame. However, if messages are appreciably shorter than the frame length no advantage results. A disadvantage of long frames is that transmission delay is increased and, if collisions occur, the effective load to be carried by the network may increase. Ideally, messages should be equal to an integral number of frames to optimize efficiency. Then no short frames occur and throughput is maximized.

The foregoing is based upon the worst case and assumes that the maximum propagation time always occurs. This is patently not the case for every transmission for the particular type of network topologies discussed. For instance, the mean propagation

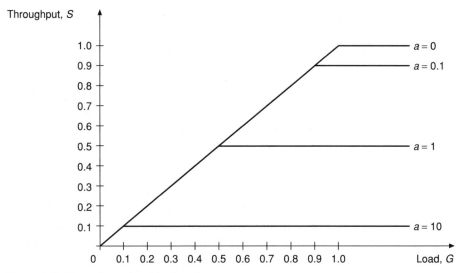

Figure 9.5 Throughput as a function of *a*.

time between two adjacent stations in a token ring releasing the token at the receiver would be considerably shorter than the maximum.

Protocol performance

To compare different types of protocol, a valid basis for comparison, or model, must be established. The model we shall use assumes the following:

- N active stations connected to the network.
- Propagation time is normalized such that it has a maximum, or worst-case value, equal to a.
- Each station is always prepared to transmit a frame. Although not true in practice, this does enable a maximum value of throughput S to be determined, which is one of the major considerations in both design and operation of a network.

Token ring performance

Ring activity, in both token ring and token bus networks, alternates between frame transmission and token passing. Consider the case of a single data frame followed by a token which we can regard as a cycle. Firstly, some definitions: let T_1 be the average time taken for a station to transmit a data frame; and T_2 be the average time elapsed between one station gaining a token and the next station receiving a token. T_2 can also be regarded as the cycle time or the average time required per station to complete the transmission of a frame.

From (9.3) it is clear that normalized system throughputs may be expressed as:

$$S = \frac{T_1}{T_2} \tag{9.12}$$

That is, the time required to transmit one frame expressed as a fraction of the total time that the medium is occupied, or cycle time. Now consider the effect that a has upon throughput. For the analysis, frame duration T_1 will be normalized to 1 and therefore, from (9.2), propagation time becomes equal to a.

Firstly, consider the case when the medium is physically short in relation to the duration of a frame: thus a is less than 1. In this case, the transmitter receives the start of its frame *before* it has finished transmitting the end of the frame. We shall assume that the token is, as is usual, released at the transmitter, in which case the station releases a token immediately it ceases transmission of its frame. Hence the time elapsed between receiving a token and releasing a token is T_1 and equal to the normalized time interval of 1. The token is received by the next station after some time interval owing to propagation between stations. The average value of time to pass a token between stations is a/N. Hence, since each station is always prepared to transmit a frame, $T_2 = T_1 + a/N$. Substituting into (9.12), and where $T_1 = 1$, yields:

$$S = \frac{1}{1 + a/N}, \, a < 1 \tag{9.13}$$

Now consider a ring of medium length where the propagation delay exceeds that of a frame, that is a greater than 1. A transmitting station receives the start of its frame after the frame has propagated the full distance of the ring, that is after time interval a, since propagation time is normalized to a. It is at this point that the token may be released by the transmitter. The average time to pass the token is, as before, a/N. S now becomes:

$$S = \frac{1}{a + a/N}, \, a > 1 \tag{9.14}$$

$$S = \frac{1}{a(1 + 1/N)}, \, a > 1 \tag{9.15}$$

We may now compare (9.13) and (9.15). When the medium is physically long, or frames are short, a is greater than 1. Throughput, if N is reasonably large, is to a close approximation degraded by the factor a compared with relatively short medium lengths or long frames, when a is less than 1. It is not surprising that throughput diminishes with increasing medium length. A new token cannot successfully be applied until the current frame has traversed the medium when token is released at the transmitter. The longer the medium, the lower the rate of application of successful frames; hence throughput is reduced.

CSMA/CD performance

The analysis of throughput for this MAC technique is more complex than that for token ring operation and relies upon probability theory. Such an analysis is beyond the scope

Table 9.1 Effect of signalling rate, frame size and medium length upon transmission coefficient, *a*.

Signalling rate (Mbps)	Medium length (m)	Frame size (bits)	Transmission coefficient, *a*
10	50	100	0.025
		1 000	0.0025
		10 000	0.000 25
	200	100	0.1
		1 000	0.01
		10 000	0.001
100	50	100	0.25
		1 000	0.025
		10 000	0.0025
	200	100	1
		1 000	0.1
		10 000	0.001
1000	50	100	2.5
		1 000	0.25
		10 000	0.025
	200	100	10
		1 000	100
		10 000	1000

of this text but it may be shown (Stallings 1991, pp413–418) that in the limit, as the number of stations N becomes very large, S has a maximum possible value:

$$S_{max} = 1, \ a < 1 \tag{9.16}$$

Or:

$$S_{max} = 1/a, \ a > 1 \tag{9.17}$$

Some typical values of *a* are shown in Table 9.1. Note that where signalling rate is less than 1 Mbps or medium length is under 1000 m, then the value of *a* becomes negligible.

Figure 9.6 shows the throughput for both types of MAC with various values of *a* (Figure 9.6a) and numbers of stations (Figure 9.6b). As might be expected intuitively, token LANs outperform CSMA/CD under almost all circumstances.

Table 9.1 uses parameters for the determination of *a* that are fairly representative of those found within CSMA/CD-based LANs today. In Figure 9.6 we saw how, in order to achieve optimal performance in terms of throughput, *a* should be much less than 1. The table illustrates how this ideal situation is more easily achieved at lower speed transmission. Increasing speeds of operation that now prevail of hundreds of Mbps, or more, mitigate against satisfactory throughput unless either frames, or medium length, tend towards being short. Fortunately, because signals deteriorate more rapidly with distance at higher speed operation, higher speed LAN standards use media of shorter length. Therefore, to some extent, acceptable throughput is retained in LANs which operate at high speed.

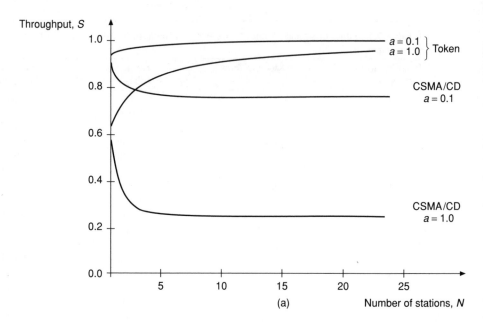

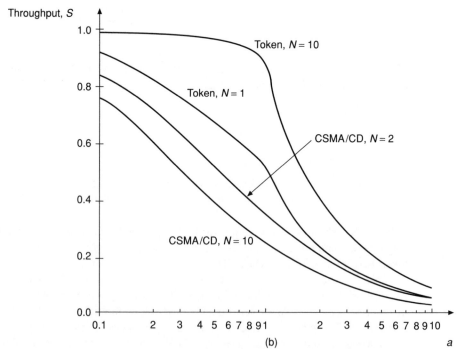

Figure 9.6 Throughput comparison of CSMA/CD and token ring: (a) values of *a*; (b) numbers of stations. Source: Stallings, William, *Data and Computer Communications*, 4th edn, © 1994, pp416, 417. Reprinted by permission of Pearson Education, Inc., Upper Saddle River, NJ.

Example 9.2

If the signalling rate is 100 Mbps and frame length 2000 bits, calculate the value of a for the following medium lengths:

(a) 250 m

(b) 4000 m

Assume signal propagation, typical of twisted-pair cable, to be 2×10^8 m/s.

(a) a is given by:

$$a = \frac{\text{propagation delay}}{\text{frame transmission time}}$$

$$\text{Propagation delay} = \frac{250 \text{ m}}{2 \times 10^8 \text{ m/s}} = 1.25 \text{ } \mu s$$

$$\text{Frame transmission time} = \frac{\text{no. of frame bits}}{\text{signalling rate}} = \frac{2000 \text{ bits}}{100 \text{ Mbps}} = 20 \text{ } \mu s$$

Therefore:

$$a = 1.25/20 = 0.0625$$

(b) If the medium length is changed from 250 m to 4000 m then a is increased by 4000/250 or 16 times. Hence a becomes 1, which would lead to a marked deterioration in throughput under heavy-load conditions.

Exercises

9.1 Distinguish between vulnerable time and collision window.

9.2 Explain two key advantages of CSMA/CD compared with CSMA which result in improved performance.

9.3 Explain why a CSMA/CD bus may be idle, even though some stations have frames to transmit.

9.4 Explain how the P-persistence algorithm used with CSMA/CD networks attempts to improve bus efficiency compared with 1-persistence and non-persistence algorithms.

9.5 Draw flowcharts to illustrate the CSMA/CD protocol, including an appropriate persistence algorithm, for:
(a) a transmitting station
(b) a receiving station.

9.6 A CSMA/CD-based LAN operates at 100 Mbps with a utilization of 30%. Calculate:

(a) the number of information bits transmitted per second
(b) the ratio between medium activity and idle time
(c) the duration in time of a frame consisting of
  (i) 18 bytes (IEEE 802.3 minimum frame length) and
  (ii) 1526 bytes.

Compare each frame's length in time with the equivalent length of cable which would produce a similar time duration. (Assume that signals propagate in a cable at approximately two-thirds of the speed of free space propagation.)

9.7 An upper bound for utilization U of a CSMA/CD-based LAN may be expressed by:

$$S = 1 \quad a < 1, \quad S = 1/a, \quad a > 1$$

where a is given by:

$$a = \frac{\text{propagation time}}{\text{frame transmission time}}$$

Estimate the utilization of a 10 Mbps network with a maximum length of 500 m if a frame is transmitted with:
(a) a size of 1526 bytes
(b) a size of 18 bytes
(c) Explain why utilization may be substantially reduced with small frame sizes or long lengths of cable.

9.8 Compare the relative merits of LANs using ring, bus and star physical media.

9.9 Consider the transfer of a file containing a million characters from one station to another. What is the total elapsed time and effective throughput for the following cases?
(a) A circuit-switched, star topology local network. Call set-up time is negligible and the data rate is 64 kbps.
(b) A bus topology local area network with two stations D apart, a data rate of B bps, and a frame size P with 80 bits of overhead. Each frame is acknowledged with an 88-bit frame before the next is sent. The propagation speed on the bus is 200 m/μs:

	D (km)	B (Mbps)	P (bits)
(i)	1	1	256
(ii)	1	10	256
(iii)	10	1	256
(iv)	1	50	10 000

(c) A ring topology with a total circular length of $2D$, with two stations a distance D apart. Acknowledgement is achieved by allowing a frame to circulate past the destination station, back to the source station. There are N repeaters on the ring, each of which introduces a delay of 1 bit time. Repeat the calculation for each case as in (b) for $N = 10$, 100 and 1000.

9.10 In token ring systems, suppose that the destination station removes the data frame and immediately sends a short acknowledgement frame to the sender, rather than letting the original frame return to the sender. How does this affect performance?

LAN standards

The previous chapter explored the two main MAC protocols used in LANs and also compared their performance. This chapter concentrates upon IEEE standards for wired LANs operating at speeds up to 10 or 16 Mbps. It concludes with an examination of standards for wireless LAN operation at up to 54 Mbps. Chapter 11 includes details on higher speed LANs, operating at 100 Mbps, and beyond.

10.1 IEEE 802.2

The IEEE 802.3, 4 and 5 LAN standards, which will be discussed in detail shortly, primarily specify details relating to the respective MAC protocol and various layer 1 arrangements, for example details relating to the medium such as transmission rate. IEEE 802.2, as discussed in Chapter 1, is a standard common to all three LAN standards above and is a **Logical Link Control** (LLC) protocol responsible for addressing and data link control. Figure 10.1 shows the three layers found in the IEEE 802 standards and their comparison with the OSI Reference Model layers.

Figure 10.2 illustrates how an *N*-layer protocol data unit (*N*-PDU) is passed from the network layer via the LLC layer to the MAC layer where a frame is formed for transmission onto the medium. The LLC layer provides a data link control function, much of which is based upon HDLC, and discussed in Chapter 5. Three types of service are offered:

1. Unacknowledged connectionless mode: No flow or error control. If required, flow and error control may be added at a higher layer.

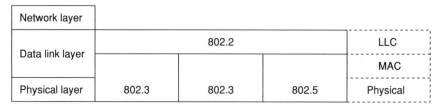

Figure 10.1   IEEE 802 and OSI.

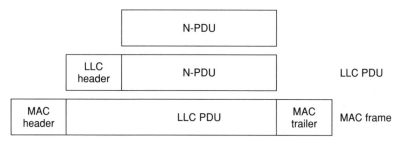

Figure 10.2   LLC layer and MAC frame.

2. Connection-oriented (CO) mode: Similar to that offered by HDLC whereby a logical connection is offered with error and flow control.

3. Acknowledged connectionless mode: A datagram service, similar to service 1, but with acknowledgement of frames.

All three types of service use a standard LLC PDU format shown in Figure 10.3. The three leftmost fields form the LLC header.

An *N*-PDU is assembled at the network layer and encapsulated into the data field of an LLC PDU at the data link layer. A **service access poin**t (SAP) defines the address of a service that a layer offers to the layer immediately above it. SAPs are necessary since the layer above may be running several independent processes, each of which is being networked via the LLC layer. The control field contains bits to implement the LLC protocol between stations in a similar fashion to that of HDLC.

LLC frames, as in HDLC, may be either I-, S- or U-frames. Only unacknowledged connectionless operation at the LLC layer will be described since this mode is used in the vast majority of instances. In connectionless mode there is no necessity to establish a connection. Hence the only user service function provided by the network layer primitive required is an L_DATA.request. This primitive defines one type of LLC PDU and is indicated using the control field. The L_DATA.request primitive is used to send a data frame over a network and contains both destinations SAP (DSAP) and source SAP (SSAP) addresses. The LLC PDU is then passed to the MAC layer where it is

DSAP (8)	SSAP (8)	Control (8 or 16)	*N*-PDU (Variable length)

() denotes no. of bits

Figure 10.3   LLC PDU.

encapsulated into an MA_DATA.request MAC primitive. Parameters associated with the MAC primitive are:

1. MAC layer destination address (DA) and source address (SA);

2. service class, for example token priority;

3. user data field length indicator.

A MAC frame is prepared and transmitted and consists of additional fields dependent upon the IEEE 802 LAN specification in use. We shall look at the MAC frames in later sections of this chapter where we shall consider IEEE 802.3, 4 and 5 in some detail.

It should be added here that for a single LAN the network layer's main functions, that is establishment of a connection and routing, are not necessary. A station originating a MAC frame transmission includes its own address and of course that of the intended recipient. The latter address is largely derived from the user's instructions. For instance, selection of an e-mail user to whom a message is to be sent implicitly provides the required address of the receiving station. We shall see specifically in Chapter 15 how a destination address is derived.

(10.2) IEEE 802.3 CSMA/CD

IEEE 802.3, which, for historical reasons, is also known as Ethernet, is the most popular type of LAN currently in use. It employs a CSMA/CD MAC protocol similar to that discussed in the previous chapter.

The standard defines a range of options for the physical media, which are summarized in Table 10.1. Earlier variants employed a bus-based topology. A star-based topology is also defined which makes use of twisted-pair conductors although the network behaves as a logical bus.

The basic, 10Base5 standard allows for a maximum segment length of 500 m and a total bus system not exceeding 2500 m. A **segment** is merely an unrepeatered section of cable. This gives rise to the **non-rooted branching tree** structure shown in Figure 10.4. It is 'non-rooted' since no head end or master station exists. Segments

Table 10.1 IEEE 802.3 bus topology variants.

	Transmission medium	Signalling technique	Data rate (Mbps)	Maximum segment length (m)
10Base5	Coaxial cable (50 Ω)	Baseband (Manchester)	10	500
10Base2	Coaxial cable (50 Ω)	Baseband (Manchester)	10	185
10BaseT	UTP	Baseband (Baseband)	10	100
10Broad36	Coaxial cable (75 Ω)	Broadband (DPSK)	10	3600
10BaseF	Fibre	N/A	10	up to 2000

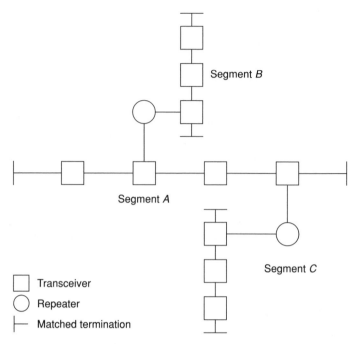

Figure 10.4 Non-rooted tree structure.

not exceeding 500 m may be interconnected via repeaters which reshape and retime data signals to overcome the attenuation and distortion introduced by the medium. In this way unacceptable signal deterioration in networks up to the maximum system length of 2500 m is avoided. However, care must be taken in building IEEE 802.3 networks comprising several segments. A further rule, known as the '5:4:3 rule', must be followed to ensure satisfactory operation. This rule states that no more than five segments may be interconnected using four repeaters and that only three of the segments may be populated with stations.

With reference to Table 10.1, the IEEE uses certain abbreviations for the various CSMA/CD derivatives. Originally IEEE 802.3 only specified the use of Radio Grade-8 (RG-8) 50 Ω coaxial cable of 0.4 inch diameter at up to 10 Mbps. Baseband transmission is used and the maximum segment length of the bus is set at 500 m. Branch cables of each station are interconnected, by means of a T-connection arrangement, to the bus using a device known as a **tap**.

A lower cost system suitable for PC networks was later specified with RG-58A/U 0.25 inch coaxial cable dubbed Thinnet, or Cheapernet, and able to support up to 30 stations. Such cable is more easily installed as it is physically more flexible. This poorer quality cable is limited in use to 200 yard (185 m) segments and fewer stations. This system is termed 10Base2 and limits the physical area which may be served. Stations are connected with cheap and simple coaxial T-connectors.

An alternative option for installation of an Ethernet network is to make use of voice-grade cable which often already exists in buildings customarily **block wired** as a matter of course and so avoid the necessity of installing additional cables. Such cabling is known as **unshielded twisted-pair** (UTP). An initial version of Ethernet using UTP was known as StarLAN and operated at 1 Mbps, the reduced speed reflecting the lower performance of twisted-pair conductors at that time compared with coaxial conductor. As its name implies, stations were connected in star fashion, a pair for each direction of transmission, to a central **hub**. Here each station has its own dedicated connection to the star point, or hub, and which is in fact a segment. Each frame transmitted by a station over its segment to the hub would normally then broadcast to all other segments, and hence stations.

A 10 Mbps standard using UTP subsequently appeared, designated 10BaseT. Two cable pairs are used, one for each direction of transmission, and baseband signalling, using Manchester encoding, is employed. The star point is a hub which provides basic repeater functions. Only one station is connected by a single cable, or segment, to the hub. In consequence the hub requires to have one port for each station. Typically a hub may have between 4 and 24 ports. It is for this reason that it may also be referred to as a **multiport repeater**. The maximum segment length is 100 m. Each frame sent by a station is repeated by the hub to every other port, except the port on which the frame originated. This means that the network effectively operates as a **logical bus** since each frame appears at every station and which, from a protocol viewpoint, operates as if it is a physical bus.

Broadband LANs, for example 10Broad36, apply data signals to the medium using some form of modulation. A variety of carrier frequencies are specified ranging from a few to several hundred MHz. Such LANs generally use readily available cable TV (community antenna TV, or CATV) technology and components. Broadband systems historically have been popular in the USA where CATV cable infrastructures are widely available. RF operation enables propagation over appreciable distances, tens of kilometres, with the aid of simple and cheap amplification.

10BaseF uses a star topology and employs two fibres, one for each direction of transmission, to support longer medium lengths than baseband operation. Up to 33 stations may be supported. Several options exist where fibres may be used for segments or interconnection of repeaters. In addition, the use of fibre means that it offers good protection against EMI and security attacks.

Figure 10.5 indicates the frame structure used by IEEE 802.3. The preamble, in conjunction with Manchester line coding, provides a period during which the receiver may synchronize its clock with that of the incoming bit stream. Once synchronized, a receiver monitors the incoming bit stream for the unique start of frame delimiter (SFD) pattern from which the receiver may then correctly align itself with that of the incoming

Preamble	SFD	DA	SA	Length	Pad (46–0)	Data (0–1500)	FCS
(7)	(1)	(6)	(6)	(2)	(0–1500)		(4)

( ) Number of bytes
SFD Start of frame delimiter   SA Source address
DA   Destination address   FCS Frame check sequence

Figure 10.5   IEEE 802.3 frame.

frame structure. Destination and source addresses (DA, SA) are 6 bytes long, although there exists an option for 2-byte addressing. Ethernet addresses, each of which is unique, are burnt into NIC cards during manufacture.

The length field indicates to the receiver how many data bytes to expect. The data field carries the LLC PDU and therefore the length depends upon its size, with a maximum of 1500 bytes. To ensure that the frame length is at least equal to twice the maximum propagation delay, or collision window, for reasons discussed in the previous chapter, the data and pad field must equal at least 46 bytes. Where there are less than 46 bytes of data to be transmitted within a frame sufficient pad bytes are added to ensure that the pad and fields in combination are made equal to 46 bytes.

Finally, 32 check bits are determined by dividing the frame's significant bits, namely both address fields, length and data and pad fields, by a cyclic code generator polynomial. The remainder of this division constitutes the check bits which are then placed in the frame check sequence (FCS) field. This process is known as a cyclic redundancy check or CRC. The following generator polynomial is used to perform an extremely thorough check which can detect error bursts up to 31 bits long:

$$x^{32} + x^{26} + x^{23} + x^{22} + x^{16} + x^{12} + x^{11} + x^{10} + x^8 + x^7 + x^5 + x^4 + x^2 + 1$$

The CSMA/CD access mechanism used by Ethernet was described in some detail in Chapter 9. A station finding the medium to be busy uses the 1-persistent algorithm. In the event of a collision occurring, stations back off for a random period of time unless an **attempt limit** has been reached (e.g. 10). If the attempt limit has been reached the frame is dropped. This guards against a station retrying endlessly and probably indicates a fault condition in the network. The back-off period is a randomly selected integral number of **slot times** where the slot time is a time slightly greater than the collision window and calculated to be:

Twice the maximum transmission path delay + safety margin

and where transmission path delay is the worst-case propagation delay between any two stations. The safety margin includes NIC and repeater processing delays. The slot time must be equivalent to at least the duration of 512 bits. Randomness is achieved by means of a **truncated binary exponential** probability distribution function (Tanenbaum 2003, pp278–279) to select the number of slot times to be used in back-off on each occasion. On average this number increases after each collision.

IEEE 802.3 does not provide a separate network management function for the detection and recovery from abnormal network conditions. Rather, each station is equally responsible for network operation; hence control is fully distributed. This also means that no initialization procedure is required to add or subtract stations.

Star-based LANs may alternatively use a **switch** at the star point instead of a hub, Figure 10.6. Any pair of nodes, for example B and F, may be interconnected, on a frame-by-frame basis, by the switch. Unlike a hub, which forwards frames to every port, a switch only forwards a frame to a *single* port, namely the port associated with the destination address indicated within the frame. The advantage of a switch is that bandwidth is not necessarily time shared between each active station. Instead, the possibility exists for simultaneous transmission of two, or more, frames through a switch, each at full bandwidth. For instance, stations B and F may be actively transferring

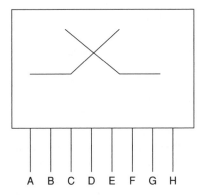

Figure 10.6 LAN switch.

frames between each other, and up to three other pairs of stations (in the case of a switch comprising eight ports) may also be transferring frames simultaneously. The only proviso is that station pairs must all of course be mutually exclusive. Mixed speed, for example 10 Mbps and 100 Mbps ports, can be supported (100 Mbps Ethernet operation is discussed in the next chapter). In the case of a 100 Mbps station sending a frame to a station operating at only 10 Mbps, the switch provides a store-and-forward function to enable the higher speed frame to be transmitted by the switch to the lower speed station at the lower data rate.

Ethernet networks operating in star topology may be extended by interconnecting star points, irrespective of whether hubs or switches are used. This facility enables a network to be expanded, subject to rules laid down within the standards appertaining to segments and the maximum number of stations, to extend distance over several segments. This is achieved by arranging the network into what is called an **extended star**, Figure 10.7. Such an arrangement also overcomes the fact that hubs, and switches, have a limit to the maximum number of supports provided. The 5:4:3 rule discussed earlier in the chapter must be adhered to.

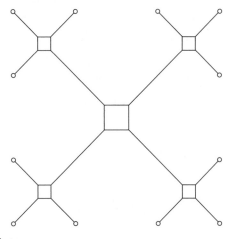

Figure 10.7 Extended star.

10.3 IEEE 802.4 token bus

This type of LAN has mainly been used in automated factory applications. It is now obsolescent and only included for the sake of completeness, but will be dealt with briefly. Physical layer specifications include a number of coaxial-based media derived from CATV technology with the idea of utilizing readily available, low-cost components. Table 10.2 shows some token bus variants.

Although a bus topology is used, a logical ring is established. Each transmitted frame appears at all stations. Stations are so arranged in a ring by declaring, for a given station, the address of the next station as a **successor** and that of the preceding station a **predecessor**. Tokens and frames then circulate around the ring passing from each station to its successor in turn. In order to effect ring-like transmission it is the responsibility of a successor station only to retransmit a frame that is not destined for itself. It would be impracticable, if not chaotic, if each station, all of which receive each frame, were also to retransmit each frame that was not destined for itself. Provision exists within the protocol for stations to be added to, or removed from, the ring and to recover from abnormal or fault conditions.

The frame structure is shown in Figure 10.8. As in most bus-based topologies, there is no continuous frame transmission on the medium. Therefore all frames commence with a preamble to enable clock resynchronization. This is followed by a start of frame delimiter (SD). Although the frame is similar to that of IEEE 802.3 it differs in that rather than specifying length, an end of frame delimiter (ED) is used. Additionally, there is a frame control (FC) field. Two FC field bits indicate:

00 MAC control frame
01 LLC data frame
10 Station management data frame
11 Special-purpose data frame

Table 10.2 IEEE 802.4 token bus physical medium variants.

	Transmission medium	Signalling technique	Signalling rate (Mbps)	Maximum segment length (m)
Broadband	Coaxial cable (75 Ω)	Broadband (AM/PSK)	1, 5, 10	Not specified
Carrier band	Coaxial cable (75 Ω)	Broadband (FSK)	1, 5, 10	7600
Optical fibre	Optical fibre	ASK–Manchester	5, 10, 20	Not specified

Preamble	SD	FC	DA	SA	Data	FCS	ED
1	1	1	2 or 6	2 or 6	≥ 0	4	1

Bytes

SD Start of frame delimiter   SA   Source address
FC Frame control   FCS Frame check sequence
DA Destination address   ED   End of frame delimiter

Figure 10.8 Token bus frame.

10.4 IEEE 802.5 token ring

Token ring has been a very popular LAN and is one of the oldest, first proposed by IBM in 1969, and commonly found in commercial environments. It is now giving way to the dominance of Ethernet with its ease of installation and ability to operate at 1 Gbps or more. The IEEE 802.5 standard enables up to 250 stations to be connected with multiple levels of priority.

Token ring uses shielded twin twisted-pair cable with baseband transmission at either 1, 4 or 16 Mbps. A ring topology is used in which stations are connected to the medium via a **trunk coupling unit** (TCU) which enables inactive or failed stations to be bypassed. A disadvantage of a ring topology is that if the medium fails at any point, the ring fails. In consequence it is very common to connect each station as a single spur to a central star point which, as with a TCU, contains facilities to bypass a faulty node, or its associated cable spur. In this way the reliability of the medium, and hence LAN, is greatly improved.

When all stations are idle, a short token circulates around the ring and the token is labelled as **free**. A station wishing to transmit awaits the arrival of a token. The station then inserts its own data and forms an I-frame, marks it as **busy** and immediately transmits. Each station receiving I-frames merely retransmits them with the exception of the receiver for whom the I-frame is destined. This station not only retransmits the frame but also copies the frame. Each I-frame eventually returns to the station that originally transmitted it, the station currently holding the token. I-frames are removed at the transmitter. The station may then transmit further frames, or reinsert another token into the ring. In the absence of a free token, no other station is able to access the ring.

The token ring frame is shown in Figure 10.9. Data is transmitted using differential Manchester encoding to enable receivers to synchronize reliably with the incoming bit stream.

Two types of frame may be transmitted, namely **token** or **normal**.

Token frame

This consists of a subset of the full token ring frame and is shown in Figure 10.10. A token frame contains SD, AC and ED fields. The ED field contains an (Intermediate) I-bit which, if set to 1, indicates that it is an intermediate frame and that another frame from the same transmitter will follow. A zero indicates that the frame is either

SD	AC	FC	DA	SA	Data	FCS	ED	FS
1	1	1	2 or 6	2 or 6	< 5000	4	1	1

Bytes

SD Start of frame delimiter   SA Source address
AC Access control   FCS Frame check sequence
FC Frame control   ED   End of frame delimiter
DA Destination address   FS   Frame status

Figure 10.9 Token ring frame.

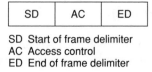

SD Start of frame delimiter
AC Access control
ED End of frame delimiter

Figure 10.10   Token frame.

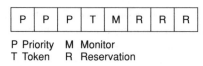

P Priority   M Monitor
T Token   R Reservation

Figure 10.11   Access control field.

the only frame, or the last. The AC field, which has 8 bits, is of particular interest and is shown in Figure 10.11. If the token bit is a zero, then it is a token. Otherwise a one indicates a data (or normal) frame.

Two sets of 3 bits, known as reservation (R) bits and priority (P) bits, permit eight levels of priority, 0 to 7, the latter being the highest. A station with a particular priority (priority being determined by a network administrator) wishes to send a frame and waits for a token. Upon receipt of a token, the priority bits are examined. If a waiting station receives a free token which has a higher priority than itself, the station then examines the reservation bits of the token and, if the station has a higher priority, it places its own priority into the reservation bits. The token is then passed on. Alternatively, providing the token's priority is not higher than that of the station, the station may seize the token. The station may then transmit information frames (I-frame) with the reservation bits set to zero.

A station which is successful in gaining the token may continue to transmit frames until either it has no more frames to send, or its *only* token holding time (THT) expires (the default holding time is 10 ms), whichever occurs first. If the station is timed out but still has frames to transmit, a free token is then released by the station with:

1. priority bits set equal to the reservation bits, and

2. reservation bits replaced by the priority bits of the station, if it has a higher priority.

It is apparent that token priority, indicated by priority bits, may so far only be increased, not decreased. In order to overcome this problem, and so allow lower priority stations to transmit eventually, an additional rule must be strictly adhered to. A station raising token priority must eventually restore it to its original value. This is achieved by a station which raised priority storing the original priority bits on a **stack**. Such a station is known as a stacking station. A stacking station will eventually receive a token of the same priority as the value to which it raised an earlier token. It may then be assumed that there are no further stations awaiting transmission at this, or higher, priority. Then, if the stacking station has no frames to transmit, it unstacks the previously stored, lower priority and places it in the priority bits. There may be a number of stacking stations active within a ring at any one time, where priority bits are successively raised by a number of stations in turn.

To summarize this priority strategy: a station may only seize a token of given priority if it has the same or higher priority. While a station is actively transmitting, other stations may bid for the next free token to be released by indicating their priority using reservation bits. Tokens are released with priority set to that of the waiting station with the highest priority in the ring. Only the highest priority station is able to seize a token. Over time high-priority stations complete their transmissions and the priority bits become replaced by lower values, obtained from the reservation bits, enabling lower priority stations to transmit.

Normal frame

Normal frames, containing all fields, are used to send either data or MAC information around the ring once a station gains a token.

An FCS field provides a 32-bit CRC error check. The FC field indicates that it is either a MAC or I-frame. MAC information relates to the following:

- usage of the token
- control of priority messages
- management of network in the case of errors or failure

All stations interpret and, if necessary, act upon MAC information. In the case of an I-frame, control bits within the FC field are interpreted only by those terminals identified by the DA field. Although the token access control is one of the MAC functions, there are a number of other functions necessary for correct operation of the ring which include initialization of the ring and designating another station as a back-up to the active monitor (to be discussed shortly).

The frame status (FS) field, consisting of two 4-bit nibbles, is shown in Figure 10.12. The originating station sets both A (address-recognized bits) and C (frame-copied bits) to zero. Any station which has the address, or is within the range of addresses, specified by a MAC I-frame sets the A bits. Station(s) for whom an I-frame is addressed may also copy the frame for further processing and set the C bits. Hence when a frame returns to the originating station it is possible, by examination of A and C, to determine if the addressed station(s) are:

- inactive;
- active but did not copy frame;
- active and copied frame.

Ring management is achieved in the following manner. Each station is active and operates as a repeater. Error detection and recovery facilities are performed by one of the stations functioning as a monitor. Any station has the potential to become a monitor. This also enables back-up in the event of a monitor failing.

Acxx	Acxx

Figure 10.12 Frame status field.

The active monitor periodically signals its presence by transmitting an active monitor present (AMP) MAC frame. The first station to receive the AMP becomes the standby monitor, resets a timer and sends a standby monitor present (SMP) frame. If at any time the standby's timer expires, it is taken as an indication that the active monitor has failed. The standby becomes the active monitor and then sends an AMP frame to produce another standby monitor.

The monitor also provides a **latency buffer**. Since the token consists of 24 bits, the ring must be at least 24 bits long. In physically short rings, this may not be the case. The latency buffer introduces additional bits as necessary to pad out the ring. The monitor also provides the master oscillator for the network from which all other stations are synchronized.

The active monitor also checks the ring for correct transmission. There are two main error conditions:

1. no token or frame circulating;

2. persistent busy frame.

Absence of a token or frame is detected by the monitor, which times the interval between tokens and frames. This interval must not exceed the propagation time of the ring; if it does a fault has occurred. The monitor then purges the ring of all frames and initiates the generation of a new token.

Under normal operation, each busy token frame passing through the monitor has a **monitor bit** set to one. It is reset by the originating transmitter. A continuously circulating busy frame would arrive at the monitor with the monitor bit already at one. In such cases, the monitor changes the busy token to free.

Other functions of the monitor are to enable the establishment of the ring and enable stations to be added or removed from the ring. If the ring has collapsed, for example if the medium is severed, no frames circulate. A station, upon discovering this condition, sends a **beacon frame**. When the ring is restored, a beacon frame returns and the ring may then be reinitialized.

(10.5) Wireless LANs

Wireless LANs do not use any wires or cables to interconnect stations physically. They operate using either infrared (IR) or radio propagation, although IR operation is rare. Current technology may only support operation at best of the order of several tens of Mbps. The dominant transmission technique by radio is in what can only be described as a hostile environment. Transmission is subject to a variety of fading, noise and interference difficulties and physical obstacles may give rise to dead spots.

We shall see in the next chapter that LANs are now available which operate at 100 Mbps or more. The question arises: why install a wireless LAN (WLAN) with relatively low speed of operation? There are a number of applications of WLANs which are attractive. In large, open areas, such as stock exchange trading floors and historic buildings, it would be impracticable or visually unacceptable to cable stations together. An area of local area networking now proving popular is that of home LANs where two, or more, computers, printers and so forth may be interconnected as a WLAN and so avoid similar difficulties of cabling to those above.

Although WLANs may be free standing, they may alternatively be connected to either a cable-based LAN serving other physical areas within the site, or a backbone. In such circumstances a WLAN offers a **LAN extension** facility for connection of more awkward areas which are then linked to a cable LAN. A single **access point** (AP) is required within the WLAN. The access point may be implemented as a station and is the 'conduit' through which the WLAN interconnects to the wired LAN or backbone. The access point is also a convenient point at which bridging or routing, discussed in Chapter 14, is provided, if required.

Another developing area for the use of WLANs is ad hoc networks where a peer-to-peer network may be quickly set up and dismantled. An example might be to network some computers quickly at a stand in a trade fair. No temporary cabling is necessary and the physical siting and mobility of computers is very flexible.

Nomadic access provides a wireless link between a LAN and a mobile computer such as a laptop or personal digital assistant (PDA). This enables easy transfer of data between a fixed network and a computer used by people who for instance travel about and need to update data upon return to a central office. Other applications enable guest users to access networks at different premises, or various stock control applications in retail stores, warehouses and so on.

Another application of WLANs is for interconnection between buildings, or **wireless interconnect**. This is suitable for buildings that are relatively close together and where conventional cabling may be impossible for a variety of reasons, for example a river may separate them. Strictly speaking, wireless interconnect is not a LAN as such. Rather it is a network in its own right but without end-users. Nevertheless this application is typically considered within the scope of WLANs. Such an arrangement would usually include bridging or routing to inhibit intra-frame traffic within the WLAN being unnecessarily forwarded over the wireless interconnect.

IEEE 802.11 recommendation

Operation may be at IR, with a range of a few tens of metres, or be radio-based and have a range about one order more. RF operation is by means of one, or other, of the unlicensed industrial, scientific and medical (ISM) bands at either 2.4 or 5 GHz. The use of 2.4 GHz is possible virtually anywhere in the world, However, although 5 GHz is available for use in North America, it is not universally available throughout Europe or Asia.

The IEEE introduced its first WLAN recommendations, IEEE 802.11 (also known as WiFi), in 1997 operating at 2.4 GHz. Since then further development has occurred. IEEE 802.11b was introduced to overcome the speed limitations of, and be compatible with, IEEE 802.11. IEEE 802.11a (also known as WiFi5 as it operates at 5 GHz) was introduced to improve further upon speed performance but, since a different transmission technique and frequency were employed, this meant that it was no longer compatible with the other two standards. The choice of 5 GHz operation, to provide the additional bandwidth for an improvement in speed, has restricted its use primarily to

North America. There is, as always, a trade-off between speed of operation and distance. IEEE 802.11a, although faster than IEEE 802.11b, has a range which is approximately one order less. Nevertheless, for a given distance, IEEE 802.11a is anticipated to outperform IEEE 802.11b on speed.

In a wired LAN there must be a high degree of security since it is relatively easy for unauthorized parties physically to access the network, or its signals. WLANs are far less secure since radio signals especially are not neatly confined to the geographical area of a network. It is relatively straightforward both to monitor radio signals and even attempt to interconnect a WLAN station, whilst outside of the building or site containing a LAN. With this in mind IEEE 802.11 includes an authentication procedure to ensure unauthorized parties do not gain access to a network. In addition the **Wired Equivalent Privacy** (WEP), a security protocol, is specified to provide encryption and privacy. The WEP algorithm (Stallings 2002, pp471–473) is specified to provide privacy and authentication. Symmetrical key encryption is provided in which communicating stations share a secret key, based upon an encryption algorithm known as RC4. In addition two levels of authentication are provided: open system authentication, whereby both parties exchange their network identities; and shared key authentication, where each party shares an agreed secret key and enables full authentication of both parties to each other.

The protocol stack for the various recommendations is shown in Figure 10.13. The LLC sublayer is broadly similar to that described in IEEE 802.2 earlier in this chapter and common to all derivatives of IEEE 802.11. However, there are significant differences regarding the MAC layer protocol, each of which will be described shortly. At the physical layer we see that transmission is by means of either IR or radio propagation using either **spread spectrum** (SS) techniques or **orthogonal frequency division multiplexing** (OFDM).

At the physical layer IR may be used, operating at a wavelength of around 900 nm. Line of sight propagation is not essential since transmission may succeed by means of diffusion. Alternatively, RF propagation centres upon a carrier frequency of 2.4 GHz. In either case data may be transmitted at 1 or 2 Mbps.

Two forms of SS operation are recommended. One form is frequency hopping SS (FH–SS) which uses up to 79 1 MHz channels. The precise number of channels is dependent upon the territory in which the WLAN is operated, for example 23 channels may be used in Japan whereas 70 are used in the USA. Different territories have

Logical Link Control					Data link layer
MAC layer					
FH–SS 2.4 GHz 1 or 2 Mbps	DS–SS 2.4 GHz 1 or 2 Mbps	IR 1 or 2 Mbps	OFDM 5 GHz ≤ 54 Mbps	DS–SS 2.4 GHz 5.5 or 11 Mbps	Physical layer
IEEE 802.11			IEEE 802.11a	IEEE 802.11b	

Figure 10.13   IEEE 802.11 protocol stack.

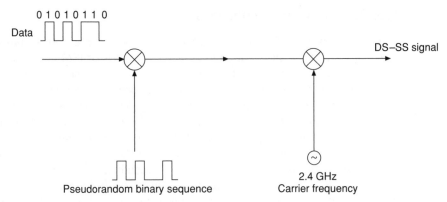

Figure 10.14 Direct sequence spread spectrum.

different numbers of channels dictated by their national frequency licensing authorities to minimize the risk of interference with other services. Data is only transmitted upon a single 1 MHz bandwidth channel at any one time at the full 1 or 2 Mbps. The carrier frequency of the channel then 'hops' from channel to channel at a certain rate. The hopping sequence across the available channels is pseudorandom both to improve transmission performance and also to help prevent eavesdropping.

The attractions of SS operation in WLANs are:

● The radio environment often has a large amount of interference and spurious noise from lighting, machinery, electrical equipment, etc. By rapidly changing channels some immunity to narrowband and frequency-dependent interference may be achieved.

● At the frequency of operation employed **multipath propagation** is common whereby signals propagate from transmitter to receiver over a number of different ray paths (due to reflections). In consequence the received signal is enhanced if the rays are constructive or reduced, or even cancelled out, if the rays are destructive. If, on a particular channel, destructive interference is experienced then, when a hop to a new frequency occurs, it is relatively unlikely that interference will continue to be destructive. Therefore a satisfactory signal is guaranteed some of the time.

The other form of SS specified, which also operates at 1 or 2 Mbps, is that of direct sequence SS (DS–SS). A number of channels may be employed, each operating at the full 1 or 2 Mbps. As with FH–SS the actual number of channels that may be used is governed by national regulation. Japan only permits one channel, in the USA seven channels may be used and most European countries use 13 channels. The data is multiplied by a higher rate pseudorandom binary sequence prior to modulation, and hence the spectrum is spread. This then modulates a 2.4 GHz carrier frequency and is then transmitted, as illustrated in Figure 10.14. DS-SS has an equivalent bandwidth to that of FH–SS and enjoys the same advantages in regard to combating noise and interference discussed earlier.

IEEE 802.11a recommendations

In 1997 a derivative of IEEE 802.11, 802.11a, was introduced. At the physical layer orthogonal FDM (OFDM) is used in the 5 GHz unlicensed ISM band. Up to 52 individual carrier frequencies, and hence subcarriers, may exist within the band. The subcarriers are orthogonal in order to minimize cochannel interference, or interchannel interference (ICI). The use of multiple, contiguous, carriers is similar to frequency division multiplexing (FDM). (This signal has similarities to that of DMT used in ADSL.) Although similar in principle to that of FH–SS inasmuch that multiple subcarriers, or channels, exist, hopping is not employed. Rather the serial data stream is converted into parallel form using an n-bit register, n depending upon the precise number of subcarriers. Each parallel bit is then used individually to modulate a single subcarrier. Finally the subcarriers are summed and then transmitted as a composite signal. Modulation is either PSK or QAM and various sizes of signal constellations are used. As a result a variety of data rates are possible and provides a much higher data rate, up to 54 Mbps, than IEEE 802.11 recommendations. The precise rate used is dynamically adapted and depends upon the quality of RF transmissions and the network loading. In addition, convolutional encoding is employed to provide FEC in order to combat errors introduced in transmission.

The advantages of OFDM are:

● As with FH–SS, the use of multiple channels means that frequency-selective interference, whereby some channels may experience significant noise and interference and others may not, is mitigated since some channels will operate satisfactorily. Therefore some data will succeed and FEC may be successful in correcting erroneous data.

● However, the main advantage stems from the fact that·for n channels the signalling rate per channel is reduced by a factor n. Therefore the symbol length is extended by the same factor. The effect of multipath propagation gives rise to multiple rays, all arriving at the receiver at different intervals in time. As a result the edges of symbols suffer significant distortion and so cause ISI (discussed in Chapter 2). Now, since symbol length is increased with OFDM, the impact of ISI can be made far less significant. This is because the time spread between the arrival of the first and the last multiple ray becomes relatively small in comparison with the length of a symbol.

IEEE 802.11b recommendation

This variant, introduced in 1999, is similar to that of IEEE 802.11 in that it too uses FH–SS, but at a higher data rate of either 5.5 or 11 Mbps, and yet retains transmissions with the same bandwidth. It achieves increased speed for the same bandwidth using a complex technique known as **complementary code keying** (CCK). CCK is beyond the scope of this text but, briefly, data is taken 8 bits at a time, encoded, reserialized and finally applied to a QPSK modulator.

IEEE 802.11g recommendation

IEEE 802.11a and b standards differ in regard to speed and frequency of operation. In addition they are incompatible with each other. The IEEE 802.11 Committee is developing a new standard, IEEE 802.11g. It is aiming to produce higher data rates at 2.4 GHz and be backward compatible with IEEE 802.11a and b. The attraction of 2.4 GHz operation is to enable widespread use in Asia and Europe and so become a universal standard available throughout the world.

If IEEE 802.11g offers comparable speed with that of IEEE 802.11a, the latter may become redundant – not least since if 2.4 GHz operation could satisfy every application, manufacture of radio components around a single frequency band would lead to larger scale manufacture and an attendant reduction in cost. Backward compatibility from IEEE 802.11g means that existing systems may still be used during migration to the newer standard. However, transmission would be limited to the maximum data rate of IEEE 802.11b, which is 11 Mbps.

IEEE 802.11 Medium Access Control protocol

The IEEE 802.11 Committee recommended a new protocol, the Distributed Foundation Wireless MAC (DFWMAC) protocol, for the control of station access to the physical layer, or medium, for use with WLANs. This protocol is used with all of the variants described above. The protocol has two elements: **Distributed Coordination Function** (DCF) and **Point Coordination Function** (PCF), both illustrated in Figure 10.15. DCF distributes the decision to transmit to each station and makes use of carrier sensing, is contention based and suitable for transmission of asynchronous frames. Optionally PCF, which uses centralized control where access is controlled or coordinated from a single point, may be overlaid upon DCF to provide contention-free access.

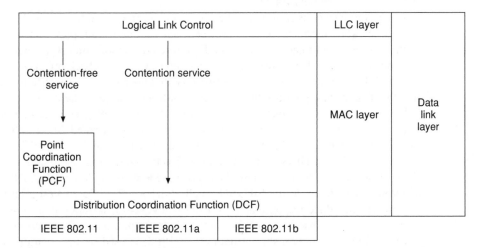

Figure 10.15 IEEE 802.11 MAC protocol.

Distributed Coordination Function

Radio systems which transmit and receive on a single frequency cannot do so simultaneously. Therefore WLANs must operate in half-duplex mode and while a station is transmitting, it is unable to monitor reception as the relatively strong transmitted signal would mask out any weak received signal. As a result, the Collision Detection aspect of the Ethernet CSMA/CD protocol is not possible with WLANs. Instead, the DCF sublayer uses CSMA with Collision Avoidance (CSMA/CA). Collision Avoidance seeks to arrange that transmitters only transmit at optimal times when it is unlikely that other stations may transmit and hence avoid, or at least minimize, the risk of a collision.

When a station wishes to transmit, the CSMA aspect of the protocol is as follows:

1. Station performs CSMA. If free, it waits out a delay known as the **Interframe Space** **(IFS)** delay and, if the medium is still free, transmits.

2. If the medium is busy (initially when CSMA is performed, or because another station transmits during the IFS delay) station defers using 1-persistence; that is, monitor until medium becomes free.

    When the medium becomes free, station then again waits out IFS delay and if the medium is still free backs off using the binary exponential back-off. The station re-examines the medium to see if it is still free and, if so, transmits.

3. If in 2 above, another station should gain access to the medium while a station is waiting out the IFS delay, the station again defers using 1-persistence and waits for the medium to go free.

The reason that the IFS delay is invoked when the medium is, or becomes, free before a frame may be transmitted is that it prevents a station sending frames continuously and so ensures fair-share operation. That is, once the medium is, or if necessary forced to be, idle by means of an IFS, any station may then contend for transmission of the next frame.

Two or more stations waiting for the medium to go free are unlikely to collide. This is because, when the medium does go free, each waiting station only transmits after waiting out a random back-off interval. Therefore one station, almost inevitably, will transmit before any other. Any other waiting stations, when their back-offs have elapsed, then find that the (first) station's transmissions are under way and so do not transmit. It is this feature that provides the collision avoidance feature of the protocol.

IFS delay has in fact one of four possible values enabling support of priority-based access. The delay values, shortest delay first, are termed Short IFS, Point Coordination Function IFS, Distributed Coordination IFS and Extended IFS, abbreviated SIFS, PIFS, DIFS and EIFS, respectively. Normal transmission of asynchronous MAC data frames as described above use a relatively large delay, DIFS, and therefore have a low priority. SIFS, the smallest delay, offers the greatest priority and is used for immediate response actions. EIFS is invoked by a station indicating it has received an erroneous, or unknown, frame. Under such circumstances priority is in effect set low. The intermediate length delay, PIFS, is used by the centralized controller in PCF operation and described shortly.

An example of the use of SIFs is in the transmission of an LLC PDU. Commonly a number of MAC frames will form a single PDU. Each PDU MAC frame is acknowledged with an ACK frame, which uses an SIFS delay. Upon receipt of the ACK the sending station of the LLC MAC frame responds immediately, after waiting out the SIFS delay, with the next MAC frame in the PDU. The use of SIFS in this way assigns higher priority to an LLC PDU enabling the LLC layer to maintain control of the medium until its transmission is completed.

If a sending station in a wired LAN appears to have succeeded in transmitting a frame onto the medium the station may reasonably assume that the frame has almost certainly reached the destination. In a wireless LAN such an assumption is less sound. A WLAN station may be confident of successfully transmitting a frame but whether or not a receiving station receives the frame depends on whether or not the two stations are within radio (or IR) contact of each other. In consequence, lost and corrupted frames due to the poorer quality transmission medium are far more frequent in WLANs.

In general such frames are either dealt with by the LLC layer at layer 2 or at layer 4, the transport layer. In Ethernet the LLC layer generally operates in unacknowledged connectionless mode, which does not afford any reliability. Therefore reliability must be implemented at the transport layer. However, appreciable time may elapse before lost or corrupted frames are recovered from this layer. IEEE 802.11 has included a more efficient reliable transfer mechanism at the MAC layer. A handshake is used which ensures that stations are logically connected prior to transmission of data. A sending station with data to send transmits a Request to Send (RTS) frame. Communication may then take place provided a Clear to Send (CTS) frame is returned by the receiving station. Each MAC data frame transmitted must be individually acknowledged. If an ACK becomes corrupted, or lost, a retransmission occurs. The use of RTS/CTS and ACKs improves efficiency, medium usage and throughput. The handshake arrangement is shown in Figure 10.16.

The above mechanism may optionally be extended further to enhance the collision avoidance feature of the MAC protocol. Other stations may monitor for RTS/CTS frames. When they have a frame to send they can allow sufficient time to elapse to ensure that the current RTS/CTS and data/ACK sequence completes before attempting transmission.

Point Coordination Function

PCF operation can override DCF's contention-based transmission of asynchronous traffic by means of a centralized master, or **point coordinator**, to poll a station. This approach contrasts with that of DCF where access control is fully distributed. Polling and responding stations use an SIF delay. Since this delay is shorter than that used in DCF, PCF polling effectively locks out normal DCF frame transmission. The use of a round-robin approach with PIF means that operation is effectively contention free.

An example of the use of PCF to effect priority is where a number of stations have time-sensitive frames to transmit. Polling in round-robin fashion ensures equal access to the medium. To guard against the point controller hogging the medium by locking

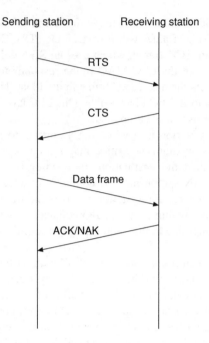

Figure 10.16 Handshake.

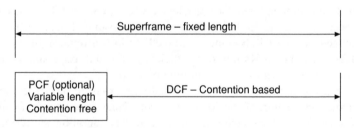

Figure 10.17 Superframe structure.

out asynchronous, or DCF, traffic indefinitely, a period of time called a **superframe** is defined, Figure 10.17. Superframes are contiguous. During the contention-free period of the superframe the point-controller polls certain stations, each of which make their response. The length of the superframe is so chosen that after one cycle of poll/response activity time remains before the next superframe commences during which contention-based DCF operation may take place. Should asynchronous traffic be using the medium at the end of, and into the next, superframe, the point-controller must defer until it is able to seize control of the medium upon cessation of DCF activity. PCF operation then commences but, since superframes are of fixed duration, the remaining time available for PCF activity is correspondingly reduced.

During PCF operation, contention-based DCF operation is suspended in favour of round-robin polling. DCF operation is suitable for networks where stations are in a

FC (2)	D/I (2)	Address (6)	Address (6)	SC (2)	Address (6)	Frame body (0 to 2312)	CRC (4)

(#) bytes
FC   Frame control
D/I   Duration/connection ID
SC   Sequence control
CRC Cyclic redundancy check

Figure 10.18 MAC frame.

peer-to-peer relationship (e.g. ad hoc networks) and no particular priority is required. If network traffic is predominantly bursty, PCF is less suitable. Bursty traffic may arise because only some stations are active, some stations only transmit irregularly, or a combination of the two. Hence PCF could waste much time, and therefore network capacity, by needlessly polling stations that have no traffic to send. PCF is most suited to time-critical and real-time frame transmission, and where frames may be reliably transmitted within a fairly narrow time window.

MAC frame

The MAC frame structure is shown in Figure 10.18. The FC field indicates whether it is a control, management or data frame and also has a number of other functions. Further details on both the fields and types of MAC frames may be found in Stallings (2002, pp467–471). Address fields include indication of source, destination, transmitting station and receiving station. The sequence control (SC) field is used to provide sequence numbers and caters for segmentation of frames. The frame body field carries the payload and contains either an LLC-PDU or MAC control information.

Services

IEEE 802.11 offers nine services. These are provided to ensure that a WLAN offers an equivalent degree of functionality to that of a wired LAN. A WLAN may be a single entity and may, or may not, be connected to a wired LAN or backbone via an access point. In such circumstances it is analogous to that of a single, isolated, cell in a mobile radio communications system such as GSM and has a single point coordinator. Alternatively two, or more, separate WLANs may be interconnected via an intermediate network called a **distribution system**.

There are five services which relate to distribution systems. They are called **distribution services** and are concerned with managing station membership within a cell and also interaction between stations in different cells interconnected by a distribution system. Four other services, **station services**, are concerned with a single cell only. These services relate to station mobility within a cell; that is, stations joining and leaving the cell. Table 10.3 illustrates the nine services, where they are provided and a brief outline of their purpose.

Table 10.3   IEEE 802.11 services.

	Service	Provider	Purpose
Distribution service	Association	DS	For a new station to associate itself to a cell
	Disassociation	DS	For a station to disassociate itself from a cell before leaving, or for a base station to alert stations it is going out of service
	Reassociation	DS	Used by a station moving from one cell to another
	Distribution	DS	Used to invoke routing (if required): frames destined for a station in another cell are transmitted to an AP station rather than intra-cell frames which are simply 'broadcast'
	Integration	DS	Used to transmit frames through an intermediate non-802.11 network. Deals with address translation, frame formatting, etc.
Station service	Authentication	Station	To enhance security, stations must be authenticated to ensure bogus stations do not attempt to join a cell
	Deauthentication	Station	Used when a station leaves a network and ensures it may not rejoin without reactivating authentication
	Privacy	Station	Manages encryption procedures for secure transmission
	Data delivery	Station	Service which provides data transmission

DS – distribution system.

HiperLAN

During the 1990s, in parallel with the IEEE 802.11 Committee, ETSI developed a WLAN standard called HiperLAN. Subsequently, ETSI has produced HiperLAN/2 which, in common with IEEE 802.11a, uses OFDM at 5 GHz with data rates up to 54 Mbps. Although their physical layers, as indicated, are similar there are significant differences at the MAC layer. HiperLAN/2 has a number of time slots and uses TDMA whereby stations are centrally allocated a time slot in which to transmit. Bidirectional operations are achieved using **time division duplexing** (TDD) whereby alternate periods of time are allocated to each direction of transmission. TDD is similar to burst-mode operation discussed in Chapter 7. The choice of a 5 GHz carrier frequency, as with IEEE 802.11a, limits the universal appeal geographically of HiperLAN/2-based products.

Exercises

10.1 Explain why the CRC check field is not applied to the preamble of the IEEE 802.3 frame.

10.2 IEEE 802.3 frames contain a pad and length field, while IEEE 802.4 and 5 token-based frames contain an ED (End-of-frame Delimiter) field only. Discuss.

10.3 Compare the operation of bus-based and star-based Ethernet LANs. What are their relative merits?

10.4 IEEE 802.4 and 5 standards both use token-based MAC protocols. Explain why the IEEE 802.4 token bus LAN has a variety of additional frames, such as 'solicit_successor', which are not found in IEEE 802.5.

10.5 In considering the frame structure of IEEE 802 standards:
(a) Indicate those fields which are common to 802.3, 802.4 and 802.5 and briefly explain their use.
(b) Indicate any fields which vary within the three standards mentioned, and explain their use and why such variation exists.

10.6 Compare the relative merits of wired and wireless LANs.

10.7 Compare the approaches of FH–SS and DS–SS to spread spectrum operation.

10.8 Briefly outline the CSMA/CA medium access technique used in wireless LANs. Explain why the earlier CSMA/CD LAN protocol does not lend itself to use in WLANs.

Chapter 11

High-speed LANs and metropolitan area networks

....

This chapter is devoted to high-speed LANs, and metropolitan area networks (MANs) that may be used to connect a number of sites and typically span an area the size of a metropolitan region. The chapter commences with an explanation of an optical-fibre-based high-speed LAN in the form of the Fibre Distributed Data Interface standard. High-speed developments of the LAN based on IEEE 802.3 CSMA/CD discussed in the previous chapter are then explained. The chapter concludes with the IEEE 802.6 and emerging IEEE 802.17 MAN Standards.

11.1 Fibre Distributed Data Interface

FDDI was originally developed by ANSI as a high-speed LAN operating at 100 Mbps. It has been defined in ISO 9314 and uses optical fibre. Its speed advantage has now been overtaken by high-speed Ethernet. However, the use of fibre with greatly reduced attenuation enables FDDI to operate over tens of kilometres. FDDI may, with its relatively high transmission speed and reach, alternatively be used as a MAN to interconnect a number of urban sites. Alternatively FDDI includes twisted-pair vari-

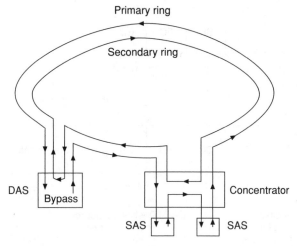

Figure 11.1 FDDI attachments.

ants (using MLT-3 line coding) with considerably reduced repeater spacing and which in consequence limits ring size to about 10 km.

FDDI employs two counter-rotating rings for reliability, with each using a token-based protocol. The dual-ring arrangement consists of a primary and secondary ring. The secondary ring may be used in the same way as that of the primary. Alternatively, it may be used purely as a back-up in the event of the primary ring failing. Node spacing may be of the order of a few tens of kilometres, if repeaters are introduced.

Stations connected to both rings are known as **Dual Attached Stations** (DASs), and are typically devices such as hubs, concentrators or servers. **Single Attached Stations** (SASs) are connected only to the primary ring and may be workstations or printers, for example. Because a single SAS device does not normally require such a high-capacity medium as afforded by FDDI, they are commonly connected instead to a multiplexer which is itself a DAS. Ring length can be of the order of 100 km, with up to 500 DASs or 1000 SASs. A typical FDDI network configuration may be as shown in Figure 11.1.

At the physical layer 4B5B line coding is used and this is followed by an NRZI encoder which produces a more spectrally efficient line signal than Manchester coding. NRZ encoding suffers the disadvantage that clock timing information in the received signal is lost if long strings of binary ones, or binary zeros, are transmitted. NRZI partially overcomes this disadvantage by arranging that no signal-level change occurs when transmitting binary ones (as with NRZ) but each transmission of a successive binary one causes a transition in the signal level (a form of differential encoding). Hence clock timing would be lost only when transmitting long strings of binary ones. However, the combination of 4B5B and NRZI coding used in FDDI ensures that the received signal contains a transition at least once in every two bits. The code is insufficiently robust to enable self-clocking. Hence frames contain a preamble to synchronize receiver clocks at the commencement of each frame and clock frequency accuracy is sufficient to guard against a clock slip for the longest frame length that may be transmitted.

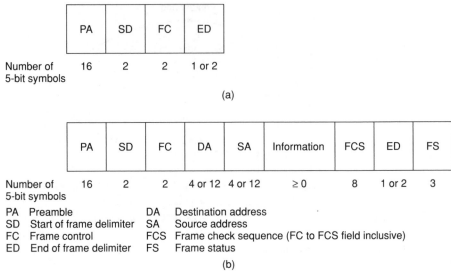

PA   Preamble   DA   Destination address
SD   Start of frame delimiter SA   Source address
FC   Frame control   FCS   Frame check sequence (FC to FCS field inclusive)
ED   End of frame delimiter   FS   Frame status

(b)

Figure 11.2 FDDI frame structures: (a) token; (b) information frame.

The frame structures for a token and an I-frame are shown in Figure 11.2 and are similar to the IEEE 802.5 token ring format. Note that, unlike IEEE 802.5, frame transmission is not continuous and therefore a response is necessary.

FDDI uses a protocol similar to that developed for token bus, but may have a ring which may be as much as 10 times longer leading to much longer propagation delays. If FDDI were to use a simple release at transmitter approach, a sending station would have to wait an appreciable period of time before its transmitted frame returned to itself. Therefore the time elapsed between gaining a token and its subsequent release would also be very long, which means that stations would have to wait an appreciable period of time to gain a token. To overcome this problem and so improve utilization, stations release a token *immediately* after sending the FS field of their last I-frame. Hence, FDDI uses what is termed an **early release** token release mechanism. Note that although stations read frames addressed to them, it is the responsibility of stations initiating I-frames to remove them from the ring.

The use of early release, coupled with the relatively large size of FDDI rings, means that more than one frame may be circulating around the ring at a time. Each station relays the SD, FC and DA fields of all received frames before it may be aware that a frame is in fact its own. If the frame is a station's own frame, subsequent fields are discarded. This gives rise to the transmission of **frame fragments** around the ring. Such fragments are removed from the ring as follows. Once a station gains a token, all subsequent frames received prior to releasing the next token are assumed to be its own frames. In this way, any frame fragments which appear while a station is holding a token are automatically discarded. Once the station releases the token one, or more, of its frame transmissions prior to release may give rise to fragments. These will be 'cleared' by the next station to seize the token in the manner described above.

Priority is similar to that used by token bus. Each station measures the **token rotation time** (TRT) which is the time interval that has elapsed between receiving a token and the last time it did so. The TRT is therefore an indication of how heavily loaded the ring is. A station may send any waiting frames if the TRT is less than a fixed time known as the **target token rotation time** (TTRT). The difference between TRT and TTRT is the **token holding time** (THT) and is the time during which frames may be transmitted. Once the THT elapses frame transmission must cease and a token be released. If the ring is heavily loaded, the TRT will be long and hence THT correspondingly shorter, so reducing the time for which a particular station holds the timer. Ultimately, as loading decreases tokens will appear at a station relatively more frequently and also the time for which they may be held increases. In this way station demand and ring loading are regulated in a fair manner for all stations.

FDDI differs from token bus in that it supports not only asynchronous data but also synchronous data, such as regularly occurring speech samples. Frames containing synchronous data are allocated highest priority. Each station is then allocated a **synchronous allocation time** which defines the maximum length of time that a station may transmit synchronous data upon gaining a token.

Example 11.1

An FDDI network has a maximum of 1000 single attached stations. Each station introduces 10 bits because of a buffer contained in the interface. Given that a 4B5B code is used, determine the minimum number of information bits which may be present in the ring at once.

Number of bits introduced by stations = $1000 \times 10 = 10\,000$ bits

However, for each 5 bits transmitted as a result of coding, only 4 bits convey any information. Therefore there is a minimum of 8000 active information bits circulating the ring at any one time.

In practice additional bits are circulating within the transmission medium as a result of the propagation delay introduced.

Figure 11.3 shows how, if a fault occurs in a link between stations or at a station, primary and secondary rings may be reconfigured to allow continued operation by arranging that a faulty section, or station, be bypassed.

When FDDI was introduced it represented a leap forward in LANs by offering high-speed operation at 100 Mbps. However, as we shall see shortly, Ethernet has subsequently surpassed FDDI in speed and become for many the LAN of choice. FDDI is relatively complex to operate and manage and somewhat expensive. In consequence FDDI as a LAN has not had a significant take-up. However, FDDI using fibre in the physical medium enables the relatively short-distance limitations of Ethernet to be overcome, which means that it has found wide appeal for use as a **backbone** to interconnect a number of LANs distributed over a relatively large area, such as a university campus. (Backbones are discussed further in Chapter 14.) Subsequently FDDI-II (Halsall 1996, pp562–568) has appeared, targeted at the synchronous market to support synchronous circuit-switched traffic such as ISDN.

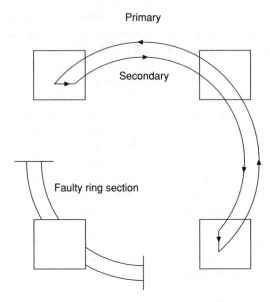

Figure 11.3 Use of dual counter-rotating ring under fault condition.

(11.2) IEEE 802.3u

IEEE 802.3u defines high-speed Ethernet standards for operation at 100 Mbps and is commonly referred to as **Fast Ethernet**. It is predominantly based upon twisted-pair cable, using star topology, which has been in use for decades, mostly in telephone cable applications between telephone exchanges and also in block-wired offices and commercial premises. Tests on early voice-grade cable pairs indicated that data could be transmitted at useful rates and cables were subsequently developed specifically for use with data transmission. Twisted pairs may, or may not, have a **shield**. This has given rise to abbreviations for shielded and unshielded twisted pair of **STP** and **UTP**, respectively. Where shielding is present, it is generally applied to each pair, within a multipair cable as well as the whole cable. Shielding reduces ingress of noise and interference and either is used where cabling is required in electrically noisy environments produced by switchgear, rotating machines, etc., or becomes obligatory at higher frequency operation.

Table 11.1 indicates the development of data cables and their associated bandwidth and data rate. One of the main differences in twisted-pair construction is the number of twists per unit length. The greater the rate of twisting the better the performance. Cat 5E is an enhanced variant of Cat 5 and may now support gigabit operation using multiple pairs. Cat 6 offers twice the bandwidth of Cat5E. Cat 7, uses shielded screen twisted pair (SSTP) cable where each pair is individually screened with a foil and the entire structure further screened with a metallic braid.

Cat 5 cable, and later versions, is installed using components and standards which in summary are known as **structured cabling**. Structured cabling has reduced cabling to that of a basic building utility comprising off-the-shelf cable and connectors and is

Table 11.1 Cable categories.

Cable type	Shielding	Bandwidth (MHz)	Data rate (Mbps)
IBM Type 1A	Shielded		4
IBM Type 2A	Shielded		4
Cat 3	Unshielded	16	16
Cat 4*	Unshielded	20	20
Cat 5	UTP and STP	100	100
Cat 5E	UTP and STP	100	100
Cat 6	UTP and STP	200	1000, or more
Cat 7	SSTP	600	1000, or more

*Cat 4 originally designed for IEEE 802.5 token ring operation at 16 Mbps.

installed in new buildings automatically in the same way as electrical cables, plumbing and heating. Structured cabling has introduced the prospect of a cheap, readily available cabling technology for LANs and has enabled the development of Fast and Gigabit Ethernet. The latter is discussed shortly.

There are a number of variants of Fast Ethernet:

1. 100Base4T

- Operates over Cat 3 or 4 UTP cable. As with 10BaseT the intention is that, in this case, a relatively high-speed Ethernet network could be installed without having to install any additional cables.

- 100 m segments.

- 100 Mbps operation is made possible by reducing the signalling rate on each pair by:

  - using multilevel coding at baseband;

  - using four pairs (hence 4T), three in any *one* direction using half-duplex operation over one of the pairs. Each pair therefore carries a data rate of $33\frac{1}{3}$ Mbps.

  In order to signal at $33\frac{1}{3}$ Mbps over Cat 3 cable pairs, 8B6T encoding is employed. This allows 3^6, or 729, codes to convey only 2^8, or 256, binary codewords. This offers considerable redundancy and therefore only codewords are selected which have at least two transitions to ensure 'clock-rich' signals for ease of clock recovery at the receiver. In addition, to minimize baseline wander, codewords with four identical consecutive leading or trailing elements are not used.

A number of 100 Mbps standards have also been developed which are generally classified as **100BaseX** where X denotes that various transmission media may be employed. In common with previously discussed UTP-based Ethernet variants, the maximum segment length is 100 m.

2. 100BaseTX

- Uses a single Cat 5 pair in each direction. UTP or STP may be used.

- MLT-3 ternary code employed. This code concentrates most of the signal energy below 30 MHz, thereby reducing interference into other nearby pairs

3. 100BaseFX

- One fibre for each direction of transmission.
- 4B5B coding (as used in FDDI) employed which, although leading to increased signalling rate, 125 Mbaud, guarantees a signal transition every 2 bits to facilitate clock recovery in the receivers.

(11.3) IEEE 802.3z

IEEE 802.3z defines Ethernet standards for operation at 1000 Mbps **Gigabit Ethernet**. Although Gigabit Ethernet will operate with the higher layers of the protocol stack without any changes, to gain full advantage of its speed such layers must be able to provide sufficiently fast processing to gain full advantage of enhanced network speed.

The design goals of Gigabit Ethernet were:

- the ability to operate at 1000 Mbps in half- and full-duplex mode;
- to retain IEEE 802.3 frame format;
- to provide backward compatibility with 10BaseT and 100BaseT technologies. This may be achieved by using existing installed cable pairs and so avoid major recabling expense, as occurred in the transition from coaxial to twisted-pair media.

Gigabit Ethernet continues to use the Ethernet protocol of IEEE 802.3. However, a problem occurs with the standard frame structure used in Ethernet. In order to satisfy protocol requirements concerning response to a collision, Ethernet requires that the frame length, in time, be in excess of twice the vulnerable time: that is, greater than twice the maximum end-to-end propagation delay.

The minimum frame length for standard Ethernet is 64 bytes (ignoring preamble and SFD fields), or 512 bits. At 10 Mbps operation this is equivalent to 51.2 μs. Now twice the vulnerable time for 10Base5 is ≈ 5 μs, and for 10Base2 ≈ 2 μs. Clearly, for both of these Ethernet standards, the minimum frame length exceeds twice the vulnerable time. Now consider Gigabit Ethernet operation by way of the following example.

Example 11.2

Calculate the maximum network span if a frame comprising 512 bits is transmitted at 1 Gbps.

At 1 Gbps, each bit is of 1 ns duration. Therefore the minimum frame duration t_f is:

$$t_f = 512 \times 1 \text{ ns}$$
$$= 0.512 \text{ μs}$$

Assuming a velocity of propagation of 2×10^8 m/s, the network span is:

$$\text{Span} = v \times t_f$$
$$= 2 \times 10^8 \times \frac{0.512}{2} \text{ μs}$$
$$= 51.2 \text{ m}$$

This means that segments are limited to about 50 m which is rather restrictive.

Preamble & SFD (8)	DA (6)	SA (6)	Length (2)	Pad & Data (46–1500)	FCS (4)	Extension (448–0)

( ) Number of bytes

Figure 11.4 Carrier-extended MAC frame.

The answer to the problem highlighted in the above example, in order to accommodate adequate segment length, is to use **carrier extension** when operating in half-duplex mode whereby the standard Ethernet frame is extended to ensure that the duration of a minimum length frame exceeds twice the vulnerable time. An extension field of 0 to 448 bytes may be added to the end of the standard frame, where necessary, to ensure that there are at least 512 bytes following the preamble and SFD fields, as shown in Figure 11.4. Whether or not an extension is required and, if so, how long it is, depends upon the size of the Pad & Data fields. If they are sufficiently long that the frame length is equal to, or greater than, 512 bytes no extension is necessary.

A disadvantage of carrier extension is that its overhead can be significant and lead to inefficiency when a station has a number of short frames to be transmitted. To overcome this **frame bursting** is used whereby a station may transmit a succession of frames, up to a predetermined limit of 8192 bytes, end on. The frames are contiguous and therefore no idle period occurs on the medium, which inhibits any waiting stations transmitting until the frame bursts have ceased. Note that neither carrier extension nor frame bursting are used in full-duplex mode. This is because, even if one station is transmitting, another may do so simultaneously without interfering with any existing transmission. In fact, the CSMA/CD protocol is no longer required or used in full-duplex operation.

Gigabit variants are summarized below:

- 1000BaseT – four Cat 5 pairs are used, each operating at 125 Mbaud/pair and use a sophisticated five-level code. Segments up to 100 m may be supported.
- 1000BaseSX – multimode fibre. Segments may be up to 550 m, depending upon the choice of fibre.
- 1000BaseLX – multimode fibre may support segments up to 550 m or, if monomode fibre is used, 5 km.
- 1000BaseCX – coaxial cable with a separate pair used for each direction of transmission. The maximum segment length is 25 m making it suitable for use in equipment rooms, for example to network high-speed devices such as servers.

Gigabit Ethernet, although a LAN in its own right, can alternatively provide a high-speed backbone for interconnection of a number of lower speed LANs.

11.4 IEEE 802.6 MAN

MANs are networks which are commonly used to interconnect a number of physically disparate LANs to overcome the distance limitations of Ethernet and token ring networks. Their geographical size is of the order of 10 kilometres in diameter. Interconnection of LAN sites in the highly regulated environment of WANs has traditionally been possible only via leased lines provided by PTTs. This is now changing as other operators, such as cable companies, enter the marketplace. FDDI was originally conceived as a high-speed LAN. It may nevertheless perform a MAN facility, but the cable infrastructure required is not standard to that of the PTT domain. A MAN using FDDI technology could be built by considerable tailoring on the part of a PTT or by the installation of a purpose-built cable network. Such approaches to the development of a MAN are expensive, cumbersome and also result in networks which are inflexible in regard to the addition and subtraction of physical nodes.

A MAN standard, IEEE 802.6, appeared in 1990 specifically to address the above issues. The specification is so arranged that a MAN can be built around standard technology offered by PTTs, making use of coaxial or optical fibre links, and be capable of adapting as technology evolves. In Europe, MANs operate at 34 or even 140 Mbps, using E3 and E4 bearers, whereas in the USA a 44 Mbps T3 bearer may be used.

The large physical size of a MAN precludes contention and token MAC protocols used by conventional LANs. This is because time wasted by collision activity is, as has already been seen, a function of the length of the medium. In token ring networks, the average time for a station to gain a token is at best half the total ring propagation time. Physically large networks such as MANs result in a reduction in utilization if contention is used. Similarly, the use of a token may result in large access times or long delay in gaining a token, and the increased time in token propagation represents reduced utilization (note that FDDI addresses the latter point by using early release). IEEE 802.6 includes a new protocol to resolve these difficulties for operation in physically large networks.

Distributed Queue Dual Bus (DQDB)

The MAC specified by IEEE 802.6 is known as the **Distributed Queue Dual Bus** (DQDB) and is illustrated in Figure 11.5. As its name implies, there are two (counter-directional) busses, and each station is connected to both busses and able to send or receive from either.

A frame generator is situated at the end of each bus. Frames are generated at a rate of 8 kHz and consist of a header followed by a number of slots. The number of slots contained in each frame is dependent on the transmission speed of the bus.

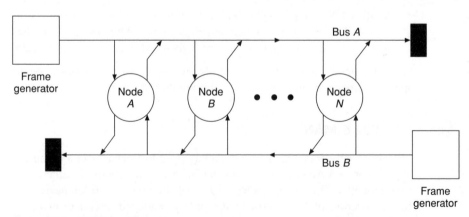

Figure 11.5   DQDB topology.

Example 11.3

A DQDB operates at 34.368 Mbps. Assume that the size of the frame header is negligible in comparison with the frame's length. Estimate the number of slots contained in one frame if each slot contains 53 bytes.

Frames are transmitted at 8 kHz and therefore each frame has a duration of 125 μs. At a transmission rate of 34.368 Mbps, the duration of 1 bit is found:

$$\text{Duration of 1 bit} = \frac{1}{34.368 \times 10^6} = 29.1 \text{ ns}$$

and, since each slot contains 53 bytes, we may now determine the number of slots:

$$\text{Number of slots} = \frac{125 \text{ μs}}{\text{duration of one slot}} = \frac{125 \text{ μs}}{53 \times 8 \times 29.1 \times 10^{-9}} = 10.13$$

Clearly the number of slots must be an integer. Hence the bus may support 10 slots per frame if the header is ignored.

DQDB has been adapted from a protocol developed by a subsidiary of Telecom Australia (Telstra). Now let us examine the MAC protocol in more detail. Each node has two queues, one for each bus, into which are placed data segments waiting for transmission. Each queue has associated with it a **countdown counter** and a **request counter**. Figure 11.6 shows the two counters associated with the queue for sending data segments on bus B for a particular node. (There are also a queue and a pair of counters associated with bus A which operate in the same manner, but are not shown.) A node wishing to send on a particular bus makes a request on one bus and ultimately is granted a free slot on the other bus.

Nodes wishing to send a data segment on bus B set the request bit (R) of the next slot to pass on bus A. Each R bit of a slot which is set increments the request counter of each node as it passes. Hence the request counter's value indicates how many downstream nodes on bus B are queuing a data segment. Each empty slot, indicated by $B = 0$, which passes on bus B is subsequently used by a downstream node queuing a data segment.

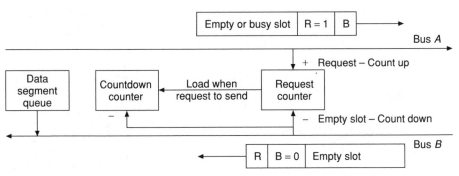

R   Request bit, 1 = set   B   Busy bit, 0 = free

Figure 11.6 DQDB MAC protocol.

Such queuing nodes are in fact the same nodes that made requests on bus *A*. Therefore, each time an empty slot appears on bus *B*, the request counter must be decremented.

To use a free slot, a node first sets an R bit, as already mentioned, and then loads the value of its request counter into the countdown counter. The latter's value represents how many nodes are currently queuing. Each time an empty slot passes on bus *B*, the countdown counter is decremented (in addition to the request counter for reasons already stated). Once the countdown counter reaches zero, all previously queuing downstream nodes have sent their data segments and emptied their queues. When the next free slot appears on bus *B*, a data segment is then 'dequeued' and placed into it and the slot marked 'busy'. The MAC protocol operates a fair-share policy by arranging that downstream data segments awaiting transmission are sent before those of any *subsequent* upstream requests are serviced.

The arrangement of a segment queue, request counter and countdown counter at each node is duplicated for both busses. Hence 'distributed queue dual bus' (DQDB). In addition, each node may have up to four levels of segment priority, each level having its own segment queue. Thus there may be as many as eight queues at each node in total if priority is used. Synchronous data is always assigned the highest level of priority. The MAC protocol is relatively simple to implement and yet offers efficient use of the medium (using a slotted technique) as well as a fair-share access arrangement.

As with FDDI, the use of a pair of counter-directional busses enhances reliability. All nodes are able to generate frames. If the network topology is arranged as a looped bus (rather than a linear open bus shown in Figure 11.5) a break in the bus can be 'healed'. Figure 11.7 shows how, simply by changing the selection of the two terminating stations, a faulty section of bus, or indeed node, may be eliminated.

The protocol is designed to support asynchronous data such as computer data as well as the synchronous data of 64 kbps voice/ISDN channels. The latter is supported by permanently assigning a particular slot, or slots, to form a connection since frames appear regularly at 8 kHz. Asynchronous data frames are arranged in blocks, known as **segments**, each of 53 bytes. Each segment has a 5-byte header and 48-byte information field. Once assembled, segments are then applied, via the MAC protocol, to non-assigned slots within bus frames. Note that asynchronous data segments, with their 53-byte structure, support ATM cells, which are discussed in Chapter 12.

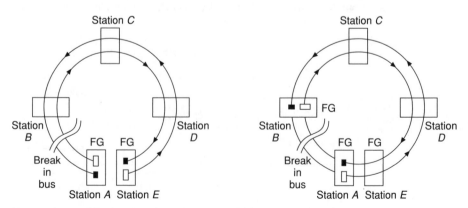

Figure 11.7 Self-healing bus (FG = frame generator).

11.5 IEEE 802.17 Resilient Packet Rings

An emerging solution for metropolitan data networks is called **Resilient Packet Ring** (RPR) technology. It incorporates two key features of SDH: efficient support for ring topology and fast recovery from link failures. At the same time RPR provides data efficiency, simplicity, and cost advantages that are typical to Ethernet. RPR also addresses issues such as fairness and congestion control that, up to now, have only been addressed in ATM networks. In the past few years there have been fibre ring deployments in most metropolitan areas. The challenge for service providers is to tap into the latent capacity available on these fibre rings and carve out as many revenue-generating services as possible. The problem of effectively managing a shared resource (in this case the fibre ring needs could be shared by thousands of customers in a metro area) is a function of the MAC layer of a protocol. A new MAC protocol is being developed for metro RPR fibre ring networks and is designated IEEE 802.17. Neither SDH Add-Drop Multiplexers nor Ethernet switches address the need for a MAC layer designed for the metropolitan area environment. SDH employs Layer 1 techniques (point-to-point connections) to manage capacity on a ring. Ethernet switches rely on Ethernet bridging or IP routing for bandwidth management. Consequently, the network is either under utilized in the case of SDH or non-deterministic in the case of Ethernet. By creating a new MAC protocol for ring networks, RPR attempts to provide efficient traffic management in metropolitan areas. At the time of writing several vendors, including Cisco Systems and Nortel Networks, are already developing and introducing metro networks incorporating RPR technologies.

Exercises

11.1 Outline the Medium Access Control protocol used in FDDI networks. Your answer should include reference to token passing, token holding and priority.

11.2 Explain why an 'early release' mechanism is used in FDDI.

11.3 Explain how frame fragments may occur in FDDI networks.

11.4 Explain how high-speed Ethernet LANs make use of twisted-pair cable technology and coding to enable data rates of 100 Mbps, or more, to be supported.

11.5 An Ethernet MAC frame is assumed to have a minimum of 512 bits. Explain, using a numerical example, how this satisfies protocol requirements regarding collisions in 10 Mbps networks. Explain what change is necessary to ensure that this requirement is satisfied in Fast Ethernet networks.

11.6 A DQDB bus operates at 140 Mbps. Assume that the size of the frame header is negligible in comparison with the frame's length. Estimate the number of slots contained in one frame.

11.7 Frames transmitted on a DQDB bus contain 20 slots. Calculate the transmission rate of the bus.

11.8 Discuss the features of the DQDB MAC protocol which give rise to short delays and high medium utilization.

Chapter 12

Packet-switched and frame relay networks

....

This chapter describes the methods used to access and switch frames and packets of data through a WAN. After a brief look at the way such networks have evolved since their inception in the late 1960s, we will look at two widely used protocols: the X.25 packet-switched network access protocol and the Frame Relay protocol.

12.1 Evolution of switched communications

When switched data communications systems were first deployed in the late 1960s and early 1970s, they utilized the existing Public Switched Telephone Network (PSTN) based on a technology known as circuit switching. Data was first converted into audio-frequency analogue signals, using a modem, and then transported across the network in the same way as voice signals. Many end-users still access the Internet in this way if they have a modem installed in their PC. However, circuit switching was never intended to support this type of traffic and a new switching technology, known as message switching, was developed at about the same time. Although widely deployed in the early 1970s, the lifespan of message switching was relatively brief. It developed fairly rapidly into a more durable technology, know as packet switching, which is still utilized to this day and forms a major element of the core structure of the Internet.

Circuit switching

The PSTN is a circuit-switched network. In this type of network the user is given exclusive use of a circuit for the duration of a call. Its main characteristics are:

- Real-time communication can take place for as long as desired.
- A finite amount of time is taken in establishing a connection. If it is not possible to establish a connection, the network generally gives no indication of when communication can be established.
- When terminal equipment establishes communication, the channel and equipment are exclusive to that connection and are not available for other communications.

Circuit switching can be an inefficient means of communication if sufficient bandwidth is not readily available. A communications channel is dedicated to the user for the duration of the connection, even if no information is being transmitted. For a typical voice transmission there will be lots of gaps in the conversation and link utilization will be well short of 100%. For a PC to server connection the channel may also be idle for much of the time. However, it has the advantage that once a connection is established it is transparent to the users. Information may be transmitted constantly at the data rate of the circuit in real time with the only delay being propagation delay.

Packet switching

As mentioned above, packet switching developed from the short-lived technology of message switching and is used extensively for computer communications. As with message switching, but unlike circuit switching, there is no direct channel established between the transmitter and receiver. Rather, a channel exists between each node in the network and the data, in the form of packets, proceeds from one node to another according to whichever route is perceived to be best. The choice of path through the network is determined by the state of the network at the time and **metrics** are used to determine the best route. Typical metrics are maximum throughput or minimum delay.

Packet switching has the following advantages:

- Link efficiency is greater than for a circuit-switched system since a single link can be shared dynamically by many connections.
- Different data rates can be used along the path of a connection allowing end-user equipment of differing speeds to be connected to a network.
- When traffic congestion occurs, connections are not **blocked** as they would be in a circuit-switched system. When a network becomes congested, packets can still be accepted although delay times will increase.
- Packets could be given priorities so that high-priority packets experience less delay than low-priority packets. This is particularly useful in a network suffering from congestion.

Connectionless routing

A packet-switched protocol that uses connectionless routing treats each packet separately, allowing a packet to find the best route through the network independently. Consequently, each packet must contain a destination address and possibly a source address which are included in a packet **header** that precedes the remainder of the packet. Since a packet header might typically have a length of 20 bytes, this technique is only efficient for fairly long packets, typically several thousand bytes. Packets routed in this fashion are sometimes called **datagrams**. The concept is illustrated in Figure 12.1, which shows a six-node network. A burst of three packets, numbered 1, 2 and 3, is to be transmitted from end-user A to end-user D. Packets will arrive at node 1 in the original order and node 1 makes an independent routing decision for each packet. When packet 1 arrives, node 1 may decide that the best route is via node 6 and packet 1 is forwarded to node 6. If the routing database of node 1 is unchanged, packet 2 will follow the same route.

However, if changes in the network such as link failures or congestion cause node 1's routing database to change then a decision could be made to forward packet 3 to node 2. Hence packets, despite having the same destination address, may not all follow the same route. Packets may even arrive at the destination in an incorrect order and for this reason they must contain a sequence number inside the packet header. End-user D would need to reorder the packets.

Connection-oriented routing

If short fixed-length packets that are sensitive to variations in delay are to be transmitted then a connection-oriented routing protocol is preferred. This is the case when voice or video traffic is transmitted through a network. With connection-oriented data transmission there is an exchange of control packets prior to the transfer of traffic. Typically, the source node or end-user will send a call set-up request, the function of which is to set up a suitable route through the network. Once a route has been established, all subsequent packets from the source follow the same route to the destination. The connection between source and destination is known as a **virtual circuit**

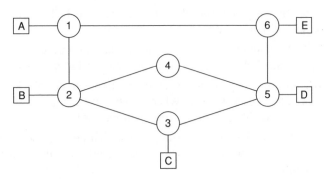

Figure 12.1   Generic packet-switching network.

since, although each packet travels over the same path, the packets do not have exclusive use of any individual link and share the available bandwidth of the link.

(12.2) X.25 packet-switched networks

X.25 is the original ITU-T standard network access protocol that defines the interface between the DTE and a packet-switched network. It is a set of protocols corresponding to the first three of the OSI layers. As it is an access protocol it covers the DTE to DCE interface. Therefore an X.25 network is only defined as this interface and the internal working of the network is up to the service provider; all that is required is that X.25 data entering the network also leaves it as X.25 data.

A typical packet-switched network consists of a number of packet switches which are linked to form a mesh as shown in Figure 12.2. Some computers are connected directly to the network but small-volume users are connected via a **Packet Assemble/ Disassembler** (PAD). A PAD takes asynchronous traffic and converts it into packets which can then be sent through the packet-switched network. Large-volume users may have a PAD on their own premises where the volume and type of traffic demands it.

The X.25 standard contains three layers of functionality:

1. The physical layer is equivalent to the OSI physical layer and lays down the rules necessary to establish a physical link between a DTE and the packet-switched network. The interface is specified by either of the ITU-T recommendations X.21 or X.21bis. X.21bis has been defined for use with analogue networks (modems). It is

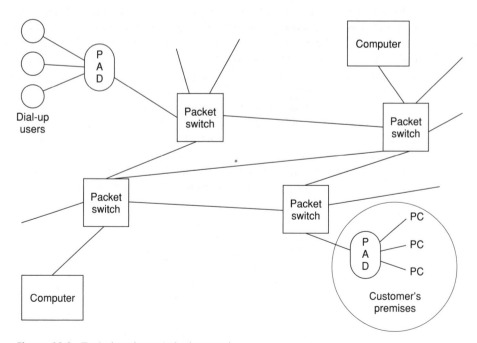

Figure 12.2 Typical packet-switched network.

a subset of EIA 232D/V.24 (which is described in Chapter 6); hence analogue equipment can be readily interfaced by use of this standard, plus the use of additional software.

2. The link layer is equivalent to the OSI link layer and its function is to provide reliable transmission of data on the link between packet switches. It achieves this by transmitting the data as a sequence of frames. The link layer standard is referred to as LAP-B (Link Access Protocol-Balanced) and is a subset of the HDLC described in Chapter 5.

3. The packet layer is broadly equivalent to the OSI network layer and is the higher level protocol that establishes the packet formats and the control procedures required to set up a call and exchange information with other terminals or computers.

The packet level

Most computers tend to send data in bursts, rather than in a steady constant flow. In many cases, unlike telephone calls, it is not essential to have a constant and short propagation time. The advantages of breaking the data into packets is that other computers can send data down the same high-speed link between packet switches. Packet switches use the virtual circuit technique mentioned in Section 12.1. A special call request packet is sent initially which carries the **Network User Address** (NUA) of both the caller and the destination in addition to a unique reference number called a **logical channel number** (LCN). The LCN and the incoming link it comes from are noted by the packet switch, which then replaces the LCN with a new number and sends it forward on an outgoing link in the direction of the destination DTE. This process is repeated at every switch until the call request packet reaches its destination DTE. Then, assuming the call is accepted, an appropriate response packet is returned to the calling DTE. At this point a virtual circuit is said to exist between the two DTEs. All subsequent packets relating to this call are assigned the same LCN values and travel over the same channel.

Each packet switch now contains a **routing table**, an example of which is shown in Table 12.1 for the packet switch of Figure 12.3. The routing table is simply a look-up table. From Table 12.1 it can be seen that a packet received from link *A* with LCN 3 will be sent down link *B* with a new LCN 5 attached to it. With this method the routing intelligence is held in the switch rather than in the packet as in a datagram system. Whenever a call request packet is received by a switch it determines the best

Table 12.1 Typical routing table.

Input link to switch		Output link from switch	
Link	LCN	Link	LCN
A	1	*B*	1
A	2	*C*	4
A	3	*B*	5
A	4	*D*	3

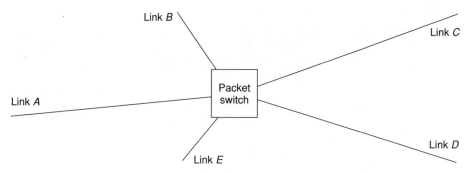

Figure 12.3   Packet-switched links.

currently available route, and updates its routing table to accommodate the new call. The path followed by a call is called a virtual circuit as each packet with the same LCN will travel over the same path. Note that virtual circuits are also bidirectional. However, a number of virtual circuits could be set up over the same physical link and the packets from these virtual circuits would be multiplexed together.

The format of a packet is specified by the ITU-T X.25 recommendation. Each packet consists of two parts: the header and the payload. The header consists of three octets and the number of octets in the data field depends on the packet type. Figure 12.4 shows the format of a call request packet:

- Octet 1 contains the general format identifier which indicates, among other things, whether the ARQ sequence count will be either modulo-8 or modulo-128. It also contains the logical channel group number indicating the type of call. Two types of call are possible:
  - **Permanent virtual circuit (PVC)**, which is established on a permanent basis, typically for a period of months.
  - **Switched virtual circuit (SVC)**, of which there are three versions: incoming only (SVC), both-ways SVC and outgoing only SVC. SVCs are established

Octets	Bits							
	8	7	6	5	4	3	2	1
1	General format identifier (GFI)				Logical channel group number			
2	Logical channel number (LCN)							
3	Packet type identifier							
	0	0	0	0	1	0	1	1
4	Calling DTE address length				Called DTE address length			
5	DTE address(es)							
					0	0	0	0
6	Facility length							
7	Facilities							
	Call user data							

Figure 12.4   Format of a call request packet.

Table 12.2   X.25 packet type identifier.

Packet type From DCE to DTE	From DTE to DCE	Octet 3 bit 8 7 6 5 4 3 2 1
Call set-up and clearing		
Incoming call	Call request	0 0 0 0 1 0 1 1
Call connected	Call accepted	0 0 0 0 1 1 1 1
Clear indication	Clear request	0 0 0 1 0 0 1 1
DCE clear confirmation	DTE clear confirmation	0 0 0 1 0 1 1 1
Data and interrupt		
DCE data	DTE data	X X X X X X X 0
DCE interrupt	DTE interrupt	0 0 1 0 0 0 1 1
DCE interrupt confirmation	DTE interrupt confirmation	0 0 1 0 0 1 1 1
Flow control and reset		
DCE RR (modulo-8)	DTE RR (modulo-8)	X X X 0 0 0 0 1
DCE RR (modulo-128)	DTE RR (modulo-128)	0 0 0 0 0 0 0 1
DCE RNR (modulo-8)	DTE RNR (modulo-8)	X X X 0 0 1 0 1
DCE RR (modulo-128)	DTE RR (modulo-128)	0 0 0 0 0 1 0 1
	DTE REJ (modulo-8)	X X X 0 1 0 0 1
	DTE REJ (modulo-128)	0 0 0 0 1 0 0 1
Reset indication	Reset request	0 0 0 1 1 0 1 1
DCE reset confirmation	DTE reset confirmation	0 0 0 1 1 1 1 1
Restart		
Restart indication	Restart request	1 1 1 1 1 0 1 1
DCE restart confirmation	DTE restart conformation	1 1 1 1 1 1 1 1
Diagnostic		
Diagnostic		1 1 1 1 0 0 0 1
Registration		
	Registration request	1 1 1 1 0 0 1 1
Registration confirmation		1 1 1 1 0 1 1 1

Note: A bit which is indicated as 'X' may be set to either 0 or 1.

and broken down as and when required by customers rather than by the network operator. They tend to be less permanent.

The X.25 standard allows up to 15 logical channel groups for each physical X.25 connection.

● Octet 2 contains the LCN and this can change as the packet passes through each switch. The logical channel group number and the LCN are normally combined to create a 12-bit field.

● Octet 3 is the packet type identifier (PTI), which specifies the function of each packet as shown in Table 12.2. Note that the designation changes according to whether the packet is being sent from DCE to DTE or vice versa. For a call request packet the PTI takes the value 00001011. When a packet with this PTI arrives at a packet switch the information in the data field is analysed, and a route is selected. The link is then chosen and a free logical channel is assigned to the call request packet. The new LCN is placed in octet 2 as described above.

● Octet 4 specifies the number of digits in the address of the calling and called DTEs.

- Octet 5 specifies the calling and called DTE addresses.
- Octet 6 (assuming only one octet is used for the calling and called DTE addresses) gives the length in octets of the facilities used.
- Octet 7 gives the facilities to be used; for example, reverse charging may be specified.
- Finally, the caller may include in the call request packet up to 16 octets of user data which, for example, could carry some user-level identification for login purposes.

Once the virtual circuit has been set up data can be sent. The PTI octet 3 will now have bit 1 set to zero for data transfer. The remaining part of octet 3 now has send, P(S), and receive, P(R), sequence numbers. These sequence numbers are used to regulate the flow of packets by a technique known as flow control. The flow control used by X.25 is almost identical to that used by HDLC and described in Section 5.4. Some aspects of HDLC will be reiterated here since they are important to the operation of the X.25 protocol. Each packet sent is numbered with a 3-bit number (modulo-8) P(S). As the system is bidirectional the receive P(R) gives an indication of the packets received. The value of P(R) is set to the number of the packet it expects to receive next. For example, if the last packet successfully received had a value of P(S) = 4 then P(R) is set to 5, that is the number of the packet it expects to receive next. So the P(R) field in the packets leaving a switch are filled with the sequence numbers of the packets the switch expects to receive next. A feature of the system is that packets in one direction along the virtual circuit carry sequence and control information for packets in the reverse direction. This system where packets in one direction carry both data and ARQ control for the reverse direction is known as piggybacking (see Chapter 7). The standard also allows for modulo-128 flow control.

The format of a data packet is shown in Figure 12.5. The GFI includes a Q bit and a D bit. The Q bit is a data qualifier bit which allows two levels of data to be sent in X.25 data packets. Although this bit is reserved it is not in fact used. The D bit is delivery confirmation and is used for end-to-end confirmation between the source and destination. A DTE can set the D bit in data packets if it wishes the returned P(R) values in received data packets to have end-to-end acknowledgement, in which case the DTE can be 'certain' that the data packets thus acknowledged have reached the destination. If the D bit is not set, the local DCE alone decides on the P(R) values to return. In octet 3 an additional feature is the **more (M) bit** which may be set to indicate to the receiving DTE that the data is longer that can be fitted into a single X.25 packet. Hence in, say, a three-packet message the M bit would be set in the first and second packets.

Octets	8	7	6	5	4	3	2	1
1	General format identifier				Logical channel group number			
	Q	D	0	1				
2	Logical channel number							
3	P(R)			M		P(S)		0
	User data							

Figure 12.5 Format of a data packet.

Octets	8	7	6	5	4	3	2	1
1	General format identifier				Logical channel group number			
	0	0	0	1				
2	Logical channel number							
3	P(R)			0	0	0	1	

Figure 12.6 Format of an RR packet.

If data is being sent in only one direction from, say, switch *A* to switch *B* then switch *B* will send a return flow control packet of the type Receiver Ready (RR), Receiver Not Ready (RNR) or Reject (REJ). The format of an RR packet is shown in Figure 12.6.

The link level

The packet level is concerned with setting up virtual circuits from one end of the connection to the other; that is, between DTEs. The link level is concerned with transporting packets from one switch to the next, with an acceptably low error rate. It is not concerned with logical channels, call set-up packets and so on. It just receives the packets and transports them to the other end of the link. When packets are sent down a link there must be a means of indicating when one packet finishes and the next one starts. This is done by sending each packet in a frame and each frame starts with a flag.

The flag has a unique pattern 01111110 which enables the ends of the frame to be identified. As there is a possibility that this pattern may occur naturally in a data stream, bit stuffing is used to prevent its occurrence (see Section 5.4). The sending end ensures that it never sends a string of six binary ones unless it is a flag. If six binary ones appear in any of the other fields then a binary 0 is inserted after the fifth bit. At the receiver a string of five consecutive binary ones is recognized and the sixth bit binary 0 is automatically removed. The format for an LAP-B information frame is shown in Figure 12.7.

In a similar manner to the packet level there are different frame types in the link level. There are three frame types: information, supervisory and unnumbered. These frames are identified by the control field which is the second octet. The information and supervisory frames are concerned with error and flow control and use a similar principle to the go-back-*n* ARQ protocol used at the packet level. Information frames carry sequence numbers N(S) and N(R) in the control field to implement the go-back-*n* ARQ protocol. The unnumbered frames are used to set up and clear down the link and do not contain sequence numbers. However, as most links are in

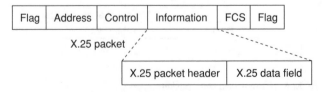

Figure 12.7 LAP-B information frame.

Format	Command	Response	1	2	3	4	5	6	7	8
							Encoding			
Information transfer	I Information		0	N(S)			P	N(R)		
Supervisory	RR (receive ready)	RR (receive ready)	1	0	0	0	P/F	N(R)		
	RNR (receive not ready)	RNR (receive not ready)	1	0	1	0	P/F	N(R)		
	REJ (reject)	REJ (reject)	1	0	0	1	P/F	N(R)		
Unnumbered	SABM (set asynchronous balanced mode)		1	1	1	1	P	1	0	0
	DISC (disconnect)		1	1	0	0	P	0	1	0
		DM (disconnect mode)	1	1	1	1	F	0	0	0
		UA (unnumbered acknowledgement)	1	1	0	0	F	1	1	0
		FRMR (frame reject)	1	1	1	0	F	0	0	1

Figure 12.8 Control field format.

operation continuously, the frame-level set-up and clear is only rarely used. The address field identifies the destination. The control field format is shown in Figure 12.8.

Figure 12.8 shows that the information frame is identified by bit 1 being set to binary 0. Bits 2, 3, 4 and 6, 7, 8 are used for sequence numbers N(S) and N(R), respectively. This is very similar to the data packet PTI field of the packet level. Again, as in the packet level, there are three supervisory frames called Receiver Ready (RR), Receiver Not Ready (RNR) and Reject (REJ). The use of these frames is similar to the packet level but they are dealing with link operation rather than end-to-end operation. They are used when there is no data flowing in the reverse direction and flow control information needs to be sent:

● An RNR frame is sent to indicate an acknowledgement of frames up to and including frame N(R) – 1 together with an indication that the receiver cannot accept any more. The maximum number of unacknowledged frames that can be in transit at any time is the window size. When the window size is reached RNR frames are sent to stop transmission of further frames. The normal window size is 8 but an extended format allows a window size of 128.

● An RR frame is used to acknowledge positively an information frame when there is no information frame to send in the reverse direction. An RR frame may also be sent to clear an existing RNR state.

● An REJ frame is used to inform the sender that a frame has been received which contains an error, and that it needs to retransmit the frame with the sequence number N(R).

There are five unnumbered frames which carry out the following functions:

1. The set asynchronous balanced mode (SABM) is used to activate the link when it has not been previously in operation.

2. If the receiving end is able to accept activation of the link it replies with an unnumbered acknowledgement (UA).

3. If the link needs to be made non-operational it is deactivated by sending a disconnect frame (DISC).

4. Once the link is deactivated, disconnect mode (DM) frames are sent to indicate that the link is logically disconnected.

5. The FRMR frame is concerned with an extended format operation. LAP-B has an extended format mode which has 7-bit sequence numbers and allows a window size of 128. The FRMR frame is sent by a receiver unable to comply with a request to set up an extended format link.

Packet Assembler/Disassembler

The prime function of a PAD, shown in Figure 12.2, is to connect asynchronous terminals to an X.25 data network. The PAD must therefore perform all the X.25 protocol functions on behalf of the terminal, its aim being to make the packet-switching network transparent to the user.

There are a number of ITU-T standards that define the operation of the PAD and the associated terminals. ITU-T recommendation X.3 defines the basic operation of the PAD. Recommendation X.28 defines the interface requirements between the terminal and the PAD. Finally, X.29 defines the interface between the PAD and a remote packet device such as another PAD or a packet mode DTE.

A common mode of operation between computer and terminal is called **echoplex**. In this mode a character transmitted from the terminal is not displayed on the screen until it has made the round trip to and from the host computer. This can cause problems for the packet-switching network as follows:

- The round-trip time delay may be relatively long.
- It may be expensive as PTTs sometimes charge on volume-oriented traffic and if the character transits the network twice the user is charged more for it.
- It generates more traffic which increases loading and delay in the network.

A function of the PAD is therefore to provide local echoing of characters rather than requiring the characters to be echoed end to end by the host. The most efficient way of operating a packet-switching system is to ensure that every packet is full. To facilitate the use of a PAD, all the parameters associated with the terminal have default values, so that only those parameters whose values differ from these need to be changed.

12.3 Frame relay networks

Despite having been approved over 25 years ago, the X.25 protocol is still in use at the time of writing. Bank cash machine networks, for example, use the protocol extensively. However, there have been great improvements in the reliability of physical circuits during this period of time and the overheads built into X.25 systems to compensate for errors are no longer necessary. These overheads included additional bits added for error checking and flow control at both end and intermediate nodes to detect and recover from errors. As a result of these overheads and also the error and flow control procedures used, the data rates achieved in networks using the X.25 protocol are quite low, typically 2 Mbps and below. In fact, the original X.25 networks were designed with a data rate to the end-user as low as 48 kbps.

The Frame Relay protocol was developed to take advantage of the improvements in transmission links that had occurred. For example, a typical optical fibre link has a bit error rate of 10^{-8}. Frame relay networks currently operate at speeds up to 34 Mbps and there is a newly approved version of **Frame Relay Forum** standard FRF.14 that allows for speeds of 155.52 Mbps over optical fibres. In order to achieve these high data rates it is necessary to remove unnecessary overheads associated with error control. Frame Relay, unlike X.25, detects frames that contain errors but performs no error recovery – frames that contain an error are simply discarded. The assumption is that higher layer protocols will cope with the loss of these frames.

The Frame Relay frame format

Frame Relay uses a structure that has some resemblance to that of X.25. The frame contains flags for marking the beginning and end of a frame, a header, a data payload and a frame check sequence (FCS). Frames associated with a particular application are said to belong to a **data link connection** (dlc) and enter a network at a **Frame Relay User Network Interface** (FRUNI) where they are multiplexed with frames from other dlcs over a single link. The frames are identified by a number in the header known as a **data link connection identifier** (dlci). A dlci can be considered as analogous to an X.25 lcn. In North America, it is common to hear the rather endearing term delsie used in place of dlci. The default frame format is shown in Figure 12.9.

The Frame Relay frame structure is based on the LAP-D protocol that, as in the LAP-B standard used with X.25, uses a flag to mark the beginning and end of each frame and a trailer consisting of a 2-byte FCS. The header has a default length of 2 bytes which can be extended to 3 or 4 bytes. The dlci, which has a default length of 10 bits, identifies a particular connection within a multiplexed link. As with X.25 connection numbers, it has local significance only. The command/response (CR) bit is application specific and is not used within the frame relay network. The **discard eligibility** (DE) bit, when set, indicates that a frame should be discarded in preference to other frames in which it is not set. It is used as part of the Frame Relay **traffic**

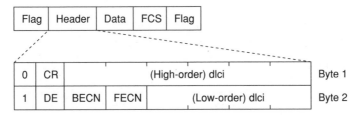

Figure 12.9 Frame Relay frame format.

management procedures, which will be explained in more detail shortly. Two further bits which can be set by a node in a frame relay network, known as forward explicit congestion notification (FECN) and backward explicit congestion notification (BECN), are used as part of the frame relay congestion control process. Finally, there is a trailer consisting of a 2-byte FCS.

Frame relay virtual circuits

As with X.25, a permanently configured frame relay connection is known as a permanent virtual circuit (PVC) and, once configured, it remains in place even when it is not being used. The originating point of the PVC will be associated with a FRUNI. The Frame Relay standards refer to an end-to-end service known as a **frame-mode bearer service**. Switch manufacturers, however, had already developed proprietary protocols for transporting X.25 traffic over their interswitch links, typically known as **trunks**. If they were to develop their switches so as to support a frame-mode bearer service, it would mean that they would no longer be able to transport X.25 traffic. In the event, many adapted their existing trunks so as to carry both Frame Relay and X.25 traffic. A PVC is illustrated in Figure 12.10.

Note that the PVC originates and terminates at FRUNIs that have been configured, in this case, on switches with a dlci 17 at one end and a dlci 18 at the other. The two dlci values do not need to be the same since, as mentioned above, they have only local significance. The term multiservice indicates that, although being used to carry Frame Relay traffic in this instance, the switches could equally carry X.25 or other types of traffic. The link between the customer's equipment (typically a router) and the switch will normally be carrying a number of different dlcs multiplexed together.

The Frame Relay standards also support the establishment of switched virtual circuits (SVCs). A calling user initiates the establishment of an SVC by issuing a call set-up request. The FRUNI receives the request, assigns a dlci, and forwards the set-up message to the destination. The SVC is set up dynamically by the frame relay network and is torn down when no longer needed. Although the multiservice switches require no additional configuration, they must support the signalling system, defined in the ITU-T Q.933 standard, that is used to set up these circuits dynamically. The call set-up signalling passes over a dedicated channel with dlci=0 and follows a similar sequence of events as in the set-up of an X.25 SVC, although the actual signals bear different names.

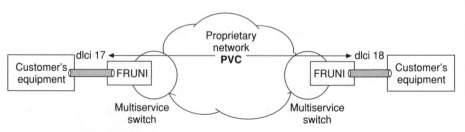

Figure 12.10   Frame relay PVC.

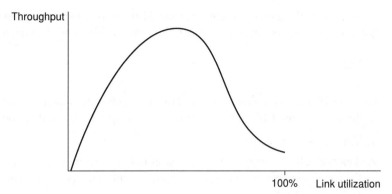

Figure 12.11 markers: Throughput, 100%, Link utilization

Figure 12.11 The effect of congestion.

12.4 Frame relay traffic management

The Frame Relay standards were streamlined in order to maximize frame throughput and consequently a frame relay switch does not need a flow control procedure as used in LAP-B, for example, to regulate traffic at the FRUNI or between switches. The higher data rates in use mean that there is a much greater potential for congestion in a frame relay network than was the case with X.25. The effect of congestion is shown in Figure 12.11. It is generally accepted that for a network to operate efficiently, link utilizations should be maintained at a levels within the range 60–70%. Congestion will normally occur as a result of link failures that will inevitably cause link throughput in the vicinity of these failures to rise.

The effect of congestion on switches is that queue lengths and subsequent delays will increase, particularly at output links. For example, if large numbers of frames arrive at a switch, all destined for the same output link, then the occupancy of the output queue this link will rise. Once the limit of the queue is reached, frames will be lost indiscriminately. This may well result in some higher, end-to-end protocol such as TCP retransmitting lost frames and the congestion can become uncontrollable, as shown in Figure 12.11. Congestion can only be successfully controlled by joint actions on the part of a network and its end-users to manage the flow of traffic in a network. However, in the absence of incentives to do otherwise, the response of end-users faced with network congestion can often be to transmit frames as frequently as possible and thus make matters even worse.

In order to foster an orderly approach to traffic management, the Frame Relay standards use the concept of a **committed information rate** (CIR). This is an average rate, in bits per second, agreed between the user and the network, at which a user can access the network. The user's traffic will actually be transferred at the line access rate in use at the FRUNI that will normally be considerably greater than the user's agreed CIR but, since each user's traffic is multiplexed with other users' traffic, the user traffic will not be transmitting continuously. Frame relay traffic will typically be transmitted in **bursts** and a second parameter known as **committed burst size** (B_c) is used. The committed burst size is defined as the maximum amount of data, in bits, that a network agrees to transfer, under normal circumstances, during a time interval T.

B_c is, in fact, the amount of data that would be transmitted during time T if the user were to transmit continuously at the CIR, which is given by the equation:

$$CIR = \frac{B_c}{T}$$

Once a CIR is agreed with a user, a network operator must decide what action to take in the event of the CIR being exceeded. In principle there are three options:

1. Take no action.
2. **Tag** the cell by setting the discard eligibility bit mentioned above, indicating that the frame may be discarded at some other point in the network in the event of congestion occurring.
3. Discard the frame immediately.

In order to assist in choosing between these options, an **excess burst size** (B_e) is defined. A user is allowed to burst beyond the committed burst size up to a value $B_c + B_e$ as long as network resources allow this. The additional frames transmitted as a result of this do not entirely escape traffic management actions as they are tagged and may be discarded at some later stage in the event of congestion. An **excess information rate** (EIR) can also be determined, from the equation:

$$EIR = \frac{B_e}{T}$$

EIR can be defined as the agreed sustainable information rate transmitted by a user, in excess of CIR, that the network will accommodate if there is sufficient bandwidth.

The different parameters agreed between a customer and a network provider constitute a **Service Level Agreement** (SLA). The relationship between the different parameters is illustrated in Figure 12.12 which is based on similar figures published in the ITU-T I.370 standard (Congestion Management for ISDN Frame Relaying Services). In each of the three graphs, the dashed line labelled 'Access rate' represents the data rate of the FRUNI connection. This is the upper bound on any information rates of individual dlcs. The other dashed line labelled 'CIR' represents the agreed committed information rate for this dlc. The solid line shows the number of bits transmitted over a period of time, T, in this dlc. Note that for this particular dlc, the data does not flow continuously since the FRUNI is shared with other dlcs. Rather, data is transmitted in bursts during which the solid line representing the data flow is parallel to the access rate line. This is because the full bandwidth of the FRUNI is available to each dlc when data is transmitted. In between bursts, the solid line is horizontal since there is no traffic flow in this dlc.

Graph (a) illustrates a customer whose data flow remains less than the CIR and the committed burst size, B_c, is not exceeded. Graph (b) illustrates the situation where B_c is exceeded but since the excess burst size, B_e, is not exceeded, the customer remains within his/her SLA. However, the discard eligibility (DE) bit in the frame(s) that caused B_c to be exceeded will be set. In graph (c), both B_c and B_e are exceeded, causing those frames that exceed B_c only to have their DE bit set and those frames that exceed B_e to be possibly discarded. If the discard is enforced, it will occur whether or not there

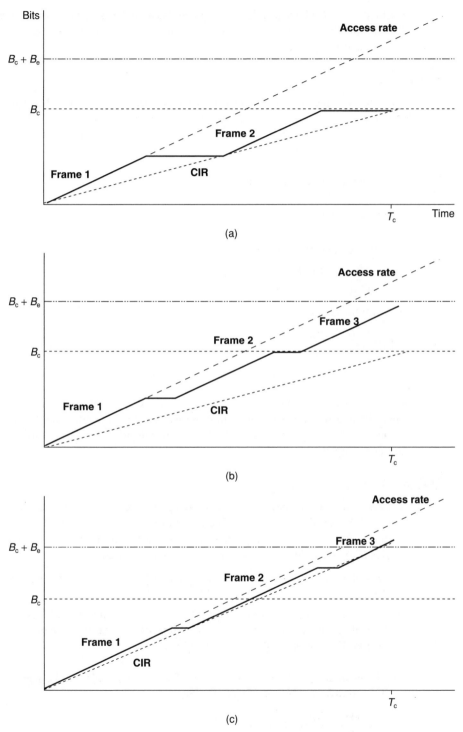

Figure 12.12   Service Level Agreement parameters.

is sufficient bandwidth available for the frames because the agreement has been breached. Whether or not to enforce discards will be a matter of policy to be decided by the network carrier/operator.

Example 12.1

A customer agrees an SLA with a frame relay network provider. The agreed committed information rate is 256 kbps and committed burst size is 6144 bytes. If network resources allow, the customer can burst for a further 2048 bytes. Determine the excess information rate.

The committed information rate is given by:

$$CIR = \frac{B_c}{T} \text{ bps}$$

The time interval is therefore:

$$T = \frac{B_c}{CIR} = \frac{6144 \times 8}{256 \times 1000} = 0.192 \text{ s}$$

Excess information rate is given by:

$$EIR = \frac{B_e}{T} = \frac{2048 \times 8}{0.192} = 85\,333 \text{ bps}$$

In the real world, a customer may not provide the SLA information in the form of CIR, EIR and so on. Customers will often work in terms of file transfers or numbers of interactive transactions. Probably the best way to illustrate this point is by way of further examples.

Example 12.2

A frame relay customer runs a file transfer application that involves the transmission of a batch of 26 files every hour. The files have an average size of 2 megabytes and are transmitted as 1024-byte payload frames, each with a frame relay overhead of 5 bytes (2-byte header, 2-byte error check and 1-byte flag).

(a) Determine a suitable CIR for this application. Round solutions up to the nearest 1 kbps.

(b) Seventeen such applications are allocated dlcis and multiplexed together over an E1 link. Assuming that the full 2.048 Mbps of the link is available for use, suggest an EIR for each of these applications.

(a) Firstly we must determine the number of frames that a file will be segmented into. The average number of frames per file is:

$$\frac{2\,048\,000}{1024} = 2000 \text{ frames}$$

Thus we have 26 files, each consisting of 2000 frames, each frame of which contains 1029 bytes, transmitted per hour. The committed information rate in bps is given by:

$$CIR = \frac{26 \times 2000 \times 1029 \times 8}{3600}$$

$$= 118\ 906 \text{ bps or } 119 \text{ kbps}$$

(b) The total bandwidth used by all 17 applications is given by:

$17 \times 119\ 000 = 2023$ kbps

The spare bandwidth remaining if all this traffic is transmitted over the E1 link at the same time is:

$2\ 048\ 000 - 2\ 023\ 000 = 25\ 000$ bps

This value of 25 kbps could be used as an EIR for each of the 17 dlcis since traffic bursting above the CIR value is not guaranteed delivery. Thus:

EIR = 25 kbps

It should be noted that these values assume that all 17 applications transmit traffic simultaneously, which is an unlikely scenario. Thus the value of the EIR could, in practice, be much higher.

<hr/>

Example 12.3

A customer uses an interactive data transaction that consists of a 128-byte query from a client to a host and a 2048-byte response from the host. The queries and responses are transmitted over a FRUNI with a 5-byte overhead. Fifty different operators make use of the transactions, each generating an average of 40 transactions per hour. Determine the total CIR.

Since the response is larger than the query, it is only necessary to determine the traffic involved in the responses. Assuming a 5-byte frame relay overhead the overall frame size for a response is:

$2048 + 5 = 2053$ bytes

$$CIR = \frac{50 \times 40 \times 2053 \times 8}{3600} = 9124 \text{ bps}$$

<hr/>

Congestion notification

A frame relay header contains 2 bits that may be set by a switch that detects congestion. The Frame Relay standard does not give details on how to detect the congestion although the ANSI standard T1.618 suggests a procedure for monitoring the length of queues at network nodes. These bits, which constitute signals from the network to the end-user, are:

● Forward explicit congestion notification (FECN): When this bit is set it informs the receiving device that there is congestion in the direction in which the frame has been travelling.

● Backward explicit congestion notification (BECN): When this bit is set it informs a receiving device that there is congestion in the opposite direction to that in which the frame has been travelling.

The intention is that the user should respond as follows:

● On receipt of a BECN signal, the user should reduce the rate at which frames are transmitted until the BECN signals cease.

● Receipt of an FECN signal should trigger the user to notify the peer end-user to reduce the flow of frames.

However, whether or not either of these actions occurs will, in practice, depend on individual vendors' implementations in their frame relay access device. Furthermore, the reluctance of some network operators to enforce SLAs may extend to taking action on congestion notification and it is possible that no corrective action will, in practice, result from the congestion notification.

Exercises

12.1 A Frame Relay Service Level Agreement provides a customer with a committed information rate of 128 kbps, measured over a time interval of 0.25 seconds. Determine the committed burst size in bytes. If an excess burst of 2000 bytes is allowed for in the SLA, determine the EIR.

12.2 A customer agrees a Service Level Agreement with a frame relay network provider. The agreed CIR is 512 kbps, the EIR is 132 kbps and the committed burst size is 6144 bytes. Calculate the excess burst size.

12.3 A frame relay customer runs a file transfer application that involves the transmission of a batch of 28 files every hour. The files have an average size of 1 megabyte and are transmitted as 2048-byte frames, each with a frame relay overhead of 5 bytes. Determine a suitable CIR for this application.

12.4 A frame relay customer in North America has an application that uses interactive data transactions that consist of a 128-byte query from a client to a host and a 4096-byte response from the host. One-hundred different operators make transactions, each generating an average of 40 transactions per hour. Determine the total CIR. A total of 40 such applications are allocated dlcis and multiplexed over a DS-1 link. If the full 1.536 Mbps of the DS-1 link are available for use, suggest a suitable EIR value for these applications.

Chapter 13

Asynchronous transfer mode

Asynchronous transfer mode (ATM) is a wide area network technology that builds on the concepts developed in frame relay networks. It takes advantage of the high speed and reliability of modern transmission links, particularly optical links, to provide high-speed cell switching. In this respect a cell can be thought of as a short fixed-length frame. Like frame relay, it allows multiple virtual connections to be established over one or more physical links. However, as well as allowing higher speeds, ATM differs from frame relay in that it does not have such a sophisticated congestion notification system but relies more on avoiding congestion in advance. The original aim of ATM was to provide a single multimedia broadband network to support all envisaged types of service, be it voice, data or video. Mainly because of the ubiquitous spread of the IP in end-system routers, ATM has not, as yet, succeeded in its original aims. It is nevertheless the predominant WAN technology used in the cores of the majority of the world's largest data networks and has been an important contributor in the drive towards data–voice convergence.

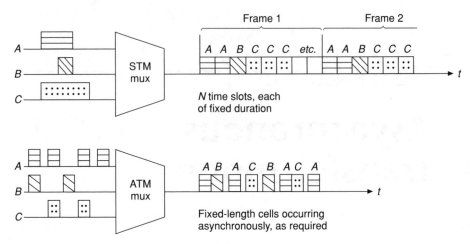

Figure 13.1   Comparison of ATM and STM transmission.

Header	Information
5 bytes	48 bytes

Figure 13.2   ATM cell.

13.1 Asynchronous and synchronous transfer

Before looking further at ATM, it is useful to consider the use of the word asynchronous in asynchronous transfer mode. At first sight it seems a bit incongruous given that a high degree of synchronization is required to switch data at rates of up to 2.48 Gbps. In order to do this it is useful to compare asynchronous transfer mode with synchronous transfer mode (STM) as illustrated in Figure 13.1.

With STM, each data stream is associated with a time slot. If a particular input to an STM multiplexer has no information to send it still has a slice of bandwidth continuously available to it, because the number of time slots allocated to each input is constant and they occur repetitively. With ATM, users generate cells as required with no need to transmit if there is no information. The cells arrive at a multiplexer and are transmitted in order of arrival and hence occur asynchronously. Cells contain 48 bytes of user data and a 5-byte header as shown in Figure 13.2. Note that there is no trailer in an ATM cell as is usual in frame-based protocols such as X.25 or Frame Relay.

13.2 ATM protocol model

ATM is sometimes referred to as a data link layer (layer 2 of the OSI reference model) protocol. This can be misleading for at least two reasons. Firstly, the ATM protocol stack does not fit readily into the OSI seven-layer model. Secondly, data link layer protocols deal with a single data link between two nodes whereas ATM involves both

Upper layers
ATM adaptation layer
ATM layer
Physical layer

Figure 13.3 The ATM protocol model.

addressing and routing throughout an entire network, both of which are associated with layer 3 of the OSI model. The ATM model is shown in Figure 13.3.

Typical upper layer protocols could be video standards such as MPEG, the IP or Frame Relay.

The ATM adaptation layer is subdivided into two sublayers: the **convergence sublayer**, which allows the different types of traffic such as data and video to converge into ATM; and a **segmentation and reassembly sublayer**, which breaks down larger blocks of data into ATM cells and reassembles them at the far end of the connection.

The ATM layer is mainly concerned with the setting up and routing of connections and the subsequent switching of cells. Cells entering a switch are switched between incoming and outgoing connections according to identification numbers in the cell header. Further functions of this layer are congestion control and traffic management.

The physical layer is also divided into two sublayers. The **transmission convergence** sublayer deals with the physical handling of cells. Prior to packaging the cells inside the underlying frame structure, an error check is carried out. A cyclic redundancy check is carried out on the cell header using the generator polynomial $x^8 + x^2 + x + 1$, resulting in an 8-bit check sequence which is inserted in a **header error control** (HEC) field of the header. At the far end of the connection the cells are extracted from the underlying frame, the error check is recalculated and if the same check sequence is not obtained then the cell header is assumed to contain errors and the whole cell discarded. Unlike other physical layer protocols, there is no delineation between cells such as the flags used in HDLC. The cell delineation is achieved by using the header error control mechanism. The error check is continuously carried out on 53-byte blocks of data until the error check indicates that there are no errors (i.e. the received check bits equal the recalculated check bits). At this point it is assumed that the 53-byte block that has just been checked is a complete cell. This is confirmed by repeating the check on several subsequent 53-byte data blocks. If all the checks are good then it is assumed that cell delineation has been achieved and from then on the beginning and end of cells is apparent to the transmission system. The other physical sublayer is called the **physical medium dependent** sublayer. This places the ATM cells on the physical cable or fibre and handles the bit timing.

ATM cell header

ATM cells multiplexed on a single cable or fibre are distinguished from each other by virtual path and virtual channel identifiers that are contained in the cell header.

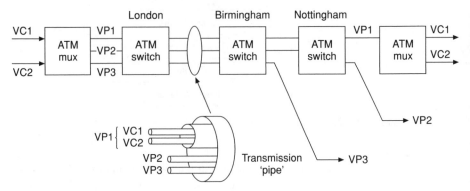

Figure 13.4 Virtual paths and channels.

Figure 13.4 shows the relationship between virtual paths (VP) and virtual channels (VC) and how a number of them can exist over the same transmission 'pipe' or link. A virtual path simply consists of a number of virtual connections, each of which has the same end-points. The path and channel numbers are used to switch cells between the incoming and outgoing interfaces of an ATM switch. **Virtual channel connections** (vcc) and **virtual path connections** (vpc), which are the basic elements of an ATM circuit, are full-duplex connections. However, the channel or path bandwidth and other traffic parameters can be configured to be different in the transmit and receive directions.

The structure of the ATM cell header varies slightly depending on whether it is entering the network from an end-user's equipment, a point known as a **user network interface** (UNI), or whether it is in the core of the network passing between two switches over a **network–network interface** (NNI). The structure of the cell header is shown in Figure 13.5.

The different fields in the cell header are used as follows:

- Generic flow control (GFC): Originally intended to be used for flow control or priority between end-users but has never been used. The field is overwritten at the first NNI encountered by the cell to provide an increased range of VPIs.

- Virtual path identifier (VPI): Used to switch cells over a virtual path. It consists of 8 bits at the UNI and 12 bits at the NNI. Thus, up to 256 virtual paths can be defined at a user interface and up to 4096 virtual paths at a network interface, although path 0 cannot be used as a complete path because channels 1 to 31 in path 0 are reserved for control functions such as signalling. Consequently path 0 is always broken down into individual channels.

- Virtual channel identifier (VCI): Selects a particular virtual channel within a path. Since the VC field contains 16 bits, up to 65 536 channels are available in principle in each path. However, this number may be restricted in practice by the hardware limitations of switches and routers.

- Payload type identifier (PTI): Indicates the type of data in a cell, for example operation and maintenance (OAM) cells or data cells.

- Cell loss priority (CLP): There is always the potential for congestion in a network, possibly as a result of link failure. The single CLP bit, which is analogous to the

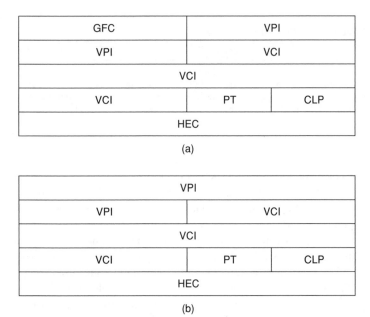

GFC		VPI	
VPI		VCI	
VCI			
VCI		PT	CLP
HEC			

(a)

VPI			
VPI		VCI	
VCI			
VCI		PT	CLP
HEC			

(b)

Figure 13.5 ATM cell header field: (a) UNI; (b) NNI.

discard eligibility bit in Frame Relay, is used to indicate whether or not a cell may be discarded in favour of another cell in order to ease the congestion. A value of 1 indicates that a cell has a lower priority and will be discarded before a cell with CLP set to 0.

- Header error control (HEC): Contains eight check bits which are used for checking the header, as explained in Section 13.2. The payload of an ATM cell is not checked for errors, with the exception of OAM cells.

13.3 ATM adaptation

In order to be able to work with and adapt between higher layer protocols such as voice and IP, ATM standards categorize the different types of end-user services into four classes of service. These are distinguished by three characteristics:

1. whether the transfer is connection oriented or connectionless;

2. whether the traffic is transmitted at a **constant bit rate** (cbr) or **variable bit rate** (vbr);

3. the requirement, or otherwise, of a timing relationship between source and destination.

The four classes of service are listed in Table 13.1 along with their respective characteristics.

Class A is suitable for constant bit rate video and for connections between PDH equipment, the latter being known as **circuit emulation.** Class B provides (real-time)

Table 13.1   Class of service characteristics.

	Class A	Class B	Class C	Class D
Bit rate	Constant	Variable	Variable	Variable
Connection mode	Connection oriented	Connection oriented	Connection oriented	Connectionless
Timing relationship required	Yes	Yes	No	No

vbr voice and video traffic such as might be used in video conferencing. Both of these classes of service require a careful timing relationship between source and destination to ensure that delay in individual cell transmission time through the network remains appreciably constant. Classes C and D are suitable for traffic arising from data transfer applications using connection-oriented and connectionless protocols respectively. This way of classifying different types of traffic was not pursued in any other areas of ATM apart from adaptation and a more commonly used categorization is by way of the ATM service categories, which will be explored in Section 13.5.

Initially, the ITU-T proposed one adaptation protocol type for each class of service and numbered them 1–4. It was soon noticed that there was no need to differentiate between connection-oriented and connectionless data traffic and ATM adaptation layer (AAL) protocols 3 and 4 were replaced by a simpler AAL5 protocol. The different AAL protocols are illustrated in Figure 13.6.

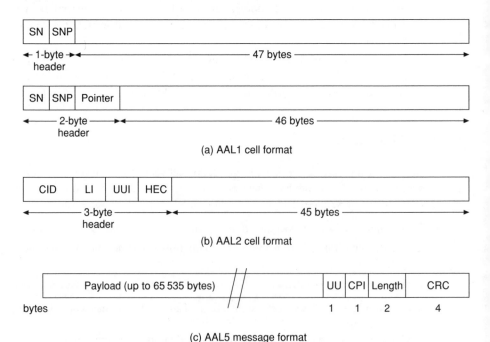

(a) AAL1 cell format

(b) AAL2 cell format

(c) AAL5 message format

Figure 13.6   ATM adaptation layer cell and message formats.

As mentioned above, AAL1 is used for adapting cbr traffic such as uncompressed video or PDH traffic. The cbr stream of traffic is segmented into either 47 or 46 bytes and a 1- or 2-byte header added as shown in Figure 13.6(a). All AAL1 cell headers contain a 3-bit sequence number (SN) and a short (4-bit) cyclic redundancy check called a sequence number protection (SNP) which checks the sequence number for errors. If the cbr traffic has no frame structure (video, for example) then it is adapted into cells with 47-byte payloads. The 46-byte payload cells are only used if a frame structure containing time slots needs to be retained, for example when connecting PDH equipment. Typically, a 46-byte payload cell is transmitted every eighth cell, the additional header byte in this cell containing a pointer which is used to keep track of the framing structure. All AAL1 cells have a single bit in the header between the SN and SNP fields which indicates the existence of a pointer when set to 1.

AAL2 is used for real-time vbr traffic (or possibly cbr traffic) which requires a more careful treatment, typically compressed video and voice. The cell structure, which is shown in Figure 13.6(b), is more complex. The 3-byte header contains an 8-bit channel ID (CID) field which identifies the user of the AAL2 channel, a 6-bit length indicator (LI) field which shows the payload size (which might be less than 45 bytes), a 5-bit user-to-user indication (UUI) and a 5-bit header error control field which is used for a cyclic redundancy check over the whole cell.

AAL5 is used for data traffic, which is typically non-real-time vbr. It differs from AAL1 and 2 in that overheads are added to a frame before it is segmented and the resulting cells contain a full 48-byte payload. The frame structure is shown in Figure 13.6(c). The user-to-user (UU) field is not used by the adaptation layer but is used by higher layers. The common part indicator (CPI) is for future use and the length field indicates the true size of the payload excluding any padding that was added to bring the frame up to a multiple of 48 bytes. There is also a 32-bit cyclic redundancy check over the entire frame including the trailer. The use of AAL5 to carry IP traffic through an ATM network is discussed in RFCs 1483 and 2684 which are entitled 'Multiprotocol encapsulation over ATM adaptation layer 5'.

(13.4) Virtual connections

ATM, like X.25 and Frame Relay, is a connection-oriented technology and involves connections being set up prior to traffic flowing. An end-to-end ATM connection is known as an **ATM bearer service** and it is worth noting that no adaptation takes place with such a service. The terminology used is similar to X.25 and Frame Relay, although there are some differences in meaning. There are three types of virtual connection possible with ATM, namely permanent virtual circuits (PVCs), soft permanent virtual circuits (SPVCs) and switched virtual circuits (SVCs).

Permanent virtual circuits

A PVC is set up manually by a carrier at the request of a customer and typically could remain in place for months or even years. This is the way that PTTs and other

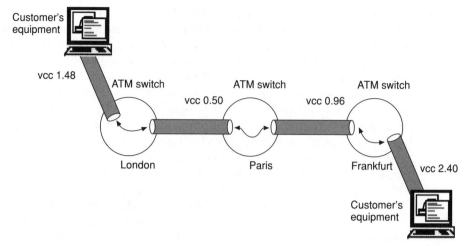

Figure 13.7   ATM permanent virtual circuit.

network providers have traditionally operated their networks, including X.25 and Frame Relay, with the PVC acting as the equivalent of a leased line. In theory, an ATM PVC is simple to set up as illustrated in Figure 13.7.

A PVC is shown between customers in London and Frankfurt, with a transit node at Paris. Note that the different hops along the path of the PVC use different vcc values: vcc 1.48 representing path 1, channel 48; vcc 0.50 representing path 0, channel 50; and so on. The task for the ATM switch at Paris is to switch between an incoming vcc 0.50 and an outgoing vcc 0.96, a process that would typically take 10–20 micro-seconds. One disadvantage of PVCs is that each hop needs to be set up manually (there could be dozens of hops) and another is that if any link along the path of the PVC were to fail then the PVC would be disconnected. In order to re-establish the PVC an alternative path would need to be chosen and set up manually again. Given that, in large networks, links between nodes will inevitably fail on a fairly regular basis, this latter disadvantage is more serious.

Soft permanent virtual circuits

SPVCs are intended to overcome the disadvantages of PVCs mentioned above. They are still permanent connections, in that they would normally remain in place for many months, but they are considerably simpler to set up. Typically, they are set up at the source switch only and the remainder of the circuit is established dynamically using signalling, the latest version of which is defined in ITU-T standard Q.2931. The values of the source and destination vccs are determined beforehand and the latter is carried through the network in a call set-up request over a signalling channel along with other information such as the required bandwidth, as illustrated in Figure 13.8.

The ATM Forum defines vcc 0.5 as a signalling channel, and this channel must exist on links between nodes prior to the SPVC being set up. The route for the circuit will normally be optimized and is determined automatically. In addition to being

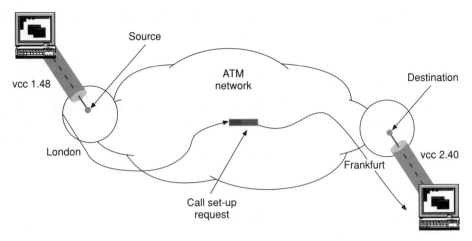

Figure 13.8 ATM soft permanent virtual circuit.

simpler than PVCs to set up, SPVCs have the added advantage that they will auto-matically re-establish in the event of a link failure.

Switched virtual circuits

SVCs, unlike PVCs and SPVCs, have the customer's equipment as their source and destination. Customers can set up and tear down circuits on demand, using the vcc 0.5 signalling channel, in a similar way in which a telephone call is made. At the time of writing, network operators have been slow in offering SVCs to customers, possibly because the responsibility for setting up the circuits would pass from the operator to the customers. Although this way of working is the norm in telephone connections, it is unfamiliar territory in the operator's world of high-speed data circuits.

13.5 ATM service categories

As was mentioned in Section 13.3, there is a need to categorize an ATM service in terms of the requirements of the different types of traffic traversing a network. After a few changes of direction, the ATM Forum has finally arrived at the following types of service category which have developed out of the classes of service mentioned in Section 13.3. They are listed in the order of priority with which they are treated within a network.

Constant bit rate (cbr)

This category is intended for a bit stream with constant intervals between cells such as would be obtained by adapting PDH circuits with rates of 2.048 Mbps (E1) or

34 Mbps (E3). Such circuits contain fixed time slots and have stringent timing requirements. It is also suitable for constant rate voice and video bit streams.

Real-time variable bit rate (rtvbr)

Voice and video traffic is often transmitted after having being compressed, resulting in a vbr stream which nevertheless still has timing requirements. Compressed video, in particular, produces widely varying bit rates as a result of the way in which the compression works, with a complete video frame often being followed by only differences between successive frames.

Non-real-time variable bit rate (nrtvbr)

Many types of data transmission have a vbr without any strict timing requirements. This category includes file transfers and IP traffic. Since WANs often use an ATM core, this category would also include other WAN protocol traffic such as Frame Relay being carried over ATM.

Available bit rate (abr)

This is the most complicated service category to implement as it involves negotiation between a user and the network. It is intended for users who have a traffic requirement that varies greatly and are prepared to take up bandwidth only when it is available. At times of heavy utilization in the network, little or no bandwidth would be allocated to such customers. At the time of writing, this service category has not been widely implemented in the WAN scenario.

Unspecified bit rate (ubr)

The final service category has the lowest priority and provides no guarantees to users as to whether traffic will be delivered or not. Ubr cells are accepted into a network without question, but at the first sign of any congestion they will be discarded. E-mails and certain types of IP traffic are suited to the ubr category since IP makes no promises about delivery. In order to make ubr attractive to customers, network providers are likely to make it cheaper than other service categories.

Tanenbaum (2003) makes a useful analogy between ATM service categories and airline travel. Cbr traffic is comparable with first-class travellers who are given the highest priority and are rarely required to wait in queues. Real-time vbr traffic is analogous to business-class travellers whose queues are normally very short and are offered a priority only exceeded by first-class travellers. In many networks, the major part of the traffic is nrtvbr. This is analogous to economy-class travellers who are guaranteed a seat on a particular flight but are often subjected to long waits in queues along with the majority of their fellow travellers. As mentioned above, abr traffic is the only service category that involves negotiations with the network. It can be compared with a standby passenger: only if there is sufficient spare capacity will the passenger be carried. If there is insufficient capacity available, such travellers must wait until such time as resources (seats) become available. Ubr traffic has the lowest priority of all. If we extend our analogy further we would have a further class of passengers who are allowed on board the aircraft even if it is fully booked and are forced to stand throughout the flight. Furthermore, if the pilot notices that the aircraft is running out of fuel as a result of being overloaded, these passengers are given parachutes and are pushed out of the emergency exit.

13.6 Traffic management

We have noted that ATM has built upon concepts developed in frame relay networks. Apart from the use of fixed-length cells rather than variable length frames, the major development has been in the area of traffic management. As we have seen in Chapter 12, Frame Relay uses the concept of a traffic contract between an end-user and the frame relay network operator. ATM networks use this same concept but much work has been done in the area of enforcing the contract in the event of a user's non-conformance with the contract. An ATM network will also monitor potential connections to ensure that there are sufficient resources to sustain the traffic levels requested by a user. This general area of concern is known as traffic management.

The traffic contract

The major aspect of an ATM traffic contract is a **traffic descriptor** which characterizes the user's traffic, normally by means of up to four **traffic parameters**. The traffic parameters used will vary according to the type of service category that the traffic belongs to. Figure 13.9 illustrates cbr traffic arriving from customer's equipment that is connected to a switch in an ATM network.

The first parameter is called **peak cell rate** (PCR) and is the maximum rate at which the end-user has agreed to transmit cells. (In fact, in this instance, it is the only rate at which the end-user proposes to transmit since, by definition, the bit rate is constant.) PCR is measured in cells/s and is defined as the inverse of the constant time interval, T, between cells. The figure shows a number of cells arriving with a constant time interval and a single cell that has arrived later than expected. This will typically be as a result of the cell having suffered additional delays waiting in queues. All cells

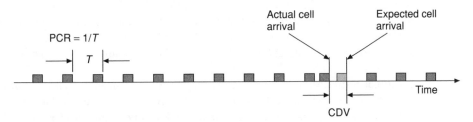

Figure 13.9 Traffic parameters for cbr traffic.

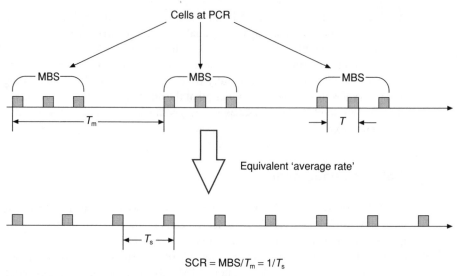

Figure 13.10 Additional traffic parameters for vbr traffic.

will have experienced some delay (simply because it takes a finite time to move from one point to another), but it is essential with cbr traffic such as voice that all cells experience the same delay. Voice traffic is often said to be delay sensitive, but in this particular respect, it is more appropriate to say that it is sensitive to variations in delay. (In fact, the one component in a voice communications system that is sensitive to delay as well as delay variation is the human ear.) In the figure, the difference between the expected and actual arrival times of this particular cell is called the **cell delay variation** (CDV). Having established that this cell has suffered additional delays, a switch must decide whether to take any action. In order to allow the switch to decide on any action, a second parameter called **cell delay variation tolerance** (CDVT) is agreed with the end-user. CDVT is defined as the maximum cell delay variation that can be tolerated (normally at the ingress point to a network) before any action is taken to enforce a traffic contract. The process of enforcing a traffic contract is known as **traffic policing** or **usage parameter control** (UPC) and is described in more detail shortly.

The other two traffic parameters that are normally utilized are only applied to vbr traffic. They are illustrated in Figure 13.10. Cbr traffic is naturally bursty and will typically consist of a series of bursts of traffic at the PCR. The fourth traffic parameter is called **maximum burst size** (MBS) and is the agreed maximum size of a burst of traffic, measured in cells. From the MBS and the mean time between bursts, T_m, an average cell rate can be determined, which is known as the **sustainable cell rate** (SCR).

Further traffic parameters are defined in the ATM standards. **Cell loss ratio** is the proportion of transmitted cells which are not delivered in a timely fashion. **Cell transfer delay** is the average end-to-end transmission time. **Cell error ratio** is the proportion of cells that arrive in error.

Example 13.1

A customer seeks to rent a circuit with the following characteristics from a public ATM network. Data transfer is in bursts of up to seven frames, each frame consisting of up to 2048 bytes of data. When the data is being transferred, the mean time between bursts is 80 ms. The maximum bandwidth required by the user is 2.048 Mbps. Determine suitable values for the following traffic parameters:

(a) Service category

(b) Peak cell rate

(c) Maximum burst size

(d) Sustainable cell rate

(a) Since the traffic consists of data, the appropriate service category will be nrtvbr.

(b) To obtain the PCR in cells/s we must divide the maximum user bandwidth of 2.048 Mbps by 8 and also by 48 since there are 8 bits in a byte and 48 bytes in an ATM cell payload. Initial instinct might lead one to divide by 53 rather 48 since there are 53 bytes in an ATM cell. In this instance of an ATM network renting bandwidth to a customer, however, dividing by 53 would relate to renting the ATM cell header to the customer, as well as the payload, with the consequence that the customer would not receive the full bandwidth requested. Thus:

$$PCR = \frac{2\,048\,000}{8 \times 48} = 5333.3 \text{ cells/s}$$

(c) Since the service category is nrtvbr, the adaptation used will be AAL5. Consequently each frame of data will have an AAL5 trailer of 8 bytes added. Thus each burst will consist of up to:

$$7 \times (2048 + 8) = 14\,392 \text{ bytes}$$

To obtain the MBS in cells/s we must divide by 48, giving:

$$MBS = \frac{14\,392}{48} = 300 \text{ cells}$$

(d) The sustainable cell rate is given by

$$SCR = \frac{MBS}{T_m} = \frac{300}{80 \times 10^{-3}} = 3750 \text{ cells/s}$$

Connection admission control

As we have already noted, there is an emphasis in an ATM network on the prevention of congestion. An important tool for preventing congestion is **connection admission control** (CAC). An ATM network will only allow a connection to be set up if there are sufficient resources available within the network to sustain the connection. Customers can then be reassured that, under normal working circumstances, the network will be able to deliver their traffic contract. (By normal working conditions, we mean the absence

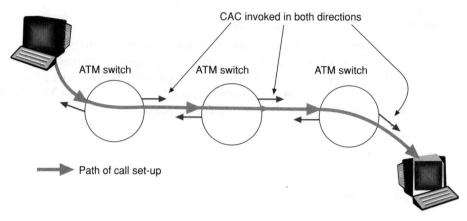

Figure 13.11   Connection admission control.

of major network failures.) Resources must be available not only at the point of ingress to the network but also at every point along the path of the connection.

CAC takes place at the time of the call set-up, at every point along the path of a connection and in both directions of traffic flow. This last point is important since the connection may be asymmetric, that is with different bandwidth in the two directions. In the case of an SPVC or SVC, the traffic parameters are carried through the network inside a Q.2931 call set-up request using VCC 0.5 and CAC will ensure that the parameters can be sustained at each node. In a busy network, multiple paths may need to be examined before a suitable path can be found. If no path can be found then the call will be rejected. Once the CAC is completed then the customer's connection is allocated the requested bandwidth. The CAC process is illustrated in Figure 13.11. The algorithm used to determine whether or not to accept a connection is complex, a commonly used example being attributable to Gibbens and Hunt (1991).

Traffic policing and shaping

Possibly the major tool for preventing congestion in an ATM network is traffic policing, also known as usage parameter control (UPC). User traffic entering a network is policed to see if it conforms to any traffic contract and, if necessary, the contract can be automatically enforced. Once it is decided to enforce the contract, the same three possible options are available to the switch as were discussed in Section 12.4 with respect to frame relay networks. These are reiterated here:

1. Take no action in enforcing the traffic contract.
2. Tag the cell by setting the cell loss priority bit mentioned in Section 13.2, indicating that the cell may be discarded at some other point in the network in the event of congestion.
3. Enforce the traffic contract strictly by discarding the cell immediately. This action may seem drastic but discarding a single cell may well affect the quality of the voice traffic less than allowing a cell to pass that suffers from excessive cell delay variation, thus risking the introduction of distortion in the voice traffic.

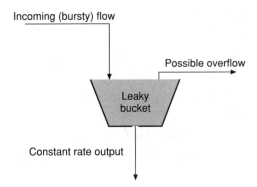

Figure 13.12   A leaky bucket.

UPC uses an algorithm known as the generic cell rate algorithm (GCRA) as outlined in ITU recommendation I.371. The process takes place in two enforcement stages, each checking two traffic parameters. In order to understand the process of enforcement it is usual to describe the process as a **leaky bucket** algorithm. A leaky bucket was used long ago in ancient Egypt to turn an erratic flow of water into a constant rate flow. The principle is illustrated in Figure 13.12.

Irrespective of the rate that water enters the bucket, it will leave at a constant rate. If the bucket fills up then any further arrival of water will cause it to overflow. When this analogy, first proposed by Turner (1986), is applied to ATM, the leaky bucket becomes a single server queue with a constant service time. Bursty traffic entering the queue is forced to leave at a constant bit rate. Once the queue becomes full, incoming cells are discarded. Since UPC requires that enforcement take place in two stages, a **dual leaky bucket algorithm** is used as illustrated in Figure 13.13. The two leaky buckets can be incorporated in a hardware interface or implemented as a software algorithm, the latter being the GCRA.

For cbr traffic, only the first bucket is required. Any bursty incoming traffic is forced to leave the bucket at the PCR. If the incoming rate is excessive then the bucket will become full and cells will be discarded. Cells can also be discarded if they exceed the agreed CDVT. A good way to think of the effect of exceeding an agreed CDVT value is if a large number of cells experience an additional delay. The effect on the bucket will be for it to empty initially and then, when the delayed cells finally arrive, to overflow. Thus the height of the bucket (i.e. the queue size) corresponds to the CDVT. Vbr traffic uses both buckets, the second of which empties at the sustainable cell rate. Since cells enter this bucket at a faster rate than they leave it, it will overflow if the input continues indefinitely at the PCR. The height of this bucket is designed so that it can only accept cells at a PCR up to the maximum burst size. Thus user traffic is discarded (or tagged) if the agreed maximum burst size is exceeded.

An end-user connected to an ATM network can avoid much of the strictures of traffic policing by choosing to **traffic-shape** their own traffic before it enters the network. This would involve the end-user's equipment, typically a router, in throttling back traffic by the use of some kind of leaky bucket mechanism. The use of traffic shaping may well cause a user to discard their own cells but this could be preferable to even harsher treatment at the hands of a public carrier's traffic policing policy.

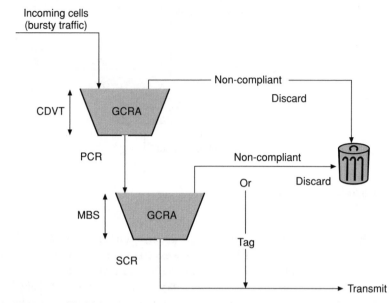

Figure 13.13   Dual leaky bucket algorithm.

Congestion control

The question arises: what if congestion starts to occur in a network despite the traffic management features of ATM that are intended to produce an orderly network? If the network is well designed congestion will normally arise only as a result of link failures. Despite advances in network technologies, link failures are still fairly common events. As mentioned in Section 12.4, once congestion sets in it can feed on itself and get worse. For example, if an output buffer becomes full and cells are lost, the loss of a single cell may result in the retransmission of a complete frame.

We have already seen the approach used in a frame relay network (see Figure 12.11) in dealing with congestion. When the Frame Relay standards were being developed, there were differing views on the nature of congestion (Bergman 1991). At that time, some researchers thought that congestion developed slowly, whereas others thought that it grew rapidly and could get out of control unless dealt with decisively. More recent opinions favour the latter scenario and there is consequently a subtle difference in the strategies employed by an ATM network. Whereas a frame relay network uses a feedback mechanism to notify end-users of the onset of congestion, there is a greater emphasis in an ATM network on preventing congestion from ever occurring by using the traffic management features mentioned above. There is general agreement amongst frame relay network operators that the use of FECN and BECN bits in the header of a frame has not proved very effective in dealing with congestion since it often relies on end-users behaving altruistically by throttling back their traffic on receipt of an FECN or BECN.

ATM networks have the ability automatically to set a single bit called the **explicit forward congestion identifier** (EFCI) bit in the PTI field of a cell headers on the onset of (normally mild) congestion. However, this is even less effective than frame relay congestion notification since there is no backward notification. A more effective

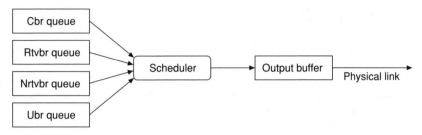

Figure 13.14 ATM queuing arrangement.

strategy is to move quickly to discarding cells as soon as congestion arises. This strategy may seem drastic but if it is handled in an intelligent fashion, it can quickly reduce congestion before it sets in and debilitates parts of a network. Having decided to use cell discard as a weapon against network congestion, a further question arises which is: how to determine the onset of congestion? Traditionally, this has been achieved by monitoring the length of queues. ATM switches will involve several stages of queuing leading to a number of output **buffers**, each of which serves a physical link. A typical arrangement is shown in Figure 13.14.

Note that cells are queued according to service category prior to entering the output buffer and there may even be a further level of queuing in which cells from different vccs (or vpcs) are queued separately. The scheduler will need to use an algorithm in order to feed cells into the output buffer in an orderly fashion. Typically, the cbr queue will be served first, followed by the rtvbr queue and so forth.

In theory, cells could be discarded from any of these queues in the event of congestion. Once again, some form of algorithm is required to ensure an orderly discard policy. Most switches will be reluctant to discard cbr cells and it is likely that they would only ever be discarded from the cbr queue if it became almost full (approaching 100% occupancy). On the other hand, switches would move quickly to discard ubr traffic at the slightest sign of congestion and a ubr discard threshold might be as low as 35% queue occupancy. The other service category queues would have different discard thresholds between these two extremes. The output buffer would require several thresholds since it queues cells from different service classes.

Of particular interest is a congestion control strategy known as **packet-wise discard**. This technique is normally only used with traffic that has been adapted using AAL5 adaptation (estimates put the proportion of AAL5 traffic in an ATM network as high as 90% at the time of writing). It is possible to detect AAL5 traffic since the segmentation and reassembly process produces beginning of message (BOM) and end of message (EOM) cells. In practice, however, it is likely that the service category of AAL5 traffic will almost always be nrtvbr. Having detected AAL5 traffic, it should then be possible to discard entire frames rather than just single cells. This has the obvious effect of reducing the congestion more rapidly and also overcomes an inherent problem associated with the discard of AAL5 cells. This problem arises from the possibility that the discard of a single cell within a frame will cause a higher level protocol such as TCP to retransmit the entire frame, thus worsening the congestion rather than easing it. There are several variations of packet-wise discard depending on precisely how the packets are chosen for discard, but such details are beyond the scope of this text.

13.7 ATM switches

The basic function of an ATM switch is to switch cells between a virtual channel (or path) on an incoming link and a preconfigured virtual channel (or path) on an outgoing link as illustrated in Figure 13.15. The central part of the switch is a non-blocking, hardware, switching matrix known as a **switching fabric**. Given that cells can enter a fabric at rates up to 2.48 Gbps, which is in excess of 5.8 million cells per second, the time spent in traversing the fabric will be of the order of a microsecond. Associated with the switching fabric will be banks of ingress and egress queues that will be physically situated on line interface cards. Cells are typically queued according to ATM service category or individual vccs and vpcs. Clearly the latter will involve far greater numbers of queues.

Traffic will arrive on incoming links at rates which will typically range from 34 Mbps (E3) to 2.48 Gbps (STM-16). The number of links supported might be between 16 and 1000 depending on the speed of the links (clearly the switch could accommodate fewer STM-16 links than it could E3 links). A switch supporting 16 STM-16 links would require a capacity of at least $16 \times 2.48 \sim 40$ Gbps. In practice the fabric's capacity would need to be in excess of this so as to avoid unnecessary queuing at the inputs to the fabric. Queuing, however, is unavoidable on egress from a switch fabric since two cells may want to go to the same output link simultaneously. Clearly one of the two cells must wait. In a well-planned ATM network, queuing should be kept to a minimum but, as mentioned in Section 13.8, link failures can cause network congestion and increased queuing. In this eventuality, the congestion control strategies described earlier will come into play.

Batcher–banyan switching fabrics

The most common form of switch fabric is based on a type of switching matrix known as a **banyan switch**, so called because its cross-connections resemble the roots of a banyan tree. A three-stage banyan switch is illustrated in Figure 13.16. Since there are eight inputs to the switching matrix, each input (and output) is numbered with a 3-bit identifier.

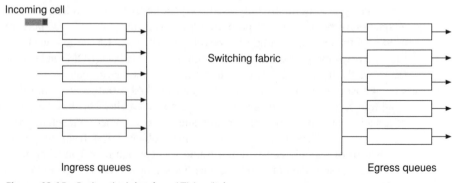

Figure 13.15 Basic principle of an ATM switch.

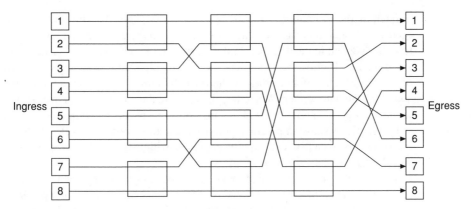

Figure 13.16 Three-stage banyan switching matrix.

At each stage, the matrix makes its switching decision by examining one of the three digits contained in the identifier in turn. It can be readily seen that each input line leads to eight output lines and, since there are eight outputs, there are $8 \times 8 = 64$ different paths through the matrix. Each of the three stages of the switch examines one of the bits of the three bit identifier. There are two outputs from each block in the swtich and an outgoing cell will choose either an upper or lower path depending on whether the relevant bit in the identifier is 0 or 1. The problem with this matrix is that it is not non-blocking and can only carry eight simultaneous connections. For it to be non-blocking it would need to be able to carry 64 simultaneous connections. A solution to this problem was found by Batcher (1968), who added a second switching matrix at the input to the banyan switch that sorted the incoming cells in such a way that the matrix could handle them without path collisions. A Batcher–banyan switch fabric with eight incoming lines is illustrated in Figure 13.17.

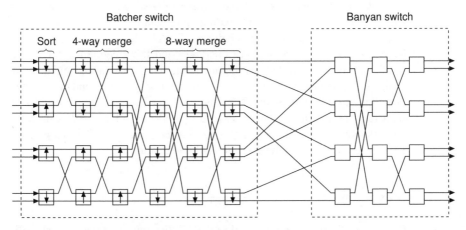

Figure 13.17 Eight-line Batcher–banyan switch fabric. (After A.S. Tanenbaum, *Computer Networks*, 3rd edn. © 1996, p. 154. Reprinted by permission of Pearson Education, Inc., Upper Saddle River, NJ.)

Each of the switching elements can switch two cells. The full output identifier of both cells is examined as they enter the matrix and the cell with the lower output identifier is switched in the direction of the arrow and the other cell is switched in the opposite direction. If only one cell enters a switching element it is switched in the direction of the arrow. The effect of the Batcher switch is to sort cells into an order that corresponds to the output lines. When they then pass to the banyan switch they will be passed to the appropriate output line without any collisions occurring within the banyan switch.

Figure 13.18 shows a practical ATM switch, the Nortel Networks' Passport 15000 ATM switch, which is extensively deployed within the ATM cores of many of the world's largest data networks.

The switch shown has a total switching capacity of 56 Gbps which is provided by two fabrics, each of 56 Gbps capacity. Thus if one fabric fails, the switch retains its full capacity, a feature known as **redundancy**. The line interface cards provide a choice of interfaces from E3 (34 Mbps) up to STM-16 (2.48 Gbps).

13.8 ATM standards

The standards necessary for ATM operation are encompassed within the ITU-T I-series recommendations for Broadband ISDN. This is because ATM was originally chosen as the underlying communications network technology to support B-ISDN. The I-series recommendations that specifically relate to ATM are I.150, I.321, I.361, I.362, I.363, I.413, I.432 and I.610.

The I.150 recommendation defines ATM functional characteristics and deals with multiplexing of cells, switching (using cell-switching techniques), quality of service of cell transmission, and payload types. I.321 defines the ATM protocol model given above in Figure 13.3. I.361 defines the specification for the ATM layer of the protocol model. This recommendation specifies the ATM cell structure that is shown in Figure 13.5. The I.362 recommendation defines the ATM adaption layer (AAL) functional description and refers to the different classes of service listed in Table 13.1. The I.363 recommendation deals with a more detailed ATM adaption layer specification that describes the interaction between the AAL layer, the layer above and also the ATM layer below. Recommendations I.413 and I.432 define the ATM user network interface. Finally, I.610 defines the operation and maintenance principles of B-ISDN.

Signalling standards have also been developed. Recommendation Q.2931 defines signalling at both the UNI and NNI and is an extension of Q.931 used for ISDN. The main function of this signalling is to set up SVCs and soft PVCs through an ATM network. Recommendations Q.2100, Q.2110 and Q.2130 collectively define the relationship between signalling and the ATM adaptation layer.

Exercises

13.1 A traffic descriptor typically contains the four parameters peak cell rate, sustainable cell rate, maximum burst size and cell delay variation tolerance. List three different features of ATM that make use of these parameters.

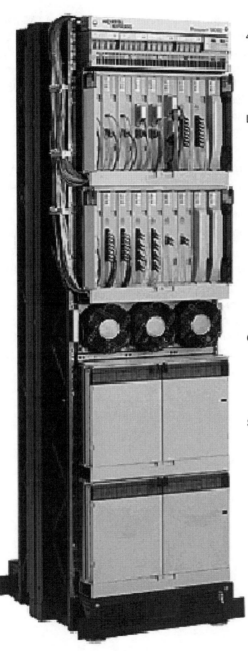

48 V dc circuit breakers

Line interface cards

Cooling units

Switching fabric

Figure 13.18   ATM switch.

13.2 A customer seeks to rent a circuit from a public ATM network with the following characteristics. Data transfer is in bursts of up to three frames, each consisting of up to 4096 bytes of data. When the data is being transferred, the mean time between bursts is 180 ms. The maximum bandwidth required by the user is 1.024 Mbps. Determine suitable values for the following traffic parameters:
(a) ATM service category
(b) peak cell rate
(c) maximum burst size
(d) sustainable cell rate.

13.3 Nrtvbr traffic from a customer connected to a public ATM network has a maximum burst size of 100 cells and a mean time between bursts of 50 ms. Determine:
(a) the sustainable cell rate;
(b) the minimum bandwidth required to accommodate this traffic.

13.4 A customer connects to an ATM network using Frame Relay to ATM interworking. At the Frame Relay end of the connection, the following parameters are used:

committed information rate	256 kbps
excess information rate	128 kbps
committed burst size	7168 bytes

Suggest suitable values for ATM service category, peak cell rate, sustainable cell rate and maximum burst size at the ATM end of the connection.

Chapter 14

Internetworking

....

The subject of this chapter is the techniques deployed to interconnect two or more networks together, generally known as **internetworking**. When discussing internetworking it is generally assumed that two, or more, dissimilar networks are required to be interconnected. The chapter will deal only with generic aspects of internetworking. Specific internetworking protocols and applications such as the widely used TCP/IP suite of protocols are dealt with in Chapter 15. Firstly the general issues and problems relating to internetworking are set out. Techniques to facilitate internetworking are then discussed. An outline of the Internet in terms of its development and organization is also presented, the Internet being the network of choice for many to achieve internetworking. Technical details of the Internet are based upon some of the ideas presented here and are described specifically in the next chapter.

14.1 Internetworking requirements

From earlier chapters it has become apparent that there are a large variety of types of both local and wide area networks. Inevitably there is a need to connect from one network to another. This may be to access services on another network not available on a local network, to extend the physical range of a network or to form a larger, or global, network. Alternatively, one may want to split a single network into two or more separate smaller networks. One reason for this might be to provide a distinct boundary for management and control to enable security features to be implemented to control access between a pair of **subnetworks**. Alternatively, a network may be split into a number of smaller networks to distribute a heavy load on a single network into a number of smaller, less heavily loaded, networks. Splitting may also be done for administrative convenience in order to separate out business functions which can then be mapped to a discrete network. This may eliminate internetwork traffic thus making it easier to administer.

The question arises as to how a number of disparate networks may be interconnected into a single, and usually large, network. In such an arrangement of interconnected networks we shall term each individual network a **subnet**. The term network will then infer two, or more, interconnected subnets. The problems that internetworking must overcome are numerous and complex. A variety of proprietary WAN protocols have been developed over the years such as IBM's Systems Network Architecture (SNA) and Advanced Peer-to-Peer Networking (APPN) and also DEC's Digital Network Architecture (DNA) none of which are directly compatible. A variety of LAN protocols also exist, such as Ethernet and Token Ring, all of which are potentially required to be internetworked.

One of the perennial internetworking requirements is LAN–WAN interconnection where a WAN is required in order to interconnect two distant LANs. The LANs themselves may also be running different protocols. For example, an Ethernet in London may be required to be internetworked with a Token Ring in Chicago. In many instances the WAN used may itself comprise a number of subnets, each of which may be different. The UK WAN might use Frame Relay and connect to the LAN by means of an ISDN connection. The US WAN might use ATM. The major example of a WAN comprising many separate subnets is the **Internet**. This is a global network formed by a large number of individual computer networks.

In broad terms internetworking must physically and logically interconnect networks; successfully route data, which is usually in packet format, across one or more intermediate networks; provide efficient management of resources and, in many cases, accounting for charging purposes. So what are the issues to be overcome in successful internetworking? Some of the main issues to consider are outlined below:

- Protocol conversion between dissimilar networks which may possibly involve different proprietary networks such as DNA to SNA.

- Some form of address translation may be required if the two distant networks use different network address strategies.

- Transmission speed may vary across a number of networks. These differences must be accommodated. In any case, the overall end-to-end speed is limited to that of the slowest network.

- Networks have a maximum packet size. Where a large packet is required to be passed over a network that uses a small maximum packet size, **fragmentation**, also known as **segmentation**, is required. This simply breaks a large packet into a number of smaller packets. Where fragmentation occurs, defragmentation must also occur at some point before packets are passed to a destination end-system.

- Some networks may only offer a connectionless service. Where a connection-oriented path is required to be established, some method of achieving connection-oriented operation is necessary by the selection of suitable networks.

- Flow control is normally employed on an end-to-end basis. Where end-system protocols that support these techniques are dissimilar, some additional effort is required of internetworking to make them compatible.

- With older WAN protocols some form of ARQ is often employed. As we saw in Chapter 5, when a sending station is awaiting an ACK, if it does not appear after an interval of time known as the 'time-out' period a retransmission occurs. Different networks have different time-outs which can present problems in internetworking.

- Increasingly end-system applications specify a class of service, particularly with multimedia applications. Different networks may support some, but different, classes of service and some networks may not specify a class of service at all. These differences need to be addressed.

Example 14.1

A message consisting of 2400 bits is to be passed over an internet. The message is passed to the transport layer which appends a 150-bit header, followed by the network layer which uses a 120-bit header. Network layer packets are transmitted via two networks, each of which uses a 26-bit header. The destination network only accepts packets up to 900 bits long. How many bits, including headers, are delivered to the destination network?

Data plus transport header = 2400 + 150 = 2550 bits

Therefore 2550 bits are passed to the internet layer. The data field of each internet packet is:

900 − 26 = 874 bits

Therefore transport layer data is encapsulated into three internet packets:

Packet 1: 874 bits of data (which leaves 1676 bits still to be encapsulated).

Packet 2: 874 bits (which leaves 802 bits still to be encapsulated).

Packet 3: 802 bits.

Packets 1 and 2 are each of 900 bits. Packet 3 is 802 + 26 bits, or 828 bits long.
    Each of the three packets has a 26-bit header appended for use by the intermediate network. Therefore, the number of bits delivered to the destination network is:

(900 × 2) + 828 + (3 × 26) = 2706 bits

Typical examples of where internetworking is required are information seeking, resource sharing and corporate communications such as e-mail and e-commerce. Information providers and on-line businesses are located on many different networks and users, particularly if private individuals, will connect to their local ISP's network. Thereafter, depending upon where the information or trading site of interest is, interconnection is made to a relevant intermediate network. Often there may not be a direct connection between the local ISP network and the target destination network. In such cases a connection may be made over one, or more, intermediate networks in tandem.

(14.2) Internetworking techniques

Let us now explore some basic internetworking devices, namely repeaters, bridges, backbones, routers and gateways.

Repeaters

Bus-based Ethernet LANs operating by means of baseband transmission (i.e. 10Base2 and 10Base5) are restricted to segment lengths of 185 m, or 500 m, respectively. Two, or more, such LANs could be interconnected to extend this length limitation by means of a device known as a **repeater**, which has been discussed earlier in Chapter 10. A repeater operates at layer 1 of the OSI Reference Model. It is primarily concerned with the transmission of electrical signals at bit level. A repeater, in its simplest form, simply reshapes and retimes data and then retransmits them. Its purpose is to restore the integrity of the signals in regard to pulse shape, amplitude and timing, all of which deteriorate with distance. In this way the length of a baseband transmission medium, and hence physical size of a network, may be extended to facilitate a larger number of users. A repeater is unintelligent, merely repeating each bit that it receives, and can therefore be regarded as transparent. The repeater function may also be thought of as **regeneration**.

A repeater is used for interconnection of LANs which are of similar type at the physical layer. End-users connected to networks which employ a ring topology are usually actively retransmitting frames that are received and therefore effectively perform a repeater function automatically. Repeaters are therefore mainly found in bus-based networks where they are used to interconnect bus segments to extend the effective medium length beyond the basic specification. Because repeaters are transparent, frames generated on any segment are passed, via repeaters, to every other segment. This can be inefficient in that frames do not necessarily always need to be presented to every other segment. As a result, frame activity and hence load on each segment is increased leading to reduced throughput and performance.

Bridges

Bridges are used to connect separate LANs together, which may or may not be similar, at the OSI layer 2, the data link layer. Bridges differ from repeaters in that they are intelligent devices and examine each frame that they receive to perform a 'filtering' function. MAC frame addresses are examined and only those frames containing addresses which indicate that they are intended to pass between networks are accepted by a bridge. All other intra-network frames are rejected by the bridge. In order to perform such filtering, frames are first buffered before any possible onward transmission to enable examination of destination addresses. Such processing can add a delay to frames passing between networks via a bridge. Frames which are permitted to pass between LANs, as with a repeater, are unaltered unless the networks are dissimilar. Bridges inherently also provide a layer 1 repeater function.

As a LAN expands in size, repeaters could be introduced to accommodate more users. However, if usage becomes high, a better option would be to separate the network into two or more identical LANs interconnected by bridges. The bridge would reduce internetwork traffic and hence loading and thus improve network efficiency. Splitting a LAN into several smaller LANs must be done carefully to ensure that users are grouped, as far as is possible, into separate **communities of interest** such that their communication requirements with other LANs do not generate excessive bridge traffic. Each LAN is now only required to support its own level of traffic and occasional inter-LAN frames via a bridge. Should bridge traffic become excessive frames may arrive at a bridge more quickly than it is able to respond, leading to a bottleneck and an attendant degradation in service or even overload leading to lost frames.

As already indicated, bridges may interconnect dissimilar LANs. Two approaches are found in practice. **Encapsulating** bridges enable interconnection of similar networks via an intermediate LAN of different type. In order to perform such a bridging operation the end-system frames are encapsulated into the frames that the bridge passes to the intermediate network. Alternatively a **translational** bridge enables direct interconnectivity between dissimilar networks. This is achieved by the bridge changing frame structures from those received by one network into a suitable form for transmission to another dissimilar network.

There are further applications, other than those purely related to loading and performance, which may warrant the use of a bridge. Where only one LAN exists, a fault may affect the entire network and put every end station out of service. If instead users are connected to one of several bridged LANs reliability may be improved since, if one LAN fails, it will only affect users on that particular network. Separate LANs are commonly configured for distinct operations within a business, for example payroll, personnel records and general application software. A bridge, by examining source addresses within frames, may reject frames based upon access privileges ascribed to an associated user. In this way access by a user to different LANs can be restricted.

A LAN may be interconnected to more than one bridge. The corollary to this is that a transmitted frame may appear on a port of two, or more, bridges. This leads to a number of difficulties, not least of which is frame duplication. Another problem is that of endlessly circulating frames caused by a loop inadvertently created within a bridge. This represents additional network loading and can, in extreme cases, seriously degrade network performance. Where multiple bridges exist on a LAN, each bridge requires knowledge of the wider interconnection arrangements and a strategy is required to ensure that frame duplication or endlessly circulating frames do not occur and also that frames are efficiently passed around the network.

Backbones

Where it is required to interconnect LANs which are physically too far away from each other, simple bridged networks are no longer appropriate. One solution is to deploy a **backbone** for use within a network. A backbone has no end stations directly attached to it. It may handle a large volume of traffic, especially if it is also connected to a WAN for internetworking beyond the local area. In most cases therefore a high-speed network is required and is often different to that of the LANs it is interconnecting. A backbone is regarded as a separate network and therefore a layer 3 protocol will be required to internetwork successfully all stations within both the LANs and the backbone to which they are connected. An FDDI or ATM network may be used as a backbone, either of which supports high-speed operation and is able to operate over relatively large physical distances compared with a conventional LAN.

Routers

We have seen how repeaters and bridges are used for internetworking of LANs at layers 1 and 2, respectively. However, to permit an internet operation, end-systems must support internet-based addressing, which is a layer 3 function. A key building block of the Internet is a **router** which is a device operating at the OSI layer 3, the network layer, and running a layer 3 protocol such as the IP to route traffic in the form of packets, based upon network-wide addresses. A router makes use of network layer addresses rather than the MAC addresses used by a bridge to interconnect similar, or possibly dissimilar, networks. Routers differ from bridges in that they typically support LAN–LAN interconnection via a WAN – that is, LAN–WAN–LAN interconnection – whereas bridges do not employ a WAN or have any need to involve themselves with network layer protocols.

Routers contain **routing tables** which indicate the mapping between the destination address contained within incoming packets and the output **port** of the router to which the packet is forwarded. In order to perform routing a router places successive packets in an input buffer associated with each port. The destination address of each packet may then be examined, normally on a first-in–first-out (FIFO) basis. The router then uses the routing table to determine the output port to be used and the packet is then passed to an output buffer associated with the required port.

Consider an internet shown in Figure 14.1 comprising the four networks listed below. Each network has a router. A set of routing tables, one for each router, are shown below. A link is defined in the form (1,3) meaning the link between network 1 and newtork 3 in this case:

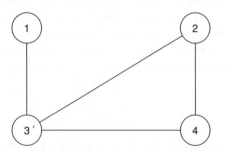

Figure 14.1

Node 1	
Destination	Next hop
1	–
2	(1,3)
3	(1,3)
4	(1,3)

Node 2	
Destination	Next hop
1	(2,3)
2	–
3	(2,3)
4	(2,4)

Node 3	
Destination	Next hop
1	(1,3)
2	(2,3)
3	–
4	(3,4)

Node 4	
Destination	Next hop
1	(3,4)
2	(2,4)
3	(3,4)
4	–

A router enables large packet-based networks to be formed by interconnecting a number of subnetworks. Each subnetwork is connected to a single router and routers are then typically interconnected by WANs. In practice each router is ideally connected to at least two other routers to provide for alternative routing strategies. It therefore follows that a router is also required to generate the routing information required for use by intermediate routers, when necessary.

In Chapter 10 we saw that LANs only operate at layers 1 and 2 and therefore have an addressing scheme which is restricted within a single LAN. These MAC addresses cannot be used as universal network addresses within an internet. In consequence, end-systems in an internet must be assigned internet-wide network addresses. In the case of LANs this means that network-wide addresses must be mapped to MAC addresses, and vice versa. We shall look at an example of how this is achieved in practice in the next chapter. By far the most common internet-wide addressing scheme is that of the IP, designed to operate with a wide range of networks. IP is commonly built upon Ethernet in a LAN scenario and would typically connect to a WAN via a serial link using the Point-to-Point Protocol (PPP). Once in the WAN, IP traffic is often encapsulated in other WAN protocols such as Frame Relay or ATM that possess the layer 2 functionality that does not exist in IP.

An extremely common scenario today is that of distant Ethernet networks internetworking by means of IP over a WAN as shown in Figure 14.2. The end-systems on each LAN are effectively networking on an end-to-end basis using the same layer 4 protocol, for example the TCP. Networking is achieved at layer 3 where all network entities are communicating via IP. End-system A communicates peer to peer with end-system A at the IP layer. In order to achieve layer 3 communication both Router X and LAN 1 communicate by means of layers 1 and 2 using an appropriate LAN protocol as do Router Y and LAN 2.

In this illustration we shall assume that LAN 1 uses Ethernet and that LAN 2 uses Token Ring. End-system A will have an Ethernet Network Interface Card and the card

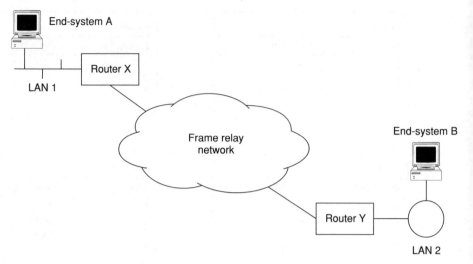

Figure 14.2   Router operation.

must support the IP. Router X connects to LAN 1 using Ethernet and may be regarded as simply another networked device on this network. The router has an Ethernet port with which it physically connects to the Ethernet medium in use. Clearly the router must also be running the Ethernet MAC protocol. Router X employs a WAN protocol for onward communication to Router Y via the WAN (Frame Relay in this example). Again the router has a Frame Relay interface, or port. Communication at layer 3 between the two routers is, as with LAN 1 to Router X, by means of IP. Similar arrangements exist between Router Y and LAN 2, the only difference being that here both the router and the LAN are now running Token Ring.

Note in this example that no direct protocol conversions take place. This is because at every node IP is being supported and implemented. In Figure 14.3 we can see how this works. At LAN 1 IP packets are encapsulated into Ethernet via LLC frames ②,

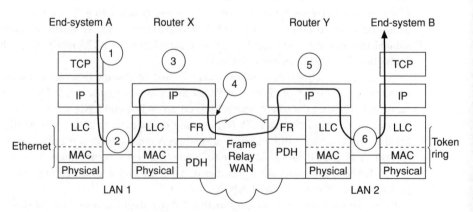

Figure 14.3   General internetworking arrangement.

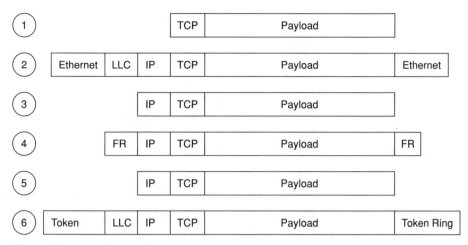

Figure 14.4 IP packet transfer.

(and indeed MAC frames, not shown). For the communication between the two routers the IP packets are further encapsulated into Frame Relay frames ④ and pass over the Frame Relay WAN. The frame relay network will require a physical medium, which would typically be PDH. Finally, packets between Router Y and LAN 2 are encapsulated into the Token Ring LLC frames ⑥.

Figure 14.4 illustrates what happens to a TCP segment in terms of different headers and trailers that are used at different points as it passes between end-system A and end-system B.

Note that, as the packet passes through the different networks, the headers (and trailers) are added and removed according to the protocol being used in the particular network. The two headers that remain in place as a segment, or packet, traverses the different networks are the TCP and IP headers. The above illustration only uses one **intermediate system** (IS), namely the Frame Relay WAN, to interconnect the two LANs. In many cases the two networks to be interconnected, irrespective of whether they are LANs or WANs, may not both conveniently be connected to the same core WAN. Many internetworking arrangements require that two or more intermediate systems are necessary. Hence the more general arrangement of internetworking is where two end-systems are interconnected using IP through a series of *cascaded* intermediate systems.

Dijkstra's algorithm

In networks comprising a number of intermediate networks, and hence routers, as discussed above, a method must be found to establish routing tables for each router. The routing tables then control which route each IP packet is forwarded over. A shortest path first algorithm known as **open shortest path first** (OSPF) to compute optimal routes to other routers in a network based upon the local topological database. The algorithm used by OSPF and other routing systems is attributable to Dijkstra (1959). Probably the best way to approach Dijkstra's algorithm is by way of an example. Figure 14.5

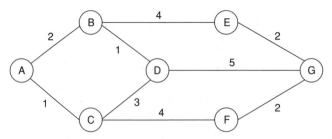

Figure 14.5 Dijkstra's algorithm example network.

Table 14.1	Link state database.					
A	B	C	D	E	F	G
B,2	A,2	A,1	B,1	B,4	G,2	E,2
C,1	D,1	D,3	C,3	G,2	C,4	D,5
	E,4	F,4	G,5			F,2

shows a seven-node network in which we will find the shortest paths between node A and all other nodes. **Metric** values are indicated on each hop that reflect the **cost** of each link.

One of the first things that OSPF (and other routing protocols such as ATM) will do is to discover neighbours. Table 14.1 shows the nearest neighbours to each of the nodes A to G, along with the metric to that neighbour. Such a table in a router using OSPF is known as a **link state database**.

Using the link state database, we build a table containing two columns, known as **tentative** and **permanent**. Starting from the root of the Dijkstra computation (node A in this case), destination nodes are entered into the tentative column as the metrics to them become known and are promoted to the permanent column if the destination is in a shortest path. Thus the table starts off as shown in Figure 14.6 (a). As a first step, only the local node A is entered into the permanent column. Nodes B and C are entered into the tentative column since, although their metrics are known, better metrics might emerge during the operation of the algorithm. In the next step, shown in (b), the entry with the smallest metric (node C in this case) is promoted to the permanent column and any new nodes that become known through the promoted node are entered in the tentative column (nodes D and F in this case) along with a metric to the source. In (c), node B is promoted to the permanent column as it has the smallest metric and this allows nodes D and E to be entered in the tentative column as reachable through B. This procedure is repeated throughout the network as shown in (d) to (g).

Once all of the nodes appear in the permanent column, the final table (g) shows the shortest path from A to all of the other nodes along with the metric of the path. This table will be stored in a routing database in routers and switches and used to forward traffic along the best available path through a network.

Tentative	Permanent
B, 2 C, 1	A, 0

(a)

Tentative	Permanent
B, 2 C: D, 4 C: F, 5	A, 0 C, 1

(b)

Tentative	Permanent
B: D, 3 C: E, 6 C: F, 5	A, 0 B, 2 C, 1

(c)

Tentative	Permanent
B: E, 6 C: F, 5 B: D: G, 8	A, 0 B, 2 C, 1 B: D, 3

(d)

Tentative	Permanent
B: E, 6 C: F: G, 7	A, 0 B, 2 C, 1 B: D, 3 C: F, 5

(e)

Tentative	Permanent
C: F: G, 7	A, 0 B, 2 C, 1 B: D, 3 B: E, 6 C: F, 5

(f)

Tentative	Permanent
	A, 0 B, 2 C, 1 B: D, 3 B: E, 6 C: F, 5 C: F: G, 7

(g)

Figure 14.6   Dijkstra computation for node A.

Gateways

The internetworking devices and systems that have been considered so far have not carried out conversions between protocols, but have encapsulated higher level protocols inside various lower level protocols. A gateway is a device that routes packets between one type of network and another, by performing the necessary protocol conversion functions. An example of a gateway is shown in Figure 14.7. The two protocols to be converted would typically operate at the same levels as each other in the ISO reference model. In this case the two protocols are Frame Relay and ATM, both of which operate at levels 2 and 3. This particular type of protocol conversion, known

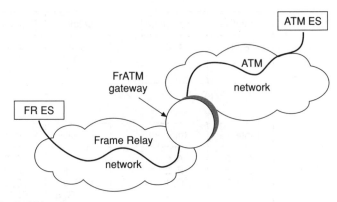

Figure 14.7 FrATM gateway.

as **Frame Relay to ATM interworking** (FrATM), is well established and is formalized in Frame Relay Forum standard FRF.8.

At first sight this arrangement looks identical to that of normal router operation. The difference is that the gateway interworks between the two protocols. Conversion between the various frame relay and ATM traffic parameters takes place and there is the possibility of interworking between the two addressing schemes used. Another example of a gateway that converts between voice and IP-based traffic is discussed in the next chapter.

14.3   The Internet

The Advanced Research Projects Agency (ARPA) of the US Department of Defense (DoD) addressed the issue of, and produced a solution for, internetworking prior to ISO's formulation of network standardization which has resulted in the Internet that we know today. The underlying design goals were to internetwork a proliferation of many different kinds of computer networks and, because the network was originally conceived primarily for military use, develop a network that would get a packet through even if the network was severely disrupted or damaged.

The DoD's developments led to the establishment in 1969 of a four-node network connected by 56 kbps links that became known as ARPANET. The Internet evolved from ARPANET over the following decade and has developed to internetwork a proliferation of many different kinds of computer networks. ARPANET was finally decommissioned in 1989. The Internet is now a global internetworking facility available on many interconnected computer networks, access to which is easily and inexpensively achieved by subscription to any of the networks which form the Internet. What had originally been a centralized core network has developed into a more diverse network operated by commercial service providers such as Sprint and MCI.

The DoD has handed over responsibility to what is now the **Internet Architecture Board** (IAB), a non-profit-making organization governed by a board of trustees, which is responsible for the further development of the Internet. The IAB has two task forces: the **Internet Research Task Force** and the **Internet Engineering Task Force**

(IETF). The IETF carries out detailed work in developing Internet protocols for routing, security and so forth. Amongst other documents it publishes **Requests For Comment** (RFCs). These were originally regarded as just technical reports but have since become *de facto* standards. In order for RFCs to become official standards they are passed by the IETF to the ITU-T for ratification. The World Wide Web Consortium (W3C), which is an industry consortium with over 150 members, was set up in 1994 to develop web standards such as HTML. In addition a variety of other protocols for use in the Internet have appeared. The Internet exploits a number of the generic concepts of internetworking discussed earlier in this chapter. However, as the Internet and its operations are so pervasive today, the next chapter is devoted to a detailed explanation of many of its technical features and operation.

(14.4) Security

Encryption, discussed in detail in Appendix 1, is widely used to secure the content of messages in transmission. The use of public key encryption is especially attractive in the Internet because it provides a simple solution to the answer of key distribution. This is particularly so in e-commerce situations where the customer base is potentially huge and where it would be impossible to assign keys, upon demand, using private key encryption.

Another technique, which involves a **firewall**, is shown in Figure 14.8. A firewall may be placed between an organization's private network and, say, a public network such as the Internet. It may then be used to control access into, and out of, the organization's network. Note that it is essential that there is only a single entry point into and out of an organization's private network so that there is no way to bypass a firewall. Access control may be achieved by **packet filtering** operating on each router within the firewall. Router A can inspect the source and destination address of each outgoing packet. A policy must be devised, and configured within the router, to establish from which source addresses packets may be forwarded by the firewall, and to which destination addresses. In this way an organization may control who has access to the public internet, and also prevent access to specified networks within the internet. Even if an outgoing packet is passed by Router A a second level of packet filtering may be implemented. Commonly, as with the IP used by the Internet, the application may be inferred from detail contained within the packet header. In the case of IP, header information includes a port address (ports are discussed in the next chapter) and a certain application is assigned to a particular port. Therefore packets may also be filtered based upon a particular service. In this way it is possible to control internet access in and out of an organization for a particular node and, where access is granted, even the type of application which may be accessed. In a similar manner Router B may be configured to provide packet filtering of incoming packets.

Packet filtering could of course be applied using a single router. However, the arrangement comprising two routers shown in Figure 14.8 means that an application gateway may additionally be inserted through which all incoming and outgoing packets must pass. The application gateway is used to implement a security policy based upon the type of data contained in packets. Although, as we have seen, packet filtering may

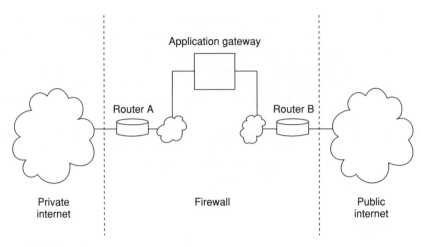

Figure 14.8 Firewall.

provide a broad-brush approach and filter services associated with a packet, for example file transfer may be inhibited for a particular node, the application gateway
enables more discriminative filtering to be implemented. For instance, an e-mail gateway may examine e-mail messages to guard against repeated messages intended
to clog up a system and so render it inoperative, a form of **denial of service**. File
transfers may be examined and certain types, or bit patterns, rejected to guard against
viruses, worms and the like.

Firewalls may also be installed within a private network. It may be that within an
organization some activities are of a sensitive nature. Users associated with these activities could be grouped into a separate network, or subnet, and connected to the rest
of the organization's network by means of a firewall.

Exercises

14.1   Discuss the issues associated with fragmentation. Include consideration of where
fragmentation and reassembly may occur and the effects upon both network
and user.

14.2   Datagrams may arrive at the destination as a series of two, or more, datagrams
due to fragmentation. Outline the action of the host to ensure that the original
datagram is correctly reassembled.

14.3   Explain why reassembly algorithms usually have a timer to guard against fragments which do not arrive at a host due to being lost within a network.

14.4   Fragmentation and reassembly occur within the network layer. If datagrams
arrive out of order, does this have any effect upon the transport service which
is being carried?

14.5   A message consisting of 1500 bits of data is passed to a transport layer for
onward transmission. Both the transport and network layers use a 160-bit header.

Datagrams are transmitted via two networks, each of which uses a 24-bit packet header. If the destination network has a maximum packet size of 800 bits:
(a) How many datagrams are produced?
(b) How many bits, including headers, are delivered to the network layer at the destination?

14.6 Explain what a bridge is and the functions it performs.

14.7 Compare and contrast a bridge and a hub.

14.8 With reference to bridged networks:
(a) What is meant by a 'loop'?
(b) Explain how a loop may occur
(c) What problems are caused if a loop occurs?

14.9 Two separate LAN segments are to be interconnected using either a repeater or a bridge. Although a bridge is more complex, and hence costly, outline the advantages it offers over that of a repeater.

14.10 Explain the term *backbone* and describe two examples where such a technique may be used.

14.11 Explain the operation of a LAN switch and a router. Discuss the differences between them.

14.12 Discuss the differences between repeaters, bridges and routers.

14.13 Construct routing tables for each of the nodes of the network illustrated in Figure 14.9. Assume that in each case the preferred route is the one containing the least number of serial hops between nodes.

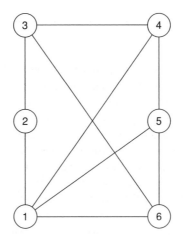

Figure 14.9 Exercise 14.13.

14.14 Explain the terms:
(a) Firewall
(b) Packet filtering.

Chapter 15

Internet protocols

The various internetworking devices, such as routers and bridges, that were discussed in Chapter 14 need to interoperate using a common group of protocols. One of the central protocols used within the Internet is simply known as the **Internet Protocol** (IP) and was originally developed to interwork with a large variety of different networks that were often proprietary. However, IP and its associated protocols such as the **Transmission Control Protocol** (collectively known as the TCP/IP suite) have proved so successful that they have developed into a *de facto* standard that is used almost universally in conjunction with the Internet.

Before examining the TCP/IP suite in detail we shall reiterate some of the original goals that the US Department of Defense sought to achieve. In broad terms an internet must interconnect networks and successfully deliver data between processes and applications on different hosts. By implication an internet must also efficiently route data via intermediate networks to ensure successful delivery to a destination. Factors which need to be considered in pursuing the above aims are that networks may have, or use, different addressing schemes, different maximum packet sizes, different network access mechanisms, different error recovery techniques, different routing techniques, and so on. In addition some networks may operate upon a connection-oriented basis and others connectionless.

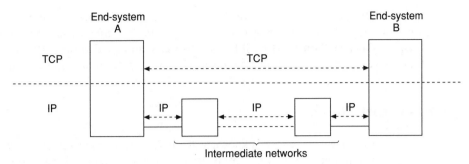

Figure 15.1 TCP/IP operation.

(15.1) ## The TCP/IP suite

TCP/IP assumes that the Internet, or some of its subnetworks, are unreliable. With reference to Figure 15.1, reliable operation on an end-to-end basis is achieved using TCP at the transport layer. TCP is only provided at the two end-systems rather than in any intermediate, and possibly unreliable, networks forming part of the connection.

The complete TCP/IP stack is shown in Table 15.1. The TCP/IP stack only offers protocols at layers 3, 4 and 7 and consequently is a lighter weight, more streamlined, model than that of OSI. Nothing is specified in TCP/IP at the presentation and session layers, or at the data link and physical layers, the latter of which Internet terms the **host-to-network** layer. In addition to TCP and IP a range of additional protocols are supported. A **File Transfer Protocol** (FTP) facility enables the transfer of files, in either direction, as well as remote viewing of files and user ID and password protection. The **Simple Mail Transfer Protocol** (SMTP) provides a basic e-mail facility and **Telnet** enables hosts to be accessed remotely, typically for interactive database enquiry services. The **HyperText Transfer Protocol** (HTTP) is used for web browsing. The **Domain Name Server** (DNS) protocol maps a domain name to its network address. DNS is discussed in more detail later in the chapter.

Other applications that are described in more detail later on are the **Simple Network Management Protocol** (SNMP) that is used to manage IP networks and the **Real-Time Transport Protocol** (RTP) that is used for transporting real-time video and

Table 15.1 TCP/IP and OSI reference models.

OSI layer	OSI model	TCP/IP model	Example protocols
7	Application	Application	FTP, SMTP, Telnet, HTTP, DNS, SNMP, RTP
6	Presentation		
5	Session		
4	Transport	Transport	TCP, UDP
3	Network	Internet	IP, OSPF, RIP, BGP
2	Data link	Host-to-network layer	
1	Physical		

audio traffic such as Voice over IP. The **User Datagram Protocol** (UDP) is an alternative, less reliable, transport protocol to TCP. The **Routing Information Protocol** (RIP), **Open Shortest Path First** (OSPF) and **Border Gateway Protocol** (BGP) are routing protocols used with IP that are dealt with in more detail later in the chapter.

(15.2) Internet Protocol

The network layer of TCP/IP is known as the Internet layer and its purpose is to establish a route through the Internet for the transmission of packets. IP was formalized in 1980 as RFC 760 and more recently as RFC 791. Considering that it was developed in the 1970s, IP has proved to be remarkably enduring and it is still the protocol of choice in routed data networks. IP is connectionless: that is, packets, which are called **datagrams**, are handled independently by routers as they pass though networks and no action is taken should a datagram be lost in transmission. A 'best effort' service is offered whereby there is no guarantee that any datagram will successfully arrive at the destination. Where reliable transmission is required, an appropriate protocol must be selected within the transport layer. Any lost datagrams may then be dealt with by a suitable protocol, such as the TCP, which is used to ensure reliable delivery of messages.

The format of an IP datagram is shown in Figure 15.2. The header contains a minimum of 20 bytes, but can accommodate further option fields, each of 4 bytes. The various fields of the header are as follows:

- Version: A 4-bit IP version number, which will be either 4 or 6.

- IHL: Internet header length, a 4-bit header length that specifies the number of 32-bit words in the header.

- Type of service: An 8-bit priority value that specifies whether the sender prefers the datagram to travel over a route with minimum delay or a route with maximum throughput.

- Total length: 16 bits that specify the total number of bytes in the datagram, including the header.

0 1 2 3	4 5 6 7	8 9 0 1 2 3 4 5	6 7 8 9	0 1 2 3 4 5 6 7 8 9 0 1
Version	IHL	Type of service		Total length
Identifier			Flags	Fragment offset
Time to live		Protocol		Header checksum
Source address				
Destination address				
Options and padding				
Data				
:				
:				
Data				

Figure 15.2 IP datagram.

Table 15.2 IP header options.

Option	Purpose
SECURITY	Provides hosts with a way to use security
LOOSE SOURCE ROUTING	Provides a list of addresses that must be included in the route
STRICT SOURCE ROUTING	Provides the complete route from source to destination
RECORD ROUTE	Records the route of a datagram as it traverses the network
STREAM IDENTIFIER	Provides a way for a stream identifier to be carried
TIMESTAMP	Provides the time and date when a router handles a datagram

- Identifier: A 16-bit sequence number that is intended to uniquely identify a datagram even if it has been fragmented.

- Flags: 3 bits that indicate whether a datagram has been fragmented or is a complete datagram.

- Fragment offset: 13 bits that tell a receiver how to order fragments within a particular datagram. It specifies where in the original datagram the fragment belongs.

- Time to live: 8 bits that are used to prevent a datagram from travelling indefinitely around a network or internet. Each router that handles the datagram decrements the time to live by 1. If the counter reaches zero, the datagram is discarded and a warning is sent back to the source.

- Protocol: 8 bits that determine whether the data is to use TCP or UDP in the transport layer.

- Header checksum: 16 bits that error check the header only. A sender computes the 1's complement sum of all 16-bit quantities in the header (excluding the checksum itself) and stores the 1's complement of the sum in the header checksum field. A receiver computes the same 16-bit sum including the checksum field. If the header is received correctly, the result should be zero.

- Source address: The 32-bit IP address of the originator of the datagram.

- Destination address: The 32-bit address of the destination.

- Options and padding: An optional field which if it exists is padded to be a multiple of 4 bytes. Five options are defined, as listed in Table 15.2. In practice, these options have rarely been used.

IP addresses

The address fields in the IP header contain 32 bits that are arranged into 4 bytes, each of which is expressed as a decimal number separated by a dot, a system known as **dotted decimal notation.** This makes IP addresses easier to handle in written form with less chance of making an error. Thus the binary address:

10000000 00000011 00000010 00000101

is expressed as the IP address:

128.3.2.5

Table 15.3 IP address formats and classes.

Class	Internet address (32 bits)			
	Code value	No. of bits		
		Code	Network	Host
A	0	1	7	24
B	10	2	14	16
C	110	3	21	8
D	1110	4	Multicast address	
E	11110	5	Reserved for future use	

Table 15.4 Classes of IP Address.

Class	Number of networks		Number of hosts		Address range
A	$2^7 - 2$	126	$2^{24} - 2$	16 777 214	1.0.0.1 to 126.255.255.254
B	2^{14}	16 384	$2^{16} - 2$	65 534	128.0.0.1 to 191.255.255.254
C	2^{21}	2 097 152	$2^8 - 2$	254	192.0.0.1 to 223.255.255.254

IP addresses fall into one of three different classes of addresses called A, B and C. The different formats that are used with these classes are given in Table 15.3. Note that for Classes A, B and C addresses are divided into two fields that distinguish between a network address and a host address. The leading, or leftmost, bits indicate the class of address. The number of networks and hosts available for the Class A, B and C address classes is illustrated in Table 15.4. Note that host bits which are all zeros and all ones are not assigned to a host address. All ones are used for IP broadcast datagrams. In the case of a further Class D a number of hosts forming a **multicast** group are assigned a multicast address. Any datagram intended for the particular group of addresses defined by a multicast uses the appropriate multicast address. A further class E is reserved for future use.

Example 15.1

A host has an IP address of 128.3.2.5. Determine:

(a) the class of address

(b) the network ID address

(c) the host address

The IP address in binary form is:

10000000 00000011 00000010 00000101

The two leftmost bits are 10. Therefore, from Table 15.3 the IP address must be a Class B address.

Hence the first two bytes define the network address. The right-hand two bytes define the host ID so that, in this case, the network ID is 128.3 and the host ID is 2.5.

Let us now consider this addressing scheme in more detail. Each entity within a network must be assigned an address. Examples of entities are a host, a terminal, or a router interface. The major function of an address is to facilitate routing a datagram through networks to ensure its correct delivery to the required destination (in a similar way that a telephone number is used as the address of a phone line). There are a number of addressing **modes** which may be used. An address defining a single entity, for example a host address, is known as a **unicast** address. Where an address relates to a number of entities, perhaps a number of hosts forming a work group, a multicast address may be used. Clearly some mapping is necessary to define the individual addresses to which multicast address communications are distributed. Where a communication is to be sent to all entities within a network, a **broadcast** address is used. Ideally, in a fully 'wired world', each entity should have a unique global address. Although this has not happened as yet, there is a possibility that it may, in time, appear. However, many networks are so long established, for example X.25 and the Internet, that global addressing of intermediate systems is perhaps a non-starter.

Domain names

The 32-bit IP addresses are unfriendly for humans to use. They are difficult to remember, work with and easy to make a mistake with. In consequence users generally work with **domain names** rather than IP addresses. For instance, the domain name for Pearson Education is pearsoned-ema.com and is shorthand for the class C IP address 194.200.102.32.

A domain is the final destination, or point of connection, on the Internet. For example, a large institution with an internal computer network connected to the Internet is the end-point of the Internet. As such, it is regarded as a domain. E-mail addresses, for instance, contain a **username** which represents the user's account name on his/her computer system, one or more **location identifiers** and a **domain**. The symbol '@' separates the username from the locations and domain. For example, consider the following e-mail address:

myname@somewhere.com

'somewhere.com' is the domain name. 'myname' is the username and normally assigned to a particular person or organizational function, for example enquiries. 'Somewhere' is the domain's location identifier (or address) on the particular network, or domain to which 'somewhere' is connected. More detail may be included in domain names. For instance, the above may be extended to:

myname@entity.somewhere.com

'entity' could, as suggested, define a particular entity at 'somewhere' and is a more specific location indentifier. 'entity' could, for instance, be a particular server. A domain name extension, .com here, indicates the particular type of network. Additionally, this can be followed by an indication of where the domain is located, e.g. .uk, .ca, Canada etc.

Subnetting

Ethernet-based LANs may use repeaters or hubs to form a larger network and connect more hosts. Any frame generated by a host on one segment is effectively broadcast to each host on every other segment. Since a destination host is only on one segment this may lead to a substantial increase in collision activity and degrade network performance. (In UTP networks this may be resolved by installing switches instead of hubs.) However, a popular solution is to use IP for networking and a router to split the network into a number of subnets, each subnet being connected to one port of the router. In this way datagrams destined for another host on the same subnet are not forwarded by the router to other subnets. Datagrams from a host on one subnet to a host on another subnet are only forwarded to the port to which the destination host is connected.

A LAN which does not use subnets, or LAN switches, may be thought of as comprising a single **collision domain** where each originating frame is passed to every segment and may collide with a frame from any other host in the network. In subnetting each subnet is regarded as a *single* collision domain and overall collision activity is greatly reduced. For maximum advantage in subnetting, users should be grouped into suitable subnets so that most datagrams are destined for the same subnet as the source. For instance, accounts personnel could be assigned to one subnet, management to another, and so on.

Subnetting is achieved by 'stealing' 2 bits or more (the leftmost significant) from the host address portion of an IP address. These bits are known as **subnet bits**. Suppose a network has a Class C address. It has eight host bits. There must be at least two subnet bits. This is because the all-zero and all-one pattern within the subnet bits is prohibited. (All ones are used for broadcast addresses and all zeros are used as a network address.) In consequence we may use 2 bits, 3 bits and so on. There is a trade-off. The more subnet bits, and hence subnets, there are, the fewer bits are available for assigning to host addresses.

(**Example 15.2**)
_____

An organization has a Class C IP network address 194.82.212.0 allocated to it. Suppose six subnets are required. Determine how many subnet bits are required and the ranges of host addresses on each subnet.

Six subnets require three subnet bits: $2^3 = 8$. Therefore the subnet patterns are 001 to 110. Remember that 000 and 111 are not available for subnetting.
This means that host addresses for each subnet are:

Subnet 1:   001 0 0001   to   001 1 1110

(note that broadcasts may occur on a subnet and all-zero and all-one patterns are not assigned for host bits) through to

Subnet 6:   110 0 0001   to   110 1 1110

It is left as an exercise for the reader to convert the above host portion addresses into full 32-bit dotted decimal format. It is also instructive to calculate how many actual host addresses are available with the above subnetting scheme and to compare this with the number of hosts possible without subnetting. You will find that subnetting comes with a price of reducing the number of host addresses available. For Class A and B users, where addresses are plentiful, this may not be an issue. Most Internet users are assigned a Class C address which only has 254 addresses available. With subnetting this is further reduced.

In the above example three subnet bits were used. Had four subnet bits been used, up to 14 subnets would have been possible, but the number of host addresses per subnet would be somewhat reduced, and also the total number of hosts that may be supported. There is thus a trade-off to be made between the number of subnets and the maximum number of hosts available to a network as a whole.

It follows from the above that even without subnetting Class C networks cannot have more than 254 host addresses and hence hosts. For many organizations more addresses than this are required. Fortunately, in time-honoured fashion, diversity may be brought into play to good effect. Suppose a Class C network requires to connect 300 hosts. For most of the time it may well be that many hosts are inactive. Indeed one may discover that it is extremely rare for more than 254 hosts requiring to be active at any one instant in time. In such cases, whether subnetting is employed or not, addresses may instead of being permanently assigned to hosts, known as **static addressing**, be assigned temporarily to hosts as required, that is **dynamic addressing**. If a host becomes active but has not currently been assigned an address, it may be assigned an address, assuming that there is one free, on the fly as it were. TCP/IP provides a protocol for assigning dynamic addresses called **Dynamic Host Configuration Protocol** (DHCP). In practice a DHCP server is connected to the network which controls and assigns addresses to hosts. Note that DHCP may still be used with subnetting. DHCP has another attraction for network administrators since no IP addresses have to be configured on each host within the network, nor is detailed record keeping required of host–IP address associations.

In order for a router which is using subnets to be able to make routing decisions, a **subnet mask** is required to be assigned for each subnet. Consider the subnet 194.82.212.128 from the previous example. This subnet address in dotted binary is:

    11000010.01010010.11010100.10000000

In that example 27 subnet bits were used and the subnet mask has all ones in the network address and in the host portion a one is set in each subnet position, that is:

    Subnet mask = 11111111.11111111.11111111.11100000

In dotted decimal form this is:

    255.255.255.224

When a datagram is received by the router it makes a copy of the destination IP address with which it then performs a logical AND operation with the subnet mask. For example, suppose the host address 194.82.212.128.161 is received:

Table 15.5	
Destination	Next hop
194.82.212.32	Subnet 1 port
194.82.212.64	Subnet 2 port
194.82.212.96	Subnet 3 port
194.82.212.128	Subnet 4 port
194.82.212.160	Subnet 5 port
194.82.212.192	Subnet 6 port
Default	WAN port

Host address   11000010.01010010.11010100.10100001
Subnet mask   11111111.11111111.11111111.11100000
Logical AND   11000010.01010010.11010100.**101**00000

It may be seen that the effect of ANDing always results in zeros in the non-subnet bit positions of the host portion of the address. What remains is in fact the subnet bit pattern for the desired subnet, 101 in this case. The routing tables of the router are now relatively simple. Instead of having an entry for each IP address of every host on the network, all that is required is an entry for each subnet address. If, as is very common, there is only one other route from a router, which is the WAN connection, the routing table for the above example would typically appear as that shown in Table 15.5. A destination address not destined for one of the subnetworks is regarded as a **default** address and must, by definition, be destined for another network. Default addresses are defined by a single entry within the routing table and datagrams containing such addresses are all forwarded to the WAN connection.

Address Resolution Protocol (ARP)

The question arises: how does IP addressing operate within a LAN network where hosts use MAC addressing? The answer is that the **Address Resolution Protocol** (ARP), defined in RFC 826, is used. Each station within a LAN, be it host or router, maintains an ARP table which is a **cache** that contains a mapping between known MAC addresses on a LAN and their associated IP address. When a host wishes to transmit an IP datagram, it examines its ARP table and finds the required MAC address of the host which has the specified destination IP address. The host then encapsulates the IP datagram into a MAC frame which is transmitted using this MAC destination address. If a node does not hold an entry for the IP address in its ARP table, an **ARP request** is broadcast to all other nodes on the network. Any host which has the required MAC address of the IP address in question in its own ARP table responds with an **ARP reply**. The node originating the request may then make use of the returned MAC address and also update its ARP table. If an ARP request is made and no response returned, perhaps because the IP address is that of a host in a different network, the router examines the destination IP address contained in the ARP request and is able

Table 15.6   ICMP messages.

Message	Purpose
Destination unreachable	Datagram cannot be delivered
Echo request	Requests a destination if it is reachable
Echo reply	Reply that a destination is reachable
Source quench	Used to indicate to a source to throttle back
Time exceeded	Time to live field has reached zero

to determine that the destination host is on a different network. The router then responds with a default MAC address which is that of the port of the router connected to the subnet upon which the ARP request orignated.

Internet Control Message Protocol (ICMP)

ARP is an example of an Internet control protocol. A more general control protocol that is used to monitor and test the operation of the Internet is called the **Internet Control Message Protocol** (ICMP). A number of ICMP messages are defined in the RFC, the most important of which are listed in Table 15.6.

The first three messages are associated with what is commonly called a **packet internet groper (ping)**. A ping is typically instigated using the command 'ping (ipaddress)' which results in an **echo request** being transmitted to the specified IP address. If the ping is successful in reaching its destination, an echo reply is returned by the host; if it is unsuccessful at some point along its path, a destination unreachable message is returned. A further facility called **traceroute** is also implemented extensively. Traceroute operates by sending out an echo request datagram to a remote destination with a time to live (TTL) of 1. The first hop then sends back an ICMP error message indicating that the datagram could not be forwarded because the TTL expired. The datagram is then resent with a TTL of 2, and the second hop returns the TTL expired error message. This process continues until the destination is reached. The purpose behind this is to record the source of each ICMP TTL expired message to provide a trace of the path the datagram took to reach the destination.

The source quench message was intended as a method of controlling congestion. In theory, a router may discard internet datagrams if it does not have the buffer space needed to queue the datagrams for output to the next hop. If a router discards a datagram, it may send a source quench message to the source host of the datagram. A destination host may also send a source quench message if datagrams arrive at too high a rate to be processed. The source quench message is a request to the host to cut back the rate at which it is sending datagrams to the destination. On receipt of a source quench message, the source host should cut back the rate at which it is sending datagrams to the specified destination until it no longer receives source quench messages from the router. The source host can then gradually increase the rate at which it sends traffic to the destination until such time that it receives another source quench message, if at all.

IP version 6

The version of IP described above is known as IP version 4 (IPv4). IP has been extra-ordinarily successful in becoming the universal choice of layer 3 protocol for internetworking. However, its very success has produced a problem. This has not, however, deterred the inexorable growth of IP as a *de facto* standard protocol. The problem is that IP is running out of addresses. Although a 32-bit address might, at first sight, seem adequate, the way that the addresses are organized is very wasteful. For most organizations, a Class A address, which allows for 16 million addresses, is too big and a Class C network, with 256 addresses, is too small. Consequently, Class B addresses, which allow 65 536 addresses, are in great demand but they only allow up to 16 384 networks. It was mainly to solve this lack of addresses that a new version of IP was first outlined in 1995 as RFC 1752. Known as IPv6 (an IP version 5 had already been proposed as an early real-time protocol), it is more recently defined in RFC 1883. The new features of IPv6 can be grouped into four main categories as follows:

1. Address size: Instead of 32 bits, IPv6 uses 128-bit addresses.

2. Header format: An IPv6 header is much simpler than the IPv4 header.

3. Extension headers: IPv6 allows for several headers, in that the basic header can be followed by a number of further extension headers, followed by data.

4. Support for multimedia traffic: Users can establish a high-quality path through an underlying network and associate voice and video traffic with that path. IPv6 terms this path a **flow** and associates a flow **label** with the datagrams in the flow. This is a dramatic departure from the traditional connectionless mode of IP working.

Despite offering some interesting solutions to the problems faced by IPv4, IPv6 has not, at the time of writing, been widely adopted. This is partly due to the overwhelming success of IPv4 and the resulting massive investment in it such that the cost of converting to IPv6 is formidable.

(15.3) Routing protocols

A major function of the Internet layer, and network layers in general, is to route traffic from a source to a destination. Routing decisions are not simply based upon destination addresses alone. They must also take account of the network topology and prevailing traffic conditions. For instance, many internet topologies contain loops and routing tables can, if correctly configured, ensure that a datagram does not follow a loop and thus reappear at a node already traversed.

Routers (and switches) operate by discovering the topology of their network and then use this topology to build routing tables containing the best routes to destinations. In order to build topology and routing tables a router cannot operate alone, it needs to exchange information with other routers. This exchange of information is achieved by routers 'talking' to each other by means of **routing protocols** which are also a part of the TCP/IP suite and reside at the Internet layer. Three routing protocols are considered here, namely Routing Information Protocol (RIP), Open Shortest Path First (OSPF) and Border Gateway Protocol (BGP).

Routing Information Protocol

Routing Information Protocol (RIP) is a simple routing protocol, originally defined in 1988 as RFC 1058 and more recently as RFC 1723, based upon the original ARPANET routing algorithm. RIP involves a router calculating the best route to all other routers in a network using a **shortest path** algorithm attributable to Bellman (1957) and Ford and Fulkerson (1962). The shortest path in this case is the one that passes through the least number of routers. Each router traversed is known as a **hop**. Therefore the shortest path is described by a **hop count**, or **distance vector**. This is a crude measure of distance or cost to reach a destination. It takes no account of other factors such as propagation delay or available bandwidth. RIP then builds a routing database that contains tables of the best routes to all the other routers. Each router then advertises its own routing tables to all other routers. Although RIP is simple to implement it is only efficient in small networks since, as the size of a network grows, RIP datagrams can become very long, thus consuming substantial amounts of bandwidth.

Open Shortest Path First

A more powerful routing protocol developed subsequent to RIP, defined originally as RFC 1131 and more recently as RFC 2178, is called **Open Shortest Path First** (OSPF). It is the preferred routing protocol for medium or large networks which, in OSPF, are referred to as **autonomous systems** (ASs). OSPF endeavours to establish a least-cost shortest route within an autonomous system. Cost does not necessarily involve monetary considerations, but means that parameters are used that are of particular importance to the network operator. They may be financial or could be based on delay or transmission rate. Such parameters are known as **metrics**. Whereas RIP is a distance-vector-based protocol, OSPF is described as a **link state** routing protocol. This is because it only advertises the changes in the state of its routing tables to other routers using **link state advertisements** rather than the full tables. Link state advertisements that are exchanged between routers produce much less traffic than is generated by RIP datagrams. Each router holds a database, each containing the same information, as a result of the exchange of link state update messages. It is worth noting that, unlike RIP, OSPF only exchanges changes in a network rather than complete topologies. This is a major advantage over RIP and results in much less information being exchanged. Cost metrics are indicated at the output ports of each router and may be deduced by router software or configured by a network administrator.

Since autonomous systems can be large, OSPF allows for them to be divided into numbered areas such that topology information is largely contained within a single area. Area 0 is a special case, termed the backbone area, and is arranged so that all other

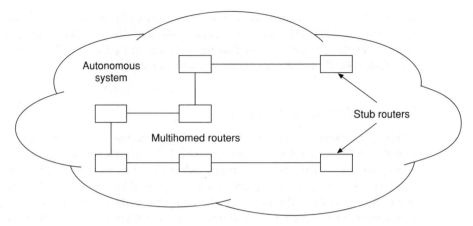

Figure 15.3   Stub and multihomed routers.

areas can be interconnected through it. Routers operating in an OSPF environment can be categorized by their connectivity with other routers and the type of traffic that they carry as illustrated in Figure 15.3. A **stub router** has only one entry/exit point to the router and all traffic passes through this one point, whereas **multihomed routers** have more than one connection to other routers.

OSPF, in common with certain other routing protocols, can also use equal-cost multipath routing to avoid some parts of the network becoming congested while other parts are not fully utilized. Such procedures are not part of the OSPF protocol and an equal-cost multipath algorithm is analysed in RFC 2992. Equal-cost multipath routing, as the name implies, is a technique for routing datagrams along multiple paths of equal cost. The forwarding algorithm identifies paths by next-hop and the router must then decide which next-hop (path) to use when forwarding a datagram. For example, a round-robin technique might be used whereby each eligible path is used in turn. However, such an approach is not suitable for TCP sessions, which perform better if the path they flow along does not change while the stream is connected. A more useful method for determining which next-hop to use is known as a **hash-threshold**. The router first selects a **key** by performing a cyclic redundancy check (known as a **hash**) over the datagram header fields that identify a flow (typically the source and destination IP addresses). With the very simplest implementation of the algorithm, the combined source and destination addresses are divided by the number of equal-cost routes and the remainder of this division is the key. The router then uses the key to determine which next-hop to use. This should result in a more balanced use of the available paths and is known as **load balancing**.

Border Gateway Protocol

The Border Gateway Protocol (BGP) is a routing protocol used to exchange network reachability information between autonomous systems. It is an example of an exterior gateway protocol rather than an internal gateway protocol such as OSPF or RIP.

Table 15.7 BGP path attributes.

Path attribute	Purpose
Origin	This indicates whether the path attribute information has been generated by an interior gateway protocol or by BGP
AS path	A list of ASs contained in a route to a destination AS
Next-hop	The IP address of the border router within the local AS that is to be used to reach the destination AS

BGP was defined in RFC 1771 and subsequently RFC 1997 and in its version 4 is currently the routing protocol of choice for the Internet. BGP provides a set of mechanisms that allow support for advertising an abbreviated IP address, known as a prefix, and thus eliminate the concept of network 'class' from an IP address. As such, it is known as a **classless** routing protocol.

Routers, known as BGP **speakers**, exchange BGP routing information over a TCP connection. The routing information contains a list of reachable autonomous systems with **path attributes** that convey routing information, such as preference for a particular hop or route. The main path attributes are listed in Table 15.7 along with a brief explanation of their use.

If the two BGP speakers are in the same AS, the connection between them uses the interior BGP (IBGP). As long as an interior gateway protocol such as OSPF is running in the AS, two speakers are reachable using IP and an IBGP connection will be established. If the two BGP speakers are in different ASs then the connection between them uses the exterior BGP. It is not necessary, and is in fact undesirable, for every router in an AS to be running BGP: as long as at least one router in an AS uses BGP, the AS will remain in contact with other ASs.

Of particular importance to BGP are what are known as **import and export policies**. These define which types of traffic can be received or transmitted by a particular BGP speaker. For example, a carrier will be willing to carry its own customers' traffic but may be unwilling to allow other carriers' customer traffic to transit through its IP network. Policies are manually configured on each router that supports BGP. Thus a BGP speaker may have policies configured that permit it to distribute addresses from one external AS within its own AS but not the addresses from another AS. These policies are not only of importance for political reasons. They also have the effect of reducing the amount of routing information that is distributed between ASs. This is important in large groups of networks such as the Internet, as the amount of routing information could otherwise become unmanageable. Import and export policies can also be used with OSPF, but they do not assume the same importance as when used by BGP, as the distribution of routing information by OSPF is contained within a single AS. BGP also shares the nomenclature used by OSPF to describe different routers as multihomed, stub, etc. An AS that has just one single connection to another AS, described as a **stub AS**, is illustrated in Figure 15.4. A further type of AS, known as a **transit AS**, in which multiple connections to other ASs exist and through which traffic can transit, is also shown. Clearly all transit ASs must be multihomed since, by definition, they connect to more than one other AS.

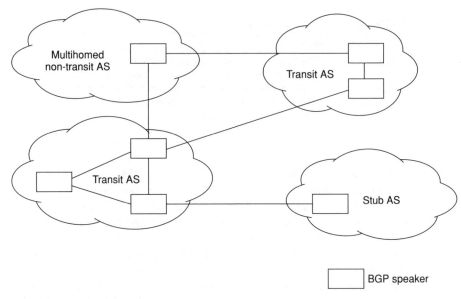

Figure 15.4 Stub and transit autonomous systems.

It is possible for an AS to have more than one connection to other ASs but for traffic to be unable to transit through the AS, in which case it is termed a multihomed non-transit AS.

15.4 Transport layer protocols

The transport layer within the TCP/IP protocol model offers similar functions to those defined by layer 4 in the OSI reference model. It is only implemented in the hosts connected to a network and is only concerned with end-to-end transmission. The transport layer offers a number of protocols which may be connectionless or connection oriented and provide reliable or unreliable services.

Transmission Control Protocol

The most common of the transport layer protocols is the **Transmission Control Protocol** (TCP) that, along with IP, gives its name to the entire TCP/IP protocol model. TCP was originally defined in RFC 761 (1980) and carries a stream of bytes from source to destination in a reliable manner using ARQ flow control techniques. A message from the application layer is ordered into bytes, a number of which form a discrete **segment** that is then passed to the Internet layer below. A segment must consist of multiples of 32 bits, known as words. The sending and receiving applications at the two end-points of a TCP connection use a **port** number to connect with TCP/IP. A port is the Transport Service Access Point (TSAP). The combination of a port number and

16-bit source port number								16-bit destination port number
32-bit sequence number								
32-bit acknowledgement number								
4-bit length header	Reserved (6 bits)	U R G	A C K	P S H	R S T	S Y N	F I N	16-bit window size
16-bit checksum								16-bit urgent pointer
Options (if any)								
Data (if any)								

Figure 15.5   TCP segment.

an IP address uniquely defines an end-point and is known as a **socket** (Halsall 2001, pp773–5). The TCP segment header is shown in Figure 15.5.

The fields are as follows:

- The source and destination ports identify the local end-points of the connection as explained above.

- A segment sequence number identifies the first byte carried in the TCP segment. (All bytes in a TCP segment are numbered.)

- The acknowledgement number field contains the sequence number of the next byte expected to be received.

- The header length is the number of 32-bit words contained in the header. Note that this is required because the option field within the header is of variable length.

- The next field contains six single-bit flags. URG is set if a segment contains a block of data that is urgent. ACK indicates a valid acknowledgement number in the corresponding field. PSH (push) indicates data to be handed to an application immediately on arrival, but is now outdated. The RST flag is used to reset a connection that has become confused. SYN is used in the handshaking used to establish connections and to set initial sequence numbers. The FIN flag is used to indicate that a sender has finished sending data.

- The window size is the number of bytes that a receiver is able to receive at a time.

- The checksum is the 1's complement of the sum of all the 16-bit words in the segment. The checksum is carried out on the complete segment including the header plus a **pseudo-header** that is only used at the time of the calculation of the checksum. The pseudo-header contains the IP addresses of both source and destination, a number indicating the transport protocol (6 for TCP), and the length of the segment in bytes. By including this pseudo-header in the checksum calculation at both the source and destination, TCP guards against the delivery of segments to the wrong IP address, since an incorrect delivery should cause the checksum to fail even though there are no errors in the segment itself.

● The urgent pointer field is used in conjunction with the URG flag and gives an off-set to the sequence number field needed to find the last byte of a block of urgent data.

● The options field is intended to be used to indicate various options, the most import-ant of which is the maximum segment size that a host can receive. It is sent in the first segment transmitted when a connection is opened.

TCP transmission is made reliable by the use of the sequence numbers and acknow-ledgements. When TCP transmits a segment, it puts a copy of the segment in a retrans-mission queue and starts a timer. When an acknowledgement for that data is returned to the receiver, the segment is deleted from the queue. If an acknowledgement is not received before the timer runs out, the segment is retransmitted. An acknowledgement by TCP does not guarantee that the data has been delivered to the end-user, only that the receiving TCP has taken the responsibility to do so. To govern the flow of data into TCP, a flow control mechanism is established. Flow control in TCP is different from that used in most data link protocols as the window size is not fixed. The data receiving TCP reports a window to the sending TCP that depends on the amount of buffer space available at that point in time. This window specifies the number of bytes that the data receiving TCP is currently prepared to receive. Once an advertised win-dow size reaches zero, the sender must stop transmitting.

To identify the separate data streams that TCP may handle, TCP provides a port identifier. Port numbers below 1024 are known as **well-known ports** and are reserved for standard services such as Telnet, which uses port 23. A list of well-known ports is given in RFC 1700. Since port identifiers are selected independently by each operat-ing system, TCP, or user, they may not be unique. It is for this reason that the socket value mentioned above is important since it will be unique throughout all networks connected together.

User Datagram Protocol

An alternative transport layer protocol is the User Datagram Protocol (UDP), defined in RFC 768 (1980), which is a connectionless protocol that is unreliable; that is, there is no flow control. UDP was originally intended for use with non-urgent data transmissions such as e-mail. However, the fact that it does not use acknowledgements has led to interest in using it with protocols designed for delay-sensitive traffic such as the Real-Time Transport Protocol discussed shortly. The 4-byte UDP header is illus-trated in Figure 15.6.

4 bytes	
Source port	Destination port
UDP length	UDP checksum

Figure 15.6 UDP header.

The UDP length field gives the length of the UDP segment. The other fields have the same functions as in TCP. Note that the UDP header is very much slimmer than the TCP header since there is so much less to be done.

15.5 Virtual private networks

In recent years, service providers have sought to capitalize on the telecommunication infrastructure that they have installed, often at huge cost, in their networks by the use of **virtual private networks** (VPNs). A VPN can be defined as the emulation of a private IP network using a shared IP infrastructure. Since IP is a layer 3 protocol, the VPN must rely on a protocol that incorporates layer 2 functionality, such as Frame Relay or ATM.

IP **tunnels** are normally used to separate one VPN from another across the shared network. A point-to-point IP tunnel is illustrated in Figure 15.7.

A point-to-point tunnel is shown that connects the two routers and carries traffic transparently through address space Y. Both the source and destination networks are in a separate address space X. In practice, address space Y represents the IP address range used by a service provider or **carrier** and address space X represents the IP address range used by a customer whose network is attached to the service provider's network. In most cases, both the service provider and the customer will use IP in their networks, as shown in the figure. In these circumstances, the IP tunnelling will use IP in IP encapsulation as specified in RFCs 1853 and 2003 and the data passing through the tunnel will have two IP headers as shown in Figure 15.8.

The customer datagram to be tunnelled has a header X that maintains its original source and destination IP addresses. The service provider's router gives the packet a second IP header Y that contains the source and destination of the tunnel end-points. The original IP header is known as the inner IP header and the carrier's IP header is

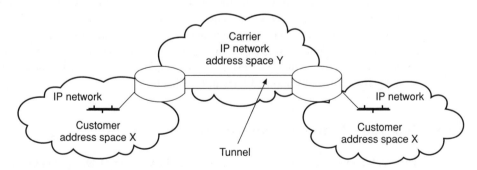

Figure 15.7 Point-to-point IP tunnel.

Header Y	Header X	IP payload

Figure 15.8

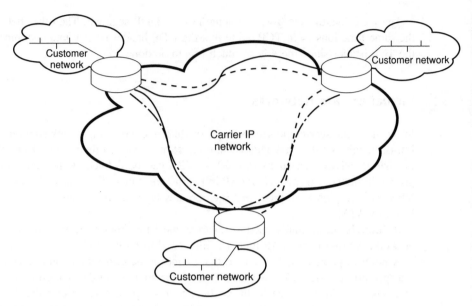

Figure 15.9   Point-to-multipoint tunnels.

called the outer IP header. When the datagram reaches the router at the far end of the tunnel, it is stripped of its outer header and is routed within the customer network to its destination. If the original customer datagram originates from a protocol other than IP, then a more generalized form of outer encapsulation, known as generic routing encapsulation, is used as specified in RFC 1701.

The point-to-point tunnel illustrated in Figure 15.7 connects two networks operated by a customer of the service provider. In order to accommodate more than two customer networks, tunnels can also be point to multipoint as illustrated in Figure 15.9.

Each router sets up a point-to-multipoint tunnel to each of the two other routers and all three customer networks operate in the same address space. It is important for VPNs that operate in this way that security is maintained within the VPN and it is for this reason that the customer address space is kept entirely separate from the carrier's address space. It is also likely that the customer will employ further security measures such as using IP security, as outlined later in the chapter.

15.6 Real-Time Transport Protocol and Voice over IP

The Real-Time Transport Protocol (RTP) is a fairly recent (1996) protocol, described in RFC 1889, that provides end-to-end delivery for real-time audio and video traffic, which might be either unicast or multicast, over an IP network. It does not, however, guarantee any quality of service nor does it provide a mechanism for recovery from errors. It typically runs over UDP, which is a connectionless protocol and therefore does not involve end-to-end acknowledgements which could introduce unacceptable delays to the real-time traffic. Typical applications for RTP might be voice over IP

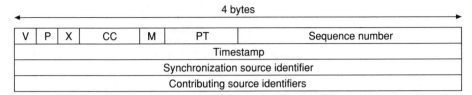

Figure 15.10   Real Time Protocol header.

and audio or video conferencing. If both video and audio are involved in a transmission, then two separate RTP sessions are required.

An important concept used within the context of a conference is that of a **mixer**. Consider the case of an audio conference where participants in one area are connected through a low-speed link to the other conference participants who have high-speed network access. Instead of forcing everyone to use a lower bandwidth, a mixer may be placed near the low-bandwidth area, which resynchronizes incoming packets to reconstruct the constant rate voice traffic from the sender and then mixes multiple audio streams into a single stream for presentation to the rest of the network. In the case of the audio streams that are in the opposite direction, the mixer translates the audio encoding into a lower bandwidth and forwards the lower bandwidth packet stream across the low-speed link.

The RTP header, which is illustrated in Figure 15.10, consists of 12 bytes that are present in all packets plus a number of optional fields. The version (V) field contains 2 bits that indicate the RTP version (currently 2). The single padding (P) bit is set to one if the packet contains any padding and the single extension (X) bit is set to one if the header is extended beyond 12 bytes. The header will only be extended if a mixer has been used to accommodate lower speed input voice streams. If this has happened then the contributing source count (CC) field of 4 bits will contain the number of contributing sources. A single-bit marker (M) bit allows significant events such as frame boundaries to be marked in the packet stream. As an example, in the case of voice over IP, it could be used to mark the start and end of speech so as to allow silence suppression to take place. The 7-bit payload type (PT) field identifies the type of payload, for example 18 denotes G.729 compressed voice and 26 denotes JPEG. The 16-bit sequence number increments by 1 for each packet transmitted. The 32-bit timestamp reflects the sampling instant of the first byte in a data packet and allows synchronization and jitter calculations to be carried out. The 32-bit synchronization source identifier identifies the synchronization source. It is determined in such a way that no two sources within an RTP session will have the same identifier. The final 32-bit contributing source list field is optional and is only used if there is more than one source contributing to the data stream.

A major application that makes use of RTP is Voice over IP (VoIP). VoIP implementations enable users to carry voice traffic (e.g. telephone calls and faxes) over an IP network. There are three main reasons for the evolution of VoIP services:

1. Low-cost phone calls that can be established using a PC or IP telephone set.

2. Merging of data/voice infrastructures.

3. Add-on services such as video conferencing.

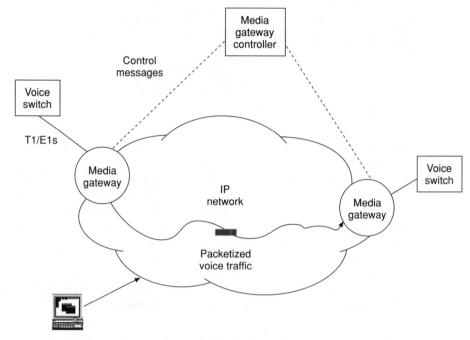

Figure 15.11   Voice over IP system.

A typical VoIP system is illustrated in Figure 15.11. The major component in terms of the conversion of voice into IP is called a **media gateway**. A media gateway is a generic term used for devices that convert media provided in one type of network to the format required for another type of network. For example, it could terminate channels from a switched circuit network and convert them into a different medium such as IP or ATM. In this instance the conversion is into IP, and the traffic is typically transported across the IP network using RTP/UDP/IP as outlined earlier.

The media gateways are controlled by an external call control element called a **media gateway controller**. Since the practical implementation of VoIP is not set in stone and remains under development, a number of competing protocols are used at present between the media gateways and the media gateway controller. Theoretically, ITU-T recommendation H.323 (1996) could be used as a basis for a VoIP control system since it specifies procedures for the transmission of real-time audio, video and data communications over packet-based networks. However, H.323 is an 'umbrella' protocol that provides for a large variety of multimedia communications over different types of packet-based network and offers far more than is required just for VoIP. The emergence of VoIP applications has resulted in new requirements, such as providing communication between a PC-based phone and a phone on a traditional switched circuit network, and has led to a revision of the H.323 specification. Version 2 of H.323 – packet-based multimedia communications systems – was introduced to accommodate these additional requirements and was accepted by the ITU-T in January 1998.

Despite this development, there is general agreement (Mier and Yocom, 2000) that H.323 suffers from being too complex and lacks scalability. The **Media Gateway Control Protocol** (MGCP), as defined in RFC 2705 (1999), also describes an application programming interface and a corresponding protocol for controlling media gateways. MGCP assumes a call control architecture where the call control 'intelligence' is outside the gateways and handled by external media gateway controllers which are also known as **call agents**. However, MGCP is perceived as having neglected multimedia applications and is already losing ground to an IETF protocol called **Megaco** which has since been adopted by the ITU-T, where it is has been renamed H.248. The H.248/Megaco protocol is gaining favour because it permits greater scalability than is allowed by H.323, and it addresses the technical requirements and multimedia conferencing capabilities overlooked in MGCP. Yet another IETF protocol, called **Session Initiation Protocol** (SIP), proposed in RFC 2543, is being trialled in a number of systems at the time of writing and there are hopes that its use will resolve the problems associated with H.323.

In summary, the ITU-T's H.323 'umbrella' standard, the first to be proposed for VoIP interoperability, proved complex and difficult to implement. As a result, other less unwieldy standards have been used in its place, and until recently, we have seen little consensus on which of several VoIP standards would be most widely implemented. It is likely that VoIP service providers will continue to use a number of standards, among them the ITU-T's H.323, the IETF's SIP and MGCP and the ITU-T's H.248. The prevailing opinion is that H.248/Megaco will be used between media gateway controllers and media gateways, although there is support for using SIP between controllers and also between media gateway controllers and residential IP phones. In other words, the situation looks as if it will be unduly complicated for some time into the near future. Clearly there will need to be coexistence among all these standards, at least in the short term.

(15.7) Multi Protocol Label Switching (MPLS)

The TCP/IP suite has been far more successful than might have been envisaged when it was first proposed in the 1970s as a means to interconnect disparate networks into the US Department of Defense ARPANET network. Its success has culminated in its being universally used by end-users accessing the Internet. However, the carrier networks that carry large volumes of traffic at the core of the Internet predominately use a 'switched' protocol, typically either Frame Relay or ATM. This use of IP to route traffic through a network and then to encapsulate the traffic subsequently in either frame relay frames or ATM cells is inherently inefficient. Not only does it result in a relatively large overhead, but also it leads to a duplication of the layer 3 addressing function since both IP and ATM/Frame Relay addresses will be used within the network.

At the time of writing, MPLS is an emerging standard that integrates layer 3 routing with layer 2 switching. It is a connection-oriented protocol that allows IP to be used in conjunction with either Frame Relay, ATM, Ethernet or the Point-to-Point Protocol (PPP). The layer 3 IP address is used to determine the path that is to be

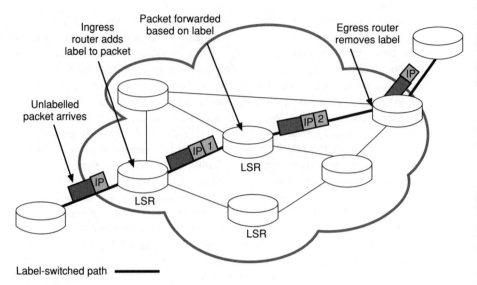

Figure 15.12   MPLS packet forwarding.

followed and a packet entering the MPLS network is routed once at the edge node and then forwarded to its destination by core nodes, known as **label-switched routers (LSRs)**, using the layer 2 switching protocol. The route through the MPLS network, which is set up using OSPF, is known as a **label-switched path** and is similar to a PVC in ATM and frame relay networks but with the major difference that the label-switched path is unidirectional. A label-switched path is illustrated in Figure 15.12.

An unlabelled packet arrives at an LSR (which in practice could be an ATM or frame relay switch with appropriate MPLS software) and has an MPLS header attached which contains a label. The labelled packet is forwarded along the label-switched path by each LSR until it reaches the path destination. The remote LSR removes the MPLS header and the packet is routed using its IP address. Note that the forwarding process at an LSR is similar to the VPI/VCI translation in ATM switches and is called **label swapping**. In fact, a VPI/VCI value may be used directly as the label within an MPLS header if the underlying technology is ATM. Individual label-switched paths can be aggregated with other label-switched paths if they share part of their paths. This is achieved by merging paths together by adding a further label for the shared portion of the path. As with IP there is the option of paths being chosen using either loose or strict routing.

It was mentioned at the beginning of this section that MPLS combines the layer 3 functionality of IP with the layer 2 functionality of ATM (or Frame Relay). Let us conclude this section by examining the advantages that this brings to a network:

● MPLS provides an evolutionary migration from separate IP and ATM networks that should prove attractive to Internet service providers and other carriers.

● An MPLS core converges the two networks that are required if IP traffic is adapted and carried over a separate ATM core. This offers the prospect of a single network management system, thus reducing design and operation costs.

● Adapted IP traffic passes through an ATM core transparently and is unaware of the underlying ATM topology. This results in the physical topology and the logical topology of the network being different. In an MPLS core the physical topology and the logical topology are the same, thus simplifying the network design.

● The traffic management capabilities of ATM, such as different classes of traffic, can be utilized by the incoming IP traffic. This differentiation of traffic types has long been talked about in connection with IP but has rarely been implemented. When used in an MPLS network it is called **traffic engineering**.

15.8 Packet over SDH/SONET

IP traffic carried over ATM using MPLS has to be adapted using one of the ATM adaptation layers (AALs). This results in an overhead which, although often exaggerated, is significant. In addition to the 5-byte header in each ATM cell (an overhead of 10.4%), there is an AAL overhead which for IP datagrams would typically be 8 bytes per datagram and the last cell in a packet would normally contain some padding. Assuming packets of length 512 bytes this would result in a total overhead of approximately 13.9%. This is in addition to the overheads involved in the SDH framing.

Much effort has been exerted in recent years in trying to transmit packet-based traffic over SDH/SONET circuits without using an intermediate ATM network, a process commonly known as **packet over SDH/SONET** (PoS), thus reducing the percentage of overhead involved in the transmission. Although this would seem an obvious approach, it is only recently that the available technology has been available to produce the necessary hardware components. At the time of writing, the current IETF specification, RFC 2615, is called Point-to-Point Protocol (PPP) over SONET. PoS takes IP packets and encapsulates them in a PPP frame that is similar to that used by HDLC according to a further RFC, 1662 (PPP in HDLC-like framing). The frame structure is illustrated in Figure 15.13 with each field size shown either as a hexadecimal number or a number of bytes.

The first 2 bytes of the PPP packet payload contain a protocol identifier that, in the case of IP, is equal to 8021hex. It is recommended that scrambling be used to prevent a loss of synchronization due to long 1- or 0-bit sequences.

We can now compare a 512-byte IP packet using PoS with the figures above for ATM multiprotocol encapsulation. The overhead in bytes will be 7 bytes per packet if we assume that a 2-byte error check is used and only one flag is required between frames. The ratio of total frame length to payload length is therefore given by:

$$\frac{512 + 7}{512} = 1.014$$

Flag 7E	Address FF	Control 03	IP Packet	FCS 1 or 2 bytes	Flag 7E

Figure 15.13 PPP over SDH/SONET frame structure.

Thus the percentage overhead is 1.4%. If we were to use ATM multiprotocol encapsulation there would be an 8-byte overhead per frame, giving a frame length of 520 bytes which would be adapted into ATM with the following number of cells:

Number of cells = ROUND(520/48) = ROUND(10.83) = 11 cells

Thus the ratio of transmitted cells to payload will be:

$$\frac{11 \times 53}{512} = 1.139$$

Thus the percentage overhead using ATM is 13.9% compared with an overhead of 1.4% when using PoS. It is anticipated that there will be considerable interest in PoS over the next few years.

(15.9) IP security

The key requirements to provide secure communication within an internet are to:

1. Guard against unauthorized monitoring. This means both eavesdropping and also monitoring traffic flow, movement and patterns.

2. Protect against the control of network traffic, for example **spoofing**, in which a third party creates datagrams containing bogus IP addresses. These may give the impression that they have been sent from a trusted party on a known network, when patently they have not and may be a way of gaining unauthorized access to a network.

3. Provide authentication and encryption mechanisms (for more details on these topics, see Appendix 1).

An important issue in IP networks, particularly when using VPNs, that are built using the Internet, is that of security. A small group of protocols, collectively known as **IPsec**, provide security services at the IP layer by enabling a system to select required security protocols, determine the algorithm(s) to use for the service(s), and put in place any encryption keys required to provide the requested services. IPsec can be used to protect one or more 'paths' between a pair of hosts, between a pair of **security gateways**, or between a security gateway and a host. (The term 'security gateway' is used throughout the IPsec RFC documents to refer to equipment that implements IPsec protocols. For example, a router implementing IPsec is a security gateway.) The set of security services that IPsec can provide includes access control and limited traffic flow confidentiality. Because these services are provided at the IP layer, they can be invoked by any higher layer protocol, for example TCP, UDP, ICMP, BGP, and so on.

IPsec uses three approaches to security, as follows:

1. The IP **Authentication Header** (AH) which is defined in RFC 2402 and provides connectionless integrity, data origin authentication and an optional anti-replay service. The authentication header is illustrated in Figure 15.14.

2. The **Encapsulating Security Payload** (ESP) protocol which is defined in RFC 2406 and can provide confidentiality (encryption) and limited traffic flow confidentiality. As with the AH, it may also provide connectionless integrity, data origin authentication and an anti-replay service. (One or the other set of these security services must be applied whenever ESP is invoked.) ESP, unlike AH, includes both authentication and encryption and, since both of these features are usually desirable, is a more likely candidate to be used. ESP encapsulates the IP datagram, which is also encrypted, as shown in Figure 15.15, to form an ESP packet. The authentication data, as its name suggests, authenticates the packet to provide an integrity check when it is received. This is to guard against the packet being tampered with, where some of its content is corrupted or changed, in transmission.

3. A key exchange function to arrange that communicating parties using encryption initialize their communication with secure keys (RFC 2409).

Both AH and ESP are also vehicles for access control, based on the distribution of encryption keys and the management of traffic flows relative to these security protocols. These protocols may be applied alone or in combination with each other to provide a desired set of security services in both IPv4 and IPv6. Each protocol supports two modes of use: transport mode and tunnel mode. In transport mode the protocols provide protection primarily for upper layer protocols and therefore the payload of an IP datagram. This is beacause IPsec is applied to a TCP segment at the transport layer. The segment is then encapsulated within the payload of an IP datagram. In tunnel mode, the protocols are applied to the entire IP datagram which is to be tunnelled, rather than simply its payload, as in transport mode above. A new secure IP datagram is then produced, into which the tunnelled IP datagram is inserted with a new pair of source and destination addresses. This means that the original, now secure datagram may not be examined by an unauthorized third party, the whole process being analogous to tunnelling.

The key exchange function uses a separate set of mechanisms for putting keys in place for both authentication/integrity and also for use in encryption. RFCs propose support for both manual and automatic distribution of keys. A public-key-based approach, known as **Internet Key Exchange** (IKE), is specified for automatic key management and is especially convenient for public use in the Internet. For instance, in e-commerce a trader arranges for a purchaser to submit credit card details in encrypted form. However, it would place an intolerable burden on both parties to have to involve

AH	IP datagram

Figure 15.14 Authentication header.

ESP header	IP datagram (encrypted)	Authentication data

Figure 15.15 ESP packet.

the purchaser in establishing a secure on-line trading facility. Rather, security is built in by embedding the encryption software within universally distributed 'Internet software' and arranging automatically, without any action on the part of the purchaser, to securely pass an encryption key to him/her, a so-called automated key distribution technique, at the commencement of the connection.

IPsec allows the user (or network administrator) to control the granularity at which a security service is offered. For example, one can create a single encrypted tunnel to carry all the traffic between two security gateways or a separate encrypted tunnel can be created for each TCP connection between each pair of hosts communicating across these gateways. IPsec management must incorporate facilities for specifying the following:

- which security services to use and in what combinations;
- the granularity at which a given security protection should be applied;
- the algorithms used to effect cryptographic-based security.

There are several ways in which IPsec may be implemented in a host or in conjunction with a router or firewall (to create a security gateway). Several common examples are provided below:

- Integration of IPsec into the native IP implementation. This requires access to the IP source code and is applicable to both hosts and security gateways.
- **Bump-in-the-stack** implementations, where IPsec is implemented 'underneath' an existing implementation of an IP stack, between the native IP and the local NIC drivers.
- The use of a separate encryption process is a common design feature of network security systems used by the military, and of some commercial systems as well. It is sometimes referred to as a **bump-in-the-wire** implementation. Such implementations may be designed to serve either a host or a gateway (or both). Usually the device is IP addressable. When supporting a single host, it is analogous to a bump-in-the-stack implementation, but in supporting a router or firewall, it operates as a security gateway.

More detail on IPsec may be found in Stallings (2000a), pp674–83.

Exercises

15.1   Make a suitable sketch showing both the TCP/IP stack and the OSI Reference Model. Compare the differences between their two approaches to networking.

15.2   With reference to IP version 4:
(a) What are the three main classes of IP addresses?
(b) How are the bits distributed between host and network in each of these classes?
(c) What is the purpose of the time-to-live field in an IP header?
(d) What happens when time-to-live reaches zero?

15.3   An IP address is expressed in hexadecimal form as CD465605. Convert it into dotted decimal format.

15.4 Explain why it is necessary to recalculate the checksum at each router.

15.5 Assuming that all routers and hosts are operating correctly in an IP network, explain some possible circumstances under which a datagram might be delivered to the wrong destination, or not find its destination.

15.6 A router is sending a series of datagrams over a particular link. If each datagram is of uniform size and equal to 2048 bytes, calculate the maximum link speed at which the router may operate if packets live for 12 seconds. *Hint*: The identifier value in the IP header must not repeat within the 12-second period.

15.7 A router is to be used to interconnect six subnetworks. Assuming a network IP address of 192.228.17.0:
   (a) State the subnet mask
   (b) Design a suitable addressing scheme for the hosts
   (c) Determine the address ranges within each subnet.

15.8 Explain, when subnetting, why some of the available IP addresses are not available for assigning to hosts.

15.9 In the case of Class C addresses:
   (a) Calculate each possible subnet mask
   (b) For each mask determine the number of subnets and how many hosts there are for each subnet mask.

15.10 With reference to the TCP/IP suite explain the following terms:
   (a) Static addressing
   (b) Dynamic addressing.

15.11 Explain the purpose and operation of the Address Resolution Protocol. Include reference to ARP caches in your explanation.

15.12 Briefly outline the features offered by ICMP. Explain how ICMP may be used in practice.

15.13 A router has built the routing table shown in the table below. The router can route packets directly to Ethernet interfaces 0 or 1, or it can forward packets to routers R2, R3 or R4. Describe what the router does with a packet addressed to each of the following destinations:
   (a) 128.96.39.10
   (b) 128.96.40.12
   (c) 128.96.40.151
   (d) 192.4.153.17
   (e) 192.4.153.90

Subnet number	Subnet mask	Next hop
128.96.39.0	255.255.255.128	Interface 0
128.96.39.128	255.255.255.128	Interface 1
128.96.40.0	255.255.255.128	R2
192.4.153.0	255.255.255.192	R3
<default>		R4

15.14 Explain, within the context of the Internet, the roles of:
(a) interior gateway
(b) exterior gateway.

15.15 Compare TCP with UDP and explain:
(a) why a user program cannot directly access IP; and hence
(b) why UDP is necessary.

15.16 Discuss some applications where connection-oriented and connectionless services are appropriate.

15.17 With reference to TCP discuss parameters that might require to be negotiated on connection establishment.

15.18 Describe how TCP uses a window mechanism. In what way does TCP's use of it vary from that described in Chapter 5?

15.19 State the maximum payload of a TCP segment and explain how this figure is computed.

Chapter 16

Network management

A data communications network needs to operate efficiently, particularly in the event of a major failure. The cost of a network ceasing to function efficiently as a result of a failure is extremely high and most major networks incorporate some form of network management system to ensure efficient operation. The functions performed by a network management system must include the monitoring of the network's performance, handling failures when they occur and reconfiguring the network as a response to such failures.

16.1 Fault management

An important feature of any network management system is the detection of faults and the subsequent repair and restoration of system performance. The first step in fault handling following the detection of a fault is normally setting an alarm indication of some kind. Traditionally, data communications equipment such as modems and multiplexers have used a crude form of alarm in which the loss of a circuit causes a lamp to extinguish. This primitive type of alarm conveys little information and can easily be overlooked. A true network management system normally provides a more positive type of alarm such as a message at a network operator's desk indicating the location and type of fault which requires some action by the operator. Some systems also set off alarms to indicate degrading situations, which may allow a serious situation to be averted.

Once an alarm has indicated a failure the next step is to restore the system to its normal operating condition. Initially, this may involve finding some short-term solution to the problem such as a fallback arrangement, but eventually the precise cause of the fault will need to be determined by using diagnostic techniques and the faulty device repaired or replaced.

System restoration and reconfiguration

System restoration following a failure involves two processes. Normally, the first step is some form of **fallback switching** which involves the replacement of a failed device or circuit by an immediately available back-up. In the case of failed circuits the back-up is normally an alternative circuit within the same network, although in some cases an alternative circuit may be provided by a separate back-up network. With equipment such as routers, switches and multiplexers, the back-up is usually provided by spare equipment. Fallback switching is normally automatic but may still be carried out manually, for example by using a **patch panel** to connect to alternative circuits temporarily. A patch panel is an arrangement that allows devices to be connected, or patched, together. Thus, a patch panel may be used to bypass faulty equipment and to patch in spare equipment in the event of failure. Similarly, a patch panel allows a limited amount of reconfiguration to be carried out, although the reconfiguration of a large network is normally beyond its capabilities.

Test equipment

Fallback switching is only a short-term solution to network failure. The more permanent repair or replacement of equipment or circuits requires testing to locate a failure precisely. Many systems provide an integrated test facility although some may only provide access for separate test equipment. Several items of test equipment, listed below, have traditionally proved useful, particularly in smaller networks in which there is no integrated test facility.

Data analyser

This is a device which can capture the status of data on a data line and display this information either on a screen or as a printout. It displays data flow in both directions of a line as well as timing information. A typical printout is shown in Figure 16.1. This printout has been produced using a software-based data analyser and shows a data signal above a corresponding clock signal.

Protocol analyser

A protocol analyser is an extension of the idea of a data analyser which, as well as displaying data, can also carry out simulations. It normally has two modes of

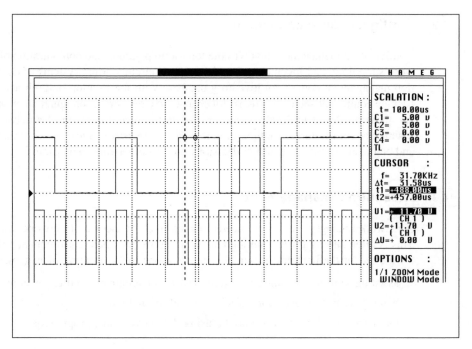

Figure 16.1 Data analyser printout.

operation, the more basic of which does little more than a data analyser. However, in simulation mode the protocol analyser can simulate the signals and responses expected from a particular piece of equipment or part of the network. In this way it can be used not only to determine the source of failures but also to analyse and hopefully improve network performance. Protocol analysers can be used with most common standard protocols such as Frame Relay, ATM and the IEEE 802 series of protocols.

Trouble ticketing

Trouble tickets have traditionally been a major constituent of network management systems. They are used as a means of logging the problems that arise in a data network. A trouble ticket is an extended log entry containing useful information such as date, time, network device involved and the nature of the problem. It also contains information on any follow-up, such as the remedial action taken and details of any equipment or parts replaced. Manual trouble ticketing has mainly been replaced by trouble ticketing databases which can play a further role in the management and planning of a network. Thus network managers or engineers may, for example, examine the fault history of a particular item of equipment or the action taken for particular types of faults to see whether the network is functioning efficiently.

16.2 Configuration management

Configuration management involves the long-term planning and configuration of a network's topology and inventory of equipment and circuits. Most systems of configuration management contain an inventory database with information on both active and back-up equipment and connections. All changes to a network's configuration are tracked and these databases updated. As well as aiding the reconfiguration of a network following network failures, configuration management systems allow network managers and engineers to make informed decisions on future network expansion.

16.3 Accounting management

A network management system needs to keep track of the use of network resources. This is often simply for accounting reasons in networks where customers are charged for the use of the network resources. Other reasons for accounting management are:

- assisting with the planning of future network development and expansion;
- helping users to make more efficient use of the network;
- the detection of users who may be using the network inappropriately.

16.4 Performance management

A number of measures of network performance were mentioned in Chapter 5 in relation to link control and management. These included link efficiency and utilization, error rates and delay times. These measures apply equally to the network as a whole and the collection of these and other statistics forms an important part of any network management system. Statistics gathered by a network management system not only aid the efficient operation of a network but also can be used to plan the future requirements of a network. Most systems use the two further performance criteria of availability and response time, as outlined below.

Availability

In most communications systems availability is an important measure of the amount of time that a system is available for use and can be accessed by the customer. Network availability is normally measured only from the originating service provider network switch node to the terminating switch node. In managed service contracts under which the customer uses the service provider's end equipment, network availability is normally measured on an end-router to end-router basis. In Internet dial-up access, availability is related to the percentage of calls that are not blocked when dialling into the Internet.

Typically availability is measured as the average amount of time a system is available per unit time. Alternatively it can be measured in terms of **mean time between failures** (MTBF) and the **mean time to repair** (MTTR) as follows:

Table 16.1 Typical MTBF and MTTR values.		
Network component	MTBF (hours)	MTTR (hours)
Router	4000	4
Modems	5000	3
Lines	3000	4
Terminals	1000	2

$$\text{Availability} = \frac{\text{MTBF}}{\text{MTBF} + \text{MTTR}}$$

Typical values for MTBF and MTBR for various network components are shown in Table 16.1.

Example 16.1

A router has a mean time between failures of 4000 hours and a mean time to repair of 4 hours. Determine the router's availability. Determine the maximum number of minutes per day that the router can experience failure in order to meet this level of availibility.

$$\text{Availability} = \frac{\text{MTBF}}{\text{MTBF} + \text{MTTR}}$$
$$= 4000/4004 = 99.9\%$$

Percentage that the router can be in failure is $100 - 99.9 = 0.1\%$.
    Number of minutes per day represented by this percentage is:

$$\frac{0.1 \times 24 \times 60}{100} = 1.4 \text{ minutes}$$

Response time

In many communications systems response time is an important measure of performance. It is a measure of the speed of operation of the system. It can be defined for systems in which humans carry out operations as the time between an operator pressing a transmit key and a reply appearing on a screen. This time is also known as **round-trip delay**. A network management system will gather response time statistics for specific devices and circuits as well as for complete networks. Once gathered, statistics are presented in a variety of ways, quite often in the form of a graphical printout. Figure 16.2 shows a typical response time chart.

This chart shows response times plotted at regular intervals, the value plotted being an average response time obtained during the time interval. Network management systems often use such statistics to produce more detailed breakdowns which allow percentiles to be obtained, as in Figure 16.3, which has been obtained from Figure 16.2.

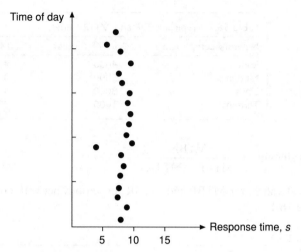

Figure 16.2 Response time chart.

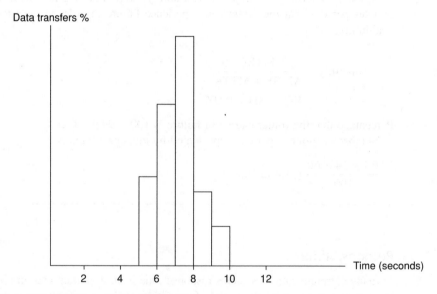

Figure 16.3 Response times as percentages.

16.5 Integrated management systems

Originally, the functions of performance, failure, configuration and accounting management were provided separately for a data communications network. More recently, network management systems integrate these management functions with reporting capabilities in a centralized computer. The computer has access to a variety of local and remote monitoring devices, typically by means of SNMP, and may itself be connected to a computer network. The monitoring devices used depend on the type of system. For example, a system assembled by a company that supplies routers will use diagnostic monitoring facilities associated with its routers.

16.6 Network management standards

Standards for network management are not as well established in practical networks as in other areas of data communications. The American National Standards Institute (ANSI) Committee X3T5.4 was tasked by the ISO to develop a management standard for OSI systems. Within the ISO itself, Study Group 21 looked at network management within the OSI model in general. In its capacity as a LAN standardization body, the IEEE 802 Committee carries out work on standards for the management of LANs.

OSI network management

As is the case with most areas of OSI standardization, the series of standards that have been developed by the ISO is both complicated and voluminous. The first of these standards, issued jointly by the ISO and ITU-T, was the X.700 recommendation entitled *OSI Basic Reference Model Part 4: Management Framework*, which specified the overall management framework for the OSI model and gave a general introduction to network management concepts. In this context the ISO prefers the term 'systems management' to what is more generally known as network management. A number of standards followed which constitute the ITU-T X.700 series of recommendations. Recommendation X.701 provides a general overview of the other standards.

The key elements of the series of documents are recommendations X.710 Common Management Information Services and X.720 Common Management Information Protocols. These form the basis for all the OSI network management functions. X.710 is the set of management services provided and X.720 provides a protocol for exchanging information between the points at which management functions are initiated and other points at the same level where the functions are carried out. Five functions are specified in the documentation as follows:

1. Fault management: The OSI fault management facility allows for the detection and identification of abnormal operation in an OSI environment. The specific facilities include the following:
   (a) The detection of faults and the passing on of error reports.
   (b) The carrying out of diagnostic tests on remote system resources. The ISO uses the term **managed object** to describe a resource or device that is managed by its management protocols.
   (c) The maintenance of a log of events.
   (d) The operation of threshold alarms which are activated if a preset threshold is crossed.

2. Configuration management: OSI configuration management allows a network manager to observe and modify the configuration of network components in an open system. The following facilities are included:
   (a) The collection of data concerning the current configuration of network components.
   (b) The alteration of network component configurations.
   (c) The initialization and closing down of network components.

3. Accounting management: OSI accounting management allows network managers to identify the use of resources in an open system and, where costs are incurred in the use of resources, to calculate and allocate such costs. Two main areas of accounting are specified, namely the transmission system including the communication medium and the end-systems.

4. Performance management: A performance management capability is envisaged which will allow for the monitoring and collection of data concerning the current performance of network resources in an open system and also the generation of performance reports. As yet, there is no facility for the prediction of performance patterns. It is possible to make performance predictions using, among other tools, the queuing theory outlined in Appendix 3. The lack of this facility is considered by some to be a disadvantage of this area of the OSI management standards.

5. Security management: The term 'security' is frequently associated with sensitive areas such as military systems in which data is often highly confidential or even secret. However, the term has a much wider meaning and a security management facility should ideally include the following functions:
   (a) The control of access by users to the various resources of a system.
   (b) The protection of both data and operations to ensure that they are carried out correctly.
   (c) The authentication of data communications to ensure that data is from the source that it claims to be.

No systems are totally secure. Even a local, isolated system is prone to some insecurity and such problems are multiplied as the size of a network increases. An open system, therefore, is particularly vulnerable in this respect.

M.3100 recommendation

Perhaps one of the more widely used applications of OSI network management can be found in the world of telecommunications management networks where much of the modelling provided is based on objects specified in the ITU-T M.3100 recommendation. M.3100 in turn bases much of its terminology on the networking nomenclature defined for the Synchronous Digital Hierarchy (SDH) by the G.803 recommendation. These recommendations provide a generic networks information model that can be used to manage **network elements** such as multiplexers, switches and routers. The managed objects could be physical components or logical components such as software. A managed object possesses **attributes** that allow a user to control and/or

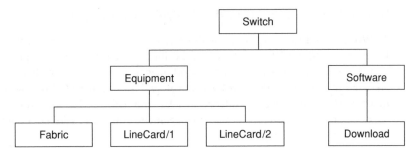

Figure 16.4 Inheritance hierarchy of a switch.

Table 16.2 Attributes of object LineCard/1.	
Attribute	Value
Administrative state	Unlocked
Operational state	Enabled
Usage state	Active
LineCard type	Eight-port E3 ATM

observe the behaviour of the object. Objects with similar attributes and behaviours may be grouped into **object classes**.

A good way to illustrate these terms is by way of a hierarchical diagram, known as an **inheritance/containment hierarchy**. An explanatory inheritance hierarchy is shown in Figure 16.4. It should be stressed that this figure is intended to be explanatory rather than typical. The network element shown is a switch. There are two object classes shown called equipment and software.

Within each object class there are one or more managed objects which may be organized into further subclasses. It may be that there is more than one example of a particular object, in which case they are enumerated. The recommendation refers to each enumeration as an **instance**. Thus in Figure 16.4 there are two instances (1 and 2) of an object called LineCard. Most objects will have a number of attributes. Typical attributes for the object LineCard/1 are given in Table 16.2 along with possible values.

The first three are examples of attributes that allow a user to observe the behaviour of the managed object and are all specified in M.3100. An object with the adminis-trative state unlocked is in service and one with the administrative state locked has been taken out of service. An operational state of enabled indicates that the object is performing its normal function and one of disabled indicates that the object is incapable of performing its normal function. The usage state of an object indicates whether it is being used or not. Active indicates that it is in use but has spare capa-city; busy indicates that it is in use but there is no spare capacity; and idle indicates that the object is not in current use. The final attribute, LineCard type, indicates the particular type of card that is represented by the object LineCard/1 and is an example of an attribute that can be changed since there may be a variety of different types of card that can be inserted into this switch.

Network management in the TCP/IP environment

TCP/IP evolved for many years without any formal network management capability. It was not until the late 1980s, when the Internet started to grow rapidly, that attention was given to this matter and a network management protocol called SNMP (Simple Network Management Protocol) was developed for use in a TCP/IP environment. The first SNMP products were produced in 1988 and their use has spread rapidly since to most major manufacturers. Network management within a TCP/IP environment is based on four key components:

1. Network management station: This is normally a standalone device which acts as the interface between a network manager and SNMP. A network management station provides typical network management functions such as data analysis, fault recovery and network monitoring facilities. It also has access to a database.

2. Agent: Network elements within a network such as routers and bridges can be managed from a network management station. The active software modules within a network element that communicate with a network management station are known as **agents**. Network management stations send various commands to agents which respond appropriately. The agents may also send important items of information, such as alarms, to a network management station even though they are not specifically requested.

3. Management information base: At each network element there is a collection of data similar to a database, which is known as a **management information base** (MIB). A network management station controls a network element by accessing its management information base and retrieving information from it or modifying its contents. Typical information contained in a MIB would be configuration data.

4. Network management protocol: This is the SNMP and it allows the management stations and the agents to communicate with each other.

(16.7) Practical network management systems

A number of manufacturers have developed practical network management systems. Hewlett Packard has a package called OpenView, which is extensively used to manage small and medium networks, and IBM has a product called Tivoli Netview. Both of these systems have the advantage of being able to manage equipment from different vendors since they are based on SNMP. Additionally, manufacturers of equipment such as switches, multiplexers and routers often use proprietary network management systems. All of these products have, to a greater or lesser extent, the same limitation in that they have been developed with a particular manufacturer's systems in mind.

As a practical example of a network management system we shall look at a product developed by Nortel Networks and called Preside Multi-service Data Manager (MDM). Preside is a proprietary range of network management products that encompass a wide range of data communications network products. MDM is a network management system that runs on a Sun workstation and is used to manage carrier data

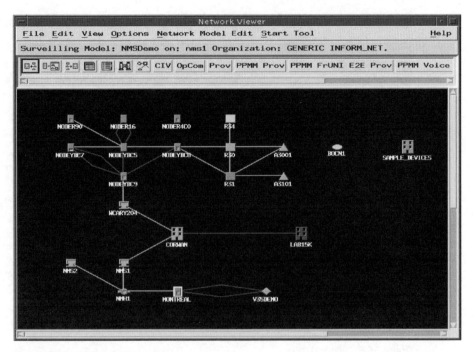

Figure 16.5   Network viewer.

networks containing multiservice and ATM switches as well as high-capacity IP routers. At the time of writing, over 600 major carrier networks use MDM, among them the world's largest networks containing thousands of nodes. The system provides all of the network management functions mentioned in this chapter and serves as a useful illustration of how these functions operate in practice. The main features of the system are summarized below under the headings of these management functions. At the highest level the system uses a **graphical user interface** (GUI) to provide a view of the network as shown in Figure 16.5.

Different types of network elements (switches, routers, etc.) are represented by different-shaped icons. The icons are colour coded according to the fault management alarm convention described in the next section. Nodes and links that are operating normally are coloured green. Nodes and links in a fault condition are typically coloured orange or red according to the severity of the fault.

Fault management

In the event of failures, MDM provides the following three main functions:

1. real-time alarm reception which indicates the nature and location of a failure;

2. access to any selected link or node so that fault conditions can be analysed;

3. access to any link or node in order to correct a fault.

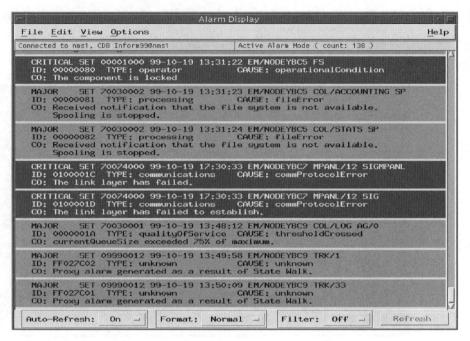

Figure 16.6 Alarm display.

A typical alarm display is shown in Figure 16.6. Displays are typically colour coded according to the severity of the fault: red for critical failures, orange for major faults and yellow for minor faults.

Configuration management

The network view of Figure 16.5 represents each node and link graphically. Any node can be accessed for configuration purposes by clicking on the node's icon. This will give rise to a more detailed graphical representation of the node. In addition to the graphical views of the network, the following activities are available:

- download of software from a central distribution site to a network element;
- configuration of various parameters associated with a network element;
- back-up of service data such as configurations from a network element to a storage site.

A typical display for software downloaded from a distribution site to a network element is shown in Figure 16.7.

The software distribution site is represented by the left-hand side of the display where different software packages are listed. The right-hand side of the display represents the network element to which software is to be downloaded, termed the target in this case. The required software is highlighted and the download started by clicking on a download button.

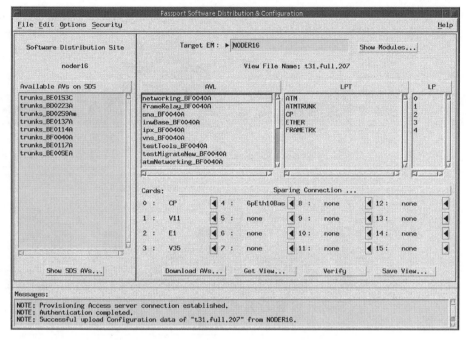

Figure 16.7 Software distribution display.

Performance management

MDM allows the performance of a network to be monitored, thus providing information that allows the following calculations to be carried out:

- availabilities of nodes and links
- numbers of active connections
- volumes of traffic
- numbers of errors.

Figures 16.8 and 16.9 show typical reports for network volume of traffic and numbers of errors.

Summary Table

Volume	(GBytes)	Errors	(×1000)
Total Volume This Day	1,053	Total Errors This Day	1
Previous Day Peak (13 Mar)	824	Previous Day Worst (17 Mar)	1
Ratio This Day To Peak Day	127.8%	Ratio This Day To Worst	95.1%
		Ratio This Day to Best (13 Mar)	130.6%

Figure 16.8 Performance summary table.

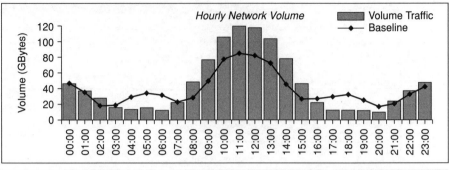

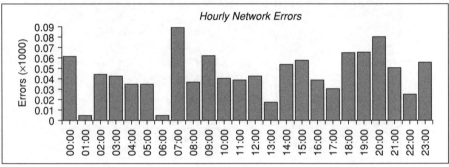

Figure 16.9   Traffic volume and error reports.

These reports will not have been produced directly by the MDM but will have involved the use of intermediate equipment. Large network carriers may provide such facilities in-house, which has the advantage that such reports can be tailored to the individual carrier's requirements.

Encryption

The widespread use, and vast number, of data networks provides enormous scope for breaches of security. This is particularly important given the increase in on-line trading in recent years, where financial transactions are made with a machine with a minimum of direct human involvement. Network security may be compromised in a number of different ways:

- **Eavesdropping**: Unauthorized persons are able to examine or obtain a copy of data which is either transmitted or stored.
- **Manipulation**: Data may be modified either in transmission, or in storage.
- **Impersonation**: Where one person or organization pretends to be, or masquerades, as another. This threat relates to the granting of access to a network, or resources, and protection against unauthorized access.

An attacker may be **passive**, as in eavesdropping for instance, or **active** as in the case where data is manipulated. Another example of an active attack is where data in a transmission, for example, is recorded and then **replayed** in the hope of tricking a receiver into believing that the replayed message is genuine. The attacker may then perhaps gain unauthorized access to a system or resources. An increasingly common form of attack, especially via the Internet, is **denial of service** in the form of **viruses**, **worms** and so forth. These can erase data to prevent work or service being conducted. They may also effectively cause communication to cease by bombarding, a site with incoming messages causing an overload and rendering the site's system powerless to respond to normal requests and activity.

E-commerce is especially concerned with eavesdropping where a third party may gain details of a credit card. Such details may then be used to obtain goods by means of traditional mail order via telephone, or by making an on-line purchase. Impersonation is also important in on-line banking, for example, where a bank must be confident that access is only granted to a bona fide customer before s/he may engage in a transaction such as a withdrawal of funds.

The aim of **encryption** is to make data, information or a message incomprehensible either in transmission, or in stored form. Ideally links conveying, and sites storing, data should be physically secure to prevent access to data by unauthorized persons. This may not always be possible. Data links may pass through many sites and nodes which may have weak physical security and/or contain personnel who may not in all cases be completely trustworthy. Even if this is not the case data may be transmitted over media where signals are easily accessed by an illicit third party. This is particularly true of systems which include a wireless link, such as WLANs.

Ideally, although very rarely found in practice, it would be even better if a transmission were made totally secret in the sense that any third party would be totally unaware of its presence. Secret communication achieved by hiding the existence of a message is known as **steganography** (Singh 2000, pp4–5). Communications systems which make use of spread spectrum techniques come very close to this and are used, although not necessarily for reasons of security, in WLANs.

A1.1 Encryption

Symmetrical encryption is illustrated in Figure A1.1. The system aims to secure a link by changing a message, known as **plaintext**, into transmissions which are rendered unintelligible and called **cyphertext**. The sender could alternatively be delivering cyphertext, or encrypted data, directly into a store such as a floppy disk, rather than a link, to prevent the data being accessed by an unauthorized party. **Encryption** is the process of performing a series of complex mathematical operations upon the plaintext to produce a cyphertext.

Even if the encryption algorithm is designed and intended to remain a secret, it may nevertheless become known to a third party, or even to the public at large. Therefore it is usual to assume that an algorithm is not a secret. In consequence, to prevent unauthorized decryption succeeding by gaining both the cyphertext and knowledge of the algorithm, the whole process is designed to be highly variable. This is achieved by having a large number of **secret keys** from which to choose in order to encrypt each message. To encrypt a message, both sender and receiver must agree which key

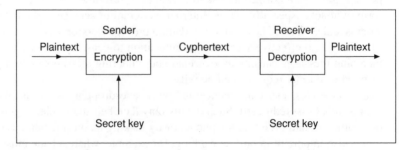

Figure A1.1 Symmetrical encryption.

is to be used. The receiving station decrypts the cyphertext by performing an inverse mathematical operation to that used for encryption and uses the same encryption key. In order for an unauthorized party who gains access to the cyphertext to decrypt the message, knowledge of which particular key was used for encryption is now necessary in order to produce the plaintext. Symmetrical encryption has been used for many decades and is so called because the same key is used for both encryption and decryption. However, as we shall see shortly, this is giving way in many applications to asymmetrical encryption.

Encryption has, as may be imagined, a parallel in door locks. Locksmiths devise a fairly universal lock mechanism that can be produced in a variety of similar ways, each of which may only be opened by its associated key. The general mechanism is analogous to an encryption algorithm and is for all intents and purposes assumed to be known, or available, to the public at large. The only thing that prevents a would-be intruder opening a lock is that the precise key required by a particular lock is not known and may be one of, hopefully, a large number of possible keys. In this way it becomes impracticable to possess all possible keys. Even if it was possible to obtain all possible keys, their number is so large that the probability of finding the correct key within a reasonable period of time is negligible.

A **brute force attack** could be made in an attempt to decipher a message by applying each key in turn to the cyphertext. To guard against this type of attack it is arranged that there is a very large number of encryption keys indeed, which means that it would take an inordinate amount of time to attack a cyphertext one key at a time. In the commercial arena it is hoped that by the time a brute force attack has succeeded, the message will be of no use or interest to a third party. Encryption is based upon binary computations and typically a binary key used in symmetrical encryption might be 56 bits long. This yields 2^{56} possible keys, which is well in excess of 10^{16}, or 10 thousand million million keys. Common examples of encryption found in practice are the Data Encryption Standard (DES) with a 56-bit key and the International Data Encryption Algorithm (IDEA) which may use a key of up to 128 bits in length.

When DES, with a 56-bit key, was devised, such a key length was considered extremely secure by the relatively slow computer processor speeds of the day. Moore's law states that computer speeds double every 18 months. In consequence, given the exponential increase in the speed of processing, the use of a 56-bit key is no longer seen as adequate for many applications. A brute force attack, with modern processor speeds, can succeed in decrypting a message in a relatively short period of time. For this reason key lengths have increased and 128 bits or more are now commonplace.

In practice secret keys are frequently changed so that even where a cipher is broken by discovering the key, use is limited until the next time the key is changed. In many systems, keys are changed for each new message interchange, transaction or session to improve security further. In order to change a key, both sending and receiving stations must be notified of the new key to be used. The generation, and distribution to sender and/or receiver, of a new key must be done in a secure manner to prevent a would-be eavesdropper gaining knowledge of the new key. This is in practice not as trivial as it may seem. Changing keys is a part of the wider topic called **key management**, which is a subject in its own right and discussed shortly.

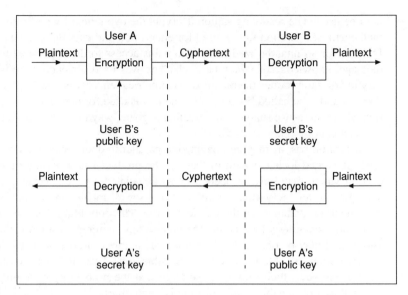

Figure A1.2 RSA encryption.

The main alternative to symmetrical key operation is ciphers based upon an **asymmetrical key** in which the sender and receiver use *different* keys. The predominant asymmetrical key cipher is that devised by **Rivest, Shamir and Aldeman (RSA)** and illustrated in Figure A1.2.

RSA makes use of a **public key** to encrypt a message and a different but related key, the **secret key**, for decryption. In order to encrypt a plaintext the sender obtains the key associated with the receiving station. This can be passed directly from receiver to sender in plaintext or **clear** form, or even be published widely in a lookup table or form of directory. It is for this reason that the key required to encrypt a message for delivery to a particular receiver is known as a **public key**, and does not have to be kept secret. This is because the strength of the cipher is predicated upon the fact that knowledge of the public key gives no insight into what the secret key is and therefore is of no use in endeavouring to decrypt a message. A cyphertext encrypted using a public key system may only be decrypted by a receiver which has the associated secret key. Clearly, as its name suggests, this key must be kept secret. For obvious reasons RSA is also termed **public key encryption** to distinguish it from its forerunner in symmetrical key encryption which may also be called **private key encryption**. Furthermore, to enhance security further, since keys may be sent to a would-be sender in clear, there is no reason why a new key may not be generated for each message transfer, or transaction. In this case, even if an eavesdropper were to gain knowledge of the secret key by some means, it would only be of assistance once.

Public key encryption algorithms make use of mathematical operations, or functions, known as **one-way** functions. This is an operation whereby it is very easy to convert a number (plaintext) into another number (cyphertext) but extremely difficult, given a cyphertext, to obtain the original plaintext, even though the algorithm is known. An analogy of a one-way function is adding a fluid to another fluid. For example, it is very easy to add milk to tea, but far more difficult to reverse the process to obtain black tea.

Public key encryption overcomes the enormous difficulty in symmetrical encryption systems of keeping keys secret. The secret key does not have to be passed to a third party. In order to encrypt a message all that is necessary is the public key, which does not need to be kept secure.

As with all key-based encryption systems RSA is still open to a brute force attack, not least since the algorithm is in the public domain. However, commercial implementations use a key of at least 128 bits in length, which offers an enormous number of keys which, even given Moore's law, results in a formidable task for any would-be eavesdropper. Ciphers for use in ultra-sensitive environments use even longer keys of 256, or even 512, bits.

Although public key encryption predates the e-commerce revolution, it turns out that it is extremely useful in on-line trading. One of the central difficulties to be overcome is how to pass a purchaser's credit card details in a secure manner to an on-line vendor. Because of the nature of on-line connections via the Internet, a private key system is totally infeasible as it would be impossible to pass a secret key swiftly and securely each time a new purchaser connects on-line. Fortunately public key encryption comes to the rescue as once a buyer connects to an on-line sales site, a public key may readily be passed, in clear, to him/her for the current transaction. Public keys are randomly selected for each transaction.

A common form of attack in many communications systems operating at a distance is that of impersonation. Often a high degree of confidence is required to accept that a message is indeed from the source or person it purports to be. In symmetrical key systems a high degree of confidence is placed upon the fact that a sender has the correct key. However, in asymmetrical encryption, the sender's key is issued by the receiver, but how does the receiver know who the sender is, or whether s/he may be trusted? Consider also, for instance, on-line trading: how can a would-be purchaser be certain, before transmitting sensitive financial data in the form of credit card details, that the receiver is bona fide? The receiver may purport to be genuine but be criminally intent on gaining credit card details for subsequent misuse to gain money or goods at someone else's expense. The use of RSA means that in principle anyone may encrypt and send a message to a receiver provided the public key is available. Public key encryption does not provide **authentication**, which is the feature that guarantees that a sender, or receiver, is in fact who s/he purports to be. One may communicate via a cyphertext but that does not prove that either party is genuine. In asymmetrical encryption a sender or a receiver may impersonate, or masquerade.

Masquerading may be prevented using a simple authentication arrangement. A feature of RSA is that a receiver may decipher a message encrypted by the sender using his/her secret key by using the sender's public key, Figure A1.3. Since A's secret key is, by definition, only known to A, B may verify that a message is encrypted by A and their secret key by using A's public key for decryption. In this way it is impossible to masquerade as A, unless of course A's secret key has become known. The feature of authenticating the sender in this way is known as a **digital signature** because it is analogous to that of a unique handwritten signature. The use of digital signatures supports **non-repudiation** in that a sender is unable to say at a later date that s/he did

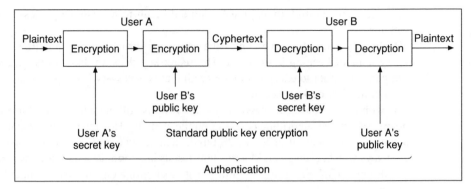

Figure A1.3 RSA authentication.

not in fact send a particular message. This is another useful feature in encryption systems for use in the financial arena. Furthermore, the entire message is also authenticated against manipulation because it may only be produced using A's secret key.

(A1.2) Key management

In private key encryption, apart from keeping the secret key secure, it is usual to change it frequently to provide greater security. Typically a new key is generated for each **session** (or connection). Some method of securely distributing a **session key** (Stallings 2003, pp214–215) to communicating parties is necessary. A number of possible ways of producing session keys are as follows:

1. One party chooses a key and physically passes it to the other party.

2. A third party chooses the key and physically delivers it to each party.

3. Where two parties have recently communicated, one may select a new key and pass it to the other party encrypted with the session key used in the last session.

4. If both parties have a secure (encrypted) link to a third party, the third party may deliver a session key to each party over the link.

The physical passing of keys is generally not an attractive proposition in terms of setting up a secure courier arrangement and the time it takes to effect a key change. The third possibility still requires a courier to deliver a secret key initially to both parties for use in encrypting the first message to be transmitted. Another disadvantage is that once an attacker gains knowledge of one session key, all subsequent key changes will also be revealed and security is, from then on, breached. In consequence many secret keys adopt the fourth option where a third party distributes keys over secure links. A typical third-party approach is by means of a **key distribution centre** (KDC).

A typical key distribution technique is shown in Figure A1.4. User A wishes to communicate with B and requires a session key. Users A and B share master keys with the KDC which we shall term K_a and K_b, respectively. A session key is then produced as follows:

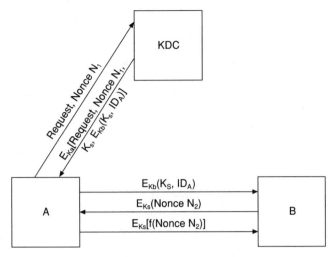

Figure A1.4 Key distribution.

1. A requests, unencrypted or 'in clear', a session key from the KDC indicating that s/he wishes to communicate with B. The request contains a **nonce** N_1 which must be different for each request and is typically a random number. Its main purpose is to prevent masquerade by an attacker and it should therefore be very difficult to guess.

2. The KDC returns an encrypted response using A's secret key K_a. (Note that where data is encrypted, the nomenclature E_{Kx}(parameter/s) is used. This means that the contents of the bracket are encrypted using the key K_x.

   The response contains the original request in order to verify that the request was not altered in transmission to the KDC; the nonce is to enable A to match the response with the request (should a number of requests be made close together). This also verifies that the response is not a replay of a previous response; the session key, K_s; and $E_{Kb}(K_s$, A's network address ID_A), the purpose of which is explained next.

3. A then extracts $E_{Kb}(K_s, ID_A)$ and transmits it directly to B. Encryption, with B's key, ensures that the session key is protected when sending from A. B decrypts this message to obtain the session key and also knows that the other party is A, based upon A's network address. The fact that B's secret key is used indicates that the message must have originated at the KDC, since no other party knows B's secret key.

4. A and B may now communicate securely. A potential danger exists at this point. How does B know that message 3 is authentic, and not simply a replay of a previous message? This is resolved by B sending his/her own nonce N_2 encrypted with the new session key to A.

5. A performs a known and agreed function, or operation (e.g. decrement), upon B's nonce and returns the result to B who checks that the prearranged operation has been performed. It is assumed that the operation would not be known to a third party and in this way A is authenticated to B.

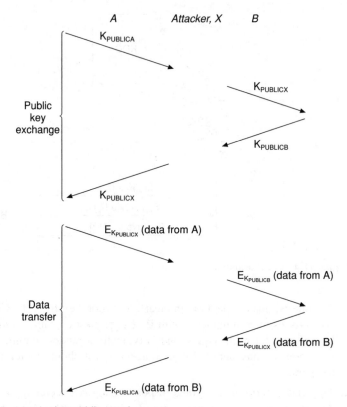

Figure A1.5   Man-in-the-middle attack.

In public key encryption each party may exchange their public keys at the commencement of a session. It appears at first glance that public key encryption overcomes the key management problem of private key encryption. However, if the public keys are published and made available electronically, or exchanged by communicating parties at the commencement of a session, the keys are subject to a so-called **man-in-the-middle attack** whilst in transit. This is best explained by a diagram, Figure A1.5.

Suppose A and B wish to communicate. Each may attempt to exchange their public keys. Each key may be intercepted by an attacker who removes each key and forwards his/her own public key (for which s/he has the secret key(s)). A and B may then exchange data using the attacker's public key(s) and which the attacker may readily decrypt. A digital signature does not overcome this problem as a would-be attacker could sign a message using his/her own secret key. Note that both A and B may be oblivious to this attack and assume that they are operating securely. The attacker meanwhile is able to decrypt all of their messages, and even corrupt them should s/he desire.

The solution to this problem is to use a **certificate**. Any party wishing to issue its public key for secure communication issues the public key and a certificate which not only contains the public key but also verifies the owner of the public key. Certificates are issued by a trusted third party known as a **Certificate Authority**. Therefore if the public key is presented along with a certificate it may be used to encrypt a message and provide confidence that only the intended, or authentic, recipient will be able to decrypt the message. An Internet standard for certificates, RFC 2459, has been produced.

Secure Sockets Layer (SSL)

Internet applications, especially web-based e-commerce, must solve the problems common to all communications at a distance of eavesdropping, manipulation and impersonation. That is, one must guard against credit card details being divulged to an unauthorized third party, data must not be changed to gain unlawful advantage, and a very high degree of confidence that a message is indeed from the source it purports to be is required.

Another way of considering web-based security is that it may be breached at a web server or browser, or within a network. We have already seen in Chapter 15 how IPsec may be implemented at layer 3, the IP or network layer, to provide security transparently to applications and end-users. Alternatively, security may be added on top of the transport layer to provide a secure and reliable connection to the application above. One example considered here is the provision of a **Secure Sockets Layer** above the TCP layer.

Figure A1.6 illustrates the standard TCP/IP stack. Applications communicate with each other by establishing a **socket** which is the interface between the application and transport layers. A socket is also known as the **Application Programmers' Interface** (API) and may be regarded as the Transport Layer Service Access Point, or TSAP. Normal practice is to use a **client–server** arrangement where one application operates as a **server** and one or more other applications, known as **clients**, may request a connection to the server. The server, as expected, acts as a central controller in granting, or denying, connection requests and controlling what service or resource is delivered to a client.

A socket is created by a programmer and in the case of a server specifies the process code to be run within an application and the TCP port number to be used. The client process additionally specifies the IP address of the server.

A Secure Sockets Layer (SSL) has been added to the TCP/IP stack, as shown in Figure A1.7, to provide security, predominantely for web-based applications. SSL provides a secure connection and offers both authentication, including certificates, at the time of connection establishment and the encryption of messages. It makes use of a reliable connection over the TCP layer. (SSL may not be used with UDP, or directly upon the IP layer.) SSL provides server-only authentication, and optionally client authentication. (In credit card transactions a client does not necessarily have

Application
TCP
IP
Host-to-network layer

Figure A1.6   TCP/IP stack.

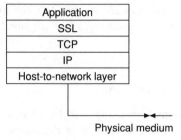

Figure A1.7   Secure Sockets Layer.

to be authenticated. Rather the trader, or server, may authenticate the credit card via a separate mechanism with the cardholder's bank.) Server authentication assures on-line purchasers that they are indeed connected to a bona fide e-commerce trader. RSA encryption is invariably used and ensures the integrity of the message interchanges and especially the credit card details to guard against fraud.

Instead of SSL being implemented on top of the TCP layer, it may alternatively be embedded within the application. Both Netscape and Microsoft Internet Explorer browsers have chosen this latter approach. Such browsers indicate that a current HTTP page has been delivered to a client securely by means of SSL by displaying on the screen the symbol for a padlock.

Current SSL implementations nearly all use version 3. SSL has been adopted by the IETF as **Transport Layer Security** (TLS) and is very similar to SSL version 3. In consequence TLS is now replacing SSL.

Line codes

The topic of line coding was introduced in Chapter 2. Various line codes have been devised to overcome the problems, especially in metallic media, of transmission of binary data. The problems such transmission has to overcome are **baseline wander**, ensuring that the receiver may synchronize its clock with the incoming signal, and matching a signal's bandwidth to that of the medium in use.

The complexity and sophistication of line codes have increased as advances in electronic circuits have occurred. Many codes have been devised, the choice of coding depending upon the characteristics of the line, or channel, over which signals are to be passed. Here we shall examine some of the common line codes. In particular our treatment will categorize codes which will enable the reader to grasp quickly other codes not specifically addressed here.

A2.1 Bit-oriented line codes

Bit-oriented line codes are a class of code where each bit is encoded on an individual basis.

Alternate mark inversion (AMI)

This line code is illustrated in Figure A2.1 and, as in RZ encoding illustrated in Chapter 2, is an example of a ternary code since the line state may be at one of three possible voltages. However, unlike RZ, each transmitted symbol employs only one signal element and therefore is an example of a 1B1T code. Intuitively it is therefore spectrally efficient. In the figure binary 1 is regarded as a 'mark' and encoded into either +V or −V. Binary 0 is encoded into 0 V, always. The polarity of any particular mark symbol is always opposite to that of the preceding mark. Hence the code's name, alternate mark inversion.

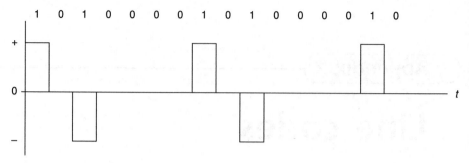

Figure A2.1   AMI code.

The main advantage of AMI is that it is a 'dc balanced' code. That is, successive non-zero voltage signal elements, or marks, are of opposite polarity and therefore the long-term mean line voltage is zero. As a result, baseline wander is eliminated. The main disadvantage of AMI is that a sustained series of binary 0 signals results in a long period of zero volts on the line which can lead to the receiver losing clock synchronization.

High density bipolar 3 (HDB3)

HDB3 is illustrated in Figure A2.2 and is based upon AMI but modified to overcome loss of synchronization due to long strings of binary 0. A rule is introduced to inhibit four successive 0 V symbols on the line. In other words, the maximum number of 0 V symbols that may be transmitted is three.

If data contains four successive binary 0 signals, the fourth zero is encoded as a mark, but with the *same* polarity as the last mark to be transmitted. Such a signal is termed a **violation** (V) pulse since the normal AMI rule is violated in this instance. In consequence HDB3 only has a maximum of three consecutive 0 V symbols, which means that sufficient transitions exist in a received signal to ensure reliable clock recovery.

The receiver may easily recognize a violation pulse and decode it as the binary 0 symbol it represents. Subsequent symbols continue with AMI operation with the

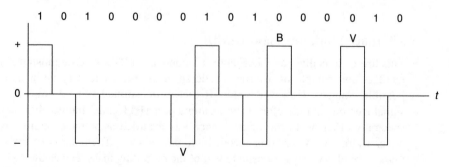

Figure A2.2   HDB3 code.

next binary 1 symbol encoded as a mark with opposite polarity to the preceding V pulse.

AMI is a balanced code and eliminates baseline wander. In HDB3 a single V pulse disturbs balance slightly, although this is not a significant problem. However, problems with successive V pulses may occur. Depending upon the binary signal sequence to be transmitted, it may be that a number of successive V pulses may be of the *same* polarity which would appreciably disturb the line balance, introducing significant baseline wander and leading to a deterioration in BER. To overcome this HDB3 makes use of a **balancing** (B) pulse. After a V pulse has been introduced, then on the occurrence of the next string of four binary zeros, if it happens that the V pulse would be of same polarity as that of the last V pulse, a B pulse is introduced in the first bit position. A B pulse simply has opposite polarity to the preceding V pulse and thereby restores the dc balance of the signal. The fourth zero is encoded as a V pulse with the same polarity as that of the immediately preceding B pulse.

Initially the receiver is unable to distinguish a B pulse from a binary 1 symbol. However, three pulses later a V pulse is received and the receiver may then deduce that the B pulse must in fact be a binary 0.

The complexity of HDB3 is increased as both transmitter and receiver, unlike AMI, need to include some storage. The transmitter cannot encode a signal fully until after 4 bits of data have appeared at its input, because only then will it be able to determine if a violation has occurred and, if so, whether also to introduce a B pulse. The receiver does not immediately recognize a B pulse and must contain a 3-bit store so that when a V pulse occurs, it may look back to see if a B pulse also occurred. If there is a B pulse the four associated zeros with the B and V pulses can then be correctly decoded.

HDB3 code is another example of a 1B1T code and may be summarized as having negligible baseline wander, supporting reliable clock recovery and, as with AMI upon which it is based, being spectrally efficient. In addition HDB3 is an example of the group of codes generally classed as BnZS codes. These codes are explained shortly.

Coded mark inversion (CMI)

At higher data rates the memory and logic circuits required to implement HDB3 become relatively more expensive. CMI was developed for use at higher data rates as it uses simpler, and therefore cheaper, circuitry. In comparison with AMI, this code overcomes the problem of strings of zeros as there is at least one transition for each symbol. The coding rules are shown in Figure A2.3. Binary 1 is chosen from one of two full-width pulses. Binary 0 is encoded into two alternate half-width pulses, as shown. As some data is encoded into two pulses of opposite polarity, the spectrum of CMI is double that of AMI and HDB3, which means that lines of larger bandwidth are required.

Figure A2.4 illustrates how a certain string of data may be encoded using CMI. Each successive binary 1, rather like AMI, simply uses the alternate symbol compared with that used by the immediately preceding binary 1 symbol, irrespective of any preceding or intervening binary zeros.

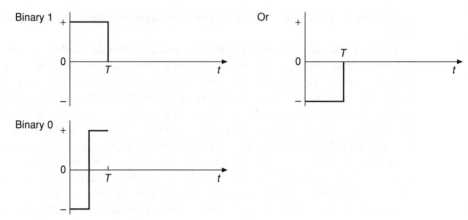

T – duration of 1 bit, or symbol

Figure A2.3 CMI coding rules.

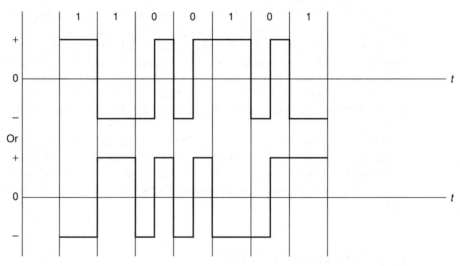

Figure A2.4 CMI example.

Binary with *n* zeros substituted code

Generically these codes are abbreviated as **BnZS**. We have already seen an example of such a code in the form of HDB3, which may be described as bipolar with the fourth successive zero substituted. Therefore HDB3 may also be classified as a B4ZS code. BnZS codes follow the same rules as HDB3 in that the *n*th successive zero is encoded as a violation pulse and a balancing pulse inserted, if required. An example of BnZS, B6ZS in this case, is shown in Figure A2.5. BnZS codes are attractive since they offer adequate clock timing and yet are spectrally efficient. The number of successive zeros may be chosen to suit the particular requirements of a system.

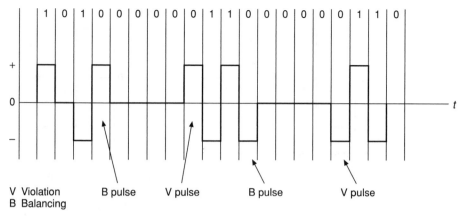

| 1 | 0 | 1 | 0 | 0 | 0 | 0 | 0 | 0 | 1 | 1 | 0 | 0 | 0 | 0 | 0 | 0 | 0 | 1 | 1 | 0 |

V Violation   B pulse   V pulse   B pulse   V pulse
B Balancing

Figure A2.5 B6ZS code.

Manchester code

The line codes discussed so far are primarily used in long-haul digital transmission line systems found within a core network. Manchester encoding, Figure A2.6, is employed for baseband line signalling in local area networks, for example some Ethernet networks. The code has similarities with CMI and is an example of a 1B2B code where a binary signal is encoded into two signal elements which are either −V and +V for binary 1 or +V and −V for binary 0 (or vice versa). Manchester encoding is also known as a **bi-phase** code as each symbol may be regarded as containing two elements of opposite phase. The polarities of each signal element are equal in amplitude but of opposite polarity and it is therefore a balanced code eliminating baseline wander. Closer inspection reveals that there is a signal transition in the centre of each symbol, which means that the code is clock rich, enabling ease of clock recovery at the receiver, its principal attraction. The price paid for this feature is a doubling of the signal's spectrum which makes it less spectrally efficient.

Differential Manchester code

The differential Manchester code is an example of a **differential code** whereby data is encoded as a difference, rather than into signal voltages. Figure A2.7 illustrates differential Manchester encoding and it may be seen that similar symbols to those used in Manchester coding, above, are used. It is still a 1B2B form of coding. However, both binary 1 and binary 0 can be encoded into either symbol. The convention used is that one binary state causes a transition at the start of the symbol whereas when the other binary state is transmitted, no transition occurs. The particular assigning of transition, or no transition, to data bits is arbitrary, although for a given implementation it must remain consistent. In the figure binary 1 causes a transition whereas binary 0 does not result in a transition. Hence we see that data is encoded into transitions, or otherwise, hence the name of the code.

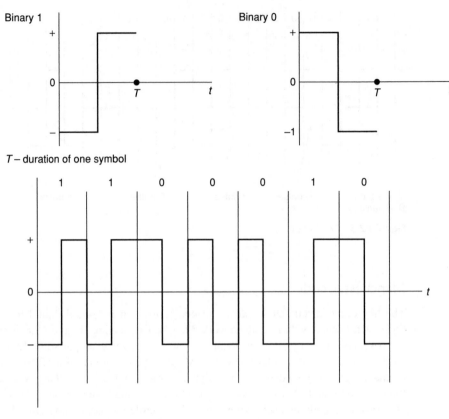

T – duration of one symbol

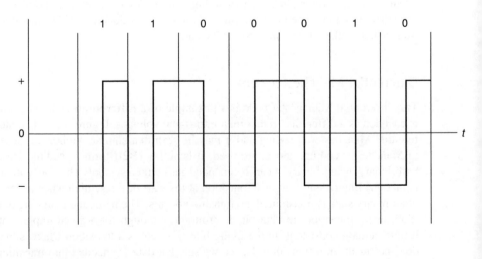

Figure A2.6   Manchester coding.

Figure A2.7   Differential Manchester coding.

A useful feature of differential coding is that the receiver does not have to be polarity sensitive. If, for instance, a fault developed in a cable pair carrying such a signal and in repair the pair became reversed, the voltages would also become reversed. However, the binary signals would still be correctly interpreted at the receiver since the same *changes* would result at the signal boundaries in terms of a transition or not, even if the direction of the change in a transition were reversed.

(A2.2) Block codes

All the line codes looked at so far are examples of bit-oriented codes where the coding rules operate on individual bits. In **block codes** the coding rules operate on a block of bits, which means that they often require more complex encoding and decoding circuitry. Like the codes previously described they are designed to prevent baseline wander and to have good timing content.

The basic principle behind the design of block codes is that blocks of input bits are encoded to give blocks of code symbols. This is different to all the codes looked at so far which involve coding a single bit to give one or more code symbols.

The encoder for a block code first has to break the incoming data stream into appropriately sized blocks (sometimes called words). It then encodes each block of input bits into a block of code symbols (codewords). Finally, it has to transmit the codewords serially. Figure A2.8 is a typical block diagram for a block encoder.

A binary block code can be specified as an $nBmB$ code, where n binary bits are encoded into m binary bits. So in the case of a 3B4B code the serial input data is first of all broken down into blocks 3 bits wide, the 3-bit blocks are then encoded into 4-bit blocks and the 4-bit blocks are then transmitted as serial data. It is also possible to have a ternary block code which can be specified as an $nBmT$ code, where n binary bits are encoded into m ternary symbols, or a quarternary block code, for example 2BIQ, where 2 bits are encoded into one of four possible quaternary symbols.

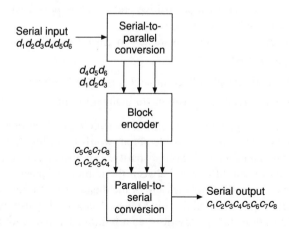

Figure A2.8 Block code encoder.

Input	Output			
	Negative	0	Positive	Disparity
001		--++		0
010		-+-+		0
100		+--+		0
011		-++-		0
101		+-+-		0
110		++--		0
000	--+-		++-+	±2
111	-+--		+-++	±2

Table A2.1 3B4B coding table.

It is not unusual for the incoming data to have no inherent block structure; the position of the initial block boundary chosen by the encoder may therefore be arbitrary. However, once the initial block boundary is chosen, the encoder can then take successive sequences of n adjacent symbols.

One of the principal attractions of block codes is that more spectrally efficient codes may be designed compared to bit-oriented codes. It is impossible, if n and m are both binary symbols, to make $n > m$ but codes where $m = n + 1$ are especially common as they are spectrally efficient, and more efficient than where $m > n + 1$.

At first glance it may seem puzzling that one may consider designing a code where $n > m$ at all. The clear implication is that more codewords are possible than the 2^n possible codewords required. The codewords ($< 2^m$) used are in fact a subset of the total number of codewords available. Use is made of this feature of block codes whereby codewords may be selected to suit a particular requirement. This may be best illustrated by examining a particular code as follows.

Consider the 3B4B block code which is one of the simplest types of block code, but illustrates all of the characteristics of a block code. Block codes are fully described in a **coding table** which shows how each input word is coded. Table A2.1 gives all the encoding rules for the 3B4B code. The table assumes that the code is implemented by some combination of four positive and negative pulses where + indicates a positive pulse and – indicates a negative pulse.

Table A2.1 has been constructed to ensure that the encoded words have the following properties:

- There is no mean voltage offset (to prevent baseline wander).
- There are frequent transitions to maintain timing.

The left-hand column lists all the possible input 3-bit binary words. The next three columns contain all the possible output words according to the coding rules. The fifth column contains the codeword disparity. The disparity, or **digital sum**, of a codeword is a count of the difference between the number of positive and negative pulses and is therefore a normalized measure of the mean voltage of the word. A word with equal numbers of positive and negative pulses has zero disparity and a zero mean voltage. A word such as this is described as a **balanced word**. **Unbalanced words** can have positive or negative disparity. For example, the codeword + + – + has a disparity of

Table A2.2   Example of a running digital sum.

Coded word	Running digital sum
--++	0
--+-	-2
+--+	-2
++--	-2
+-++	0
-++-	0

+2. To ensure that there is no mean voltage offset, balanced codewords are used in Table A2.1 for the output where possible, that is for input words 001 to 110. The remaining two input words have to be encoded to unbalanced words. To maintain the zero mean offset, each of these two input words can be encoded to a word with either a positive mean voltage or a negative mean voltage. The choice between the two for a particular input word is made at the time of encoding and depends on the value of the **running digital sum**. During encoding the encoder keeps a record of the running digital sum of each transmitted word. Table A2.2 shows how the value of the running digital sum changes during the transmission of some coded words.

The encoder consults the value of the running digital sum whenever an unbalanced word must be transmitted. If the sum is negative or zero, the positive disparity option is selected; if it is positive the negative disparity option is selected. When the input word is encoded into a balanced word then no choice needs to be made and the running digital sum is unchanged.

Following the above encoding rule and assuming that a register holding the running digital sum initially contains 0, the running digital sum is always either 0 or -2 between the transmission of words. So the encoder can be regarded as having two different states, defined by the current running digital sum.

Table A2.3 illustrates how the data sequence 000 001 111 101 111 is encoded on the assumption that prior to this sequence the running digital sum is zero.

The output sequence is therefore:

++-+ --++ +-++ +-+- +-++

In order to decode a 3B4B code the decoder needs to break the incoming serial data sequence into 4-bit words. The decoder must know where to break the serial data into words to get the correct blocks of code symbols; this is known as **block alignment**.

Table A2.3   Example of 3B4B encoding.

Input word	Running digital sum before encoding	Encoded word	Running digital sum after encoding
000	0	++-+	+2
001	+2	--++	+2
111	+2	-+--	0
101	0	+-+-	0
111	0	+-++	+2

Table A2.4 Decoding for 3B4B codes.

Received codeword	Decoded to	Most likely transmitted word	Number of bits in error
----*	001	000 or 111	1 or 2
---+*	000	001 or 010 or 100	1
--+-	000		
--++	001		
-+--	111		
-+-+	010		
-++-	011		
-+++*	011	001 or 010 or 011	1 or 0
+---*	100	100 or 101 or 110	0 or 1
+--+	100		
+-+-	101		
+-++	111		
++--	110		
++-+	000		
+++-*	111	011 or 101 or 110	1
++++*	110	000 or 111	2 or 1

Once the alignment has been carried out, the decoding may be completed using a look-up table which consists of all the possible binary forms. A decoding table is shown in Table A2.4.

Codewords marked with an asterisk are called **forbidden words**; these are words which are not used in the coding table. However, they might appear in the coded data arriving at a decoder as a result of errors in the received data. The decoder needs to know how to decode them; therefore an entry must be included in the decoding table. The forbidden words are chosen, not on the basis of nearest neighbour, but rather to produce the lowest average number of errors in the output.

(A2.3) Error detection

As noise is present in all transmission systems it is more than likely that errors will occur in a received data stream. Line codes use a particular coding rule that may also be used as a means of error detection. The received data stream can therefore be checked to see if it is consistent with the particular rule. Consider, say, an AMI code that is used to encode the data 1011001. This produces the code:

$$+ 0 - + 0\ 0 -$$

Now suppose an error were to occur in the fifth symbol such that the received code became:

$$+ 0 - + - 0 -$$

A violation has occurred in the coding rule and an error can be detected. In this system we have error detection but not error correction, and although single errors can be detected multiple errors may be missed.

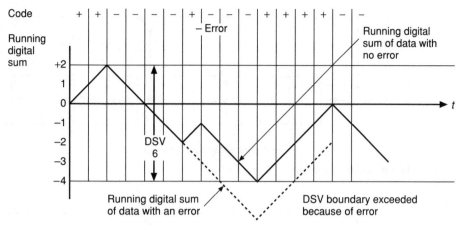

Figure A2.9   Digital sum variation.

In block codes, the **digital sum variation** (DSV) can be used to detect errors. Suppose a running digital sum can vary between 0 and −2 between words and by ±2 during words. Its total variation can be from −4 to +2. Therefore, the total DSV is 6 with bounds of −4 and +2. A single error will eventually cause the measured running digital sum to exceed its bounds. Decoders can monitor the DSV bounds and if they are exceeded an error can be indicated.

Figure A2.9 shows how the DSV varies on receipt of a particular data stream and the effect of a single error. For this situation the DSV exceeds its bounds and therefore an error can be detected. Again, this system gives error detection, not error correction.

A2.4   Scramblers

Many subsystems in data communications systems, such as equalizers, work better with random bit sequences. Strings of binary ones or zeros, or periodic sequences, may appear in the output of any information source; therefore such sequences need to be coded for transmission if the data transmission systems are likely to have difficulty in conveying them. A device used to randomize the input data is called a **scrambler**. Scramblers are often used in conjunction with some of the line codes described earlier in order to ensure that undesirable sequences, e.g. long strings of same binary code, are not present in the data to be encoded. When a scrambler is used at the transmitter a descrambler must be used at the receiver to reconstitute the input data.

A typical scrambler consists of a feedback shift register and the matching descrambler consists of a feed forward shift register. In both the scrambler and the descrambler the outputs of several stages of shift register are added together modulo-2 (exclusive OR), and then added to the data stream again in modulo-2 arithmetic. The contents of the shift register are shifted at the bit rate of the system. A block diagram of a typical scrambler is shown in Figure A2.10 and its associated descrambler in Figure A2.11.

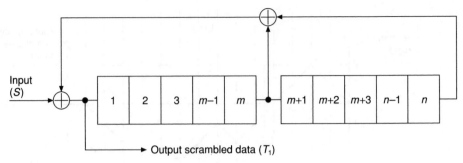

Figure A2.10   Scrambler.

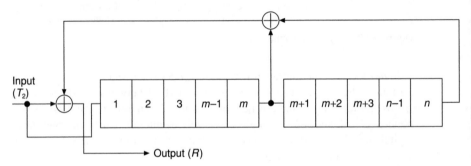

Figure A2.11   Descrambler.

The operation of a scrambler may be analysed by allowing the operator D to represent a 1-bit delay. Thus DS represents a sequence S delayed by 1 bit and $D^k S$ represents a sequence S delayed by k bits. Using this method the scrambler and descrambler shown in Figures A2.10 and A2.11 can be analysed as follows.

The output of the scrambler is given by:

$$T_1 = S \oplus (T_1 D^m \oplus T_1 D^n)$$
$$= S \oplus F T_1 \quad \text{where } F = D^m + D^n$$
$$= \frac{S}{1 \oplus F}$$

The output of the descrambler is given by:

$$R = T_2 \oplus (T_2 D^m \oplus T_2 D^n)$$
$$= T_2 \oplus F T_2$$
$$= T_2 (1 \oplus F)$$

In the absence of errors $T_2 = T_1$ and therefore the unscrambled output is given by:

$$R = \frac{S}{1 \oplus F} \times (1 \oplus F)$$
$$= S$$

Thus the output is an exact replica of the input.

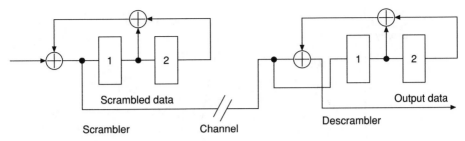

Figure A2.12 Two-stage scrambler and descrambler.

ITU-T specifies a scrambler by use of a **tap polynomial** which gives the position of the feedback taps. For example, the scrambler of Figure A2.10 has feedback taken from stages m and n, so it may be described by listing its feedback taps as (m, n). Its tap polynomial is:

$1 + D^m + D^n$

Then from the analysis above it can be seen that:

$T_1 = S$ (divided by the tap polynomial)

and:

$R = T_2$ (multiplied by the tap polynomial)

Note that the selection of n for a given m is non-trivial and is outside the scope of this book, see Peterson (1961).

An example of a scrambler and descrambler with a tap polynomial of $1 + D + D^2$ is shown in Figure A2.12.

In general, an appropriately designed scrambler of length n will respond to an all-zeros input with an output that is a repeating sequence of length $2^n - 1$, provided that it is not latched, see shortly. A scrambler of this type is called a **maximal-length scrambler**.

A situation can occur in a scrambler where if all the storage elements contain zero and the input is all zeros, then the output will be all zeros. In this (generally undesirable) state the scrambler is said to be **latched**, and the effect is described as **scrambler lock-up**. It is possible to prevent this condition by using additional circuitry, but an all-zeros input is still possible. More complex scrambler configurations ensure that the input conditions that cause lock-up are less likely to occur.

(A2.5) Frequency spectra characteristics of common line codes

One of the main characteristics of a line code is that the spectra of the transmitted data should be appropriate to the line characteristics. We therefore need to examine the spectrum of the various line codes we have looked at in order to determine their suitability for transmission. In comparing line codes we need to take care when evaluating the spectral characteristics as, for most cases, the spectral diagram of

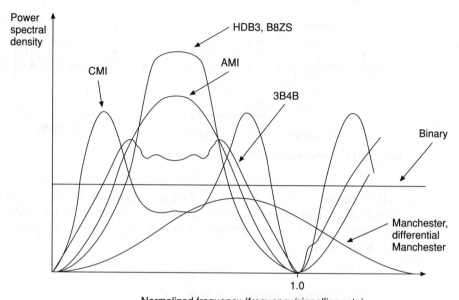

Figure A2.13   Frequency spectral characteristics of some line codes.

each code is dominated by a particular pulse shape. Figure A2.13 shows the frequency characteristics of the line codes already considered. The graphs are obtained by using impulses as digits. The spectrum of randomly encoded data using such impulses is constant (flat). Hence for any such data encoded by the normal coding rules the deviation from a flat spectrum is due entirely to the code.

The spectral characteristics of the codes can now be compared using the information contained in Figure A2.13. For the straightforward binary code the spectrum is flat and includes dc and low-frequency components, thereby may result in baseline wander.

AMI code has some very attractive properties; the spectral diagram shows no dc component and very little low-frequency content, thereby reducing considerably likelihood of baseline wander. The bandwidth required is equal to the transmission rate. It is a very simple code to implement but does have the big disadvantage of poor timing content associated with long runs of binary zeros.

HDB3 and B8ZS have similar characteristics to AMI but have superior timing content. Their main disadvantage, as already mentioned, is that they are more complex to implement and this means greater cost, particularly at high data rates.

CMI has a power spectrum that is fairly evenly distributed throughout the spectral band, but there are large power spectral density components at the low-frequency end of the spectrum, which again can lead to baseline wander problems.

3B4B has a spectrum that is fairly evenly distributed throughout the spectral band. It also has good timing content. It is, however, a fairly complex code to implement but, because this class of code can be spectrally efficient, it does have application in long-distance transmission.

Manchester encoding, compared with the previous codes, has most of its energy situated at relatively high frequencies. This means that it requires a correspondingly higher bandwidth for transmission. However, as already discussed, it is very attractive in as much that it is a balanced code and therefore does not give rise to baseline wander. In addition it is clock-rich making for ease of clock recovery at a receiver.

(A2.6) Codes in practice

Table A2.5 indicates commonly found data rates in PDH and SDH digital transmission systems and some examples of the codes typically employed. At lower speed Europe favours HDB3 and CMI. In the USA, with relatively longer links, BnZS codes are preferred since longer intervals can be permitted between repeaters with attendant reduction in cost.

Table A2.5 Codes found in practice.

Data rate (kbps)	Code used
1 544	AMI with scrambling or B8ZS
2 048	HDB3 (B4ZS)
6 321	B6ZS or B8ZS
8 448	HDB3
34 368	HDB3
44 736	B3ZS
139 264	CMI
155 520	CMI
565 148	CMI

So far in this appendix line code examples have centred upon those found in metallic line systems. Much of the core network comprises high-speed optical links where line coding requirements are slightly different. The simplest form of modulation in optical transmission is OOK where a binary 1 is equivalent to maximum light intensity and binary 0 to no light transmitted. In practice, it is more satisfactory to operate between, say, 70% and 30% intensity, rather than 100% and 0% as described above. This reduces the transition time of devices between binary states enabling operation at the highest possible speed. There is no particular need to choose a spectrally efficient code since the relatively high bandwidth of optical fibre is not a limiting factor. Binary, rather than ternary or quaternary, coding is therefore adequate for use in optical line transmission. The main considerations of a line code for optical transmission are:

- Provision of error detection capability.
- Timing information to support clock recovery at the receiver.

Line codes that are used in optical line transmission include CMI and nBmB such as 3B4B. The transatlantic optical fibre system TAT-8 operates using a 24B1P line code which is where 24-bit blocks have one parity bit added. It is therefore an example of a 24B25B block code, and thus spectrally efficient, and provides a degree of error detection capability.

Applications of queuing theory

A3.1 Introduction

An important measure of performance of a data communications network is the average delay while transmitting data from source to destination. Furthermore, delay considerations play an important part in network functions such as flow control and routing. (These are dealt with in some detail in Chapter 5.) Queuing arises naturally in both packet-switched and circuit-switched networks. Packets at a node in a network will join a queue whilst waiting to be connected to an outgoing transmission link to the next node along the route. Much of the theory of queuing was developed from the study of telephone traffic at the beginning of the twentieth century by A.K. Erlang. The simplest queue, in which data, shown as packets, arrives randomly at an average rate of λ packets per second, is shown in Figure A3.1. The packets are held in a queue while a server deals with them at a rate of μ per second and then are transmitted.

This type of system is known as a single-server queue, although there may be more than one server in a system. It is important that the arrival rate λ is not allowed to exceed the service rate μ, or the queue will build up (to infinity in theory, but to a maximum size in practice).

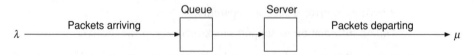

Figure A3.1 Single-server queue.

A3.2 Multiplexing

When a number of streams of data come together over a single link they need to be multiplexed. The most common arrangement in data communications is statistical multiplexing in which traffic from a number of data streams is merged into a single queue and then transmitted over the link on a first-come first-served basis. Alternatively, each stream may have its own queue and each queue is served in sequence. If a queue is empty the server moves on directly to the next one. Two types of multiplexing are often used in a circuit switched system. In time-division multiplexing (TDM) the time available on the transmission link is divided into fixed-length time slots which are each allocated to an input stream. In frequency-division multiplexing (FDM) the available frequency bandwidth of the transmission link is divided into fixed-frequency bands each of which is allocated to an input stream. The reason for the popularity of statistical multiplexing in data communications is that it produces a smaller average delay. This is because both TDM and FDM allocate time (or frequency) to an empty input stream even if other input streams have data waiting for transmission.

A3.3 Little's theorem

This simple theorem provides the basis for much of queuing theory. It arises out of a queuing model in which blocks of data (normally in the form of packets) arrive randomly at a network node. While at a node they are held in a queue awaiting service (retransmission). The time taken to retransmit the packet (equal to the packet length in bits divided by the transmission rate) is often called the **service time** in this context. The theory applies equally to a circuit-switched telephone system in which packets are replaced by calls and the service time is equal to the duration of a call. Little's theorem states that the average number of packets in the system, N, the average delay, T, and the average arrival rate, λ, are related as follows:

$$N = \lambda T \tag{A3.1}$$

The usefulness of this theorem is that it applies to almost every queuing system. Everyday examples spring to mind. For example, slow-moving traffic (large T) produces crowded streets (large N); a fast-food restaurant (small T) needs fewer tables (small N) than a normal restaurant for the same customer arrival rate (λ). The theorem can also be used to find the average number of packets in a queue rather than the overall system. If we define the following:

W, the average time spent waiting in the queue
N_q, the average number of packets found waiting in the queue by packets on arrival

then Little's theorem leads to:

$$N_q = \lambda W \tag{A3.2}$$

Example A3.1

A fast-food restaurant is operating with a single person serving customers who arrive at an average rate of two per minute and wait to receive their order for an average of 3 minutes. On average, half of the customers eat in the restaurant and the other half eat take-away. A meal takes an average of 20 minutes to eat. Determine the average number of customers queuing and the average number in the restaurant.

Customers who eat in the restaurant stay on average for 23 minutes, and customers who eat take-away for 3 minutes. Arrival rate, λ, is two per minute.

Average customer time in restaurant, $T = 0.5 \times 23 + 0.5 \times 3 = 13$ minutes
Average time in queue, $W = 3$ minutes

From Little's theorem:

Average number of customers queuing, $N_q = \lambda W = 2 \times 3 = 6$
Average number in restaurant, $N = \lambda T = 2 \times 13 = 26$

A3.4 Single-server queues

The simplest type of queue is that shown in Figure A3.1 in which there is a single server. To take our analysis further it is assumed that the arrival of packets at a network node occurs randomly and independently of each other. This type of arrival process is called a memoryless or Poisson process. The best way of illustrating this is using the probability distribution shown in Figure A3.2, where $P(n)$ gives the probability that the number of packets arriving in a particular time interval will equal n.

Suppose now that the packets are dealt with from the queue in the order in which they arrive (first in, first out). The different service times are assumed to be independent of the arrival times and mutually independent. The average service time is denoted by S and the service rate, μ, when the server is busy is given by:

$$\mu = \frac{1}{S} \text{ packets per second} \tag{A3.3}$$

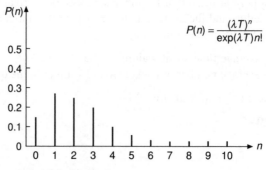

$$P(n) = \frac{(\lambda T)^n}{\exp(\lambda T)n!}$$

Figure A3.2 Poisson probability distribution.

The average number of packets being retransmitted at any one time equals the arrival rate times the average service time:

$$\lambda S = \frac{\lambda}{\mu}$$

Since one packet is the most that can be transmitted at any one time in single-server systems then this value is also a utilization factor ρ:

$$\rho = \frac{\lambda}{\mu} = S\lambda \qquad (A3.4)$$

We now introduce the concept of residual service time. By this we mean that if packet i is already being served when packet j arrives, R_j is the time remaining until packet i's service time is complete. If no packet is being served (the queue is empty when packet j arrives) then $R_j = 0$. Thus when a packet arrives at a queue, the average time spent waiting in the queue is equal to the average residual service time, R, plus the product of the average service time and the average number of packets found in the queue:

$$W = R + SN_q$$
$$= R + \frac{N_q}{\mu} \qquad (A3.5)$$

From Little's theorem:

$$N_q = \lambda W$$

and substituting for N_q gives:

$$W = R + \frac{\lambda}{\mu} W$$
$$= R + \rho W \quad \text{where } \rho \text{ is the utilization factor}$$

Therefore:

$$\text{Average time spent waiting, } W = \frac{R}{1 - \rho} \qquad (A3.6)$$

The simplest way to determine R is graphically, as shown in Figure A3.3, by plotting the residual service time $r(t)$ against time. When a new service of duration S begins,

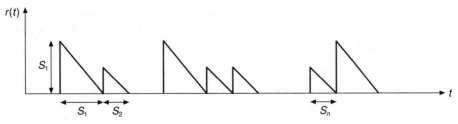

Figure A3.3 Plot of residual service time against time.

the value of $r(t)$ starts at S_1 and falls linearly until it reaches zero after a period of time equal to S_1. As can be seen, the plot resembles a series of 45° right-angled triangles with gaps occurring when the queue is empty. The average value of $r(t)$ can be found by integrating and extending the time scale to infinity.

This gives the result for average residual service time, R, as:

$$R = \frac{1}{2}\lambda \overline{S^2} \tag{A3.7}$$

where $\overline{S^2}$ is the mean square service time. Substituting for R in (A.3.6) gives:

$$W = \frac{\lambda \overline{S^2}}{2(1-\rho)} \tag{A3.8}$$

This is the Pollaczek–Khinchin (P–K) formula which along with Little's theorem provides much of the theoretical basis for queuing theory.

The total time spent both waiting in the queue and being serviced (transmitted) can now be written as:

$$T = S + \frac{\lambda \overline{S^2}}{2(1-\rho)} \tag{A3.9}$$

The average number of items in the queue, N_q, and the average number in the system, N, can be obtained by applying Little's theorem to (A3.8) and (A3.9):

$$N_q = \frac{\lambda^2 \overline{S^2}}{2(1-\rho)} \tag{A3.10}$$

$$N = S\lambda + \frac{\lambda^2 \overline{S^2}}{2(1-\rho)}$$

But from (A3.4), $S\lambda = \rho$, so that:

$$N = \rho + \frac{\lambda^2 \overline{S^2}}{2(1-\rho)} \tag{A3.11}$$

This P–K derivation assumes that packets are served in the order of arrival (FIFO). However, the formula holds even if packets are served in a different order as long as the order of service is independent of the service times.

(Example A3.2) _____

Packets arrive at a single-server node for transmission at random with an average arrival rate of 15 per second; 80% of packets contain 1024 bits and 20% contain 64 bits. If the transmission rate is 19.2 kbps and the system is error free, determine:

(a) average transmission time

(b) average time spent waiting in queue

(c) average number in the queue

(d) average number in the system

(a) Average transmission time for long packets $= \dfrac{1024}{19.2} = 53.3$ ms

Average transmission time for short packets $= \dfrac{64}{19.2} = 3.3$ ms

Average transmission time $= 0.8 \times 53.3 + 0.2 \times 3.3$
$$S = 43.3 \text{ ms}$$

(b) Mean square service time $= 0.8 \times (53.3)^2 + 0.2(3.3)^2$
$$= 2275.5 + 2.2$$
$$= 2277.7 \ \mu s^2$$

(Note that in calculating the mean square service time, the short packets could have been ignored without much affecting the result. This is not always the case, particularly when errors are taken into account.)

Utilization factor, $\rho = \lambda S$
$$= 15 \times 43.3 \times 10^{-3}$$
$$= 0.65$$

The average time spent waiting in the queue is obtained directly from P–K:

$$W = \frac{\lambda \overline{S^2}}{2(1 - \rho)} = \frac{15 \times 2278 \times 10^{-6}}{2 \times 0.35} = 48.8 \text{ ms}$$

(c) The average number in the queue is obtained from Little's theorem:

$N_q = \lambda W$
$$= 15 \times 48.8 \times 10^{-3}$$
$$= 0.732 \text{ packets}$$

(d) Average number of packets in the system:

$N = S\lambda + N_q$
$$= 43.3 \times 10^{-3} \times 15 + 0.732$$
$$= 0.649 + 0.732$$
$$= 1.3815$$

(A3.5) ## Further queue types

The P–K formula can be used to analyse most types of queue. Each type of queue is specified by three letters and numbers. The type considered up to now is known as M/G/1 which has the following meaning:

1. The first letter gives the nature of the arrival process: M for memoryless (i.e. a Poisson probability distribution); G for general (unspecified); D for deterministic (at predetermined time intervals).

2. The second letter stands for the nature of the probability distribution of the service (i.e. transmission times), again M, G or D.

3. The final number is the number of servers.

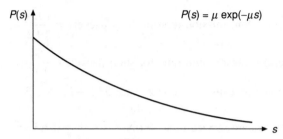

Figure A3.4 Exponential probability distribution.

The M/M/1 queuing system

This is similar to the M/G/1 system discussed above except that the service process has the same memoryless (Poisson) process as the arrival process. This has the effect of giving the service times an exponential probability distribution, as shown in Figure A3.4.

This is often considered the worst-case situation since it involves a wide range of service times. The mean square value of the service time can be determined from the exponential distribution. This gives the following result:

$$\text{Mean square service time, } \overline{S^2} = \frac{2}{\mu^2} \tag{A3.12}$$

The P–K formula and related equations then become:

$$P\text{–}K, W = \frac{\lambda 2}{\mu^2 2(1 - \rho)}$$

$$= \frac{\rho}{\mu(1 - \rho)}$$

$$\text{Average time spent in the system, } T = S = \frac{\rho}{\mu(1 - \rho)} = \frac{1}{\mu} + \frac{\rho}{\mu(1 - \rho)}$$

$$= \frac{1 - \rho + \rho}{\mu(1 - \rho)} = \frac{1}{\mu(1 - \rho)}$$

$$\text{Average number waiting in queue, } N_q = \lambda W = \frac{\lambda \rho}{\mu(1 - \rho)}$$

$$= \frac{\rho^2}{1 - \rho} \qquad \text{since } \frac{\lambda}{\mu} = \rho$$

$$\text{Average number in system, } N = \lambda T = \frac{\lambda}{\mu(1 - \rho)}$$

$$= \frac{\rho}{1 - \rho}$$

Example A3.3

A node in a half-duplex multipoint system has the following characteristics:

Single server
Arrival rate, $\lambda = 750$ messages per hour
Average transmission time, $S = 1.5$ seconds

Determine the worst-case average time spent waiting in queue and the corresponding average number of messages waiting in the queue.

Since a worst-case value is required, we assume that an M/M/1 queue is used.
Utilization factor, $\rho = \lambda S$

$$= \frac{750 \times 1.5}{3600}$$

$$= 0.3125$$

Service rate, $\mu = \dfrac{\lambda}{\rho} = \dfrac{750}{3600 \times 0.3125}$

$$= 0.667 \text{ per second}$$

Mean square service time, $\overline{S^2} = \dfrac{2}{\mu^2}$ (Equation A3.12)

$$= 2/0.667^2 = 4.5 \text{ s}^2$$

From the P–K formula:

Average time waiting in queue, $W = \dfrac{\lambda \overline{S^2}}{2(1 - \rho)} = \dfrac{750 \times 4.5}{3600 \times 2 \times (1 - 0.3125)}$

$$= 0.68 \text{ s}$$

Average number in queue, $N_q = \lambda W = \dfrac{750}{3600} \times 0.68$

$$= 0.142$$

It can be seen that messages spend an average of 0.68 seconds waiting in the queue, which is a long time in a data communications system, yet the utilization factor is only 0.3125 which is fairly low. Why is this? The reason is that the average transmission time of 1.5 seconds is slow. To improve the efficiency and throughput of this system it is necessary to increase the transmission rate of the half-duplex link.

The M/D/1 queuing system

This type of system has predetermined equal service times for all packets and thus gives a best-case situation since there is no deviation from an average value of service time. The mean square value of service time is given by:

$$\overline{S^2} = S^2$$

$$= \frac{1}{\mu^2} \qquad \text{from (A3.3)}$$

Note that this is half the value of the M/M/1 case.
This gives a result from the P–K formula of:

Average time in queue, $W = \dfrac{\lambda}{\mu^2 2(1 - \rho)}$

$$= \frac{\rho}{2\mu(1 - \rho)}$$

Average time in the system, $T = S + \dfrac{\rho}{2\mu(1 - \rho)}$

$$= \frac{1}{\mu} + \frac{\rho}{2\mu(1 - \rho)}$$

$$= \frac{2(1 - \rho) + \rho}{2\mu(1 - \rho)}$$

$$= \frac{2 - \rho}{2\mu(1 - \rho)}$$

Average number in queue, $N_q = \lambda W = \dfrac{\lambda \rho}{2\mu(1 - \rho)}$

$$= \frac{\rho^2}{2(1 - \rho)}$$

Average number in system, $N = \lambda T = \dfrac{\lambda(2 - \rho)}{2\mu(1 - \rho)}$

$$= \frac{\rho(2 - \rho)}{2(1 - \rho)}$$

Multiple-server queues

In practice some nodes in a system may have more than a single outgoing transmission link. For example, consider the case of two outgoing transmission links connecting a packet-switching node to a neighbouring node. Packets use either link randomly. Such a system will use an M/M/2 queuing system at the first node. This will produce double the service rate as an M/M/1 queue and will be able to handle twice the arrival rate. Adding a second server thus improves both the time delays and throughput performance. This is illustrated in Figure A3.5, showing time delay, T, plotted against utilization for the M/M/1 queue of Example A3.3 along with the corresponding M/M/2 queue and an M/M/1 queue with doubled service rate.

Note that the M/M/2 queue gives lower delay times. It is clear, however, from the corresponding curve for an M/M/1 queue with a doubled service capacity that

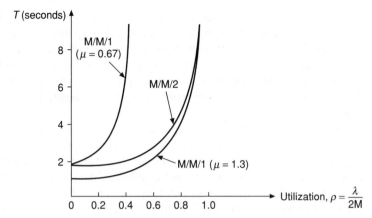

Figure A3.5 Plot of time delay against utilization.

this queue outperforms the M/M/2 queue at low utilizations since, when traffic is low, only one of the two links in the M/M/2 system is being used. As a general rule it is better to double the transmission capacity of a link rather than to add a second link.

(A3.6) Effects of errors on delays

If errors occur in a system and Automatic Repeat on Request (ARQ) is used for error correction to retransmit erroneous packets, then the average transmission time will increase. This will, in turn, result in increased delays and queue lengths. In determining an average transmission time, both the error rate and the type of ARQ strategy need to be taken into account. The greater the error rate, the more packets will need to be retransmitted, and the greater will be transmission and queuing times and queue lengths.

(A3.7) Networks of transmission links

In a data communications network there are large numbers of transmission queues which interact with each other, in that traffic leaving a queue at one node may enter one or more other queues, possibly merging with traffic leaving further queues on the way. This tends to complicate the arrival process at the subsequent queues. As a simple exercise, consider the case of two links with equal capacity, connected in series as shown in Figure A3.6. Packets of equal length arrive at node A at a rate of λ per second with a Poisson probability distribution. Although the packets arrive at node A in

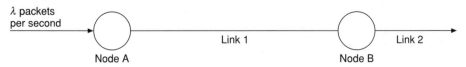

Figure A3.6

random fashion, as soon as a queue forms at the node input, they are transmitted across link 1 in a systematic fashion, so that the queuing system at node A is M/D/1 and can be modelled using the P–K formula. Since there is no reason that the packet transmission time (service time, S) should not be the same at both nodes, the queuing system at node B will complete its packet transmission at the same time as, or before, the next packet arrives. In other words, other factors apart, there will be no queuing at node B.

The main factor affecting the operation of the queuing system at node B is, in fact, the packet length. Even if the incoming packets have exponentially distributed lengths, so that the queuing system at node A is M/M/1, the action of the queue at node B will depend in some way on the length of the packets. Consequently it is not possible to apply the (relatively) simple type of analysis explored in this appendix to whole networks. Bertsekas and Gallagher (1992) take the analysis of networks of queuing systems further, but any such analytical approach becomes unwieldy in networks consisting of more than a few nodes. However, computer simulation packages are available, such as CACI's Comnet package, which uses queuing models as part of their network simulation. These packages can be run on PCs, but become slow and expensive in computer time if the network modelled is large.

Glossary

Address resolution protocol (ARP)   Used by IP to determine the physical MAC adress of a host (or router) given its IP address.

Advanced Research Projects Agency (ARPA)   *see* ARPANET

American Standards Committee for Information Interchange (ASCII)   In normal usage this refers to the character code defined by this committee for the interchange of information between two communicating devices. The ASCII character set is in widespread use for the transfer of information between a computer and a peripheral device such as a visual display unit or a printer.

Amplitude modulation (AM)   A modulation technique to allow data to be transmitted across an analogue network, such as a switched telephone network. The amplitude of a single (carrier) frequency is varied (modulated) between two levels – one for binary 0 and the other for binary 1.

Amplitude shift keying (ASK)   A type of modulation in which two binary values are represented by two different amplitudes of a fixed carrier frequency.

ANSI   American National Standards Institute.

Application layer   This corresponds to layer 7 of the ISO reference model for open systems interconnection. It comprises a number of application-oriented protocols and forms the user interface to the various distributed information processing services supported.

ARPA   *see* ARPANET

ARPANET   The wide area network funded by the former Advanced Research Projects Agency (ARPA) and now known as the Defense Advanced Projects Research Agency (DARPA).

ASCII   American standard code for information interchange. *See also* American Standards Committee for Information Interchange.

Association control service element (ACSE)   A protocol entity forming part of the application layer. It provides the generalized (common) function of establishing and clearing a logical association (connection) between two application entities.

Asynchronous transfer mode (ATM)   A popular wide area network protocol. All information to be transmitted – voice, data, image, video – is first fragmented into small, fixed-sized frames known as cells. These are switched and routed using packet-switching principles – also known as cell switching.

Asynchronous transmission   Strictly, this implies that the receiver clock is not synchronized to the transmitted clock when data is being transmitted between two devices connected by a transmission line. More generally, it indicates that data is being transmitted as individual characters. Each character is preceded by a start signal and terminated by one or more stop signals, which are used by the receiver for synchronization purposes.

ATM adaptation layer (AAL)   The upper layer of the ATM protocol model. It involves the adaptation into ATM of end-user services such a voice, video and data applications.

ATM bearer services   A service in which the traffic consists of ATM cells at every point along the path of an end-to-end correction.

Automatic Repeat Request (ARQ)   A technique used for error control over a transmission line. If errors in a transmitted message are detected by the receiving device, it requests the sending device to retransmit the message together with any other messages that might have been affected.

Autonomous System   A group of networks and routers under a single technical administration. The routers use an interior gateway protocol such as OSPF to communicate within the autonomous system.

Backward explicit congestion notification (BECN)   A notification used in Frame Relay networks to indicate that congestion has occurred in the backward data path.

Bandwidth   The difference between the highest and the lowest sinusoidal frequency signals that can be transmitted across a transmission line or through a network. It is measured in hertz (Hz) and also defines the maximum information-carrying capacity of the line or network.

Baseband   A particular operating mode of a transmission line: each binary digit (bit) in a message is converted into one of two voltage (sometimes current) levels – one for binary 1 and the other for binary 0. The voltages are then applied directly to the line. The line signal varies with time between these two voltage levels as the data is transmitted.

Batcher-banyan switch   A non-blocking switch matrix often used in ATM switches.

Baud   The number of line signal variations per second. It also indicates the rate at which data is transmitted on a line, although this is strictly correct only when each bit is represented by a single signal level on the transmission line. Hence, the bit rate and the line signal rate are both the same.

BER   *see* Bit error rate

Bit error rate (BER)   The probability that a single bit, when transmitted over a link, will be received in error.

Bit stuffing (zero bit insertion)   A technique used to allow pure binary data to be transmitted on a synchronous transmission line. Each message block (frame) is encapsulated between two flags, which are special bit sequences. If the message data contains a possibly similar sequence, then an additional (zero) bit is inserted into the data stream by the sender, and is subsequently removed by the receiving device. The transmission method is said to be data transparent.

Border Gateway Protocol   A routing protocol used in large IP networks for routing traffic between autonomous systems.

Bridge   A device used to link two homogeneous local area subnetworks, that is, two subnetworks utilizing the same physical and medium access control method.

Broadband   Describes data rates in excess of 2 Mbps and distinguishes between rates below this which are termed narrowband. Alternatively, in the context of LANs, broadband refers to variants that apply data signals to the medium at radio frequencies using some form of modulation and distinguishes them from baseband operation.

Broadcast   A means of transmitting a message to all devices connected to a network. Normally, a special address, the broadcast address, is reserved to enable all the devices to determine that the message is a broadcast message.

Bus   A network topology used to interconnect communities of digital devices distributed over a localized area. The transmission medium is generally a single coaxial, or optical fibre, cable. In the former, transmissions propagate the length of the medium and are received by all devices connected to the medium. Alternatively, transmission in fibre is strictly uni-directional.

CCITT   International Telegraph and Telephone Consultative Committee (now ITU-T).

CCR   Commitment, concurrency and recovery.

Cell delay variation (CDV)   Variation in the delay experienced by cells in an ATM bearer service.

Cell delay variation tolerance (CDVT)   A traffic parameter, used in an ATM bearer service, that sets a maximum CDV value that can be tolerated.

CEPT   European Conference of Posts and Telegraphs.

Circuit switching   The mode of operation of a telephone network and also some of the newer digital data networks. A communication path is first established through the network between the source (calling) and destination (called) terminals, and this is used exclusively for the duration of the call or transaction. Both terminals must operate at the same information transfer rate.

CMIS   *see* Common management information system

Coaxial cable   A type of transmission medium consisting of a centre conductor and a concentric outer conductor. It is used when high data transfer rates (greater than 1 Mbps) are required.

Commitment, concurrency and recovery (CCR)   A protocol entity forming part of the application layer. It allows two or more application processes to perform mutually exclusive operations on shared data. It also provides control to ensure that the operations are performed either completely or not at all. It uses the concepts of an atomic action and a two-phase commit protocol.

Common management information protocol (CMIP)   The ISO application layer protocol used to retrieve and send management-related information across an OSI network.

Common management information system (CMIS)   The set of management services provided in the ITU-T X.710 recommendation which forms the basis for the OSI network management functions.

Community antenna television (CATV)   A facility used in the context of local area data networks, since the principles and network components used in CATV networks can also be used to produce a flexible underlying data transmission facility over a local area. CATV networks operate using the broadband mode of working.

Concentrator   A process whereby a number of data sources are combined in order to share a single channel to improve channel utilization.

Committed information rate (CIR)   A transmission rate, in bits per second, agreed between a customer and a Frame Relay network, at which a user can access the network.

Connection admission control (CAC)   A process that determines whether to admit or reject a new connection to an ATM network.

Constant bit rate (CBR) A category of ATM service that describes an ATM cell stream that has constant time intervals between cells.

Convolutional code A type of error correcting code that operates on data continuously as it is received, rather than waiting until a complete block of data has been received.

CRC *see* Cyclic redundancy check

Crosstalk An unwanted signal that is picked up in a conductor as a result of some external electrical activity.

CSMA/CD Carrier Sense, Multiple Access with Collision Detection. A method used to control access to a shared transmission medium, such as a coaxial cable bus to which a number of stations is connected. A station that wishes to transmit a message first senses (listens to) the medium and transmits the message only if the medium is quiet – no carrier present. Then, as the message is being transmitted, the station monitors the actual signal on the transmission medium. If this is different from the signal being transmitted, a collision is said to have occurred and been detected. The station then ceases transmission and tries again later.

Cyclic code A type of block error detection and correction code used extensively in data communications networks. The codewords of a cyclic code are distinguished in that if their bits are shifted, either right or left, they produce another code word.

Cyclic redundancy check (CRC) A technique used for the detection of errors in transmitted data which uses a cyclic code. A numeric value is computed from the bits in the data to be transmitted which is placed in the trailer of a block of data. A receiver is able to detect the presence, or otherwise, of errors by repeating the check.

DARPA *see* ARPANET

Data circuit terminating equipment (DCE) The equipment provided by the network authority (provider) for the attachment of user devices to the network. It takes on different forms for different network types.

Data link layer This corresponds to layer 2 of the ISO reference model for open systems interconnection. It is concerned with the reliable transfer of data (no residual transmission errors) across the data link being used.

Data terminal equipment (DTE) A generic name for any user device connected to a data network. It includes such devices as visual display units, computers and office workstations.

Datagram A type of service offered on a packet-switched data network (*see also* Virtual circuit). A datagram is a self-contained packet of information that is sent through the network with minimum protocol overheads.

Defense Advanced Research Project Agency (DARPA) *see* ARPANET

Delay distortion Distortion of a signal caused by the frequency components making up the signal having different propagation velocities across a transmission medium.

Demultiplexer Performs the opposite process to that of a multiplexer.

Differential Phase Shift Keying (DPSK) A form of phase shift keying in which the phase of a carrier signal is shifted according to differences in an incoming bit stream.

Digital signal processing (DSP) A digital technique, often by means of a computer, to process signals which are in sampled data representation. Analogue signals are often converted into such a form by means of an analogue-to-digital converter (ADC) to enable processing by means of DSP.

Digital subscriber line (or loop) A connection between subscriber and local exchange, or central office, that carries signals in digital form.

Distributed queue, dual bus (DQDB) An optical-fibre-based network that can be used as a high-speed LAN or MAN that is compatible with the evolving Broadband ISDN. It operates in a broadcast mode by using two buses, each of which transmits small, fixed-sized frames – known as cells – in opposite directions. Each bus can operate at hundreds of megabits per second.

DMT Discrete multitone transmission.

DNA Digital Network Architecture.

DSP *see* Digital signal processing

EIA Electrical Industries Association.

EIA-232D Standard laid down by the American EIA for interfacing a digital device to a PTT-supplied modem. Also used as an interface standard for connecting a peripheral device, such as a visual display unit or a printer, to a computer.

Entropy Average information content of a codeword.

Equalizer A device (or circuit) used to make a channel's response uniform within its bandwidth. Typically used to make gain or attenuation constant, or phase shift linear, with frequency.

Ethernet The name of the LAN invented at the Xerox Corporation Palo Alto Research Center. It operates using the CSMA/CD medium access control method. The early specification was refined by a joint team from Digital Equipment Corporation, Intel Corporation and Xerox Corporation, and this in turn has now been superseded by the IEEE 802.3 – ISO 8802.3 – international standard.

ETSI European Telecommunication Standards Institute.

Excess information rate (EIR) A transmission rate that a Frame Relay service provider will accept in excess of a committed information rate, as long as a sufficient bandwidth is available to carry the excess traffic.

Explicit forward congestion indication (EFCI) An indication in an ATM cell header that reports congestion occurring in the forward path of an ATM bearer service.

Extended binary coded decimal interchange code (EBCDIC) The character set used on all IBM computers.

Fibre distributed data interchange (FDDI) A ring-based optical fibre network traditionally used in metropolitan area networks that supports a bit rate of 100 Mbps.

Fibre optic *see* Optical fibre

File transfer access and management (FTAM) A protocol entity forming part of the application layer. It enables user application processes to manage and access a (distributed) file system.

Filter A device which selectively passes some frequencies and rejects others. Typically may pass high frequencies, low frequencies or a band of frequencies. Alternatively may suppress a particular band of frequencies.

Flow control A technique to control the rate of flow of frames or messages between two communicating entities.

Forward explicit congestion notice (FECN) A notification used in Frame Relay networks to indicate that congestion has occurred in the forward data path.

Frame The unit of information transferred across a data link. Typically, there are control frames for link management and information frames for the transfer of message data.

Frame check sequence (FCS) A general term given to the additional bits appended to a transmitted frame or message by the source to enable the receiver to detect possible transmission errors.

Frame relay   A packet-switched data service operating at higher speed than X.25 networks and commonly used in wide area networks.

Frequency shift keying   A modulation technique to convert binary data into an analogue form comprising two sinusoidal frequencies. It is widely used in modems to allow data to be transmitted across a (analogue) switched telephone network.

FTAM   File transfer access and management.

Full duplex   A type of information exchange strategy between two communicating devices whereby information (data) can be exchanged in both directions simultaneously. It is also known as two-way simultaneous.

Gateway   A device that routes traffic, normally in the form of datagrams (packets) between one network and another. Typically, the two networks operate with different protocols, and so the gateway also performs the necessary protocol conversion functions.

Generic cell rate algorithm (GCRA)   A software algorithm used to control ATM traffic parameters in accordance with a traffic contract at a user interface with the network.

Half duplex   A type of information exchange strategy between two communicating devices whereby information (data) can be exchanged in both directions alternately. It is also known as two-way alternate.

Hamming code   An early error correcting code attributable to R.W. Hamming.

High-level Data Link Control (HDLC)   An internationally agreed standard protocol defined to control the exchange of data across either a point-to-point data link or a multidrop data link.

Host   Normally a computer belonging to a user that contains (hosts) the communication hardware and software necessary to connect the computer to a data communications network.

IEEE   Institute of Electrical and Electronic Engineers.

Integrated Services Digital Network (ISDN)   The new generation of worldwide telecommunications network that utilizes digital techniques for both transmission and switching. It supports both voice and data communications.

International alphabet number 5 (IA5)   The standard character code defined by ITU-T and recommended by ISO. It is almost identical to the ASCII code.

Internet   The abbreviated name given to a collection of interconnected networks. Also, the name of the US-government-funded internetwork based on the TCP/IP protocol suite.

Internet Control Message Protocol (ICMP)   A protocol within the TCP/IP suite of protocols used by hosts and routers to exchange control messages across an internet.

Internet Protocol (IP)   The protocol that provides connectionless network service between multiple packet-switched networks interconnected by gateways.

Intersymbol interference (ISI)   Caused by delay distortion introduced in transmission which results in a dispersion (in time) of a received symbol such that it overlaps the time periods of adjacent symbols.

IP security (IPsec)   A small group of protocols that provide security services in an IP environment.

ISI   *see* Intersymbol interference

ISO   International Organization for Standardization.

ITU   International Telecommunications Union.

Joint Photographic Experts Group (JPEG)   The name of a committee that produced a video standard used to compress single still images by means of spatial compression.

JTAM   Job transfer, access and management.

Link management   A function of the data link layer of the OSI Reference Model which is concerned with setting up and disconnection of a link.

Local area network (LAN)   A data communications network used to interconnect a community of digital devices distributed over a localized area of up to, say, 10 km². The devices may be office workstations, mini- and microcomputers, intelligent instrumentation equipment, and so on.

Logical Link Control (LLC)   A protocol forming part of the data link layer in LANs. It is concerned with the reliable transfer of data across the data link between two communicating systems.

Management information base (MIB)   The name of the database used to hold the management information relating to a network or internetwork.

Manchester encoding   A 1B2B code which converts each single binary 1 and binary 0 into two respective equal, and opposite, binary signal elements.

Mark   A term traditionally used in telegraph systems to indicate a logic 1 state of a bit.

Maximum burst size (MBS)   A traffic parameter, agreed between an ATM network and a customer, that is the agreed maximum size of a burst of cells with variable bit rate that can be accepted by the network.

Media gateway   A device that converts media provided in one type of network to the format required for another type of network.

Media Gateway Control Protocol   A protocol for controlling media gateways.

Medium access control (MAC)   A method of determining which device has access to a shared transmission medium in a local area network.

Metropolitan area network (MAN)   A network that links a set of LANs that are physically distributed around a town or city.

Modem   The device that converts a binary (digital) data stream into an analogue (continuously varying) form, prior to transmission of the data across an analogue network (MODulator), and reconverts the received signal back into its binary form (DEModulator). Since each access port to the network normally requires a full-duplex (two-way simultaneous) capability, the device must perform both the MODulation and the DEModulation functions; hence the single name MODEM is used. As an example, a modem is normally required to transmit data across a telephone network.

Moving Picture Experts Group (MPEG)   An ISO committee that generates standards for digital video compression. It also gives its name to their standards.

Multidrop   A type of network configuration that supports more than two stations on the same transmission medium.

Multiplexer   A device to enable a number of lower bit rate devices, normally situated in the same location, to share a single higher bit rate transmission line. The data-carrying capacity of the latter must be in excess of the combined bit rates of the low bit rate devices.

Multi Protocol Label Switching   A standard that integrates layer 3 routing using IP addresses with a layer 2 switching technique such as ATM or Frame Relay.

Network interface card   A physical interface in an end system such as a computer that connects to a transmission medium.

Network layer   This corresponds to layer 3 of the ISO reference model for open systems interconnection. It is concerned with the establishment and clearing of logical or physical connections across the network being used.

Network management A generic term embracing all the functions and entities involved in the management of a network. This includes configuration management, fault handling and the gathering of statistics relating to usage of the network.

Noise The extraneous electrical signals that may be generated or picked up in a transmission line. Typically, it may be caused by neighbouring electrical apparatus. If the noise signal is large compared with the data-carrying signal, the latter may be corrupted and result in transmission errors.

Non real-time variable bit rate (NRTVBR) A category of ATM service that describes a cell stream, carrying non real-time traffic, in which the bit rate varies with time.

NRZ/NRZI Two similar (and related) schemes for encoding a binary data stream. The first has the property that a signal transition occurs whenever a binary 1 is present in the data stream and the second whenever a binary 0 is present. The latter is utilized with certain clocking (timing) schemes.

OFDM Orthogonal frequency division multiplexing.

On-off keying (OOK) A type of modulation in which two binary values are represented either by the presence of a fixed carrier frequency or not.

Open shortest path first (OSPF) An internet routing protocol that determines a least cost shortest path within a network.

Open system A vendor-independent set of interconnected computers that all utilize the same standard communications protocol stack based on either the ISO/OSI protocols or TCP/IP.

Open Systems Interconnection (OSI) The protocol suite that is based on ISO protocols to create an open systems interconnection environment.

Optical Carrier (OC) A level within the Synchronous Optical Network (SONET) hierarchy which defines a transmission rate. The base rate of 51.84 Mbps is termed OC-1 and other levels use multiples of this rate.

Optical fibre A type of transmission medium over which data is transmitted in the form of light waves or pulses. It is characterized by its potentially high bandwidth, and hence data-carrying capacity, and its high immunity to interference from other electrical sources.

Orthogonal In the context of signals, a pair of coexisting signals which are mutually independent.

PABX Private automatic branch exchange.

Packet Assembler/Disassembler (PAD) A device used with an X.25 packet-switching network to allow character mode terminals to communicate with a packet mode device, such as a computer.

Packet internet groper (PING) An IP control packet used to test whether a host or router is operational by sending a query and receiving a confirmation.

Packet switching A mode of operation of a data communications network. Each message to be transmitted through the network is first divided into a number of smaller, self-contained message units known as packets. Each packet contains addressing information. As each packet is received at an intermediate node (exchange) within the network, it is first stored and, depending on the addressing information contained within it, forwarded along an appropriate link to the next node and so on. Packets belonging to the same message are reassembled at the destination. This mode of operation ensures that long messages do not degrade the response time of the network.

PAM Pulse amplitude modulation.

Parity A mechanism used for the detection of transmission errors when single characters are being transmitted. A single binary bit, known as the parity bit, the value (1 or 0) of which is determined by the total number of binary ones in the character, is transmitted with the character so that the receiver can determine the presence of single-bit errors by comparing the received parity bit with the (recomputed) value it should be.

PCM Pulse code modulation.

Peak cell rate (PCR) An ATM traffic parameter that defines an agreed peak rate at which a customer may access a network.

Permanent virtual circuit (PVC) A term used in X.25, Frame Relay and ATM networks to describe an end to end connection across a network that has been established on a permanent basis.

Phase shift keying (PSK) A modulation technique to convert binary data into an analogue form comprising a single sinusoidal frequency signal with a phase that varies according to the data being transmitted.

Physical layer This corresponds to layer 1 of the ISO reference model for open systems interconnection. It is concerned with the electrical and mechanical specification of the physical network termination equipment.

Piggybacking A technique to return acknowledgement information across a full-duplex (two-way simultaneous) data link without the use of special (acknowledgement) messages. The acknowledgement information relating to the flow of messages in one direction is embedded (piggybacked) into a normal data-carrying message flowing in the reverse direction.

Pixel The smallest picture element, or cell, which may be physically resolved on a CRT screen.

Plesiochronous digitial hierarchy (PDM) A hierarchy of transmission rates traditionally used in telephony networks. The base rate in North America, termed DS-1, is 1.544 Mbps. The base rate in Europe and elsewhere, termed E-1, is 2.048 Mbps.

Postal, Telegraph and Telephone (PTT) The administrative authority that controls all the postal and public telecommunications networks and services in a country.

POTS Plain old telephone system.

Presentation layer This corresponds to layer 6 of the ISO reference model for open systems interconnection. It is concerned with the negotiation of a suitable transfer (concrete) syntax for use during an application session and, if this is different from the local syntax, for the translation to and from this syntax.

Primitive A type of PDU, such as a request or response.

Protocol A set of rules formulated to control the exchange of data between two communicating parties.

Protocol data unit (PDU) A packet of data transmitted across a network and normally associated with a specific layer of a protocol.

PSK Phase shift keying.

PSTN Public Switched Telephone Network.

Public Data Network (PDN) A packet-switched communication network set up and controlled by a public telecommunications authority.

QAM Quadrature amplitude modulation.

Quadrature In the context of signals, two signals, or carriers, which are orthogonal.

Real-time variable bit rate (RTVBR)   A category of ATM service that describes a cell stream, carrying real-time traffic, in which the bit rate varies with time.

Remote operations service element (ROSE)   A protocol entity forming part of the application layer. It provides a general facility for initiating and controlling operations remotely.

Request for comment (RFC)   Numbered Internet information documents, originally regarded as just technical reports but now regarded as *de facto* standards.

Ring   A network topology in widespread use for the interconnection of communities of digital devices distributed over a localized area, such as a factory or a block of offices. Each device is connected to its nearest neighbour until all the devices are connected in the form of a closed loop or ring. Data is transmitted in one direction only and, as each message circulates around the ring, it is read by each device connected in the ring. After circulating around the ring, the source device removes the message from the ring.

Router   A device used to interconnect two or more networks together, each of which may possibly use different protocols.

Routing Information Protocol (RIP)   A simple Internet routing protocol, based on the original ARPANET routing algorithm, that determines the shortest path to a destination as a number of hops

Scrambler   A device that randomizes binary data. That is yields signals that are equiprobable. May be used to minimize the number of consecutive binary 1s, or binary 0s in a bit stream.

Segmentation and reassembly (SAR)   A sub-layer of the ATM adaptation layer that breaks down larger blocks of data into ATM cells and reassembles them at the far end of a connection.

Server   A facility found in many local area networks where file access, printing or communication functions are provided to other stations.

Service access point (SAP)   The subaddress used to identify uniquely a particular link between two protocol layers in a specific system.

Session Initiation Protocol (SIP)   An Internet protocol, used in voice over IP systems.

Session layer   This corresponds to layer 5 of the ISO reference model for open systems interconnection. It is concerned with the establishment of a logical connection between two application entities and with controlling the dialogue (message exchange) between them.

Simple Network Management Protocol (SNMP)   The application protocol in a TCP/IP suite used to send and retrieve management-related information across a TCP/IP network.

Simplex   A type of information exchange strategy between two communicating devices whereby information (data) can be passed only in one direction.

Slotted ring   A type of local area network. All the devices are connected in the form of a (physical) ring and an additional device known as a monitor is used to ensure that the ring contains a fixed number of message slots (binary digits) that circulate around the ring in one direction only. A device sends a message by placing it in an empty slot as it passes. This is read by all other devices on the ring and subsequently removed by the originating device.

SNA   Systems Network Architecture.

Space   A term traditionally used in telegraph systems to indicate a logic 0 state of a bit.

Star   A type of network topology in which there is a central node that performs all switching (and hence routing) functions.

Statistical multiplexer (stat mux)   A device used to enable a number of lower bit rate devices, normally situated in the same location, to share a single, higher bit rate transmission line. Data is transmitted on the shared line on a statistical basis rather than, as is the case with a basic multiplexer, on a preallocated basis. It endeavours to exploit the fact that each device operates at a much lower mean rate than its maximum rate.

Subnet   A part of a network, which may or may not be a physically separate segment, that shares part of an IP address range with other subnets.

Sustainable cell rate (SCR)   An ATM traffic parameter that defines an agreed average cell rate at which a customer may access the network for sustained periods of time.

Switch fabric   A non-blocking switching matrix that forms the central part of an ATM switch.

Switched virtual circuit (SVC)   A term used in X.25, frame relay and ATM networks to describe a connection between end users that is established by end users using a signalling system.

Synchronous digital hierarchy (SDH)   An international hierarchy of transmission rates, used with optical fibres. The base rate, known as STM-1, is 155.52 Mbps.

Synchronous Optical Network (SONET)   A broadband standard for high speed transmission using optical fibres at rates that are multiples of 51.84 Mbps. SONET is the North American equivalent of SDH.

Synchronous transmission   A technique to transmit data between two devices connected by a transmission line. The data is normally transmitted in the form of blocks, each comprising a string of binary digits. With synchronous transmission, the transmitter and receiver clocks are in synchronism; a number of techniques are used to ensure this.

Synchronous transport module (STM)   A numbered level within the synchronous digital hierarchy. Transmission rates range between 155.5 Mbps (STM-1) and 39.81 Gbps (STM-192).

Syndrome   The result of a computation undertaken to detect whether or not errors have occurred in a data transmission which uses an error detection or correction code.

TCP/IP   The complete suite of Internet protocols, including IP, TCP and the associated application protocols.

Teletex   An international telecommunications service that provides the means for messages, comprising text and selected graphical characters, to be prepared, sent and received.

Time-division multiplexing (TDM)   A technique to share the bandwidth (channel capacity) of a shared transmission facility to allow a number of communications to be in progress either concurrently or one at a time.

Time to live (TTL)   A field in an IP header that indicates the number of further hops that this packet should be allowed to make before being discarded.

Token bus   A type of local area network. Access to the shared transmission medium, which is implemented in the form of a bus to which all the communicating devices are connected, is controlled by a single control (permission) token. Only the current owner of the token is allowed to transmit a message on the medium. All devices wishing to transmit messages are connected in the form of a logical ring. After a device receives the token and transmits any waiting messages, it passes the token to the next device on the ring.

Token ring   A type of local area network. All the devices are connected in the form of a (physical) ring and messages are transmitted by allowing them to circulate around the ring. A device can transmit a message on the ring only when it is in possession of a control (permission) token. A single token is passed from one device to another around the ring.

Transmission Control Protocol (TCP)   The protocol in the TCP/IP suite that provides a reliable full-duplex message transfer service to application protocols.

Transmission medium   The communication path linking two communicating devices. Examples are metallic or optical cable.

Transport layer   This corresponds to layer 4 of the ISO reference model for open systems interconnection. It is concerned with providing a network-independent, reliable message interchange service to the application-oriented layers (layers 5 to 7).

Unshielded twisted pair (UTP)   A type of transmission medium consisting of two insulated wires, normally twisted together in order to reduce interference due to induction from electromagnetic fields in close proximity, but without an external shield.

Usage parameter control (UPC)   A form of traffic policing used to monitor and control incoming traffic into an ATM network.

User Datagram Protocol (UDP)   A transport layer protocol used in the Internet to transport end to end user traffic without using any flow control.

Variable bit rate (VBR)   A type of traffic in which the bit rate is variable with time.

Videotex   A telecommunications service that allows users to deposit and access information to and from a central database facility. Access is through a special terminal comprising a TV set equipped with a special decoder.

Virtual circuit   A connection through a WAN in which sequent packets from the same source follow the same route through the network, which is called a virtual circuit. These packets do not, however, have exclusive use of the circuit. Packets from a number of different sources may share the use of each link.

Virtual private network   A virtual network that emulates a private IP network by using a shared IP infrastructure, typically provided by a network carrier.

Viterbi algorithm   An algorithm used to decode convolutional codes.

Voice over IP (VoIP)   A technology that provides voice services over IP connections.

WEP   Wireless equivalent privacy.

Wide area network (WAN)   Any form of network – private or public – that covers a wide geographical area.

Wireless LAN   A LAN that uses either radio or infrared as the transmission medium. Requires different MAC methods from those used with wired LANs.

xDSL   x is a generic term representing a range of different Digital Subscriber Line (DSL) services, and speeds.

Bibliography

....

Batcher K.E. (1968). Sorting networks and their applications. *Proceedings of the 32nd Spring Joint Computer Conference*

Beker H. and Piper F. (1982). *Cipher Systems*. Northwood Books

Bellman R. (1957). Notes on the theory of dynamic programming – transportation models. *Management Science*, **4**, April

Bergman W. (1991). Narrowband Frame Relay Congestion Policy, *Proceedings of the 10th Annual Phoenix Conference on Computers and Communications*, March

Bertsekas D. and Gallager R. (1992). *Data Networks*, 2nd edn. Prentice Hall

Beyda W.J. (2000). *Data Communications: From basics to broadband*, 3rd edn. Prentice Hall

Black U. (1997). *Emerging Communications Technologies*, 2nd edn. Prentice Hall

Black U. (2002). *Uyless Black's Networking 101*, Prentice Hall

Brewster R.L. (ed.) (1994). *Data Communications and Networks*, 3rd edn. IEEE

Clark G.C. and Cain J.B. (1981). *Error-Correction Coding for Digital Communications*. Plenum Press

Comer D.E. and Droms R.E. (1999). *Computer Networks*, 2nd edn. Prentice Hall

Dijkstra E.W. (1959). A note on two problems in connexion with graphs. *Numerische Mathematik*, **1**, 269–271

Dunlop J. and Smith D.G. (1994). *Telecommunications Engineering*, 3rd edn. Chapman & Hall

Ferouzan B.A. (2000). *Data Communications and Networking*, 2nd edn. McGraw-Hill

Flood J.E. (1997). *Telecommunication Networks*, 2nd edn. IEEE

Ford L.R. Jr and Fulkerson D.R. (1962). *Flows in Networks*. Princeton University Press

Ghanbari M. (1999). *Video Coding: An introduction to standard codecs*. IEEE

Gibbens R.J. and Hunt P.J. (1991). Effective bandwidths for the multi-type UAS channel. *Queueing Systems*, **9**, 17–27

Gillespie A. (2000). *Broadband Access Technology, Interfaces and Management*. Artech House

Glover I.A. and Grant, P.M. (1998). *Digital Communications*, Prentice Hall Europe

Goralski W. (1999). *ADSL and DSL Technologies*. McGraw-Hill

Goralski W. (2002). *Sonet/SDH*, 3rd edn. McGraw-Hill

Griffiths J.M. (1998). *ISDN Explained: Worldwide Network and Applications Technology*, 3rd edn. John Wiley

Halsall F. (1996). *Data Communications, Computer Networks and Open Systems*, 4th edn. Addison-Wesley

Halsall F. (2001). *Multimedia Communications*. Addison-Wesley

Hamming R.W. (1950). Error detecting and error correcting codes. *Bell Systems Technical Journal*, **29**, 147–160

Handel R., Huber M.N. and Schroeder S. (1998). *ATM Networks: Concepts, Protocols, Applications*, 3rd edn. Addison-Wesley

Held G. (1998). Data Communications Networking Devices: Operation, Utilization and Lan and Wan Internetworking, 4th edn. John Wiley

Kurose J.F. and Ross K. (2003). *Computer Networking: A top-down approach featuring the Internet*. Addison-Wesley

Lechledier J.W. (1989). Line codes for digital subscriber lines. *IEEE Communication*, September, 23–32

Mazda F. (ed.) (1998). *Telecommunications Engineers' Reference Book*. Butterworth–Heinemann

Meggitt J.E. (1961). Error correcting codes and their implementation for data transmission systems. *IRE Transactions on Information Theory*, **IT-7**, 234–244

Mier E.E. and Yocom B. (2000). Too many VoIP standards. *Business Communications Review*, June

Nyquist H. (1928). Certain topics in telegraph transmission theory. *AIEE Transactions*, **47**, 617–644

Peterson L. and Davie B.S. (2000). *Computer Networks: A systems approach*. Morgan Kauffman

Peterson W.W. (1961). *Error Correcting Codes*. Cambridge: MIT Press

Read R. (1998). *The Essence of Communications Theory*. Prentice Hall

Rescola E. (2001). *SSL and TLS*. Addison-Wesley

Roden M.S. (1996). *Analog and Digital Communication Systems*, 4th edn. Prentice Hall

Schwartz M. (1990). *Information Transmission, Modulation and Noise*, 4th edn. McGraw-Hill

Shanmugam K.S. (1979). *Digital and Analog Communication Systems*. John Wiley

Shannon C.E. (1948). A mathematical theory of communication. *Bell Systems Technical Journal* **27**

Singh S. (2000). *The Science of Secrecy*. Fourth Estate

Stallings W. (1991). *Data and Computer Communications*, 3rd edn. Prentice Hall (Upper Saddle River, NJ)

Stallings W. (1993a). *Networking Standards: A Guide to OSI, ISDN, LAN and MAN Standards*. Addison-Wesley

Stallings W. (1993b). *SNMP, SMP, and CMIP*. Addison-Wesley

Stallings W. (2000a). *Data and Computer Communications*, 6th edn. Prentice Hall

Stallings W. (2000b). *Local and Metropolitan Area Networks*, 6th edn. Prentice Hall

Stallings W. (2002). *Wireless Communications & Networks*. Prentice Hall

Stallings W. (2003). *Cryptography & Network Security*, 3rd edn. Pearson Education

Stamper D.A. (2001). *Local Area Networks*, 3rd edn. Prentice Hall

Starr M., Cioffi J.M. and Silverman P. (1999). *Understanding Digital Subscriber Line Technology*. Prentice Hall PTR

Tanenbaum A.S. (2003). *Computer Networks*, 4th edn. Prentice Hall PTR

Thomas S. (2000). *SSL and TLS: Securing the Web*. John Wiley

Viterbi A.J. (1967). Error bounds for convolutional codes and asymptotically optimum decoding algorithm. *IEEE Transactions on Information Theory*, **13**, 260–269

Waters A.G. (1991). *Computer Communication Networks*. McGraw-Hill

Zeimer R.E. and Tranter W.H. (1995). *Principles of Communications*, 4th edn. John Wiley

Index